Reneé Coleman

Political Questions
Political Philosophy from Plato to Rawls
Second Edition

Larry Arnhart
Northern Illinois University

WAVELAND

PRESS, INC.

Prospect Heights, Illinois

To Susan

In te ravviso il sogno
Ch'io vorrei sempre sognar.

For information about this book, write or call:
Waveland Press, Inc.
P.O. Box 400
Prospect Heights, Illinois 60070
(708) 634-0081

Cover: Engraving of a Rubens drawing of Socrates

Copyright © 1993 by Waveland Press, Inc.

ISBN 0-88133-728-5

All rights reserved. No part of this book may be reproduced, stored in a retrieval system, or transmitted in any form or by any means without permission in writing from the publisher.

Printed in the United States of America

6 5 4 3 2 1

Prologue

For this second edition, I have made minor changes throughout the book; and I have added sections on three new topics: law as the joint product of nature, custom, and stipulation (chapter 4, section 5), women's rights (chapter 8, section 9), and the end of history (chapter 10, section 7).

My primary intention is still to help students who are studying the history of political philosophy for the first time, but even scholarly experts might find something here to stimulate (if not provoke) them. I hope that both novices and initiates can benefit from the way this book combines four major features: (1) a reliance on questions, (2) an emphasis on primary texts, (3) references to issues in American political history, and (4) some use of material from modern science.

(1) To stimulate readers to think for themselves, I raise a series of enduring political questions, and I leave the readers free to work out their own answers. As much as possible, I avoid imposing my own point of view.

(2) Because there is no good substitute for reading the original works of political philosophy, I tie my questions to specific texts. This book is only supplementary to reading the primary sources themselves.

(3) Because it is important for students to see how the study of political philosophy can illuminate their political experience, I indicate how the questions raised by political philosophers clarify issues in American politics. In particular, I draw out some of the philosophic implications of the Declaration of Independence.

(4) At various points in this book, I show how knowledge gained from the modern natural and social sciences deepens our understanding of the classic texts of political philosophy. For example, biology, economics, anthropology, and psychology can contribute to our knowledge of human nature in ways that confirm the insights of political philosophers.

In the first edition, I listed the many people who had helped me in various ways during the time I was writing the book. In this second edition, I thank the students (at both the undergraduate and graduate levels) who have been in my courses in the Department of Political Science at Northern Illinois University. They have helped me to think through many of the questions in this book.

Larry Arnhart
DeKalb, Illinois

Contents

Introduction
From the Declaration of Independence to Political Philosophy

When Americans celebrate the Fourth of July as their national political birthday, they recognize their political identity as arising from the principles of the Declaration of Independence, particularly the principle of equality of rights. Any serious reflection on what that document means for American political life becomes an introduction to the enduring questions of political philosophy. To understand what it means for a political community to be devoted to equal rights one must trace this idea back through the history of political philosophy. John Locke is particularly important, but the questions raised by the Declaration of Independence have been debated by all political philosophers.

At the base of any political community, there are some principles of justice and the common good that are so widely shared, so pervasive throughout the community, that they are rarely questioned. These principles are not usually subject to debate because they constitute the very grounds on which ordinary political debate occurs. To reflect on them is to engage in political philosophy by thinking through the fundamental questions of political life. Why is it that Americans find it difficult to discuss any political issue without speaking about "rights" that should be enjoyed by all? Is it not because our basic principles have to do with equality of rights as being "self-evident" and "unalienable"? We cannot grasp the meaning of American politics—at the deepest level—unless we revivify those philosophic questions in response to which the American regime first arose. Of course, even as we concentrate on the Declaration of Independence as a statement of American principles, we should keep in mind that it is part of a long tradition of American political documents stretching back to the Mayflower Compact of 1620.[1]

1

Consider the beginning of the Declaration of Independence.

> When in the Course of human events, it becomes necessary for one people to dissolve the political bands which have connected them with another, and to assume among the powers of the earth, the separate and equal station to which the Laws of Nature and of Nature's God entitle them, a decent respect to the opinions of mankind requires that they should declare the causes which impel them to the separation.

The appeal to reasoned argument is apparent. The signers of the Declaration tried to give a rational justification for their deeds. They assumed that good political action is supported by good political reasoning. Yet they surely knew that to found a political community on such an assumption would be a rare achievement. That was the claim of Alexander Hamilton in the opening number of *The Federalist*:

> It has been frequently remarked that it seems to have been reserved to the people of this country, by their conduct and example, to decide the important question, whether societies of men are really capable or not of establishing good government from reflection and choice, or whether they are forever destined to depend for their political constitutions on accident and force.[2]

Does politics depend on rational deliberation, or is political life usually determined by brute force? Does political power reflect political wisdom? Or is power ultimately an exercise in tyranny, even if usually disguised, in which rulers use force and fraud to exploit the ruled? We shall hear these questions echoing throughout the history of political philosophy—from Plato to Machiavelli to Marx—and they have to do with the very possibility of political philosophy: To what extent—if at all—can the political philosopher guide the political ruler?

If one wanted to shape political life according to a rational standard, what would that standard be? The Declaration appeals to "the Laws of Nature and of Nature's God." Beginning with Socrates, one of the enduring themes of political philosophy has been the distinction between nature and convention—nature referring to the universal and permanent elements of reality, convention referring to the more particular and evanescent aspects of the social world. The great concern of the Socratic political philosopher was not to be satisfied with the merely conventional side of politics, but to discover how political life might be brought into harmony with nature. As far as politics is concerned, it is not physical nature but *human* nature that is important. Human beings at different times and in different places are never quite the same.

Are there, however, some fundamental similarities among human beings—needs, emotions, capacities, and such like—so that we can properly speak of an unchanging human nature? Can we then judge conventional political arrangements by how well they harmonize with this human nature? The Declaration of Independence seems to be founded on the premise that there are universal principles of nature by which political action can be directed.

How does one discover these principles of human nature? Can they be grasped by the unassisted human mind? Or are they revealed by God only to the faithful? What are the predominant features of human nature? Are human beings so naturally selfish and competitive that the only realistic aim of government is to keep them from injuring one another, while leaving them free in all other respects to live as they please? Is it also natural for human beings to share in conceptions of justice and the common good so that government can promote human excellence? On the other hand, is it perhaps incorrect to assume that there is an unchanging realm of nature? All of these questions might occur to the careful reader of the Declaration, and all have been debated by political philosophers. Here, I shall only indicate briefly how these questions are suggested by the language of the Declaration. Then, in the rest of the book, we shall work through the questions in a more detailed manner.

First, by referring to "the Laws of Nature and of Nature's God," the Declaration implies some connection between the natural order and divinity. St. Augustine insisted that insofar as nature depends completely on God's creative will, human beings cannot fulfill their nature except by yielding themselves in faith to the divine source of nature. The Declaration refers to God four times. At the beginning of the document, appeal is made to "the Laws . . . of Nature's God" and to God's creation of men as equal and endowed with rights. At the end, the authors appeal "to the Supreme Judge of the world," and they affirm their "firm reliance on the protection of Divine Providence." Would it be fair to infer from these passages that the Declaration assumes a rational piety? That is, God is presented as caring for human beings in a lawful and thus rational way that is manifest in the nature of the world he has created. Is it implied also that because God reveals himself in the things he has made, human beings can find guidance for their lives—even without revelation—by a rational understanding of nature? Some religious believers would deny that a purely intellectual grasp of nature uninformed by religious faith is a sufficient guide for political life.

Having seen the invocation of nature in the opening sentence of the Declaration, we move to the next section to see exactly what nature dictates for politics.

> We hold these truths to be self-evident, that all men are created equal, that they are endowed by their Creator with certain unalienable Rights, that among these are Life, Liberty and the pursuit of Happiness. — That to secure these rights, Governments are instituted among Men, deriving their just powers from the consent of the governed, — That whenever any Form of Government becomes destructive of these ends, it is the Right of the People to alter or to abolish it, and to institute new Government, laying its foundations on such principles and organizing its powers in such form, as to them shall seem most likely to effect their Safety and Happiness.

It seems that holding these "truths" as "self-evident" constitutes the political identity of the American people. How do such principles, which by implication are derived from "the Laws of Nature," come to be known as "self-evident"? Or must Americans "hold" them to be self-evident even if they really are not self-evident?

What *is* a self-evident truth? In *Federalist* Number 31, Hamilton speaks of "certain primary truths, or first principles, upon which all subsequent reasonings must depend, [and that] contain an internal evidence which, antecedent to all reflection or combination, commands the assent of the mind." As examples of such truths, he cites axioms of Euclidean geometry such as "the whole is greater than its parts; things equal to the same are equal to one another; two straight lines cannot enclose a space; and all right angles are equal to each other."[3] One way of explaining why such axioms are self-evident is to say that they are tautologies — that is, the object is contained within the definition of the subject. So, "the whole is greater than its parts" is obviously true to anyone who knows the meaning of "whole" because being greater than its parts is implied in the definition of "whole." To see the truth of such statements one need only understand the meaning of the words used.

Could this be the case for the statement that all people are equal? How does this contain its own internal evidence? In fact, one might wonder whether this is not self-evidently *false*. For are not people so different in an endless number of ways that it is hard to find any two human beings who are exactly the same? Presumably the signers of the Declaration did not mean to assert that human beings were equal in intelligence, character, beauty, strength, or in any number of other respects. How, then, are human beings all the same? Why not say that *all human beings are equally human beings?* Despite all the important differences, they all are members of the human species. The equality of all human beings is self-evident insofar as all are human.

So, as far as the Declaration is concerned, the first principle of the law of nature is the equality of all human beings as human. The validity of the principle becomes evident to anyone who understands it. It is a universal truth because it holds for all people at all times and in all places. Is this principle so abstract and general, however, as to be empty of content and thus of little use for the guidance of politics?

The implications become clear only by considering what follows from the principle of human equality. In the Declaration, it is inferred that from the fact of equality it follows that all people possess "certain unalienable Rights, that among these are Life, Liberty and the pursuit of Happiness." In accordance with the simple notion of justice as requiring that like cases be treated alike, human beings should be treated as human beings: we all have rights to that without which we could not be human. Although these rights cannot be completely enumerated—perhaps because the conditions of humanity vary somewhat—some of these rights are especially clear: life, liberty, and the pursuit of happiness. These rights are essential conditions for human beings to secure their humanity. To fulfill oneself as a human being one must preserve oneself, control the course of one's life, and strive to make it a good life. To figure out more precisely what these rights might entail, one needs to work through the philosophic debate about this question. The most obvious source for the natural rights teaching of the Declaration is John Locke's *Second Treatise of Government.*[4] When Jefferson listed those political philosophers whose thought lay behind the Declaration, he included Locke, but also Aristotle. Later, we shall consider in some detail the points at issue between Aristotle and Locke, but here we need only see the general character of the dispute.

Aristotle and Locke would agree that government should promote those conditions necessary for human beings to fulfill their humanity. But Locke, according to some interpreters,[5] would think that it is sufficient for government to secure peace by prohibiting physical injuries among humans, then leaving them free to live as they please without shaping their moral character according to any standard of the common good. Aristotle, on the other hand, would insist that government should provide the conditions not only for living, but also for living well. In the pursuit of happiness, Aristotle believes, human beings seek to fulfill their natural potentialities, of which the capacity for reasoning is the highest, being that which is most distinctive of the human species, and the perfection of reason is possible only through sharing in a common culture. The aim of an Aristotelian regime is not just to keep the peace, but also to make human beings better by shaping their character and thought to promote the common good.

The problem with Aristotle's position is that human beings often seem to be so naturally selfish and competitive as to have no conception of the common good that would go beyond their own private interests. The problem with Locke's position is that if there are no standards of justice beyond the selfish desires of individuals, it seems difficult to justify any exercise of governmental power as something other than the personal domination of some by others. How, for example, could Locke persuade people to risk their lives in defense of their government if they have been taught that the only purpose of government is to secure their rights, of which the most essential is the right to life? People must allow their rights to bear limitations in order to secure the sort of powerful government necessary to protect their rights. Similarly, for a community to act in unison, majority rule must prevail, inherently jeopardizing the rights of those in the minority.

These two Lockean problems — the conflict of individual rights versus governmental powers and the conflict of minority rights versus majority rule — also emerge in the Declaration of Independence. These difficulties arise from the need that human beings have for the government to protect their rights. For it is held to be self-evident not only that all are equally endowed with rights, but

> that to secure these rights, Governments are instituted among Men, deriving their just powers from the consent of the governed, — That whenever any Form of Government becomes destructive of these ends, it is the Right of the People to alter or to abolish it, and to institute new Government, laying its foundation on such principles and organizing its power in such form, as to them shall seem most likely to effect their Safety and Happiness.

What does it mean to move from the rights of "Men" to "the Right of the People"? Who speaks for the people? How is "the consent of the governed" expressed? Could the people consent to nondemocratic or even tyrannical government? And how can the powers of government be organized so as to best secure rights?

The Declaration opens by proclaiming the rights of *men*; but with the reference to establishment of government, attention shifts to the rights of the *people*. In fact, from this point to the end of the

Declaration, the word "men" is never used again, and all rights are said to be possessed by the people. Individuals find that to secure their rights they must establish a government; to do that they must join with others to form a people. (Here the Declaration seems to assume the Lockean teaching regarding the movement from the state of nature to civil society by way of a social contract.) This means that the members of a society are no longer free to exercise their rights as individuals. The ultimate instrument for insuring that government will protect rights—the right to revolution— belongs to the people, not to solitary individuals. It is for the people to decide whether and when a government has become so subversive of rights as to justify its abolition and replacement by a new government. Assuming that unanimity is impractical, the decision of the people will reflect the will of the majority. What then is to prevent the majority from tyrannizing over all minorities?

What is to keep the majority of the people from consenting to a popular despotism? Indeed, Machiavelli advises princes that the best way to secure their power is to rely on the people. Because most people would prefer to devote themselves to the economic comforts of a private life without the burdens of self-government, they will give virtually unlimited power to a ruler who provides them the peace and prosperity they seek. Even Locke suggests that princes can increase their power by encouraging the people in their endless accumulation of property, which, as a private activity, diverts their attention from public issues.

Is it perhaps the case that a regime founded on the conflict of selfish interests tends naturally to tyranny—either the tyranny of one group over another or the tyranny of a benevolent government that provides the people with comfortable private lives in exchange for their political liberty? This is the charge leveled against the Lockean regime by those followers of Rousseau who advocate participatory democracy. They insist that true democracy can be achieved only in a small community of self-governing citizens who share some conception of the common good. The character of the people must be shaped according to a common standard so as to discourage conflicts between people with different interests. With all the citizens participating directly in the government, public decisions would emerge as a consensus of all. In such a situation, no group would be permitted to tyrannize over another. Because all citizens would be actively engaged in political life, they would not be so preoccupied with the comforts of private life that they allow themselves to be excluded from the government. There are, however, problems with this scheme. A small community of self-governing citizens is as hard to establish as it is to maintain, especially in a world dominated by large nation-states. Its success would require transforming self-seeking individuals into public-spirited citizens, which might necessitate an authoritarian suppression of personal liberty.

In any case, the underlying issue is clear — how to devise political arrangements that conform to human nature. Are human beings so divided by selfish passions that government should not be expected to do more than police their conflicts? Or is there, in addition to the selfish and competitive side of human nature, a social and cooperative inclination such that the fulfillment of human potentiality requires a communal sharing of common purposes? On the other hand, is it correct to even ask questions that assume there is an unchanging human nature?

Is the character of human beings more a product of history than of nature?

> Prudence, indeed, will dictate that Governments long established should not be changed for light and transient causes; and accordingly all experience hath shown, that mankind are more disposed to suffer, while evils are sufferable, than to right themselves by abolishing the forms to which they are accustomed. But when a long train of abuses and usurpations, pursuing invariably the same Object evinces a design to reduce them under absolute Despotism, it is their right, it is their duty, to throw off such Government, and to provide new Guards for their future security. — Such has been the patient sufferance of these Colonies; and such is now the necessity which constrains them to alter their former Systems of Government. The history of the present King of Great Britain is a history of repeated injuries and usurpations, all having in direct object the establishment of an absolute Tyranny over these States. To prove this, let Facts be submitted to a candid world.

There follows a long list of factual grievances that takes up approximately two-thirds of the entire document (see appendix for a copy of the Declaration of Independence). This part of the argument cannot be founded on a "self-evident" grasp of nature. Rather, the reasoning here depends on "prudence," "experience," and the "facts" of "history." Apparently, the signers of the Declaration think that to justify their revolution they have to combine self-evident reasoning about nature with probabilistic reasoning about history. That the aim of just government is to secure equal rights is declared as a necessary and unchanging truth deducible from the universal principles of nature. But that King George III has acted contrary to this standard is at best a probable conclusion from particular facts. Although the equality of rights for all is a universal norm, determining whether a particular government is despotic requires prudence in judging variable circumstances of history.

By contrast, some Marxists would dismiss this separation of nature from history as illusory on the premise that human beings' ideas about nature arise from their historical conditions. Do not human beings take as true whatever universal principles will best serve their interests? One might then explain the American Revolution as dictated by the historical circumstances: the revolution occurred because it allowed those with newly acquired economic power to become the ruling class. Thus, the talk about "the Laws of Nature and of Nature's God" could be seen as a rationalization of the dominant economic interests of the time. The laws of nature are only the reflection in human minds of the laws of history as grounded in the material interests of human beings.

If appeals to nature are replaced by appeals to history, does this deprive us of any fixed standard for political life? The Declaration appeals to the absolutes of nature in order to defend the idea of rights and reject tyranny. Yet if there are no natural absolutes, if everything is relative to changing historical circumstances, tyrants cannot be judged to be good or bad, just or unjust. If tyrants enjoy historical success, how can they be condemned?

It will be our task in this book to think through these and other questions. By beginning with the Declaration of Independence, I want to stress that the questions posed by political philosophers are the questions that dominate modern politics. My claim is that because political philosophy goes to the roots of political life, we cannot understand clearly our political existence without reviewing the history of political philosophy from which modern political life arose. I do not mean to suggest, however, that the relation of political thought to political action is obvious, for the issue as to how political wisdom might bear on political power is the fundamental question of political philosophy, as should be evident to any reader of Plato.

Notes

1. For the history of American political documents from the Mayflower Compact to the Constitution of 1787, see Donald S. Lutz, *The Origins of American Constitutionalism* (Baton Rouge: Louisiana State University Press, 1988), who suggests that the ideas of the Declaration of Independence could be seen as "the result of radically extending the logic inherent in the Protestant Reformation, especially as the process occurred in colonial America" (120). Some scholars (like Willmoore

Kendall) have argued that the popular emphasis on the Declaration and its principle of equality is a "derailment," initiated by Lincoln, from the earlier tradition of American politics. See Willmoore Kendall and George W. Carey, *The Basic Symbols of the American Political Tradition* (Baton Rouge: Louisiana State University Press, 1970); and the criticisms offered by Harry V. Jaffa, *How to Think About the American Revolution* (Durham, NC: Carolina Academic Press, 1978).

2. Alexander Hamilton, James Madison, and John Jay, *The Federalist*, ed. Edward Mead Earle (New York: Random House, Modern Library, n.d.), No. 1, p. 3.

3. Ibid., 188.

4. Locke's influence on Jefferson has been denied by Garry Wills in *Inventing America: Jefferson's Declaration of Independence* (Garden City, NY: Doubleday, 1978). But he ignores the clear echoes in the Declaration of language in Locke's *Second Treatise* (e.g., secs. 210, 225, 230). Shortly before his death, Jefferson commented on the purpose of the Declaration and mentioned both Aristotle and Locke as sources of its ideas. (Letter to Henry Lee, 8 May 1825, in *The Life and Selected Writings of Thomas Jefferson*, eds. Adrienne Koch and William Peden [New York: Random House, Modern Library, 1944], 719). See chap. 8, n. 3.

5. Leo Strauss, for example, emphasizes Locke's departures from Aristotelian thought; but Richard Ashcraft sees important continuities. Compare Strauss, *Natural Right and History* (Chicago: University of Chicago Press, 1953), and Ashcraft, *Locke's Two Treatises of Government* (London: Unwin Hyman, 1987). Algernon Sidney, another author cited by Jefferson as a source for the ideas in the Declaration of Independence, seems closer to Aristotle than was Locke. See Algernon Sidney, *Discourses Concerning Government*, edited by Thomas G. West (Indianapolis: Liberty Classics, 1990), and Alan Craig Houston, *Algernon Sidney and the Republican Heritage in England and America* (Princeton: Princeton University Press, 1991).

Chapter

1

Political Knowledge and Political Power

Plato's *Apology, Crito,* and *Republic*

Key Readings

Apology, Crito, Republic, 327a–379a, 414b–417b, 432b–445e, 504d–525a.

Political philosophy begins in ancient Greece. Even the words "politics" and "philosophy" are derived from ancient Greek. *Politike* denotes the affairs of the Greek city (*polis*). *Philosophia* means literally the love of wisdom. Of course, we could trace the history of politics farther back: to ancient Egypt or to ancient Mesopotamia or even back to the nomadic bands of Stone Age people. But prior to the Greek city, social order arose from custom, and it was explained through religious myths rather than through independent human reasoning. Unlike previous civilizations, the Athens in which Socrates lived required its citizens to create and maintain order by deliberating about public affairs. The center of life was the *agora*, the public space in which citizens debated political questions according to the standards of human rationality. Thus Athens gave birth to rational political thought.[1]

In the fifth century B.C., the Greek cities — particularly Athens — reached one of the highest peaks of human history. During the first half of the century, the Greeks were threatened by a series of wars with the Persian Empire. But their defeat of the Persians in 449 B.C. allowed them to flourish during a period some historians call the Age of Pericles. Some suggest that the cultural brilliance of the Greeks—in art, poetry, history, philosophy, and politics—has never been surpassed.

Plato (427–347 B.C.) was born a few years after the beginning of the Peloponnesian War (431–404 B.C.), a conflict between Athens and Sparta that eventually was disastrous for Athens. By the time of Plato's death, Athens was near the bottom of its decline. A few years after his death, Athens was conquered by the Macedonians.

During Plato's life, the Athenians were divided into factions that ranged from radical democrats to radical oligarchs. He was probably exposed to political debates at an early age as all the major political groups were represented in his family. His own political activity was most evident in Sicily because of his friendship with Dion, a political leader in Syracuse. He had hopes of shaping Sicilian political life as a political advisor, but he never succeeded.

Evidently, his conversations with Socrates (470–399 B.C.) influenced his life more than anything else. He extended the work of Socrates by founding the Academy, a center of higher learning until the sixth century A.D. The universities of the Western world have continued, in some manner, the educational curriculum of the Academy.

A large portion of Plato's writings are dialogues, most of which feature Socrates as the main character.[2] Thus the life of Socrates is important for Plato's philosophizing, and a central theme of Plato's work is the conflict between Athenian politics and Socratic philosophy manifested in the trial and execution of Socrates in 399 B.C.

1. What is the political lesson of the trial of Socrates?

We cannot consider this question without also considering many of the fundamental questions about the nature of political life. Socrates exemplifies an individual who wants to know the best way of life for a human being. Such a person will prefer those political arrangements that offer support in this pursuit. To some extent, this person represents all of humankind. Don't we all seek to live the most fulfilling lives possible? And, consequently, don't we judge our political life by how well it supports us in this search? Surely, this is why Americans can hold it to be "self-evident" that the aim of any just government is to secure our "pursuit of happiness." But how is this to be done? Some would say that a political community should shape the lives of its citizens according to some shared standard of the good life. But can human beings discover any reliable standard of goodness? Even if they can, is it feasible to establish politics on such a foundation? Those on the opposing side of this issue would say that government best promotes the pursuit of happiness by leaving people free to live according to their own personal views of the good life (as long as they do not harm others). It might be argued that there are no absolute standards of goodness discoverable by human reason, so people should be free to live by whatever moral conceptions they choose. Yet if there are no moral absolutes, how can human freedom be justified as an absolute? Is it possible to have a free society without defending human freedom as an absolute value grounded on ''the Laws of Nature''?

Thus, from the beginning, the trial of Socrates leads us to consider two closely related lines of thought that will be important throughout this book. Some of the leading citizens of Athens regard Socrates as a threat to their political life simply because of the way he discusses with his fellow citizens ideas about the best way to live. We might wonder, first, what do philosophic ideas have to do with politics? Does every political community depend on certain shared ideas about the good life, so that a person who questions those ideas must always be a political threat? Or can a community that cherishes freedom refrain from imposing on its citizens any communal standards of goodness, so that a person like Socrates would not be perceived as politically dangerous?

This might lead us, then, into a second line of questioning. What does a citizen's individual pursuit of happiness have to do with political life? The Athenians seemed to assume that the happiness of an individual's life is intertwined with the happiness of the political community. But is it possible to separate the two, to restrict politics to a limited realm of life, so that individuals can be free in their private lives from political concerns? Oddly enough, those who have debated these questions raised by the trial of Socrates have been unable to agree as to where Socrates—or perhaps more exactly, Plato's Socrates—stands on these issues.

Not only do we want to figure out what Socrates is saying, we also want to understand Plato's thoughts. This is quite difficult as Plato himself never *speaks* in his dialogues! Trying to discover Plato's thought in his dialogues is like trying to find Shakespeare's thought in his plays. We must consider every statement in the dramatic context in which it appears. We must ask why this person says this in this particular situation. Thus, far from being an abstract and dogmatic philosopher, as is commonly assumed, Plato writes in such a way that his ideas are conveyed through the concrete action of a dramatized conversation. I emphasize, therefore, that what we shall do in this brief introductory chapter is no substitute for a close study of the particular details of the Platonic dialogues. With this cautionary note in mind, let us turn to Plato's *Apology of Socrates* and consider the questions we have already raised.

The Athenian jurors had at least three choices in dealing with Socrates. They finally chose to silence him. Alternatively, they could have changed the Athenian way of life in accord with his wishes, or they could have tried to tolerate him. Many modern readers of the *Apology* assume that the last choice would have been the best and that Plato would have agreed. Indeed, John Stuart Mill in *On Liberty* takes the case of Socrates as an obvious illustration of the dangers that come from not allowing complete freedom of speech.[3] Moreover, those who read the *Apology* in this way tend to see Socrates as a relativist who doubted that there were any fixed norms of truth or morality, and therefore he challenged the traditional dogmatism of his city. Socrates appears, from this perspective, to be a defender of an open society in which all are free to think and speak as they wish, unrestrained by the community.

What evidence is there in Plato's account of the trial of Socrates to support this view? Socrates challenged the leaders of his time for not being as wise as they thought they were. He claimed to be wiser than they, in that he at least knew that he knew nothing (*Apology* 21a–22e). In questioning the commonly accepted moral and religious beliefs of his time, Socrates caught the interest of those young people who were eager to challenge the traditions of their elders; thus, he appeared to many to be a corrupter of the young. From all this, we might conclude that Socrates was only asking the Athenians to be tolerant of all ideas no matter how new and shocking they might be.

On the other hand, it could be argued that Socrates actually assumed a highly intolerant stance. In claiming that those who think they are wise are not wise, and that he himself is wise only in knowing he knows nothing, he is implicitly claiming that he knows what it would mean to know. That is to say, in order to be so confident in recognizing ignorance—his own and that of others—Socrates must be certain of his own knowledge of the standards of truth. To look for wisdom and to expose as unfounded the claims of those who appear to be wise presupposes that one knows what wisdom would be like (17a–b, 22c–e).

Socrates also claims to know that even though he may never fully *possess* wisdom, the *search* for wisdom is the highest human

But this is a matter of Space + gov. limit- ations

activity. This, he holds, is the answer to that most important question, what is the best life for a human being? Knowing the answer to this question, he condemns the Athenians for seeking money, material comfort, and social status rather than devoting themselves wholly to thinking about the fundamental questions of life (30a–b, 36b). In doing this, he makes it difficult — perhaps impossible — for the Athenians to simply tolerate him. For he insists that he will continue to use his freedom to transform the Athenian way of life (28e–30b, 37e–38b).

The Athenian jurors think the very existence of their community depends on certain commonly accepted beliefs about the purpose of human life, of which beliefs about the gods in their relationships with human beings are especially important. They cannot, therefore, allow Socrates to question these common opinions if they wish to preserve their community. (To see what opinions Socrates was thought to have subverted, compare the various accusations at 18b, 19b, 23d, and 24b.)

Socrates agrees that one should not tolerate the public teaching of false opinion about what is good and bad, because corrupt opinions make people dangerous to their neighbors (25c–26a). The health of a community depends on its citizens holding right opinions about matters of conduct. Socrates insists, however, that by teaching the supreme importance of rational self-examination and inquiry, he is improving his fellow citizens. The true source of corruption, he maintains, is the commonly accepted belief that one ought to seek wealth and status above all. It would seem that far from advocating an open society, as some have thought, Socrates is advocating a closed society ruled by philosophers who would shape public opinion to conform to their orthodoxy.[4]

We must turn to the *Crito*, because in this dialogue, Socrates considers how a citizen's freedom of thought and action might be justly limited by the laws.

2. How far is a citizen obligated to obey the laws?

At first glance, the Socratic answer to this question in the *Apology* seems to contradict the answer in the *Crito*. In his trial, Socrates refuses to give up his philosophic conversations as commanded by the Athenian authorities; later, as he awaits execution, he insists in the *Crito* that he is obligated by the laws not to try to escape. Even while resisting a particular legal command as being unjust, Socrates is still subject to the laws in other respects. Once again, the more general question is how one reconciles one's yearnings as a human being and one's obligations as a citizen.

In the first half of his discussion with Crito, Socrates says that he strives to act by a rational standard that goes beyond popular opinions. What is truly right and wrong is not necessarily the same as what most people think to be right and wrong. But what makes common opinions unreliable? And exactly what is the norm to which Socrates appeals? Satisfactory answers to these questions would require a careful reading of this and other Platonic dialogues. Here we can draw some tentative conclusions from a few of the hints that Socrates gives us.

Most people were surprised that Socrates at this trial was unafraid of being sentenced to death. Now they are surprised that he does not try to escape with his life. For most people, death is the worst of evils; and so it is to be avoided at all costs. But for Socrates the important thing is not merely to live, but to *live well*. He would choose a noble death over an ignoble life. Socrates differs from most people in that they care about the body, its preservation and comfort; he cares about the mind, that distinctively human capacity for understanding one's self and one's world. For Socrates, the greatest of evils is not death, but self-deception.[5]

How might an Athenian respond? Surely, the bodily needs of life must be satisfied as a precondition for cultivating the mind. Anyone who pursues the life of the mind is indebted to the community for providing the physical security — if not even luxury — that makes possible intellectual activity. Not only does the community secure the bodily existence of philosophers, it also provides for their education. Even Socrates is largely a product of Athens and of that rare combination of security, freedom, and high culture that distinguishes the Athenian way of life. The Athenian patriot might well demand of Socrates that he honor the city that has made his philosophic life possible. Even the intellectual independence that leads him to challenge Athenian traditions was instilled in him by an Athenian education.

Far from ignoring these arguments, Socrates presents them to Crito as reasons to accept his prescribed punishment rather than to escape. Socrates asks Crito to imagine what the laws of Athens might say if they could speak to them (50a–b). The laws would oppose an escape attempt by saying that a city could not continue to exist if individual citizens were free to nullify legal judgments against them. To which Socrates might respond that the judgment against him was unjust, implying that even if citizens should obey the *just* decrees of the laws, they should be free to resist those that are *unjust*.

Can any legal system work if its judgments may be disobeyed by any citizen who thinks them unjust? If every final decision of the laws must be accepted until legally changed, does this mean that justice is whatever the lawmakers and judges say it is? Can Socrates appeal to a standard of justice that goes beyond the legal conventions of his city and still be a good citizen?

In the speech attributed to the laws, Socrates is reminded that both his birth and his education were made possible by the laws. When he reached adulthood, he was free to leave and take his property with him. By staying he showed his acceptance of the laws and the way of life of Athens, which could be considered a tacit agreement to abide by the conditions of Athenian citizenship. Moreover, Athens gave Socrates the chance to persuade the jurors that the demands made on him were unjust, but he failed to convince them that his position was in accord with "the just by nature" (51c).

With these points in mind, the Athenian patriot might argue that Athens is as open to debate about questions of justice as any community can be, but that no community can allow disputes about fundamental political issues to continue indefinitely. Socrates complained at his trial (*Apology* 37a–b) that he had not been given enough time to state his case. He was, however, permitted to live to the age of seventy, which in itself would suggest that the Athenians had been patient with him for a long time.

Socrates seems to be convinced by the arguments of the laws that to escape his punishment would violate his obligations as a citizen. He seems, then, to agree that the philosopher's devotion to endless, radical inquiry into the most fundamental questions of life must be limited — at least in public — for the sake of a stable political order. Yet, though he *seems* to be so persuaded, the careful reader of the *Crito* might still doubt this.

We note that Socrates distinguishes between his own reasoning in the first half of the dialogue and the arguments in the second half that he attributes to the laws. He says the words of the laws have so overwhelmed him that he cannot even listen to opposing arguments (54d), which contradicts his usual assumption that all sides of an issue should be presented before a decision is made. Is it possible that Socrates thought that the teaching of the laws would have a good effect on Crito and those like him? Would his apparent acceptance of this teaching make people think that Socratic philosophers are not politically subversive after all? Would Socrates have been more receptive to plans for an escape if he had been younger, with many years of philosophizing ahead of him, and if there had been another city suitable for pursuing his work?[6]

Considering subtleties such as these is essential for an accurate understanding of the text.

But let us return to the general question at issue. To what extent is the individual's pursuit of natural fulfillment limited by the political order that secures the conditions for such a pursuit? Have we not already seen this demonstrated in the Declaration of Independence? Human beings possess by nature those rights necessary to fulfill their humanity, but they must depend on a government to secure those rights; and the proper organization of the power of government is determined not by individuals, but by the people acting under majority rule. There is, then, an absolute standard of justice by which government may be judged, but individuals cannot nullify governmental acts by appealing to this standard unless they can persuade the people of the rightness of their cause. How can the moral claims of individual human beings be given some political recognition without violating the minimal conditions of a stable political order by leaving all people free to judge their own claims?

This question has been raised at various points in American history by individuals who have claimed the right to disobey laws they considered unjust. This sort of argument was made, for example, by Henry David Thoreau in his essay "Civil Disobedience."[7] Thoreau opposed the injustice of slavery by refusing to support any law that protected it. He opposed the war with Mexico in 1846 because he thought it would extend the area for slaveholding, and he was jailed when he refused to pay a tax that he thought might indirectly support the war. To justify his disobedience he appealed to the Declaration of Independence, arguing that the right to revolution included the right of any individual to make a "peaceable revolution" by refusing to obey a government that sanctions injustice. He thought this could easily be done by self-reliant individuals like himself who had little or no need for government. "It is not many moments that I live under a government, even in this world," he explained.[8]

Would Socrates agree with Thoreau? Surely he would agree that there are standards of justice beyond the laws and that individuals ought to resist unjust laws. But as we have seen, Socrates allows the case for obedience to Athens to be made in the *Crito*. Clearly, he takes law and government much more seriously than does Thoreau, who irreverently suggests that he has no need for government. Socrates is reminded in the *Crito* that his intellectual development, even his ability to question the opinions of the Athenians, is itself a product of Athenian culture, which obligates him to respect the law. Should Thoreau have been reminded that *his* intellectual life had also been nurtured by the cultural life of America? One of the marks of the individualistic spirit of America is that Americans are more inclined than the Athenians were to separate individual life and political life. Americans such as Thoreau might say that the ancient Athenians failed to appreciate the importance of individual freedom. The Athenians might respond that Americans fail to appreciate the extent to which a good life depends on living in a civilized community.

Whatever differences there might be between the views of Socrates and Thoreau, the underlying problem is the same. How do citizens maintain their independence of moral judgment while fulfilling their obligations to the political order that secures their lives? Martin Luther King, Jr., pointed to the same issue in his "Letter from the Birmingham Jail" of 1963. Justifying his illegal acts to protest racial segregation, he explained:

> Just as Socrates felt it was necessary to create a tension in the mind so that individuals could rise from the bondage of myths and half-truths . . ., so must we see the need for nonviolent gadflies to create the kind of tension in society that will help men rise from the dark depths of prejudice and racism.[9]

But what would Socrates have to do to insure that individuals "rise from the bondage of myths and half-truths"? At times he suggests that the best answer would be for Athens to be ruled by a philosopher such as himself. Instead of being governed by traditional opinions of what is good for men, Athens might then be ordered according to the philosopher's grasp of the true needs of human nature. But Socrates' confession (or rather his boast) that he only knows that he knows nothing should make us wonder whether a philosophic ruler would have any clear substitute for the traditional political opinions. Would it be sufficient for a Socratic ruler to take as his only norm the promotion of endless philosophic inquiry as the highest human activity? These and related questions lead us to Plato's *Republic*, in which the difficulties in uniting philosophic wisdom and political rule become evident.

3. In defining justice, how do we move from opinions to knowledge?

Socrates challenges the commonly accepted opinions by which Athens is governed. He seeks a definition of political justice that arises not from the traditions of a particular community, but from the universal and unchanging principles of human nature. We can understand why he would do this. We have all noticed that different people have different opinions about justice and that the differences are especially evident when people do not belong to the same cultural tradition. This makes us wonder whether there is any universal standard of justice at all, or whether someone's conception of justice is merely a product of upbringing. Where should we look for a universal definition of justice? If we take Socrates as our guide, we should start with that which we wish to transcend—the common opinions about justice.[10] Socrates pursues justice by asking people what they think about it, and each person answers in a way that reflects his or her character. Never being satisfied with the first answer anyone gives, Socrates moves through a series of questions in which he assumes that the most rigorous knowledge comes from a refinement of the common-sense opinions of human beings. For this reason, the readers of a Platonic dialogue cannot be sure that they understand what is going on unless they follow carefully the dramatic details of each conversation. We cannot do that here, but we can at least glance at a few of the passages in Book One of the *Republic* to get some provisional impressions about how Socrates works with the opinions of those he meets.

In the *Republic*, the first view of justice is that of Cephalus, who defines justice as telling the truth and giving back what one has borrowed from another (331a–d). Because this is an ordinary view of justice taken by many people, Socrates starts here. He does not totally reject Cephalus's definition, but he does offer an example of a case where it would seem not to apply. If a man has borrowed a weapon from a friend, who later asks for it to be returned when he is drunk or deranged and likely to harm himself, the borrower would be just if he refused to return the weapon and deceived his friend until the friend recovered his reason. Cephalus immediately sees that Socrates is right. Thus Socrates has shown that Cephalus's opinions about justice are contradictory.

But why is Cephalus reluctant to broaden his definition of justice to include the kind of situation that Socrates presents? Perhaps it is his understandable hesitation to acknowledge the justice in some cases of lying and stealing. This may help to illustrate why Socrates was thought to be a corrupter of the youth. Cephalus is a respectable old man, surrounded by his children, showing them parental wisdom by teaching them that justice is telling the truth and paying one's debts—honesty is the best policy. Socrates forces him to admit that sometimes it is just to lie and steal from one's friends. Socrates shows the children that the traditional moral maxims of their father are not absolutes because they do not apply to every conceivable case.

Cephalus thinks it best to teach his children to obey habitually the ordinary moral rules without considering the exceptional cases to which the usual rules do not apply. He knows that there are exceptions to the rules, just as any person of experience would, but he hesitates to draw attention to them. Consider the difficulties that arise from taking the approach of Socrates. Socrates believes that returning someone's property can be harmful because people do not always use their property wisely. The reluctance of Cephalus to acknowledge this publicly is understandable. Socrates implies that it would be best for people to have only that property which they can properly use as determined by the judgment of the wise. One cannot do good to one's friends unless one knows what is good for them, which requires that one know what is good for human beings as such. This, however, suggests the need for philosopher-kings!

Socrates assumes, provisionally, that justice is doing good to one's friends. Why only *friends*? Why not *all people*? We should remember the admonishment of Jesus that although it is easy to love those who love us, it is a higher achievement to love even our enemies (Matthew 5:43–48). We enjoy doing good to our friends because friendship is rewarding; thus our *duty* coincides with our *interest*. We have no such motive for helping those who are not our friends—especially if they are enemies—unless as Christians we anticipate the rewards of heaven. Because Socrates does not have the benefit of Christian revelation, he cannot rely on the motives of Christian piety. Should we conclude, therefore, that Socratic justice depends ultimately on self-interest?

In any case, Polemarchus picks up Socrates' suggestion and defines justice as doing good to friends and harm to enemies (332d). One of the questions that Socrates raises in response has to do with the difficulty of recognizing true friends. Those who *seem* to be good to us may not be so in truth, and those who are truly good to us may not seem so (334c). Thus, Socrates indicates one of the major themes of the *Republic*—the importance of moving from appearance to reality, from opinion to knowledge. Socrates points out the dependence of good conduct on genuine knowledge. To act properly we must know what people are like and what is appropriate for each. Habitual acceptance of the common moral opinions falls short of this knowledge, but the common opinions do reflect the truth and must therefore be the starting point for philosophic inquiry. Again, we are compelled to challenge Socrates to show us how we can gain knowledge of the truly just. Some of us might even suggest that Socrates is naive in talking about some ideal of justice that has no application to the harsh realities of politics. In fact, this is exactly the objection made at this point in the dialogue by Thrasymachus.

Before looking at the argument of Thrasymachus, we should consider what it is that stirs up his anger. Socrates gets Polemarchus to agree that although he was right in saying that justice means helping friends, he was wrong in saying that it is just to harm enemies. The just person harms no one (335a–336a). Of course, to *refrain from injuring* one's enemies is still a long way from the Christian duty to *love* one's enemies; even so, it does seem unrealistic to think that people could completely avoid harming their enemies. Must not a good citizen of any country be willing to injure the enemies of that country in war? Or is Socrates saying that a truly just person would be a pacifist? Although he implies that here, later, in describing what he thinks would be the "best city," he says that the soldiers should be trained to be gentle to their fellow citizens but cruel to their enemies (375c). This seeming contradiction should interest us because it illustrates a general problem in the interpretation of the *Republic*.

Some readers have thought that Socrates is so idealistic as to be blind to the unpleasant necessities of political life, such as the harshness of war, that often require the violation of ordinary rules of moral conduct. We shall see that people such as Machiavelli have criticized the ancient political philosophers for ignoring how war exhibits the ignoble reality of politics as being founded on force and fraud. Yet, in various portions of the *Republic*, Socrates takes a tough-minded Machiavellian view of the grim necessities of politics. Perhaps what he intends to teach us is the political need for combining — as in the training of good soldiers — gentleness and cruelty. Political leadership requires being capable of ruthlessness without being vicious.

This might help to explain why Socrates argues early in the *Republic* against harming enemies, even though later on he concedes that even the best city might have to fight its enemies. Although war is necessary, one should see it as a necessary *evil*. This attitude promotes as much moderation as is realistically possible. It discourages aggressive, imperialistic wars, but does not undermine the capacity for defense against attacks. (It should be noted that Athens had just been defeated in an imperialistic war with Sparta.) Is it possible that Socrates knows everything that Machiavelli knows without being Machiavellian? If so, then what does Socrates know that Machiavelli does not?

Some hints about how we should answer these questions arise in Socrates' discussion with his Machiavellian friend Thrasymachus. What is said by Thrasymachus represents the characteristic teaching of the Sophists. The Sophists were teachers who traveled from one city to another, and they were best known for teaching people how to use rhetoric to defend whatever cause they wished. Like Machiavelli, they had the reputation—perhaps not entirely justified—for being unscrupulous individuals who, for a fee, would show people how to gain and use political power for selfish purposes.[11] So, in confronting Thrasymachus, Socrates must deal with the sort of person that we today might call a political realist, a person for whom justice is simply the interest of the stronger.

4. Is justice the interest of the stronger?

Thrasymachus insists that whoever is strong enough to gain political rule will dictate the rules of justice to promote selfish interests (338c–339a). Later, Thrasymachus explains that true justice does not exist because human beings are so divided by selfish competitiveness that they seek only to exploit one another whenever they can (343a–344c). What is thought to be justice is actually a tool for injustice, for those who rule exploit their subjects and call this justice. In fact, all would prefer to do injustice if they could get away with it; but only a few are strong enough and clever enough to fulfill this human desire for complete injustice, and they become tyrants. Justice is whatever the rulers say it is, and all rulers are tyrants—even if disguised—in that they rule for their own benefit at the expense of the ruled. Justice, therefore, is the interest of the stronger.

As he did with Cephalus and Polemarchus, Socrates questions Thrasymachus about the problems that arise if his conception of justice depends on mere *opinions* about how things seem to be rather than on *knowledge* of how things really are (339c–340c). According to Thrasymachus, justice is doing whatever the rulers command; and they will command whatever serves their interests. But what happens when the rulers are mistaken about their interests and command their subjects to do what in fact is harmful to the ruling group? In that case, the subjects are not serving the rulers' interests by obeying their commands. Thrasymachus is thus caught in a contradiction when he claims that justice is obeying all commands of the rulers, thereby advancing their interests. He justifies this by saying that "a ruler in the precise sense" never makes mistakes. To the extent that leaders possess the art of ruling, they know what they are doing; and to the extent that they misunderstand what they are doing, they lack the art (340d–341a).

This turns out to be Thrasymachus's fatal mistake because, by agreeing that "a ruler in the precise sense" has perfect knowledge of ruling, he gives Socrates what he apparently needs to win the argument. Because Socrates shows that in accepting the obligation to act according to the perfect *knowledge* of the art of ruling, the ruler must rule not simply to satisfy selfish *interests*, but for the perfection of the art of ruling as a form of *knowledge*.

Thrasymachus cannot present political rule as combining power and knowledge without contradicting his view of ruling as essentially tyrannical—that is, serving the good of the ruler at the expense of the ruled. To seek knowledge is to seek a good that implies standards of truth common to all thinking people; thus it is a good that rests on agreement with others. But the tyrant seeks to dominate others rather than to win their agreement to common purposes. In denying that the goods most worth seeking are attained in cooperation with others, a tyrant cannot be a seeker of knowledge because this is a good held in common with others. This defect in tyranny becomes clearer by considering the character of Thrasymachus, who apparently sees himself as the sort of great tyrant that he praises.

Why doesn't Thrasymachus show his superiority by beating Socrates up rather than arguing with him? Is it not inconsistent for him to ask for agreement with a position that denies all grounds for agreement? By trying to persuade Socrates and the others to agree with him that he knows the truth about justice, Thrasymachus shows that he wants their assent to his claims. Would a true tyrant make himself dependent on the consent of those who were to be his victims? It might have been a more accurate demonstration of the superior power of tyranny for Thrasymachus to shut Socrates up by slugging him. This, however, would have only demonstrated the power of a big thug, and Thrasymachus would not have been satisfied with that. Why does he want to present tyranny as founded not just on the physical force of a bully, but on genuine knowledge of what life is like?

Perhaps Thrasymachus thinks it is in his self-interest to show that tyranny is an art that requires a special sort of knowledge. If he wants to be employed as an advisor to rulers, he must convince those with political ambitions that he has the knowledge that they need to win and hold political power. This assumes, however, that power without knowledge is defective and thus leads to the problems indicated by Socrates.

Another possible explanation of Thrasymachus's behavior is that the bad like to think they are clever and that the good are naive (see 343a, 348c–d, 349b). Thrasymachus would like to think the tyrannical-minded are smart, and those like Socrates are childishly ignorant of the ways of the world. This would explain why Thrasymachus blushes when Socrates seems to defeat him in the argument (350d). For Thrasymachus to have been outwitted or even tricked implies that Socrates is smarter.

Simply by engaging in a conversation about justice, Thrasymachus implicitly agrees that reason rather than mere force should rule in human life. By conceding that a true ruler should govern with perfect knowledge of the art of ruling, Thrasymachus accepts—without fully recognizing that he does so—the Socratic teaching that the best political rule would combine philosophic knowledge and political power. We should remember a similar thought in the Declaration of Independence. By appealing to "the Laws of Nature" and to rational standards held to be "self-evident," the signers of the Declaration imply that, because political action is ultimately guided by some first principles, the reliability of political rule depends on the reasonableness of those principles. To differing degrees, every political regime depends on some principle of justice to sustain its authority.

5. Is justice the fulfillment of natural needs?

Toward the end of his conversation with Thrasymachus, Socrates argues that politics aims at justice because justice is a condition for human beings in fulfilling their natural inclinations. Political rule should be guided by a knowledge of the various inclinations characteristic of human nature and of how these inclinations can be satisfied to the fullest. To make justice the highest political standard is to see the purpose of political life as the actualization of human potential.

To clarify what Socrates is saying, we should consider two of the Greek terms he uses here. *Ergon* can be translated as work, activity, or function. *Arete* can be translated as virtue or excellence. "The work [or function] of each thing," Socrates says, "is what it alone can do, or can do more finely than other things"; and there is "a virtue [or excellence] for each thing to which some work is assigned" (353a–b). We would say that it is bad for a horse to have a broken leg because it cannot perform the work for which it is naturally fitted; and we would say that it is bad for eyes to be blinded for the same reason. We would say that a good horse is one that can run well, and good eyes are those that can see well. We have standards of goodness here because we know what these things are naturally suited to do. The virtue of each thing is its doing well whatever activity is most appropriate to its nature. If we knew the activity for which human beings are best fitted by their nature, then we would have a standard of the human good for political life.

Later in the dialogue, Socrates will distinguish three parts of the human soul—appetite, spirit, and reason—and he will claim that all three parts reach their fullest activity when they are well ordered under the rule of reason as the highest part. At this point in the dialogue, he alludes to this teaching by stating that what is distinctive about the human soul is its capacity for ruling through rational deliberation (353d). In having bodily appetites and spirited emotions, we are like all other animals; but we are distinguished from them by our ability to reason. Justice, therefore, exists in an *individual soul* when each power is fully active under the rule of reason. Justice exists in a *community* when each citizen does well what he or she is best suited for in cooperation with the others under the rule of the wisest.

The key point here is the idea of justice—and of goodness in general—as being the fulfillment of natural tendencies. Figuring out the exact meaning of this idea and then trying to decide whether it is correct or not would lead us into a number of difficult questions. We can postpone this discussion until we come to Aristotle and later to Aquinas, who clarify the ideas of natural justice and natural law.

What should we make of the thought that the goal of politics is justice understood as the realization or completion of the natural tendencies of human beings? It is claimed that human beings can discover moral standards in *nature*, which are not, therefore, simply arbitrary or artificial human products. These moral norms of nature are expressed in certain inclinations or needs shared by all members of the human species. We must satisfy our natural needs in order to be fully human. Food, socialization, and education are examples of such needs. Without food, we could not survive. Without social activity and some development of our minds (such as learning to speak), we might survive, but our growth as human beings would be stunted and deformed.

If justice is viewed as the fulfillment of natural needs, then our moral duties coincide with our personal interests. To do what we *ought* to do is to do what we naturally *desire* to do. There can be conflicts, however, between our natural needs and our accidental wants. Someone's pleasure in enslaving people may conflict with the need for social cooperation; though the latter should take precedence over the former because a social life is essential to human development, whereas enslaving others is not. To insure the proper satisfaction of their basic needs, individuals have to use their capacity to reason to understand their needs and how best to fulfill them. This rational ordering of human inclinations is as important for a just *community* as it is for a just *individual*. We should remember the argument of the Declaration of Independence that, according to the "Laws of Nature," any just government must secure the conditions necessary for each human being to satisfy those needs that are shared equally with all other human beings.

Can we be sure that Socrates is correct in presenting justice as the completion of our natural tendencies under the rule of reason? Does this depend on our common-sense experience of human nature? Some would insist that unbiased observations of how human beings act do not support Socratic teaching. People often seem to be so narrowly passionate and selfish in their desires as to lack all the natural inclinations to justice of which Socrates speaks. From this viewpoint, justice might seem to be little more than an artificial set of rules created by human beings to pacify the natural conflicts among themselves. Of course, Plato is fully aware of this view of justice, as we have seen from the arguments he attributes to Thrasymachus. At the beginning of Book Two of the *Republic*, another version of this position is given by Glaucon and Adeimantus.

6. Is justice conventional rather than natural?

Because Glaucon and Adeimantus are not satisfied with Socrates' apparent refutation of Thrasymachus's claim that most would naturally prefer to do injustice if they could escape detection, they restate the Thrasymachean argument. If justice is natural, then Socrates should show them that people naturally take pleasure in doing justice for its own sake. The common opinions and behavior of human beings, however, appear to deny this. It seems that people find doing injustice to be naturally good and suffering injustice bad. Yet, since most people cannot freely do injustice to others without suffering injustice themselves, and the pain of the injustice they endure is greater than the pleasure of inflicting injustice on others, they are generally willing to agree to a kind of contract that establishes laws to prohibit all people from injuring their fellow citizens. Whatever the law decrees is called justice (348e–359b). Justice, then, is more conventional than natural, because it is the arbitrary product of human agreement to keep the natural selfishness of human beings from leading to violent anarchy. Justice is natural, therefore, only in the sense that the natural desire for self-preservation leads people to want to escape the violence that results when they are unrestrained by law. This differs, however, from Socrates' conception of natural justice. Socratic justice is a good in itself that fulfills natural human inclinations; but Thrasymachean justice (as described by Glaucon and Adeimantus) is only a lesser of two evils that people choose because they cannot satisfy their natural desire for injustice without suffering injustice themselves. While the aim of Socratic justice is to perfect human nature in its highest capacities, the aim of Thrasymachean justice is to restrain the viciousness of human nature. Socratic justice makes human beings better. Thrasymachean justice simply keeps the peace.

The tyrant, as representative of those in the natural state, does what others would like to do if they could: dominate others for the satisfaction of selfish desires. Glaucon and Adeimantus recognize that if Socrates is to refute this view, he must show that living justly is more intrinsically pleasurable than living the life of a tyrant.

By responding to the Thrasymachean view of justice, Socrates will also be responding to the arguments of modern political philosophers such as Machiavelli and Hobbes. As we shall see, they also deny that there is any natural inclination to justice beyond the desire to be free from the natural war of each against all. As in Glaucon's account of justice (359a), Hobbes envisions justice as the product of a social contract through which people create an artificial restraint on their own natural rapaciousness.

This same issue as to whether political justice is natural or conventional has been important in American political history. The debates in 1858 between Stephen Douglas and Abraham Lincoln illustrate this. Douglas argued that because the Constitution gave *legal* support to slavery, the *moral* question of whether slavery was right or wrong should not be discussed. To argue about the moral status of slavery would only promote conflict, he insisted; therefore, to keep the peace, we ought to leave the people of the new states in the West free to decide by majority vote whether their states will have slavery or not. Thus Douglas was close to the Thrasymachean claim that justice is the rule of the stronger, which in this case meant the rule of the majority as embodied in the conventional legal arrangements of the society. Lincoln argued that there could be no *right* to hold slaves if slavery was *wrong*. He appealed to the equality of rights in the Declaration of Independence as a moral absolute grounded in natural justice that should be respected. Lincoln conceded that it was impracticable to abolish slavery immediately, which was why the Constitution gave at least temporary protection for the institution. Nevertheless, he insisted, as an abstract principle equality should be the goal toward which we would move as quickly as circumstances permitted.[12] Like Socrates, Lincoln ascribed to a standard of *natural* justice by which all *legal* justice would be measured.

There is a plausible argument for the position of Douglas and Thrasymachus. If the limitations of human nature, including the inability of human beings to agree about moral principles, make it impossible to reach moral perfection in politics (and both Lincoln and Socrates would have to admit this), then is it not dangerous to push political life toward that unattainable goal? Won't such unrealistic moral idealism promote unceasing political conflict, a universally agreed-upon evil? Would it not be better, therefore, to secure political peace by lowering the aims of political justice?

In response to this challenge, as presented by Glaucon and Adeimantus, Socrates must defend justice as naturally desirable in itself. To do this he offers to construct a "city in speech" in accordance with the natural needs of human beings, with the hope that true justice might come into view in this imaginary city (368b–369b). Without considering all the elements of this city, we should at least consider a few points that bear on the general questions we have raised.

Socrates sees the city arising from two principles of human nature. First, "each of us isn't self-sufficient but is in need of much" (369b). That we live in communities is natural because we must cooperate with one another in order to satisfy our needs. Food is the first and greatest need; of course, housing and clothing are also needed. The second principle of our nature that determines the shape of every community is that "each of us is naturally not entirely like anyone else, but rather differs in his nature; one man is fitted for one work, and another for another" (370b). According to this principle of the natural division of labor, all benefit when each does whatever each is most suited for by nature to do well. One individual is a farmer, another a carpenter, another a weaver, and so on. All are naturally equal in their needs, but they are naturally unequal in their capacities. The specialization of labor is more productive in both the quantity and the quality of its products.

The question of whether the social division of labor is demanded by technical efficiency and human nature has been debated throughout the history of the social sciences. Adam Smith, for example, defends the division of labor as the basis for capitalism, while Rousseau and Marx warn of the degrading effects of dividing labor so that it becomes monotonous and dehumanizing (see chapter 11, section 3).

Socrates defends the social division of labor as manifesting the natural human need for social cooperation. Are human beings naturally inclined to social cooperation? The anthropological evidence is conflicting, as we shall see when we consider Aristotle's claim that we are political beings by nature. There is, however, some support for Socrates in certain contemporary theories of human origins. Some anthropologists have argued, for example, that it was the urge for cooperation and sharing that distinguished human evolution from that of the other primates.[13] The most decisive element—just as in the Socratic account—is said to have been food sharing. The sharing of food might have supported all the other distinctive characteristics of our first human ancestors— erect posture, verbal communication, grouping around home bases, the use of tools, and long-term mating and kinship categories. Food sharing also gave rise to a natural division of labor based on sex. The men would hunt and scavenge while the women—being encumbered with children, and therefore lacking the speed and mobility for hunting—would gather plants and small animals. Rather than consuming the food as soon as they found it—like the apes—they brought it back to a home base for sharing. (Consider the implications of the many social rituals associated with food sharing as a gesture of hospitality.) This anthropological theory supports to some extent the Socratic view of human nature, whereas other theories that stress the natural violence and aggressiveness of our human ancestors seem to support Thrasymachus. No one would deny that violent conflict has almost always been part of human life, especially when circumstances force human beings to compete for survival. But the issue here is whether aggression is the predominant characteristic of human nature. How one answers this question will shape one's view of political life.

Socrates recognizes the natural aggressiveness of human beings when he describes the move from a "healthy city" to a "feverish city" (372e). At the beginning, his "city in speech" is a small community with a simple life. Because people are satisfied with the minimal necessities of life, there is enough to go around; in such circumstances, it is easy to have a cooperative community. But as the city becomes larger and more complex, and as people begin to desire luxuries so that their wants are never satisfied, competition grows, and there are wars. From this perspective, the move to the "feverish city" would seem to be a decline. From another perspective, it would seem to be an ascent, because in the city of luxury the highest cultural pursuits—such as philosophy—become possible. Yet if philosophy is not possible in a "healthy city," a question is raised about the goodness of philosophy. Is the "healthy city" more natural, in that it reflects the natural necessities of existence? Or is the "feverish city" more natural, in that it allows the highest faculties of human nature to flourish?

We begin to wonder whether or not philosophy is compatible with a good political life. We must ask ourselves what Plato intended his readers to conclude from Socrates' description of a city ruled by philosophers.

7. Is the rule of philosopher-kings meant to be a realistic political goal?

This may seem to be an odd question to ask about the *Republic* because the most famous—or infamous—teaching of this book is that the only cure for our political ills would be for philosophers to become rulers (473b–e). Yet some interpreters of the *Republic* (particularly, Leo Strauss and his students) have concluded that Plato intended to show how unrealistic it would be to combine philosophic wisdom and political power.[14] When Socrates sets down as requirements for his city measures so seemingly contrary to human nature—especially the bodily appetites—as to be comical, these interpreters regard this as evidence that Plato wants his serious readers to see how ridiculous it would be to adopt the *Republic* as a program for political action (e.g., see 450a–473a, 540e–541b, 546a–547a). What would be the value of such a teaching for understanding politics? An image of such a "city in speech," even if not fully realizable in practice, might still serve as a standard for judging political proposals as better or worse (472b–473b). Plato could be warning against the dangers of expecting too much from politics. Utopian projects can produce the greatest political disasters. Plato might be a teacher of moderation insofar as he teaches that the highest human needs—as manifested in philosophic pursuits—go beyond the limits of political life (591b–592b). But if Plato believes the highest life is philosophic, does he thus denigrate the moral life? If Plato believes morality is subordinate to philosophy, does that mean Thrasymachus was right in denying that morality is naturally good as an end in itself?[15]

Some commentators have challenged this interpretation of the *Republic*.[16] They insist that the "city in speech" is, in fact, intended by Plato to be an ideal political order. The Platonic teaching, therefore, is that far from being in conflict with political rule, philosophic perfection can be achieved only in a good political order founded on the rule of reason. These interpreters deny that Plato believes there to be a sharp conflict between the theoretical life and the practical life or between the rational, the spirited, and the appetitive elements of human nature.

To decide which of these interpretations of the *Republic* is correct requires a careful reading of the text itself. But let us keep in mind one of the principles that we shall stress throughout this book: every important question about interpreting a work of political philosophy is also likely to be an important question about how we should think about politics. The question here concerns the extent to which politics can be truly rational.

Every political community rests on certain fundamental beliefs, of which the principle of equality of rights in the Declaration of Independence might be an example. Is the nature of politics such that these fundamental beliefs must be accepted by the citizens in an unreflective way as unexamined opinions? If so, then politics can never become philosophic, for philosophy requires radical inquiry into the most important questions of life. If it were possible to transform political life so that it would be grounded not on opinions, but on knowledge or at least on the rigorous pursuit of knowledge, politics could become philosophic.

Thus, we return to the predicament of Socrates standing before the Athenian jurors. Because for him "the unexamined life is not worth living," he cannot accept without question the traditional opinions by which Athens is governed. Yet it is hard to see how the Athenians could devote themselves fully to the Socratic way of life without political disaster. It seems that the possibility for a few people to live like Socrates depends on the stable political order secured by the very opinions that he questions.

Would this problem be solved in a community ruled by philosophers? Could such a community exist without any reliance on unexamined opinions, which are usually mixtures of truth and falsity? The difficulty of achieving this is evident in a number of places in the *Republic*. We will glance at only two examples: the account of the "noble lie" and the image of the cave.

8. Why does Socratic statesmanship require a "noble lie"?

The Socratic "city in speech" requires a program of civic education. As one element of that education, the citizens must be told what Socrates calls a "noble lie." Many readers of the *Republic* have been shocked by this. Does this show that Socrates—or Plato—was willing to use propaganda to establish a totalitarian state? How can anyone who believes in political freedom accept the idea of indoctrinating citizens with lies? Socrates has distinguished a "noble lie" from a "true lie" (382a–d). A "true lie" hides the truth, and it should be avoided at all costs. But a "noble lie"—or a "lie in speech"—resembles the truth in some manner, and it is told for a good purpose. Yet why is there any need for even a "noble lie"? Why can't the citizens be told the unequivocal truth?

The "noble lie" suggested by Socrates has two parts (414b–415b). First, the citizens must be told that their childhood was like a dream, that they were actually under the earth, and that with the completion of their education the earth, which is their mother, sent them up. They should think of themselves as siblings born of the earth, and they should defend their land as their mother. Second, they must be told that even though they are siblings, they were formed of three different natures by the god. Those with gold in them are to be the rulers; those with silver the soldiers (or auxiliaries); and those with iron and bronze the farmers and other workers. Although those of each class will generally produce offspring like themselves, sometimes a gold child will be born to silver parents, or a silver child to gold parents, and so on. In these cases, the children are to be removed and placed in the group for which they are naturally suited.

Socrates admits that this story seems so fantastic that it would be difficult to convince people to accept it. Still, he thinks it conveys a truth about political life. Is this silly story true? Why shouldn't we conceive of our childhood education as a process of being born to personhood, as a fetal stage during which our society gives us the language, the habits, and the culture that shape us into full human beings by the time we reach adulthood? Isn't this why every society distinguishes between minors and adults and treats the passage into adulthood as a birth into real life? Imagine infants left to themselves from birth with no human contact. Even if they could survive physically, we might doubt whether they could ever become fully human without having been nurtured by society.

Isn't it common for political communities to be spoken of as families bound together by blood ties? We talk of the "fatherland" or the "mother country."[17] Consider the words that hundreds of millions of American schoolchildren were once required by their teachers to memorize:

> Four score and seven years ago our fathers brought forth on this
> continent, a new nation, conceived in Liberty, and dedicated to
> the proposition that all men are created equal.

Thus, we Americans have been taught from our youth that we are all brothers and sisters because we are the children of those "fathers" who signed the Declaration of Independence. It is even implied that "Liberty" is our mother in whose womb we were "conceived." Does the completion of our birth as Americans come only with our dedication to the proposition of equality? Moreover, doesn't Lincoln's speech resemble the speech of the laws of the *Crito*, particularly when the laws claim that Socrates owes them the obedience due to parents because they are responsible for his birth and his upbringing (51c–52a)?

But what about the second part of the "noble lie," the story of the metals that divide the citizens into three groups? Some readers have criticized this as the establishment of a caste system. We should keep in mind, however, that Socrates insists that people should belong to whatever group they are best fitted for by nature no matter who their parents are. He is actually teaching the importance of equality of opportunity. Still, it is hard to see how the rulers will be able to recognize gold children when they are born to iron-and-bronze parents. Don't children need the proper education before their natural abilities become apparent? That the difficulties with this scheme are so obvious suggests that Plato thought the "city in speech" to be unrealizable in practice.

Every political community seems to need some social division of labor—different people doing different jobs. As a result, power, privilege, and property are distributed unequally. The purpose of the story about the metals is to convince the citizens that the assignment of jobs and the distribution of benefits is based on merit, and Socrates has to assume that this can be done on the basis of natural abilities rather than artificial distinctions (such as wealth and family background).

Would such inequalities be contrary to the principles of equality of rights as set forth in the Declaration of Independence? Jefferson did not think so, for he thought that the aim of American democracy was to promote that "natural aristocracy among men" based on "virtue and talents" while eliminating that "artificial aristocracy, founded on wealth and birth." He thought that an educational system was needed that would allow the most talented few to rise to the top even if they were born poor and of low social status.[18] The equality to be sought is the equality of each person to develop natural talents without artificial restraints, allowing the social division of labor to be based on merit.

Yet, as we shall see, Marx later argued that only in a completely classless society could genuine freedom and equality be achieved. As long as there is any division of labor based on a class structure, human beings are not free to develop themselves without constraint and in cooperation with others. Although Plato does describe a kind of communism that anticipates Marx, it is restricted to the rulers; the division of labor by classes is not abolished. What explains these conflicting versions of communism? Does Plato think that completely abolishing the social division of labor and private property would be contrary to human nature?

Should the hierarchical class structure defended by Socrates be taken as natural? Does the story about those of gold ruling over those of silver and those of bronze and iron have any grounding in nature? Or is it simply a ruse to support the illegitimate claims of the ruling class?

9. Is there any justification in nature for the hierarchical ordering of the city and soul into three parts?

Socrates argues that the just city will have a natural division of labor corresponding to the natural tripartition of the just soul. As reason rules over the spirited and appetitive parts of the soul, so should those with political wisdom rule over the soldiers and the moneymakers (432a–443e). Those who are to rule must have a special education, the character of which is vividly depicted by Socrates in his analogy of the cave (514a–525b).

He compares political life to a dimly-lighted cave in which everyone is bound, so that they can only look at one wall. Behind them is a fire, and objects carried in front of the fire cast shadows on the wall. The prisoners assume the shadows to be the whole of reality. Only a few people with the best natures can turn around to see the fire; eventually, a very few can even rise out of the cave to see the sun. These few undergo a philosophic education so as to view the true principles of reality rather than the shadows that occupy most people. As much as they would like to remain outside the cave, the philosophers are compelled to return so that they can take turns in ruling over the cave dwellers.[19]

Human beings are naturally unequal in their moral and intellectual capacities, and those few who have reached the peak of human development seem to have a justified claim to rule over the others at lower stages of development. Modern readers of the *Republic* are inclined to raise at least two objections to this. Socrates presents his hierarchical arrangement of the levels of human development as a universal truth of human nature, but many readers would dismiss this as an artificial construction with no universal validity. Many would also regard this Platonic teaching as unduly elitist and antidemocratic and therefore contrary to modern liberal democracy. One possible response to these criticisms would be to argue that Plato's account of human psychology is supported by certain contemporary theories that have some claim to being both scientifically valid and consistent with democracy.

Lawrence Kohlberg, who was a prominent social psychologist at Harvard University, argued that Plato's view of the moral and intellectual development of human beings had been confirmed by the findings of developmental psychology.[20] Without deciding the truth or falsity of Kohlberg's theory—his work *is* controversial— we should at least consider his testimony as evidence that the questions raised by Plato's psychology remain alive today. Kohlberg distinguishes six stages of cognitive moral development. Each stage represents a particular structure of thought, a way of thinking about moral problems. Kohlberg claims that every human being begins at the lowest stage of infancy and then moves through the higher stages in later years. The six stages can be divided into three levels: the *preconventional* level, the *conventional* level, and the *principled* level. We all begin at the preconventional level where our only concern is our own selfish pleasures and pains. We see morality as simply a matter of reward and punishment. If we help others, it is only because they have promised to help us in return. But by age nine or later, many of us have moved to the conventional level; at this point, we see ourselves not just as isolated individuals, but as members of society. We see the value of a family, a group, a nation. We want to be approved by others, and we obey authority because it preserves social order. Most people don't rise any higher than this in their moral reasoning. But a few in their early adulthood reach the principled level, at which stage they look to universal moral principles that go beyond the authority of a particular group or society. The appeal of the Declaration of Independence to the "Laws of Nature" and to the equality of human rights illustrates this level of moral judgment.

If Socrates had decided to obey the Athenian authorities simply because of the threat of physical punishment, he would have been at the preconventional level. The argument that he attributes to the laws of Athens in the *Crito*—that he should accept his punishment as part of his obligations to his city—is an example of reasoning at the conventional level. His own decision that his pursuit of truth is higher than his loyalty to Athens manifests moral reasoning at the principled level.

But why should the higher levels be considered better than the lower? Why should one even speak of higher and lower levels? One reason is that, if Kohlberg's empirical studies are correct, people prefer to reason at the highest level of which they are capable. This natural preference for the higher levels rests on the fact that as one ascends the hierarchy of stages, one's reasoning becomes more differentiated, more integrated, and more universal. The reasoning is more differentiated in that one can distinguish between different goods — for example, life and property. It is more integrated in that one can rank these various goods: Life ranks higher than property because property is a means for sustaining life, not the reverse. And the reasoning at higher stages is also more universal, in that appeal is made to broad principles (such as justice and equality) applied to broader contexts (from isolated individuals to group and family members, then to citizens, and finally to human beings as such).

The political importance of all this becomes clear if one agrees with Kohlberg that to be a good citizen one must be able to reason at least as high as the conventional level. Because the Declaration of Independence requires reasoning at the principled level — appealing as it does to universal rights grounded in the nature of humans as such — a full understanding of the American regime requires moral judgment at the highest levels of cognitive development. Kohlberg estimates from his empirical studies that very few people have reached the principled level by the time of high school graduation; and even among adult Americans, he doubts that more than 10 percent have attained the highest stages.

Kohlberg agrees with the Platonic teaching that people must be educated for citizenship. He influenced the training of high school teachers who tried to move their students to higher levels of cognitive moral development. But does the failure of most people to reach the peak — even by Kohlberg's measurements — suggest natural inequalities? If only a few can comprehend the reasoning of the Declaration of Independence, does that mean that full participation in political rule should be restricted to a few? If most American citizens are unable to grasp directly the logic of the fundamental principles of their regime, how can these ideas be put into a form they can understand? Must our rulers — as shocking as it might seem — resort to "noble lies"?

We are assuming, however, that those at the highest levels of cognitive development see things that cannot be seen — or at least not as clearly — by those at the lower levels. If so, what are these ultimate objects of knowledge? And what exactly do they have to do with politics? Kohlberg has little to contribute here because he deals more with the *form* or *structure* of each cognitive stage rather than its *content*. Plato, however, does have an answer; but it is not easy to understand. The ultimate objects of human knowing — seen by the philosophers when they leave the cave — are the "Forms" or "Ideas" (505a–511e).[21]

At the simplest level, the idea of something is the visible shape or look by which something is recognized as being of a certain kind. (The Greek words *eidos* and *idea* are related to the word *idein*, which means to see.) For example, to recognize my pet Tippy as a *dog*, I have to recognize by his looks that he is a certain type or kind of thing. He shares certain essential characteristics with other dogs that distinguish them from cats, trees, and rocks. I don't confuse him with my friend Rick because as a *human being* Rick differs essentially from dogs. At a higher level of generality, however, Rick and Tippy do share certain characteristics that distinguish them as animals from plants and nonliving things. Obviously, no two dogs are ever completely alike. Tippy is unique, as I indicate by giving him a proper name. But to think about him, I have to compare him with other things as I look for similarities and differences. This process of classification is the foundation of all knowledge. Even the simplest act of perception requires categorization. To perceive something I name it; and by naming it with a common noun (*dog*), I apply an elaborate system of classification.

The wondrous mystery of this activity is suggested by the opening chapters of the Bible. Human beings participate in God's creative ordering of the world by naming things. (There is a good reason for parents to become excited when their infants utter their first words!) Is this system of names an arbitrary creation, or is it somehow inherent in the nature of things, in the order that human beings (or God?) discover? This is a critical question. In fact, it may be the most critical question that human beings can ask. It is certainly a fundamental question for politics because how we view the natural order of things will influence how we view political order.[22]

The doctrine of the Ideas is an attempt to explain what it means to order things according to their names. But in Socrates' more precise use of the word, the things we perceive through the senses are what they are on account of the Ideas.[23] To recognize someone as just I must have some understanding of the Idea of Justice, by virtue of which this particular person *is* just. To make sense of the *visible* world I must appeal to *invisible* concepts. I can *see* this just person before me and his or her just acts, but only if I also "see" the meaning of justice. From this sort of experience, Socrates concludes that the visible world is an image of those invisible Ideas on account of which the world is as it is.

One can see why philosophic materialists have rejected Plato's teaching about the Ideas as airy nonsense. But consider what can be said in favor of Plato's thought. Doesn't all reasoning about the world require an explanation of the visible by reference to the invisible? To understand reality we have to organize our visible experience according to some invisible conceptual framework. We do this whenever we sort things out into various kinds of things:

SAME AS THE
UNCONCIOUS

dogs, trees, acts of justice, and so on. We continue to do this at the most abstract levels of thought. For example, Newton's law of gravity—that the force of attraction between any two bodies is directly proportional to the product of their masses and inversely proportional to the square of the distance between them—is an invisible principle that explains something about the visible world. In this sense, modern science is clearly Platonic. Werner Heisenberg, in commenting on scientific theories of the behavior of elementary particles, said: "I think that on this point modern physics has definitely decided for Plato. For the smallest units of matter are in fact not physical objects in the ordinary sense of the word; they are forms, structures or—in Plato's sense—Ideas, which can be unambiguously spoken of only in the language of mathematics."[24]

For a political illustration of this point, let us think again of the Declaration of Independence. The principle of the equality of human rights is a standard of justice that pervades American political debate. Americans take this principle for granted even as they argue about how best to put it into practice. We cannot make sense of American political life in its distinctness without some reference to this abstract principle of equality. Later in this book, we shall evaluate the reasoning behind this particular principle of justice. But the deeper question here is whether it is reasonable to view politics in the light of *any* abstract standard of justice.

Does the Platonic concern with the Idea of Justice distract us from the harsh realities of political life? Does it also hide the fact that our conceptions of justice are only projections of the interests of those who happen to rule? We have not exhausted all the implications of these Thrasymachean questions, which will continue to echo through this book. But Plato has helped us to formulate and clarify the questions, and in that he has given us a good start.

Notes

1. See Henri Frankfort et al., *Before Philosophy* (Baltimore: Penguin Books, 1949); and Jean-Pierre Vernant, *The Origins of Greek Thought* (Ithaca, NY: Cornell University Press, 1982).
2. Some excellent translations can be found in Plato and Aristophanes, *Four Texts on Socrates: Plato's "Euthyphro," "Apology," and "Crito" and Aristophanes' "Clouds,"* trans. Thomas G. West and Grace Starry West (Ithaca, NY: Cornell University Press, 1984).
3. John Stuart Mill, *On Liberty* (Indianapolis: Bobbs-Merrill, 1956), 29–30.
4. On Plato as a totalitarian, see Karl R. Popper, *The Open Society and*

Its Enemies (Princeton: Princeton University Press, 1950). For criticisms of this view, see John Wild, *Plato's Modern Enemies and the Theory of Natural Law* (Chicago: University of Chicago Press, 1953). That this debate is still alive is clear in Stephen T. Holmes, "Aristippus In and Out of Athens," *American Political Science Review* 73 (March 1979):113–29; and James H. Nichols, "On the Proper Use of Ancient Political Philosophy," ibid., 129–33.

5. See Plato, *Apology* 25d–26a, 28a–30b, 32b–3, 35b–d, 36b–38b, 40c–42a; *Crito* 43a–b, 44c–d, 48a–49b.

6. Another student of Socrates—Xenophon—wrote his own version of Socrates' defense at his trial, in which Socrates indicates his willingness to die because his mental powers were beginning to fade with age. Xenophon, *Apology* 5–9. Compare Plato, *Apology* 41d.

7. Henry David Thoreau, *Walden and Other Writings* (New York: Random House, Modern Library, 1937), 635–59. See George Anastaplo, "Citizen and Human Being: Thoreau, Socrates, and Civil Disobedience," in *Human Being and Citizen* (Chicago: Swallow Press, 1975), 203–13.

8. Thoreau, *Walden and Other Writings*, 638–39, 647, 656.

9. Martin Luther King, Jr., "Letter from the Birmingham Jail," in Richard D. Heffner, ed., *A Documentary History of the United States*, 3rd ed. (New York: New American Library, 1976), 335.

10. See David Miller, *Social Justice* (Oxford: Clarendon Press, 1976), who argues that the definitions of justice commonly depend on three conflicting criteria—rights, deserts, and needs. Compare William A. Galston, *Justice and the Human Good* (Chicago: University of Chicago Press, 1980); and Michael Walzer, *Spheres of Justice* (New York: Basic Books, 1983).

11. See G. B. Kerferd, *The Sophistic Movement* (Cambridge: Cambridge University Press, 1981); and Mark Backman, *Sophistication: Rhetoric and the Rise of Self-Consciousness* (Woodbridge, CT: Ox Bow Press, 1991). Backman argues that in the modern world we can see the triumph of the five principles of sophistic rhetoric: "Words are tools. Images are real. Information is power. Change is inevitable. Truth is relative."

12. Paul Angle, ed., *Created Equal? The Complete Lincoln-Douglas Debates of 1858* (Chicago: University of Chicago Press, 1958), 303–4, 332, 343–44, 351.

13. See Glynn Isaac, "The Food-Sharing Behavior of Protohuman Hominids," *Scientific American* (April 1978): 90–108; Richard E. Leakey and Roger Lewin, *People of the Lake: Mankind and Its Beginnings* (New York: Avon, 1979), 213–37; and Bernard Campbell, *Human Evolution*, 3rd edition (Hawthorne, NY: Aldine, 1985), 270–76. For criticisms, see Richard G. Klein, *The Human Career: Human Biological and Cultural Origins* (Chicago: University of Chicago Press, 1989), 172–80.

14. See Leo Strauss, *The City and Man* (Chicago: University of Chicago Press, 1977), 50–138. Allan Bloom, a student of Strauss, has developed

this interpretation in the essay for his translation of the *Republic* (New York: Basic Books, 1968).

15. That this is Strauss's interpretation of Plato has been argued by Shadia Drury in *The Political Ideas of Leo Strauss* (New York: St. Martin's Press, 1988). According to Drury, Strauss and his students promote a "Socratic hedonism" that "regards the good as something other than the morally good or noble" (p. 82).

16. See Dale Hall, "The *Republic* and the 'Limits of Politics'," *Political Theory* 5 (August 1977): 293–313; Allan Bloom, "Response to Hall," ibid., 315–20; and M. F. Burnyeat, "Sphinx Without a Secret," *New York Review of Books* 32 (30 May 1985): 30–36.

    If we took seriously the proposal in the *Republic* for the rule of philosopher-*kings*, we would also have to take seriously its proposed rule of philosopher-*queens* (449c–473e). According to Natalie Harris Bluestone, in *Women and the Ideal Society: Plato's "Republic" and Modern Myths of Gender* (Amherst: University of Massachusetts Press, 1987), the feminist arguments for the equality of women and men can be found in the *Republic*, although many male scholars find this incredible. Bluestone shows that Plato understood all the basic questions raised in the modern debate over feminism. She also shows the sociobiological assumptions in Plato's view of justice as each person doing what he or she is biologically best suited to do. For the issue of sexual equality, see chap. 8, sec. 9.

    For an example of how Plato's *Republic* might be used for the instruction of rulers, see Desiderius Erasmus, *The Education of a Christian Prince*, trans. Lester K. Born (New York: Norton, 1968); and Erasmus, *The Praise of Folly*, trans. Hoyt H. Hudson (Princeton: Princeton University Press, 1969), 22–23, 36–41, 63–65, 114–25.

    If the "city in speech" in the *Republic* exists only as a mental image that can never be fully actualized in political practice, is Plato engaged in a poetic activity? Is he challenging Homer? Consider the parallels between Plato's *Republic* and Shakespeare's *Tempest*. See Paul A. Cantor, "Prospero's Republic: The Politics of Shakespeare's *The Tempest*," in John Alvis and Thomas G. West, eds., *Shakespeare as Political Thinker* (Durham, NC: Carolina Academic Press, 1981), 239–55; and Barbara Tovey, "Shakespeare's Apology for Imitative Poetry: *The Tempest* and *The Republic*," *Interpretation* 11 (September 1983): 275–316. See also chap. 5, n. 33; chap. 10, n. 22.

17. For the argument that Plato's "noble lie" is "utterly true," see Joseph Tussman, *Government and the Mind* (New York: Oxford University Press, 1977), 51–73. According to Mircea Eliade, "that human beings are born of the earth is a universally disseminated belief." *The Sacred and the Profane* (New York: Harcourt, Brace & World, 1959), 140. On the importance of fairy tales and children's books for the moral and political education of children, see Bruno Bettelheim, *The Uses of Enchantment* (New York: Random House, Vintage Books, 1977); and Isaac Kramnick, *Republicanism and Bourgeois Radicalism* (Ithaca: Cornell University Press, 1990), 99–132.

18. Thomas Jefferson, Letter to John Adams, 28 October 1813, in *The Life and Selected Writings of Thomas Jefferson*, eds. Adrienne Koch and William Peden (New York: Random House, Modern Library, 1944), 632–33; Jefferson, *Notes on the State of Virginia*, query 14, ibid., 262–66. Consider the influence that Parson Weems's *Life of Washington* had on the young Abraham Lincoln. See *The Collected Works of Abraham Lincoln*, ed. Roy A. Basler et al., 9 vols. (New Brunswick, NJ: Rutgers University Press, 1953–1955), 4:235–36, 4:240–41.

19. Does the cave art of Paleolithic human beings suggest the importance of image-making for the emergence of humanity? See Hans Jonas, "Image-making and the Freedom of Man," in *The Phenomenon of Life* (New York: Dell, 1966), 157–75; John E. Pfeiffer, *The Creative Explosion: An Inquiry into the Origins of Art and Religion* (New York: Harper & Row, 1982); Paul G. Bahn and Jean Vertut, *Images of the Ice Age* (New York: Facts on File, 1988), 149–90; Eva T. H. Brann, *The World of the Imagination* (Savage, MD: Rowman and Littlefield, 1991); and Ellen Dissanayake, *Homo Aestheticus: Where Art Comes From and Why* (New York: Free Press, 1992).

   Would Plato's allegory of the cave be useful today in considering how the mass media create *our* images of the world? See George Anastaplo, "Self-Government and the Mass Media: A Practical Man's Guide," in Harry M. Clor, ed., *The Mass Media and Modern Democracy* (Chicago: Rand McNally, 1974), 192–232; Jerry Mander, *Four Arguments for the Elimination of Television* (New York: Quill, 1978); Todd Gitlin, ed., *Watching Television* (New York: Pantheon Books, 1986); and Neil Postman, *Amusing Ourselves to Death: Public Discourse in the Age of Show Business* (New York: Penguin Books, 1986). See also chap. 8, n. 21.

20. See, for example, Lawrence Kohlberg, "Education for Justice: A Modern Statement of the Socratic View," in *The Philosophy of Moral Development* (New York: Harper & Row, 1981), 29–48. Compare Jerome Kagan, *The Nature of the Child* (New York: Basic, 1984), 112–53, and William Damon, *The Moral Child* (New York: Free Press, 1988).

   Carl Sagan (*The Dragons of Eden* [New York: Ballantine Books, 1977], 53–83), has suggested that Plato's psychology is supported by neurophysiology. Paul MacLean's tripartite division of the brain into "reptilian complex," "limbic system," and "neocortex" corresponds to Plato's tripartition of the soul into "appetite," "spirit," and "reason." See Paul D. MacLean, "A Triangular Brief on the Evolution of Brain and Law," in Margaret Gruter and Paul Bohannan, eds., *Law, Biology and Culture: The Evolution of Law* (Santa Barbara: Ross-Erikson, 1983), 74–90; and MacLean, *The Triune Brain in Evolution* (New York: Plenum, 1990). The research of "humanistic" psychologists indicates that human happiness does indeed require a proper ordering of the soul with the higher parts ruling the lower. See Abraham H. Maslow, *Toward a Psychology of Being* (New York: Van Nostrand Reinhold, 1968), 149–61.

21. Why do the guardians begin with the study of arithmetic (*Republic* 521b–526b)? In counting must we move from concrete plurality to abstract number and thus experience our first glimpse of the Ideas? Are we the only animals who can count? See Georges Ifrah, *From One to Zero: A Universal History of Numbers*, trans. Lowell Bair (New York: Viking, 1985), 3–30. On Plato's Idea of the Good as expressed in mathematics, see Alfred North Whitehead, "Mathematics and the Good," in Paul Arthur Schilpp, ed., *The Philosophy of Alfred North Whitehead*, 2nd ed. (LaSalle, IL: Open Court, 1951), 666–81. Whitehead observes:

    The notion of the importance of pattern is as old as civilization. Every art is founded on the study of pattern. Also the cohesion of social systems depends on the maintenance of patterns of behavior; and advances in civilization depend on the fortunate modification of such behavior patterns. Thus the infusion of patterns into natural occurrences, and the stability of such patterns, and the modification of such patterns, is the necessary condition for the realization of the Good. (677–78)

    Compare Scott Buchanan, *Poetry and Mathematics* (Chicago: University of Chicago Press, 1962), 33–40, 43–45, 62–63, 95–100, 140–41, 154–56. Are scientists, artists, and philosophers alike in their search for Platonic patterns in nature? See Peter S. Stevens, *Patterns in Nature* (Boston: Little, Brown, 1974); K. C. Cole, *Sympathetic Vibrations: Reflections on Physics as a Way of Life* (New York: Morrow, 1985), 219–31, 279–96; James Gleick, *Chaos* (New York: Penguin, 1987); Roger Penrose, *The Emperor's New Mind: Concerning Computers, Minds, and the Laws of Physics* (Oxford: Oxford University Press, 1990), 112–16, 149–62; and Eva Brann, "The Music of the *Republic*," *Agon* 1 (April 1967): 1–117. Lynn Arthur Steen (in "The Science of Patterns," *Science* 240 [1988]: 611–16) concludes that "the reason why mathematics has the uncanny ability to provide just the right patterns for scientific investigation may be because the patterns investigated by mathematicians are *all* the patterns there are" (616).

22. For the typically modern affirmation of the arbitrariness of naming, see Murray Edelman, *The Symbolic Uses of Politics* (Urbana: University of Illinois Press, 1964), 131, 158, 178–79; Michel Foucault, *The Order of Things* (New York: Random House, Vintage, 1973), xv–xxiv; and Murray Edelman, *Political Language: Words That Succeed and Policies That Fail* (New York: Academic Press, 1977), 23–26, 58, 62–63, 152–55.

23. See Robert B. Williamson, "*Eidos* and *Agathon* in Plato's *Republic*," in *Essays in Honor of Jacob Klein* (Annapolis, MD: St. John's College Press, 1976), 171–87.

24. Werner Heisenberg, *Across the Frontiers* (New York: Harper & Row, Harper Torchbooks, 1975), 116. See also Paul Friedlander, "Plato as Physicist," in *Plato: An Introduction* (New York: Harper Torchbooks, 1958), 246–60; and D. H. Fowler, *The Mathematics of Plato's Academy* (Oxford: Oxford University Press, 1987).

Chapter

2

Political Science as the Study of Regimes

Aristotle's *Politics*

Key Readings

Politics, 1252a1–1256a1, 1260b25–1264b26, 1274b30–1284b35, 1288b10–1289b26, 1293b22–1297b35, 1301a20–1302a16, 1313a34–1315b39, 1323a14–1325b33.

Aristotle (384–322 B.C.) saw the political decline of Greece that had begun during the lifetime of Plato. In 338 B.C., the Greek cities were conquered by Philip II, King of Macedon. After the assassination of Philip in 336 B.C., his son Alexander assumed the throne and eventually extended his empire to the borders of India before his death in 323 B.C.

Aristotle had ties to the Macedonian throne. His father was the court physician, and Aristotle was Alexander's tutor. This aroused the suspicions of Greeks opposed to Macedonian power. After Alexander's death, Aristotle was forced to leave Athens; he was, however, able to spend twenty years in Athens in Plato's Academy and later established his own school, the Lyceum. His studies were as diverse as Plato's, but he also gave much attention to biology and to the constitutional history of the Greek cities. Traditionally, Aristotle's political thought is considered more practical than that of Plato. Aristotle considers not only what might be politically best in theory, but also what is politically necessary in practice when the best is unattainable.[1]

1. Is the best regime good enough?

Although there may be good reasons for theorizing on what the best political community would look like, there is one major problem with such a regime: it doesn't exist. Presumably, the political philosopher should not be so preoccupied with the sort of "city in speech" sketched in the *Republic* that existing regimes are neglected. Plato does, in fact, comment on the variety of actual regimes in Books Eight and Nine of the *Republic*, where Socrates speculates as to how the decay of his best city would give rise to a sequence of bad cities. But we have to turn to Aristotle's *Politics* to find a comprehensive and detailed account of the practical problems of existing regimes. Aristotle criticizes the unrealistic expectations of the *Republic*. He insists that the leader should understand not only what would be the best regime generally, but also what would be best in certain circumstances — even what must be done to preserve a bad regime. Sometimes a leader must make the best of a bad situation (1288b10–1289a25).

We shall see, however, that Aristotle cannot escape the fundamental questions posed by Plato. If we agree, for example, that political action (at least in practice) cannot be guided by the norms of nature as grasped by a philosophic ruler, does that suggest that there are no minimal or natural standards for politics?

In describing the regimes that might emerge after the collapse of his philosophic city, Socrates is clearly most fascinated with the city that is next to the worst — democracy — and the one that is simply the worst — tyranny. If the best regime is not possible, then the philosophic student of politics must reconsider the claims of the worst. For if political life is not to be governed by rational standards of the good for human beings, then why not give people the political freedom to live as they please? Democracy allows such freedom, and Socrates concedes that it is "the fairest of the regimes" and even "divinely sweet for the moment" (*Republic* 557c–558a). Its beauty and sweetness come from the spontaneous variety of lives that it allows, people being free to live from moment to moment just as they wish with no particular way of life imposed on them by the laws. Such a situation should be attractive to the philosopher because it would allow the freedom to pursue the philosophic life without political constraints (561c–d). But if freedom to seek one's pleasures just as one wishes is the only good, why shouldn't a person of strength and cleverness strive for tyranny in order to use fellow human beings to secure personal pleasure? Thus, tyranny might seem the logical outcome of extreme democracy (562a–569c). Again, we are forced to consider the argument of Thrasymachus.

Is it possible to acknowledge the impracticality—if not impossibility—of Plato's philosophic city without a drastic lowering of the aims of politics? Modern political philosophers such as Hobbes and Locke argued for just such a reduction in political goals. They thought it was enough for politics to simply provide the security for people to pursue their selfish desires without inflicting or suffering violent injuries. Later, Nietzsche questioned why those persons superior in will and intelligence should refrain from dominating others inferior to them. If human life is a selfish pursuit of power unlimited by natural standards of justice, why shouldn't political rule go to the most powerful?

What is Aristotle's response to this problem? Can he combine that realistic, tough-minded attitude for which he is well known with a devotion to high moral standards? Can he overcome the political conflict between the harsh ruthlessness of the person of action and the noble principles of the person of thought?

With these questions in mind, we should begin by considering what Aristotle means by his famous statement near the opening of the *Politics* that humans are by nature political animals.

2. Does political life fulfill a natural human end?

Like Plato, Aristotle appeals to nature as a standard for his political thought. In the *Politics*, he frequently identifies something as "by nature," which indicates some essential feature of reality that is not simply a product of human will. The natural must be distinguished from the merely conventional. Sometimes, instead of a simple dichotomy of nature and convention, Aristotle speaks of a trichotomy of nature, custom (or habit), and reason (1332a36–b11).[2] But how does he know that something is natural rather than conventional? Some readers of the *Politics* have suspected that Aristotle's idea of nature depends more on the prejudices of the ancient Greeks than on the objective criteria of truth. It is often said that Aristotle's view of nature as having purposes or goals, as aiming toward ends, contradicts what we know today from modern natural science. Does not natural science present the universe as governed by mechanical laws, so that it makes no sense to speak of nature's purposes or ends? Aristotle's conception of nature is teleological, but it is commonly believed that modern science rejects all teleology. We shall have to see whether Aristotle's work can withstand this criticism. Let us begin by considering what he says about the "naturalness" of political life.

The first human association is the sexual union of male and female (1252a24–b14). This arises from an innate desire for procreation that human beings share with other animals and—in some manner—with plants. From this springs the family as a means to provide for the daily wants of life. It is not hard to see why Aristotle calls this natural, because we can see evidence of the spontaneous, biological needs and desires that gave rise to the family. Nor is it difficult to see how natural it is for families to group themselves into villages that are subject to the traditional authority of patriarchal rule that is thought to reflect the authority of the gods (1252b15–26). Anthropologists might recognize this as a traditional society such as is commonly found in primitive communities. But the last stage of development as Aristotle sketches it may be more controversial. He writes (1252b28–1253a5):

> The final community composed of several villages is the city [*polis*]. At this point the community has attained the limit of full self-sufficiency, so to speak, arising for the sake of living but existing for the sake of living well. For this reason every city is by nature, if indeed the first communities are so. For the city is the end [*telos*] of these, and nature is an end. For what each thing is when its genesis is complete, this we say is the nature of each, such as with a man, a horse, a household. Further, that for the sake of which something is—its end—is the best. And self-sufficiency is an end and the best. From these things, it is clear therefore that the city belongs to the things of nature, and that man is by nature a political animal.[3]

Sexual coupling, the family, and associations to provide for physical needs arise from the natural desire for self-preservation. Furthermore, it is natural, Aristotle claims, for human beings to desire not only *life*, but also a *good life*. The true political community—the city (*polis* in Greek)—is natural for human beings because it fulfills that natural desire to live in accordance with some shared conceptions of human goodness. In speaking of the city as "by nature," Aristotle denies implicitly that it is simply "by art"— that is, a human construction—or that it is "holy"—a divine product. (Later, we shall see that St. Thomas Aquinas distinguishes natural law from human law on the one hand, and from divine law on the other.)

Everything depends on Aristotle's assumption that by nature each thing seeks its end (*telos*). Just as an acorn is inclined by nature to grow into an oak tree, so human beings are inclined by nature to fulfill their potentialities by living in political communities. The city is natural because it is the end of the human striving to live together with others, and nature is an end. Aristotle was a biologist, and he speaks here of the political nature of human beings as a biological fact, as a characteristic of the human species. But wouldn't the modern Darwinian biologist have to reject this teleological biology?

On the fiftieth anniversary of the publication of Charles Darwin's *Origin of Species*, John Dewey delivered a lecture on "The Influence of Darwin on Philosophy."[4] According to Dewey, Darwin exerted his greatest influence by refuting Aristotelian teleology. Aristotle believed that nature conformed to a rational design such that each thing served some purpose in the order of the universe, but Darwin showed that species evolved through the struggle for existence without any preordained plan or purpose. Therefore, if we accept Darwinian biology, it would seem, we have to reject Aristotelian political thought insofar as it rests on an unscientific view of nature.

Yet consider how a modern Aristotelian might respond to this argument. On the centennial anniversary of Darwin's *Origin of Species*, John Herman Randall delivered a lecture on "The Changing Impact of Darwin on Philosophy." Contrary to Dewey, Randall concluded that, as a result of Darwin's influence, "nature is once more for us, as for the Greeks, full of implicit ends and ideals." Randall argued, "When Darwin led men to take biology seriously once more, they had to reintroduce these functional concepts that physicists had forgotten — means and ends, function, teleology, and time."[5] Obviously, there is confusion among Darwin's interpreters as to whether evolutionary biology *denies* Aristotelian teleology (as Dewey says) or *confirms* it (as Randall says).

A modern Aristotelian might explain this confusion by arguing that Darwin denied one form of teleology but affirmed another, and it is only the failure to distinguish the various kinds of teleology that makes it appear that Darwin rejected Aristotelian teleology.[6] We can distinguish between *artificial* (or external) teleology and *natural* (or internal) teleology. The first applies when something has been consciously intended by some agent; the second applies to goal-directed activity that is not intended by an agent. An individual making something or doing something for a purpose illustrates artificial teleology. The development of a fertilized egg into a mature adult or birds possessing wings for the purpose of flying illustrates natural teleology. Of course, the Christian would deny, in some sense, the validity of this distinction by claiming that all purposefulness in nature originates as a conscious purpose of the Creator. This is the sort of teleological view that Darwin would deny. No matter what God may have done to create the universe at the beginning, Darwin would say, the subsequent evolution of species through natural selection was not the work of a conscious designer. Notice that on this point Darwin and Aristotle would agree.

Further clarification requires another distinction between two kinds of natural teleology—one being *determinate*, the other *indeterminate*. The teleological development of a fertilized egg is determinate in the sense that the end (the mature adult) is predetermined from the beginning by the genetic program in the egg. But the teleological adaptation of birds for flight is indeterminate in the sense that nothing in the remote reptilian ancestry of birds dictated this result. The path of growth from a fertilized egg is predetermined, but the path of natural selection from the first forms of life to birds is not. Darwin's teaching of evolution by natural selection denies any form of cosmic teleology, which would present the evolution of the world as a progressive unfolding of a design somehow inherent in the beginning. To concede that this sort of *cosmic* teleology lacks Darwinian support, the modern Aristotelian might argue, does not subvert Aristotelian teleology.

Ernest Mayr, one of the leading biologists of the twentieth century, insists: "Aristotelian why-questions have played an important heuristic role in the history of biology. 'Why?' is the most important question the evolutionary biologist asks in all of his researches."[7] Perhaps Aristotle was correct, then, in thinking that one cannot fully understand living things without asking about their natural purposes or goals. He thought that one could not explain the development of unorganized matter into a complex organism except by postulating that some potential form (*eidos*) is thereby actualized. Although many people once dismissed Aristotle's *eidos* as nonsense, the modern discovery of how a genetic program regulates growth has apparently confirmed the truth of Aristotle's insight. A prominent molecular biologist has even written an article with the title "How Aristotle Discovered DNA."[8]

Although the Darwinian biologist has to be sceptical about any cosmic teleology, Aristotelian teleology can be seen in the goal-directed activity of organic entities and processes. Aristotle, therefore, does not violate the spirit of modern biology in claiming that the human species has certain unique natural potentialities and that the actualization of these human potentialities in political life conforms to nature's purposes. In fact, contemporary sociobiologists and behavioral ecologists, who study the biological roots of human nature, might be seen as reviving Aristotle's biological naturalism.[9]

It is still questionable whether Aristotle's specific biological claims could be supported by modern science. In particular, we might wonder about his assertion that the only truly political animals are human beings because only they are endowed with the capacity for speech that makes political life possible.

3. Are human beings the only animals with the capacity for symbolic speech?

Aristotle explains (1253a8–19):

> It is clear why man is more a political animal than is any bee or any gregarious animal. For, as we say, nature does nothing in vain; and man is the only animal that has reasonable speech [*logos*]. Voice is a sign of pleasure and pain, and so it is possessed by other animals; for their nature has reached such a point as to have sensation of pleasure and pain and to signify these to others. But reasonable speech is for indicating the useful and the harmful, thus also the just and the unjust. For with reference to other animals, it is peculiar to man that he alone has sensation of the good and the evil and the just and unjust and other things of this sort, and a community of these things makes a household and a city.

Contrary to the common reading of this passage, Aristotle does not say human beings are the *only* political animals; rather, he says human beings are the *most* political animals. In his biological writings, he explains that there are other political animals, such as bees, wasps, ants, and cranes.[10] Human beings are *more* political than these animals because only human beings have the capacity for *logos*.

Political life is natural for human beings because it permits the actualization of that potentiality that is most distinctive to human nature—the capacity for speech or reason. The Greek word *logos* denotes either speech or reason and can, therefore, be translated as reasonable speech. This suggests that thinking and speaking are two sides of the same activity and that the fullest expression of human nature is both rational and social. Are we social beings even in our most private moments? To what extent does thought consist of a kind of silent conversation with oneself? How far can individuals develop their rational abilities without learning a language?

Because of their possession of *logos*, human beings can live together in a more intimate and profound way than is possible for other political animals. The deepest association comes from mutual understanding through speech. Other animals can express to one another their immediate and particular sensations of pleasure and pain, but human beings can come to agreement about the meaning of life. For human beings living together means not just sharing in things of the body, but sharing thoughts. A human community is a state of mind.

Theodosius Dobzhansky, an influential modern biologist, has said that science now confirms these insights of Aristotle.[11] Although other animals (such as the social insects) are more "social" than human beings, we are the only political animals, in the sense that only we can consciously choose to live with other members of our species through symbolic communication. The evolution of the human brain, in both size and complexity, has reached a point such that we have an ability for thought and speech that other animals do not. Aristotle may also have suspected the neurological basis of this difference: "of all the animals," he observes in the *Parts of Animals* (653a27–28), "man has the largest brain in proportion to his size."

Although there is some disagreement among scientists about what exactly makes human cognitive ability unique, there is wide agreement about two points. Human beings have a capacity for symbolic speech that other animals do not, and this linguistic ability reflects a high level of abstract thought unattained by other animals. Clearly, however, as Aristotle and Darwin recognized, many animals do communicate in some manner; and many have some ability for reasoning.[12] We need to make some precise distinctions. Although some nonhuman animals, we might say, can communicate through *signs*, only human beings can understand and use *symbols*. This reflects different levels of cognition. Some other animals possess *perceptual thought*, but only human beings possess *conceptual thought*.

Aristotle believes, as we have seen, that although other animals can use their voices to signify their sensations of pleasure and pain, only human beings use "reasoned speech" to symbolize their concepts of expediency, justice, and goodness. This is a consequence of the fact, as Aristotle explains in the *De Anima* (414a28–415a12), that the higher animals have some mental capacity for perceptual thought, but only human beings possess intellect (*nous*). This difference between animal communication and human speech has been observed by ethologists such as Konrad Lorenz.[13] Perhaps we can see this in our own experience with animals.

If I approach a dog and say "food," it might look around for its dinner. The dog can be conditioned to respond to the sound of the word "food" by expecting a meal. But if I say "food" to a human being, he or she is likely to ask, "What about food?" Instead of simply responding to the word "food" as a *sign* of something in the *immediate environment*, the human being understands the word as a *symbol* conveying a *meaning*. If I clarify my meaning by explaining that I meant to announce that dinner was ready, the human might salivate just like the dog. But if I explain that I want to talk about the sociological significance of table manners or that I want to tell a story about food, the human would show (I hope) an intellectual curiosity in what I have to say, whereas the dog would be incapable of such curiosity.

When the dog somehow recognizes that the sound of the word "food" uttered by different people at different times always points to its being fed, it has made a *perceptual abstraction* that directs its attention to something in its present environment or in its immediate future. But it would be futile to discuss with the dog the sociology of table manners because this would require *conceptual* thought that goes beyond immediate sense experience. Similarly, I could train the dog to respond in a certain way whenever it sees a triangle, but I could never train it to think about geometry. Unlike perceptual abstractions, symbolic concepts cannot be based simply on generalized sensible images. Through concepts human beings can even think about things that do not exist at all as objects of sense experience. This world of purely conceptual meaning is forever closed to other animals.

The radical difference between animal signs and human symbols becomes clear in the autobiography of Helen Keller, who from early infancy was both blind and deaf. Annie Sullivan, her teacher, first taught Helen to communicate with signs. When she wanted a piece of cake, she spelled the word in Annie's hand. At this point, she was simply responding like any other intelligent animal. She did not understand language as an instrument for conceptual thought. Then one day something happened. She describes the experience in her autobiography:

> We walked down the path to the well-house, attracted by the fragrance of the honeysuckle with which it was covered. Someone was drawing water, and my teacher placed my hand under the spout. As the cool stream gushed over one hand, she spelled into the other the word *water*, first slowly, then rapidly. I stood still, my whole attention fixed upon the motions of her fingers. Suddenly I felt a misty consciousness as of something forgotten—a thrill of returning thought; and somehow the mystery of language was revealed to me. I knew then that "w-a-t-e-r" meant the wonderful cool something that was flowing

WHEN A CAT SEES A DOG FOR FIRST TIME

over my hand. That living word awakened my soul, gave it light, hope, joy, set it free! There were barriers still, it is true, but barriers that could in time be swept away.

I left the well-house eager to learn. Everything had a name, and each name gave birth to a new thought. As we returned to the house every object which I touched seemed to quiver with life. That was because I saw everything with the strange, new sight that had come to me.[14]

Previously, she had been conditioned to use words as signs of objects in her environment, but only at this point did she learn that words were also symbols of *meaning* and thus instruments of *thought*: "Each name gave birth to a new thought." Henceforth, she could use the word "water" not just as a sign of something wanted or expected, but also as a symbol of a concept about which she might think. She accomplished that because as a human being she had an innate potentiality for it: "I felt a misty consciousness as of something forgotten." Other animals do not have that potentiality.

There's no way of knowing

There have been attempts, however, to teach language to other animals. Some of the most publicized recent experiments have been efforts to instruct chimpanzees in the use of sign language. In surveying this work, many experts have concluded that there is no clear evidence of success. One group of researchers has reported: "Apes can learn many isolated symbols (as can dogs, horses, and other nonhuman species), but they show no unequivocal evidence of mastering the conversational, semantic, or syntactic organization of language."[15] Aristotle might be correct, therefore, in taking it to be a biological fact that, although other animals have some capacity for communication, the power of speech belongs only to human beings.

What does all of this have to do with politics? At the very least, it suggests that politics could be rooted in the biological nature of human beings. Could political science include the comparative study of other social and political animals? Would it be reasonable, for example, to speak of "chimpanzee politics"?[16]

What difference would it make for politics if we discovered that other animals—apes or dolphins, for example—could think and speak in their own way at a level comparable to that of human beings?[17] Would we, as some scientists have suggested, have to give them citizenship with all the political rights we give to human beings? Would we have to change the Declaration of Independence to recognize that all animals are created equal and endowed with rights? Would we have to take seriously those who argue for "animal liberation"?

When we think about politics, we commonly assume that it is a uniquely human activity. We don't think of dogs, dolphins, or apes as having any political claims. Thus, we take it for granted that politics expresses certain capacities of human beings that are not possessed by other animals. If that is so, then we should clarify what those capacities are in order to deepen our understanding of politics.

If we agreed, for example, with Aristotle's claim that human beings are the most political animals because they are the only animals endowed with the ability for "reasoned speech," we might conclude that politics expresses somehow the perfection of human nature through the rule of reason. But this would bring us back to Plato's recommendation of rule by philosophers as the consummation of political life, and we would have to wonder whether Aristotle has any answer to Thrasymachus's claim that politics manifests not the rule of reason, but the natural human desire to dominate others for selfish ends. After all, Thrasymachus might argue, isn't the human capacity for speaking and reasoning a powerful weapon for practicing deception in the quest for power over others?

By declaring that we are political animals by nature, Aristotle stresses the natural cooperativeness of human beings. But aren't human beings also naturally selfish? And, if so, doesn't that impede their cooperation with one another in a political community?

4. How do selfishness and aggression influence political life?

Aristotle concedes that although people are naturally inclined to share a common life, they are also thrown into conflict by their selfish desires.

> By nature, therefore, there is an impulse in all men to such a community. But the one who first established such a community was the cause of the greatest goods. For just as man when he is complete is the best of animals, so when he is separated from law and justice is he the worst of all. For injustice possessed of weapons is the most troublesome, and man is born possessing weapons for prudence and virtue that it is possible to use for entirely opposite things. For without virtue he is the most unholy and the most savage of animals and the worst with respect to sexuality and food. (1253a30–38)

Though we have a natural impulse for political life, the fulfillment of the impulse depends on the proper conditions, the securing of which is the aim of leadership. When circumstances are not conducive to the political inclinations of humanity, people can turn into savage beasts dominated by the appetites of hunger and sex. It is important to see this in Aristotle, otherwise he might seem naively optimistic in his judgment of human nature.

But does Aristotle go far enough in recognizing the natural viciousness of human beings? In recent decades, some anthropologists and ethologists have depicted human nature as primarily dominated by an instinct for aggression.[18] From this it would seem that far from being naturally inclined to social cooperation, the natural condition of humanity is a war of all against all such as that described by Thrasymachus or Hobbes. One example of this viewpoint is the work of the prominent anthropologist Colin Turnbull in his book *The Mountain People*.[19]

He describes the Ik of northern Uganda. The Ik lived a hunting-and-gathering way of life that was primitive yet sufficient for their needs; but when they were excluded from their major hunting ground, so that it could be turned into a National Park, they were forced to struggle just to avoid death from starvation. Turnbull found them to be so utterly selfish as to be bereft of any social affections. Starving children and old people were thrown out of their homes by their relatives, who laughed at their suffering. Turnbull was ridiculed when he shared his food or did anything to help someone in need. No one helped anyone else unless some favor was expected in return. Turnbull concluded that the Ik "have disposed of virtually all the qualities that we normally consider are just those qualities that differentiate us from other primates." He decided "that society itself is not indispensable for man's survival, that man is not the social animal he has always thought himself to be, and that he is perfectly capable of associating for purposes of survival without being social."[20]

How would Aristotle reply? From the passages in the *Politics* quoted earlier, we might infer that he would agree with Turnbull as to "how impossible it is, in certain circumstances, to be a beautiful human being,"[21] but Aristotle would stress the words "in certain circumstances." The social inclination of human beings is a natural *propensity* but not a natural *necessity*. When people are beaten down by harsh circumstances—especially when one person's survival competes with another's—their desire for self-preservation may overcome their social impulses. (Turnbull indicates that there is evidence that the Ik possessed the virtues of social life before they were deprived of the traditional hunting grounds that had always sustained them.) The problem, then, as far as Aristotle is concerned, is how to maintain a balance between the *natural selfishness* and the *natural sociality* of human beings. This viewpoint seems to be confirmed by certain contemporary theories of human nature advanced by some biologists and ethologists.

Aggression is only one of many drives characteristic of the higher vertebrates. Aggressive behavior is likely to arise in those circumstances that create intense competition for mates or for natural resources. Yet there is no reason to deny the existence of widespread social inclinations.[22] One ethologist has concluded "that both aggressive and altruistic behavior are preprogrammed by phylogenetic adaptations and that there are therefore preordained norms for our ethical behavior." He has also argued "that the disposition to cooperation and mutual aid is innate, as are many specific behavior patterns of friendly contact."[23]

How can a political community recognize both the selfish and the social inclinations of human beings? An illustration of how this might be done is in Aristotle's account of property. He argues that because of natural selfishness the communism of Plato's *Republic* is unrealistic (1261b33–1262a2, 1263a21–1263b2). Individuals care for the property that they can own privately, but they are indifferent toward property owned in common. Yet to nurture the natural sociability of human beings, there should be some communal element in the system of property. Aristotle's proposal, then, is that property should be private in ownership but common in use. Private ownership is a necessary concession to the self-regarding inclinations of human beings. If there is a civic education in the fundamental principles of the regime, the social bonds of the people will be strong and property will be shared in use as among friends, even though ownership is private. Perhaps an example of what Aristotle has in mind is his later suggestion in the *Politics* (1320a33–b16) that to preserve a democracy the poor should be saved from extreme poverty and, therefore, that the rich should contribute to a public fund for assistance to the most needy. Although this sort of measure may soften the conflict between rich and poor, it is likely that there will always be some conflict as long as the private ownership of property produces economic inequality. Won't this lead many observers to conclude that some form of communism is the only final solution? In any case, the inescapable question concerns the proper balance between the competitive and the cooperative, the selfish and the social, inclinations of human nature.

We have seen that Aristotle believes human beings to be naturally political insofar as it is only in a political community that they can fulfill their distinctive potential for rational discourse. However, if the aim of politics is to promote the rule of reason, should only the most rational people share in ruling? This would lead us back to Plato's philosophic rulers and to the problem of deciding who has the rational capacity for rule. Although Aristotle does not speak directly about the need for philosophic rulers, he does speak about the need for excluding from citizenship those without the rational ability for rule, those who are natural slaves. Also, what he says about women suggests to many readers that he would exclude them from citizenship as well.

5. Does Aristotle show the prejudices of his culture in his views of slaves and women?

Aristotle, like Plato, assumes that a philosopher can go beyond conventional political opinions in the pursuit of truth. Some, however, would argue that a person's thought is always the product of historical circumstances and that it is only through historical progress that the mistakes of earlier periods become obvious. Do Aristotle's views of slaves and women illustrate this? Is it possible for us, because we live in modern times, to see the injustice of slavery and the oppression of women, which Aristotle could not see because he was blinded by the prejudices of ancient Greece? Or can we see ambiguities in Aristotle's remarks on slaves and women that suggest he did not believe these individuals to be naturally inferior human beings?

Although most scholarly commentators have assumed that Aristotle endorses the Greek practice of slavery as natural, a few have concluded differently: "Aristotle was the first political thinker to realize that slavery *needed* a defense. In fact, his defense of slavery is a critique of the institution of slavery as it existed in Athenian society."[24] Aristotle's remarks are ambiguous in that they point to the fundamental contradiction in the practice of slavery: some human beings are treated as if they were not human.

Aristotle recognizes the biological unity of humankind as a single species, "simple and having no differentiation" (*History of Animals*, 490b18). As members of the human species, all normal human beings are potentially rational and political animals (*History of Animals*, 488a7–10; *Politics*, 1253a8–19). There can be sympathy among animals of the same species, and this is especially so for human beings, so that "we praise those who love their fellow human beings" (*Nicomachean Ethics*, 1155a20–21). For Aristotle, therefore, human beings are equal in their shared humanity. This allowed the early advocates of modern republicanism, like Algernon

Sidney in the seventeenth century, to cite Aristotle in support of equality of rights understood as equality of opportunity.[25]

Aristotle distinguishes natural slavery from conventional slavery. If there were natural masters and natural slaves, he explains, they would have to differ "as much as the soul differs from the body and the human being from the brute animal" (*Politics* 1254b16–17). It is hard to see how this could be so, because he makes it clear that slaves *do* have souls, and that they *are* human beings (1253b33, 1259b29). He says "the relation between master and slave, whenever they deserve by their nature to be called such, should be one of friendship and of benefit to both; but if their relation is not such but exists by law and is forced, it leads to contrary results" (1255b13–16). He also says, however, that citizens need military training "to hold despotic power over those who deserve to be enslaved" (1334a3). He argues that since friendship is possible only between human beings, "there can be no friendship with a slave as a slave, though there can be with him as a human being" (*Nicomachean Ethics* 1161b5–8). To justify slavery as natural, the master would have to be a friend to the slave, but the very possibility of friendship presupposes the humanity of the slave and therefore the injustice of enslaving people as though they were not human.

When Aristotle describes his "best regime," he recommends that *all* the slaves should have their freedom held out to them as a reward (*Politics* 1330a33–34). To commentators who assume Aristotle endorses slavery as natural, this makes no sense, because surely slaves with the desire and the capacity for freedom cannot be slaves by nature. Yet if we see the ambiguity in his account of slavery, we see that his apparent endorsement of slavery as natural establishes theoretical standards for natural slavery that can never be fulfilled in practice, thus implying that slavery as actually practiced is unnatural and therefore subject to reform.

There is a similar ambiguity in Aristotle's remarks on women and men. Many feminists assume that he was the founder of the patriarchal tradition in the Western world in which women have been treated as if they were naturally inferior to men.[26] For example, when Aristotle compares the virtues of rulers and ruled to different parts of the soul, he explains (1260a10–14): "The free rules the slave, the male the female, and the man the child in a different way. And all possess the parts of the soul but possess them differently. For the slave does not have the deliberative part at all; the female has it, but it is without authority [akuros]; and the child has it, but it is undeveloped." That a woman's reason is "without authority" in relation to her husband's rule could mean that her reason is too weak to rule over her emotions, and therefore she needs the help

But then the reverse must also be the case

of her husband. This could also mean, however, that her husband's spirited love of rule will not allow her reason to exercise authority in the marriage. When Aristotle compares males and females in his biological texts, he never says females are less intelligent than males. On the contrary, he claims that females tend to be "more capable of learning" and "cleverer" than males (*History of Animals*, 608a10–19).

In the subsequent history of the debate over the nature of slaves and women, the ambiguity of Aristotle's remarks becomes evident. In the sixteenth century, when the Spanish invaded the New World, some of the scholarly advisors to the Spanish leaders argued that the native American Indians were natural slaves as defined by Aristotle. Yet other scholars (like Francisco de Vitoria and Bartolomé de Las Casas) could argue that by Aristotle's standards, the only natural slaves, if they existed, would be freaks of nature who lacked the mental capacity of normal adults; and since such deviations from nature's normal pattern must be rare, it would be impossible for an entire race or society of human beings to be natural slaves.[27] Similarly, at about the same time, in France and Italy, when scholars debated whether men and women were morally and intellectually equal, Aristotle was cited on both sides of the argument.[28] (On the question of sexual equality, see chapter 8, section 9.)

It is not clear, therefore, that the prejudices of ancient Greek culture kept Aristotle from seeing the injustice in the exploitation of slaves and women. The larger question at issue here is the extent to which thought is determined by the historical conditions of the thinker. Of course, all thinkers are to some degree products of their social and economic circumstances. But if this means that even the most rigorous thinkers cannot question the unexamined opinions of their time, then Socratic political philosophy is impossible.

Aristotle's understanding of citizenship might seem to some readers to reflect the peculiar prejudices of the ancient Athenians. Athenian citizens had to be free from all labor in order to fulfill their public responsibilities, which is why slavery seemed essential as a way to give them the leisure they needed. Citizenship in the Greek *polis* was quite different from citizenship in a modern democratic state. Again we have to ask whether Aristotle's political thought is so tied to his historical circumstances as to be inapplicable to modern political life.

6. Does Aristotle's understanding of citizenship have any application to modern democratic politics?

There are at least four important differences between citizenship in the ancient *polis* and citizenship in the modern democratic state. In the *polis*, citizens participated directly in public affairs; but in a modern democracy, like that of the United States, citizens are represented by others who act for them in the government. A second difference, closely related to the first, is the small size of the *polis* as opposed to the large size of the modern state. A third difference is that although the state is distinguished from society, no such distinction was made in the *polis*. More needs to be said about this, but let it suffice here to say that the claims of the *polis* permeated all areas of social life—family, education, religion, and so on—whereas the claims of the modern state are limited with respect to society. The final difference between ancient and modern citizenship is that unlike modern citizens, ancient citizens were relative to their regime. That is to say, those who would be citizens in a democratic *polis* would not necessarily be citizens in an oligarchic *polis*; in a modern state, almost every adult is a citizen regardless of the form of government.

Should we conclude that Aristotle has nothing to teach us about citizenship because his ideas do not apply to modern politics? There is some truth to this insofar as it is unrealistic to expect a revival in the modern world of the ancient *polis*. On the other hand, Aristotle gives reasons for his conception of citizenship; and thinking through his reasons may force us to recognize problems with modern citizenship that would otherwise escape our attention.

Is there, for example, any justification for the Athenian claim that full citizenship comes only from direct participation in the affairs of a small community? Does genuine citizenship require something more than casting a vote every few years on election day? Rousseau even criticized the modern institution of representation as disguised slavery because it deprives all citizens of the experience of governing themselves (see chapter 9, section 6). Similar criticisms of liberal democracy have been expressed in the United States by those of the Jeffersonian tradition, including contemporary advocates of participatory democracy.[29] The same line of thinking is suggested by all those who criticize modern government for being too big and too distant from the people. Ralph Nader, for example, has said that his aim is to revive the Greek conception of citizenship by convincing people to devote more time to political activity. Aristotle might give us some guidance, therefore, in thinking about problems with the liberal view of citizenship.

The major argument in favor of the liberal version of citizenship is that when the duties of citizens are minimal, people are left free to pursue their private activities without political interference. Aristotelian citizenship, on the other hand, seems to demand such total devotion to public service as to suppress individual liberty. The danger to personal freedom seems particularly clear when Aristotle claims that every regime should shape the moral character of its citizens according to a common goal. Do we see here the superiority of modern democracy over the Aristotelian regime insofar as the modern democratic state allows for individual freedom?

7. Does Aristotle's regime go too far in restricting individual liberty?

This question is closely related to the question as to whether Aristotle's ideas hold true for modern liberal politics. Because individual freedom is a primary concern of the modern democratic state, Aristotelian political thought would seem to be irrelevant to modern conditions if it does not provide for such freedom. We need to consider more generally what Aristotle believes the purpose of a regime to be.

"Regime" is a translation of the Greek word *politeia*, which might also be translated as constitution, government, or simply polity. The importance of this term is suggested by the fact that every book of the *Politics* except the first begins with some reference to it.

A regime, according to Aristotle, is "the organization of offices in a city, by what mode they are to be distributed, and also what is to be the authoritative power in the regime and what is to be the final purpose of each community" (1289a15–17). The regime is the form of a city as distinguished from its matter. The form is higher than the matter, because the form shows the end or purpose to which the city is directed as determining everything else (1267a7–b15). This explains why even when the population and geography of a city have changed, we consider it to be the same city it was previously so long as its form of government—its regime—is the same. Similarly, although the United States has changed greatly since 1776 or 1789 in its material elements, it is still the same in form as the principles of the Declaration of Independence and of the Constitution continue to shape the political life of the country.

On the other hand, some people would insist that the modern state—of which the United States is surely an example—is not truly a regime in Aristotle's sense. They would argue that although the modern state has a formal structure of power, the aim of that governmental structure is not to promote some common moral purpose as would be required for an Aristotelian regime. The goal of the modern democratic state may be nothing more than to keep the peace so that people can pursue their private selfish interests, which reflects the teaching of Hobbes and Locke. Aristotle insists that although this may be one of the conditions for a regime, it is not by itself sufficient. He explains that the ultimate aim of a regime is a community bound together by some common conception of the good life so that there arises among the citizens a political form of friendship (1280b30–1281a8), which requires a common moral character in the citizenry. For every regime, there is a particular type of character that sets the moral tone of the community. Oligarchy promotes the oligarchic character, democracy the democratic character, and so on. But doesn't this mean a sacrifice of individual freedom insofar as everyone is forced to conform to the same pattern of life? Doesn't the modern democratic state allow for greater freedom by not prescribing a particular way of life for its citizens?

Perhaps the best formulation of the modern principle of liberty is John Stuart Mill's *On Liberty*. By comparing Mill's view of politics with Aristotle's, we may see more clearly the difficulties in applying Aristotle's theory of the regime to modern circumstances. The contrast with Aristotle is obvious when Mill asserts that the social control of the individual should be governed by "one very simple principle":

> that the sole end for which mankind are warranted, individually or collectively, in interfering with the liberty of action of any of their number is self-protection. That the only purpose for which power can be rightfully exercised over any member of a civilized community, against his will, is to prevent harm to others. His own good, either physical or moral, is not a sufficient warrant. . . . The only part of the conduct of anyone for which he is amendable to society is that which concerns others. In the part which merely concerns himself, over his own body and mind, the individual is sovereign.[30]

Mill adds immediately, however, as a qualification of this principle, that it applies only to "human beings in the maturity of their faculties." Children or young people below the legally fixed age of adulthood must be protected against their own actions because they are not yet able to care for themselves properly. He indicates, also, that for the same reason, his principle of individual liberty does not apply to "those backward states of society" in which humanity is still in its childhood. Full liberty should not be given until people are mature enough to be "capable of being improved by free and equal discussion."

Although no modern state has ever adhered fully to Mill's principle of liberty, it does express the spirit of modern liberal democracy. Every individual adult should be free from social control except to the extent that an individual's actions might harm others; although society may restrict the individual in that which "concerns others," each should be absolutely free in that which "concerns himself."[31] Mill's principle expresses the modern liberal denial of the Aristotelian claim that the formation of the moral character of citizens is a necessary and rightful concern of government. (In some of his other writings, it should be noted, Mill's thinking is not as "individualistic" as it is in *On Liberty*.)

What would the Aristotelian have to say about Mill's principle? Considering Aristotle's emphasis on the political character of human nature, the Aristotelian might challenge the fundamental assumption of Mill's principle, that one can distinguish clearly the self-regarding and other-regarding actions of human beings. Can the self be separated from others? Or is the self by its very nature relational? Aristotelians might invite us to strip away from the individual everything that comes in one way or another from society—including language, moral training, and intellectual education—and then ask us if the naked, shivering being that remains is fully human. The simple point, of course, is that the self-development of the individual depends so decisively on social life that it is hard to see any clear separation between the life of the individual and the life of that individual's community.

Mill recognizes this. He concedes, for example, that even if a person's action affects no one else "directly and in the first instance," it may still "affect others through himself." The Aristotelian might add that most of what one does to or for oneself is determined by what effects one thinks it will have on others. Even freedom of speech, which Mill is so concerned to defend, cannot be classified as a purely self-regarding activity with no effects on others. As Mill admits, no one would express opinions in public unless doing so would have some influence on others.

Another problem is evident in Mill's qualification of his principle of liberty as limited to mature adults. Doesn't he thereby concede that a political community does have a just power to shape the character of its citizens through the education of the young? In fact, Mill suggests that the best way for society to insure the proper conduct of adults is to use well its "powers of education" with the young. Society has no right to deprive adults of their freedom because it "has had absolute power over them during all the early portion of their existence; it has had the whole period of child-hood and nonage in which to try whether it could make them capable of rational conduct in life."[32] This might remind us of our earlier look at the work of Lawrence Kohlberg, who would argue that even the freest and most democratic society cannot avoid the duty of shaping the young according to some standard of citizenship.

Is it the case, then, that because of its openness to different ways of life, modern liberal democracy is not a regime in Aristotle's sense? Or does even liberal democracy fulfill Aristotle's claim that every regime shapes the character of its people to conform to its principles? A liberal democracy may be open to different ways of life, but how can it be open to nonliberal, nondemocratic attitudes and beliefs? Does the very possibility of liberal democracy depend on the formation of liberal democratic citizens? If we were correct earlier in seeing the Declaration of Independence as the fundamental expression of the American political consciousness, then instilling in citizens a respect for the principles of the Declaration might be the sort of civic education that Aristotle would regard as essential for the regime.[33]

Recently, some political scientists (like James Q. Wilson) have rediscovered Aristotle's insight that the aim of politics is to shape the moral character of citizens. Some of the most serious problems for American public policy—such as crime, drug addiction, and poor schools—may reflect the failure of our regime to instill good moral habits conforming to the common good.[34]

Let us assume for the moment that we were persuaded by Aristotle that every political community requires agreement to some regime-defining principles of justice, and that the young must be habituated to conform to these principles. Even then we would be left wondering by what standard we should judge these principles, because the nature of justice is open to dispute. If every political community seeks a shared conception of justice, and if justice is always debatable, then political life is inherently controversial. This is apparent in Aristotle's *Politics* because so much of the book is devoted to disputes about justice, disputes that give rise to a variety of regimes competing for our acceptance. The most common form of this controversy, to which Aristotle devotes much of his attention, is the debate between the oligarch and the democrat.

8. How should we settle the conflict between oligarchic and democratic views of justice?

The most visible of the differences among human beings in their social relations is their relative wealth or poverty. It is understandable, therefore, that disputes about justice often reflect conflicts between the rich and the poor. In considering the variety of regimes, Aristotle is largely preoccupied with various solutions to this problem.

Aristotle begins with the common opinions about this issue as expressed by the partisans themselves — the democratic poor and the oligarchic rich. He assumes that "all those who dispute about regimes express some part of justice" (1281a9–11). Both sides of the debate represent a partial grasp of justice that is distorted by self-interest. People tend to assert as an absolute principle that element of justice that favors their own interests (1280a14–15). Therefore, the first question is, what are the kernels of truth in the opposing claims of democratic and oligarchic justice? Second, what standard of justice can encompass both sides of this debate? Finally, through what sort of political arrangements can democrats and oligarchs be brought together without conflict?

Aristotle assumes that justice requires like cases to be treated the same, unlike cases differently — or, phrased another way, equals should be treated equally, unequals unequally.[35] The principle might be put even more simply: justice demands that each person get what he or she deserves (1281b15–1283a20). Is this principle, as Aristotle suggests, implied in all the common opinions about justice? How does this differ — if at all — from the Platonic view of justice as doing that for which one is naturally best suited?

Even if we accept as a general principle that equals should be treated as equals and unequals as unequals, we cannot apply this to particular cases without asking, equality or inequality of what? Human beings can be equal or unequal in an infinite number of respects, and disputes about justice commonly involve questions as to what equalities or inequalities are relevant to the case at hand. In deciding how to distribute flutes among flute players, equality or inequality of birth, of beauty, or of strength is irrelevant; ability in flute playing is the decisive factor. What factor is relevant in deciding who will share in political rule?

The democratic poor say that all those *equal in being born free* (that is, not enslaved) should participate equally in political rule. The oligarchic rich say that those *unequal in wealth* should have unequal political power. By what standard of merit do the democratic poor justify their political claims? The fact of being needy would not seem to be sufficient because many nonhuman animals might be even more needy. There must be some distinctly human quality possessed by the poor that would be a standard of dignity. On the other hand, to what do the oligarchic few appeal? If wealth is the only standard, then the one person who is the wealthiest should rule all of the people. What does the mere quantity of wealth have to do with political rule?

Aristotle argues that because the final end of politics is to promote a good or noble life, any claim to rule should be based on the possession of "political virtue" (1280b32–1281a8). But a regime founded on *perfect* virtue would be as difficult to establish as Socrates' "city of speech." By speaking of "*political* virtue," Aristotle suggests that in practice virtue will be interpreted according to whatever standards of conduct prevail in a particular community. He also indicates that the sort of virtue he has in mind is displayed in the multitude of common people if they are reasonably decent; this, then, would support the claims of democracy (1281a39–1282a41).

Yet even if Aristotle is willing to settle for a low-level conception of virtue as the standard for political justice, is this a realistic solution to the conflict between the democrats and the oligarchs? Or will competing views of virtue give rise to further conflict? Would the final resolution of this problem, as Hobbes would argue, necessitate lowering the needs of politics? High goals—such as justice and virtue—may be as controversial in their definitions as they are difficult to actualize in practice. But low goals—such as security and comfortable self-preservation—are easier to define in thought and easier to attain in practice because everyone can quickly agree to them. It would seem that Aristotle would never be willing to lower the goals of political life this far, because he insists that every regime must have some shared conception of the good and the just. Yet, as we have noted earlier, he is concerned not only with the goodness of regimes, but also with their practicality.

9. How does the Aristotelian leader handle a regime that is less than the best?

This question brings us back to the problem indicated at the beginning of this chapter. If Aristotle turns away from the Platonic preoccupation in the *Republic* with the best regime, by what standards will he guide leaders in working with regimes that fall short of perfection?

At the beginning of Book Four of the *Politics*, Aristotle indicates the range of political possibilities that should be understood by the politician. The adept leader should know not only what would be the best regime in the best of circumstances, but also what would be the best in most cases and what would be the best that is practicable in a given set of circumstances. Thus Aristotle may seem more "realistic" than Plato, but he is just as concerned with standards of perfection as Plato. The difference is that Aristotle's standards are graduated. Even when the Aristotelian leader is prevented by practical circumstances from pursuing the simply best regime, the ranking of regimes helps to determine what would be the best in the given conditions.

Without going into the details of Aristotle's analysis, we can see as a general principle that the leader should moderate the excesses of each bad regime by introducing elements of other regimes. A democratic regime can be improved by making it somewhat oligarchic, and an oligarchy is improved by pushing it toward democracy. What makes a regime bad is that it serves the interests of the ruling group at the expense of other groups. By mixing elements from different regimes, there is a movement toward protecting the common interests of all, which creates stability by eliminating the serious grievances of oppressed groups.

When the best regime is not possible, the second best alternative for the Aristotelian is some form of mixed regime. As both the poor and the wealthy have legitimate claims to rule, neither pure democracy nor pure oligarchy is as good as a judicious mixture of both in what Aristotle calls the "polity" (1293b2–1294b41). When even this is not possible, the next choice is a regime with a strong middle class that can soften the conflict between the rich and the poor (1295a25–1296b2).

We could easily find in American political history this same concern for balancing the power of the few rich and the many poor, so that neither class could exploit the other.[36] Some scholars have argued that the American Founding Fathers intended to establish a mixed regime along Aristotelian lines that would combine democratic and oligarchic elements.[37]

In any case, the American founders were certainly Aristotelian in the sense that they were prudent in accepting the harsh limitations of practical politics. But isn't there a temptation here to fall into unprincipled expediency? Aristotle himself seems to slip into this when he says that a leader should know how to preserve a bad regime even when it is not the best under the circumstances (1288b28–33). In many cases, a bad regime may be necessary

(1286b4–23, 1296a22–26, 1296b25–35). Aristotle even goes so far as to advise tyrants how best to preserve their power!

But it the Tyrant is in the Best

10. Why does Aristotle teach tyrants how to preserve their regimes?

Common interest of the People, why not?

Aristotle sketches two different ways for tyrants to protect their power. The first is the traditional method practiced by most tyrants, which is to intensify their tyranny by depriving the people of the inclination or the ability to rebel; tyrants do this by humiliating their subjects, getting them to distrust one another, and keeping them powerless (1313a34–39, 1314a15–29). For contemporary illustrations of this, we might consider the actions of tyrants such as Hitler and Stalin.[38]

Some readers are shocked that Aristotle explains the techniques of tyrants. It could be said in his defense that insofar as he indicates that these have been the traditional practices of most tyrants, he does not think that he is teaching tyrannical individuals anything they do not already know. For what purpose, then, does he talk about such things? Does he wish to show tyrants that he knows everything that they know? Does he teach the tricks of the base to the good so that they can protect themselves?[39] Does he also intend thereby to dispel the smug assumption of the bad that the good must be naive?

Perhaps the ultimate justification for what Aristotle does here becomes clear as one considers what he says about the second method for preserving tyrannies. Aristotle says the first method is vicious and brutalizing, but he also indicates—probably with the recognition that this will catch the tyrant's attention—that this method is not very successful. Generally, tyrannies are less durable than all other regimes, but the longest-lived tyrannies have followed the second method (1315b5–39). The general rule of this second approach is that the tyrant should cleverly appear to be a monarch rather than a tyrant. Tyranny should be moderated so that the ruler appears to be ruling for the common interests of the people. Yet it is hard to see how a tyrant could follow all of Aristotle's suggestions for pretending to be a monarch without actually becoming one!

Aristotle adheres throughout the *Politics* to the principle that the durability of a regime is *directly* proportional to its goodness and *inversely* proportional to its badness (1302a4–7, 1309b15–1310a12). The underlying reasoning is a model of Aristotelian common sense. The less oppressive a regime is, and the more the ruling group respects the claims of competing groups, the more durable the regime is likely to be. For that reason, tyranny is the worst regime and the least stable of regimes, and the only way to make it more enduring is to make it better by making it less of a tyranny. How realistic is Aristotle's reasoning? Has he underestimated the ability of tyrants to preserve themselves through sheer terror? When we look at Machiavelli, we shall have to ask how he might have replied to Aristotle.

In any case, Aristotle agrees with Plato, and with the Declaration of Independence, that we can recognize tyranny as evil because it fails to conform to the natural needs and capacities of human beings. Freedom of action and freedom of thought are conditions for the fulfillment of human nature. But what would be the political implications of a belief that the deepest human yearnings find satisfaction neither in political activity nor in philosophic thought, but only in religious devotion to God? That is the question posed by Christianity, which we can see in the work of St. Augustine.

Notes

1. In their debates over methodology, most contemporary social scientists choose between the "positivist" and the "hermeneuticist" positions. But Aristotle may offer a third choice superior to both. See Stephen G. Salkever, *Finding the Mean: Theory and Practice in Aristotelian Political Philosophy* (Princeton: Princeton University Press, 1990), 57–104. Recently, the "communitarian" critics of liberalism have looked to Aristotle for a defense of participatory democracy; while the "aristocratic" critics of liberalism have looked to him for a defense of virtue and elite rule. For a survey of these positions and an argument that Aristotle's position combines the partial truths in each, see Mary P. Nichols, *Citizens and Statesmen: A Study of Aristotle's Politics* (Savage, MD: Rowman and Littlefield, 1992).

2. See James Bernard Murphy, "Nature, Custom, and Stipulation in Law and Jurisprudence," *Review of Metaphysics* 43 (June 1990): 751–90. See also chap. 4, sec. 5.

3. All translations of the Greek texts are my own. I have used the Greek text of the *Politics* edited by H. Rackham (Cambridge: Harvard University Press, Loeb Classical Library, 1932). We do not know how Aristotle composed the *Politics*. He might have written it as a collection of lecture notes, as a handbook for his students, or as a finished book. See Carnes Lord, "The Character and the Composition of Aristotle's *Politics*," *Political Theory* 9 (November 1981): 459–78.

4. John Dewey, *The Influence of Darwin on Philosophy and Other Essays* (Bloomington: Indiana University Press, 1965), 1–19. For criticisms of the Darwinian arguments, see Gertrude Himmelfarb, *Darwin and the Darwinian Revolution* (New York: Norton, 1962), 312–78; and

Philip E. Johnson, *Darwin on Trial* (Washington, DC: Regnery Gateway, 1991). For defenses of Darwinism against these criticisms, see Douglas J. Futuyma, *Science on Trial: The Case for Evolution* (New York: Pantheon, 1983); and Philip Kitcher, *Abusing Science: The Case Against Creationism* (Cambridge: MIT Press, 1982).

5. James H. Randall, "The Changing Impact of Darwin on Philosophy," *Journal of the History of Ideas* 22 (October 1961): 456–59.

6. On the different kinds of teleology, see James G. Lennox, "Teleology," in Evelyn Fox Keller and Elisabeth A. Lloyd, eds., *Keywords in Evolutionary Biology* (Cambridge: Harvard University Press, 1992), 324-33; Peter A. Corning, *The Synergism Hypothesis* (New York: McGraw-Hill, 1983), 41–51, 201–205, 245–54; Ernst Mayr, *The Growth of Biological Thought* (Cambridge: Harvard University Press, 1982), 48–51; Mayr, *Toward a New Philosophy of Biology* (Cambridge: Harvard University Press, 1988); and Mayr, "The Idea of Teleology," *Journal of the History of Ideas* 53 (1992): 117–35. On Aristotle's biology, see Marjorie Grene, "Aristotle and Modern Biology," in *The Understanding of Nature* (Boston: D. Reidel, 1974), 74–107; Allan Gotthelf, ed., *Aristotle on Nature and Living Things* (Pittsburgh: Mathesis Publications, 1985); and Allan Gotthelf and James G. Lennox, eds., *Philosophical Issues in Aristotle's Biology* (Cambridge: Cambridge University Press, 1987). On Aristotle's teleology, see Allan Gotthelf, "Aristotle's Conception of Final Causality," in Gotthelf and Lennox, 204–42.

7. Ernst Mayr, *Biological Thought*, 89.

8. Max Delbruck, "How Aristotle Discovered DNA," in Kerson Huang, ed., *Physics and Our World: A Symposium in Honor of Victor F. Wiskopf* (New York: American Institute of Physics, 1976), 123–30.

9. See Larry Arnhart, "Aristotle, Chimpanzees, and Other Political Animals," *Social Science Information* 29 (1990): 479–559; Arnhart, "Feminism, Primatology, and Ethical Naturalism," *Politics and the Life Sciences* 11 (August 1992): 157–78; and Roger Masters, *The Nature of Politics* (New Haven: Yale University Press, 1989). The clearest defense of sociobiology is Timothy Goldsmith's *The Biological Roots of Human Nature* (Oxford: Oxford University Press, 1991). The best critique is Philip Kitcher's *Vaulting Ambition: Sociobiology and the Quest for Human Nature* (Cambridge: MIT Press, 1985). The best empirical application of sociobiology is Martin Daly and Margo Wilson's *Homicide* (Hawthorne, NY: Aldine de Gruyter, 1988). For diverse applications of sociobiology in the humanities and the social sciences, see Mary Maxwell, ed., *The Sociobiological Imagination* (Albany: State University of New York Press, 1991). See also Carl N. Degler, *In Search of Human Nature: The Decline and Revival of Darwinism in American Social Thought* (Oxford: Oxford University Press, 1991).

10. *History of Animals*, 487b32–488a14, 588a15–589a10. See Wolfgang Kullmann, "Man as a Political Animal in Aristotle," in David Keyt and Fred D. Miller, eds., *A Companion to Aristotle's Politics* (Oxford: Basil

Blackwell, 1991), 94–117. Aristotle's claim that some nonhuman animals are political should be contrasted with the modern assumption — as stated, for example, by Immanuel Kant (*Critique of Judgment*, trans. J.H. Bernard [New York: Hafner, 1951], secs. 83–84) — that humanity transcends animality because culture transcends nature. Recent biological research suggests that many animals are capable of cultural learning. See John T. Bonner, *The Evolution of Culture in Animals* (Princeton: Princeton University Press, 1980); T. M. Caro and M. D. Hauser, "Is There Teaching in Nonhuman Animals?" *The Quarterly Review of Biology* 67 (June 1992):151–74; Jane Goodall, *The Chimpanzees of Gombe* (Cambridge: Harvard University Press, 1986); W. C. McGrew, *Chimpanzee Material Culture* (Cambridge: Cambridge University Press, 1992); and Alexander H. Harcourt, "Cooperation in Conflicts: Commonalities Between Humans and Other Animals," *Politics and the Life Sciences* 11 (August 1992): 251–59.

11. Theodosius Dobzhansky, *The Biology of Ultimate Concern* (New York: New American Library, 1967), 82, 130–31. For surveys of the pertinent scientific research, see Roger D. Masters, "Politics as a Biological Phenomenon," *Social Science Information* 14 (Feb., 1975): 7–63; and Richard Passingham, *The Human Primate* (San Francisco: W. H. Freeman, 1982). Social scientists have gathered evidence of a universal social instinct. Human beings long for social bonds with their families, friends, and workmates. Those who lack such bonds are likely to experience physical and mental illness, alcoholism, suicide, and other ills. See Raoul Naroll, *The Moral Order* (Beverly Hills: Sage Publications, 1983), 129–43. It is not surprising that Aristotle has been called "the world's first published social psychologist" (Elliot Aronson, *The Social Animal*, 4th ed. [New York: W. H. Freeman, 1984], 72).

12. See Charles Darwin, *The Origin of Species and the Descent of Man* (New York: Random House, Modern Library, 1936), 459–70, 704–14. Compare Aristotle, *History of Animals*, 488a30–35, 504b1–6, 535a28–36b24, 608a10–18; *Parts of Animals*, 660a1–b6, 664a36–b6; *Generation of Animals*, 786b6–88a32.

13. See Konrad Lorenz, *King Solomon's Ring* (New York: Thomas Y. Crowell, 1952), 76–91; and Lorenz, *The Foundations of Ethology* (New York: Springer-Verlag, 1981), 338–44.

14. Helen Keller, *The Story of My Life* (New York: Doubleday, Page & Co., 1927), 23–24. See Susanne K. Langer, *Philosophy in a New Key*, 3rd ed. (Cambridge: Harvard University Press, 1957), 53–78.

15. H. S. Terrace et al., "Can an Ape Create a Sentence?" *Science* 206 (23 November 1979): 901. For the argument that Terrace and his colleagues used methods that failed to reveal the true conversational ability of their chimpanzee (named Nim), see Chris O'Sullivan and Carey Page Yeager, "Communicative Context and Linguistic Competence: The Effects of Social Setting on a Chimpanzee's Conversational Skill," in R. A. Gardner et al., eds., *Teaching Sign*

Language to Chimpanzees (Albany: State University of New York Press, 1989), 269–79. For the scientific debate over animal communication, see Derek Bickerton, *Language and Species* (Chicago: University of Chicago Press, 1990); Jane Goodall, *Through a Window: My Thirty Years with the Chimpanzees of Gombe* (New York: Houghton Mifflin, 1990), 12–23, 206–9; Philip Lieberman, *Uniquely Human: The Evolution of Speech, Thought, and Selfless Behavior* (Cambridge: Harvard University Press, 1991); Donald R. Griffin, *Animal Thinking* (Cambridge: Harvard University Press, 1985); and Carolyn A. Ristau, ed., *Cognitive Ethology: The Minds of Other Animals* (Hillsdale, NJ: Lawrence Erlbaum, 1991).

Consider Alfred North Whitehead's comment:

> You can observe animals choosing between *this thing* or *that thing*. But animal intelligence requires concrete exemplification. Human intelligence can conceive of a type of thing in abstraction from exemplification. The most obvious disclosures of this characteristic of humanity are mathematical concepts and ideals of the Good — ideals which stretch beyond any immediate realization. ("Mathematics and the Good," in Paul Arthur Schilpp, ed., *The Philosophy of Alfred North Whitehead*, 2nd ed. [LaSalle, IL: Open Court, 1951], 672–73)

See also Hans Jonas, "Image-making and the Freedom of Man," in *The Phenomenon of Life* (New York: Dell, 1966), 157–82.

16. See Frans de Waal, *Chimpanzee Politics: Power and Sex among Apes* (New York: Harper & Row, 1982); and Glendon Schubert and Roger D. Masters, eds., *Primate Politics* (Carbondale: Southern Illinois University Press, 1991).

17. See Carl Sagan, *The Dragons of Eden* (New York: Ballantine Books, 1977), 126–27, 130–31. Legal rights and duties apply only to "persons." On the difficulties in recognizing different kinds of persons, see John Chipman Gray, *The Nature and Sources of the Law*, 2nd ed. (Boston: Beacon Press, 1963), 27–64.

18. For a popular survey of this research, see Robert Ardrey, *The Territorial Imperative* (New York: Atheneum, 1966). Compare Ashley Montagu, *The Nature of Human Aggression* (Oxford: Oxford University Press, 1976); and Aronson, *The Social Animal*, 181–224.

19. Colin Turnbull, *The Mountain People* (New York: Simon & Schuster, 1972). Compare the effects of the plague in Athens as described by Thucydides, *History of the Peloponnesian War*, bk. 2, secs. 47–54.

20. Turnbull, *Mountain People*, 234, 289.

21. Ibid., 12. That one can be "a beautiful human being" even in a primitive society is the theme of Colin Turnbull's earlier book, *The Forest People: A Study of the Pygmies of the Congo* (New York: Simon & Schuster, 1961).

22. See Edward O. Wilson, *Sociobiology: The New Synthesis* (Cambridge: Harvard University Press, 1975), 242–55; David P. Barash, *Sociobiology and Behavior* (New York: Elsevier, 1977), 209–46; and

Edward O. Wilson, *On Human Nature* (Cambridge: Harvard University Press, 1978), 99–120.

23. Irenäus Eibl-Eibesfeldt, *Love and Hate: The Natural History of Behavior Patterns* (New York: Schocken Books, 1974), 5. See also Eibl-Eibesfeldt, *Human Ethology* (Hawthorne, NY: Aldine de Gruyter, 1989).

24. Jonathan Lear, *Aristotle: The Desire to Understand* (Cambridge: Cambridge University Press, 1988), 197.

25. See Algernon Sidney, *Discourses Concerning Government* (Indianapolis: Liberty Classics, 1990), 51–52, 77–87, 132–34, 191–95, 452–54.

26. For the interpretation of Aristotle as the founder of patriarchy, see Maryanne C. Horowitz, "Aristotle and Woman," *Journal of the History of Biology* 9 (1976): 183–213; and Susan M. Okin, *Women in Western Political Thought* (Princeton: Princeton University Press, 1979). For criticisms of this interpretation, see Harold L. Levy, "Does Aristotle Exclude Women from Politics?" *The Review of Politics* 52 (1990): 397–416; Mary P. Nichols, *Citizens and Statesmen*, 29–35; and Stephen Salkever, *Finding the Mean*, 165–204.

27. See Francisco de Vitoria, *Political Writings* (Cambridge: Cambridge University Press, 1991), 239–40, 250–51; and Bartolomé de Las Casas, *In Defense of the Indians* (DeKalb: Northern Illinois University Press, 1974), 32–48.

28. See, for example, Baldesar Castiglione, *The Book of the Courtier*, trans. Charles S. Singleton (Garden City, NY: Doubleday, Anchor Books, 1959), book 3.

29. See, for example, Benjamin Barber, *Strong Democracy: Participatory Politics for a New Age* (Berkeley: University of California Press, 1984); and William M. Sullivan, *Reconstructing Public Philosophy* (Berkeley: University of California Press, 1982).

30. John Stuart Mill, *On Liberty* (Indianapolis: Bobbs-Merrill, 1956), 13.

31. Ibid., 16.

32. Ibid., 100. For an interpretation of Mill's defense of individual liberty as an Aristotelian argument, see Albert William Levi, "The Value of Freedom: Mill's Liberty," *Ethics* 70 (1959): 37–46.

33. Joseph Tussman, in *Government and the Mind* (New York: Oxford University Press, 1977), argues: "Democracy is not . . . the natural or universal habit of the human mind; it is a cultivated spirit. And if we wish to maintain a democracy, we cannot neglect its constant cultivation" (143). For the argument that Aristotle's political theory can support liberal democracy, see Martha Nussbaum, "Aristotelian Social Democracy," in R. Bruce Douglass et al., eds., *Liberalism and the Good* (New York: Routledge, 1990), 203–52; and Douglas B. Rasmussen and Douglas J. Den Uyl, *Liberty and Nature: An Aristotelian Defense of Liberal Order* (La Salle, IL: Open Court, 1991). One can see Aristotelianism in the "eudaemonistic ethics" of Ludwig von Mises, *Socialism* (Indianapolis: Liberty Classics, 1981), chaps. 5, 27, 32.

The character formation required for a democratic regime became evident during the American occupation of Japan from 1945 to 1950. General Douglas MacArthur used his dictatorial power to force the Japanese to adopt democratic practices such as the emancipation of women, liberal education, individual rights, and a capitalist economy. He saw this transformation of a feudal culture into a democratic culture as a "spiritual revolution" (MacArthur, *Reminiscences* [New York: McGraw-Hill, 1964], 310). On Japanese culture, see Ruth Benedict, *The Chrysanthemum and the Sword* (Boston: Houghton Mifflin, 1946); and Kyoko Inoue, *MacArthur's Japanese Constitution* (Chicago: University of Chicago Press, 1991). For a comparison of American and Chinese culture, see Francis L. K. Hsu, *Americans and Chinese*, 3rd ed. (Honolulu: University Press of Hawaii, 1981). On the diverse national cultures of Europe, see Luigi Barzini, *The Europeans* (New York: Penguin Books, 1983).

34. See James Q. Wilson, *On Character* (Washington, DC: The AEI Press, 1991); James Q. Wilson and Richard Herrnstein, *Crime and Human Nature* (New York: Simon & Schuster, 1985); and William A. Galston, *Liberal Purposes: Goods, Virtues, and Diversity in the Liberal State* (Cambridge: Cambridge University Press, 1991).

35. On the need for different principles of justice for different spheres of life, see William A. Galston, *Justice and the Human Good* (Chicago: University of Chicago Press, 1980); and Michael Walzer, *Spheres of Justice* (New York: Basic Books, 1983). For an application to American politics of Aristotle's concept of the common good, see Arthur Maass, *Congress and the Common Good* (New York: Basic Books, 1983), 3–31.

36. See, for example, Theodore Roosevelt's comments on the "conflict between the men who possess more than they have earned and the men who have earned more than they possess" ("The New Nationalism," in Richard D. Heffner, ed., *A Documentary History of the United States* [New York: New American Library, 1976], 227).

37. See Paul Eidelberg, *The Philosophy of the American Constitution* (New York: Free Press, 1968); and Harvey C. Mansfield, Jr., *The Spirit of Liberalism* (Cambridge: Harvard University Press, 1978), 1–15.

38. See, for example, Charles L. Sherman, "A Latter-Day Tyranny in the Light of Aristotelian Prognosis," *American Political Science Review* 28 (June 1934): 424–35; and Alan Bullock, *Hitler and Stalin: Parallel Lives* (New York: Alfred Knopf, 1992).

39. That good people need to be well-armed with a knowledge of the tricks used by the base might justify Aristotle's *Rhetoric*, which explains all the techniques of rhetoric, including the fallacious and manipulative techniques of the sophists. See Larry Arnhart, *Aristotle on Political Reasoning: A Commentary on the "Rhetoric"* (DeKalb: Northern Illinois University Press, 1981).

Chapter

3

The Political Realism of Christian Theology

Augustine's *City of God*

Key Readings

The City of God, I, 8, 28–29; II, 7; IV, 3–4; V, 12–21,
24–26; VIII, 3–12; IX, 15–17; X, 24, 28–29, 32; XI, 2–4;
XIV, 13; XIX, 21, 24–28; XX, 7–9.

In the history of Western civilization, the writings of St. Augustine (A.D. 354–430) have provided a bridge between the classical culture of ancient Greece and Rome and the Christian culture of Western Europe. Augustine was supremely qualified for this role because, as a teacher of rhetoric, he had studied the Greek and Roman classics before he converted to Christianity and later became a bishop in the Christian Church.

The City of God was the first attempt to elaborate a Christian view of politics. In the New Testament, Jesus had taught that Christians were to render "to Caesar the things that are Caesar's, and to God the things that are God's" (Matthew 22:21); and St. Paul had exhorted Christians to obey their rulers as being ordained by God (Romans 13:1–7). This was interpreted to mean that Christians should obey all laws so long as this did not violate their religious

77

duties. Their primary concern was to serve the heavenly kingdom. Eventually, however, as the political influence of the Christian Church grew, it became necessary to clarify the meaning of worldly political activity for the Christians.

The last Roman persecutions of the Christians (A.D. 303–305) occurred under the Emperor Diocletian. Then, during a period of civil wars (305–324), the emperor Constantine gained control of the western part of the Roman Empire in 312. He was converted to Christianity the same year. The following year Christianity became a legal religion. In 393, the emperor Theodosius made it the official religion of the empire. When the Visigoths and Alaric sacked Rome in 410, some people suggested that this was punishment for having forsaken the traditional gods. This charge against Christianity stirred Augustine to write *The City of God*.

1. Was Augustine the first political realist?

As odd as it may sound, we should consider the suggestion of theologian Reinhold Niebuhr that Augustine was "the first great 'realist' in western history."[1] This seems a strange comment if we think about the moral ideals of Christianity, but it may seem less strange if we remember the Christian doctrines of the Fall and Redemption, which were crucial for Augustine's theology. All people bear the marks of that original sin of pride through which Adam fell from perfect union with God, and therefore they strive vainly to fill the emptiness in their souls. Their only path to fulfillment is the redemption in heaven offered by Christ. From the viewpoint of these doctrines, the Christian might well be deeply pessimistic about the political life of human beings. In their fallen state, people are too selfish to attain true goodness in their political arrangements; and consequently, to strive for political justice in this life is futile. With this kind of reasoning, Augustine's Christian theology might support the claim of Thrasymachus that in politics what is called justice is simply the rule of the stronger. By considering how even a Christian could be driven to such a harsh view of politics, we can begin to understand the issues in that perennial debate between political realists and political idealists.

Idealists, we might say, adhere to abstract, universal principles, whereas realists look at concrete, particular circumstances. Political idealists would insist on fixed principles of political justice, but political realists would demand flexibility in responding to the flux of political events. Moreover, idealists want to direct political action to high moral ends, but realists see politics as a conflict of selfish interests settled by an appeal to force with little concern for moral principles. Idealists would criticize realists for promoting the cynicism and nihilism that encourages brutality in political life. Realists would criticize idealists for the blind sentimentality that leads them to impose their own moral abstractions on political circumstances with no regard for the often harmful consequences. There is certainly some truth to both sides.

In the twentieth century, we have seen the dangers of *both* excessive idealism and excessive realism. Idealists have seduced us with visions of a cooperative world community forever free of war and injustice, yet in some cases these utopian dreams may have created opportunities for unprecedented violence and oppression. Realists, on the other hand, seem to have legitimated crude tyrannies both of the Left and the Right by affirming that politics is nothing more than the pursuit and exercise of power. We hope that political philosophers such as Augustine can help us to understand this modern dilemma.

To consider Augustine's position, let us look first at the unifying theme of *The City of God* as expressed in the idea of the two cities. Augustine opens his book by contrasting the humility of the City of God and the pride of the City of Man. Later he explains:

> Two cities have been formed by two loves, the earthly city evidently by love of self even to the contempt of God, the heavenly city truly by love of God even to the contempt of self. In short, the former glories in itself, the latter in the Lord. For the one seeks glory from men; but for the other the greatest glory is God as the witness of conscience. (XIV, 28)[2]

In the City of Man, he goes on to say, rulers rule for the glory of ruling; but, in the City of God, rulers find their true reward in the glory of heaven. In the City of Man, the wise glory in their own wisdom, even though this darkens their minds; in the City of God, the wise see that true wisdom is not human but divine. The City of Man arises from the corruption of Adam's sin of pride; the City of God arises from the humble believer's hope in salvation by Jesus Christ. Thus, in speaking of the two cities, Augustine uses the Christian doctrines of the Fall and Redemption to illuminate the human condition. Without the light of those doctrines revealed by God to the faithful, we cannot, Augustine claims, make sense of the world or our place in it.

We might conclude from this that, contrary to the earlier suggestion, Augustine exhibits a radical idealism, if we assumed that the City of God can be established on earth as a Christian empire guided by the Christian Church. In fact, this interpretation of

Augustine influenced some of the political activity of the Middle Ages. But there is evidence in *The City of God* that this reading of the book is profoundly mistaken. Augustine makes it clear that the City of God achieves its eternal peace only in heaven. On earth, Christians must submit to the earthly city, which provides only "the temporal peace, which is shared by both the good and the bad" (XIX, 26).

Perhaps we should say that Augustine *combines* idealism and realism. He is an idealist in his view of the City of God as the perfect city, but he is a realist in his account of the earthly city as weighted down by the desperate wickedness of people without God. Doesn't this resemble what we have already seen in the works of Plato and Aristotle? Don't they also lament the difficulty of actualizing the best regime, which usually exists only in the mind of the philosopher? Why, then, shouldn't they be considered just as realistic as Augustine?

Plato and Aristotle are certainly political realists in thinking that what is politically best by nature is rarely, if ever, attained fully in political practice. Still, they are idealists, in contrast to Augustine's realism, because of their confidence that nature provides a standard of political perfection discoverable by human reason, a standard that can guide political philosophy as a norm for judgment, even though it cannot be put completely into practice. The Socratic political philosophers had to make the optimistic assumption that although our knowledge of nature is always incomplete, the natural world is, in principle, rationally comprehensible as a self-sufficing and self-explanatory whole.

Augustine would dismiss this view of things as showing a naive blindness to the fact that the natural world is, at its core, a mystery. Even if we could see every part of nature in its relationship to the whole, nature would still be incomprehensible because it is not a self-sufficient whole. Because the natural universe depends for its existence on a supernatural cause, the universe is not fully intelligible on its own terms. This leads Augustine to a much more pessimistic assessment of politics than can be found in the works of Plato or Aristotle. Rather than saying that nature's standards of perfection are rarely satisfied in political life, Augustine insists that nature itself, in its present state, is imperfect, because, as far as nature is concerned, political justice does not exist anywhere, not even in the mind of the political philosopher.

Nature becomes a reliable guide only when we see by faith that it points to a supernatural source of order.

> Great it is and very rare, after one has looked at the whole creation, corporeal and incorporeal, and has discerned its

> mutability, to go beyond it by the stretching of the mind, and
> to arrive at the unchangeable substance of God, and there to
> learn from God Himself that the whole of nature — that which
> does not belong to His essence — no one but He has made. (XI, 2)

Because of nature's "mutability," it cannot be adequately explained
without reference to the immutable Creator. Therefore, when nature
is considered independently of its supernatural cause, as it was by
Plato and Aristotle, it cannot provide dependable norms for either
political philosophy or political leadership.

Because Augustine's reasoning relies on faith in the divinely
revealed doctrines of the Bible, we cannot through human reason
alone adequately judge his argument. But we can at least assess
the surface plausibility of his claims. We can ask ourselves, without
any appeal to religious faith, whether pagan philosophers such as
Plato and Aristotle failed, as Augustine says, to make sense of the
natural world without the assistance of Christian doctrine.

If the Christian teaching is correct, nature must be so mutable,
so contingent, that it cannot be made intelligible as a self-contained
whole. This Christian thought is expressed well in the questions
raised by G. W. Leibniz in 1714 in his *Principles of Nature and
Grace*: Why is there something, why not nothing? And why are
things as they are and not different? It is a sign of the shallowness
of our thinking that we commonly prefer to ignore such questions
because we find them too troubling. We would rather ask easier
questions about *how* things work than to ask *why* they work as they
do or *why* they exist at all. Leibniz offered an answer to his
questions: "This final reason of things is called *God*."[3] We are not
entitled to reject his answer unless we have a better answer of our
own.

To Leibniz's two questions — Why is there something, why not
nothing? Why are things as they are and not different? — there are
only two possible answers. Either we answer, as Leibniz did, God
wills it; or we answer, it *has* to be so. If we say that the universe
has to exist and *has* to exist in the form that it does, then the
universe needs no supernatural cause because, being a *necessary*
universe, it is its own cause. But if we say that this is only one
possible universe of many, that it does not have to exist or exist
in the form that it does, then we must conclude that because the
universe has no internal cause for its own preservation, the universe
must depend on a supernatural cause for its preservation. Notice
that Christians do *not* have to assume that there ever were or will
be other universes; they only have to assume that there could have
been or could be other universes.

The strength of the Christian position should be clear. For it seems plausible that, at least in principle, our universe is only one possible universe of many. The laws of physics *could* be different from what they are; if they were, we would live (let us hope *we* would be part of it!) in a different universe. Yet if a radically different universe is possible, then it is also possible for there to be *no* universe at all because our universe does not exist by necessity. Therefore, the continuing existence of the universe from one moment to another can be sustained only by a power beyond the natural universe itself, a supernatural cause of some sort.[4]

What does all of this metaphysical speculation have to do with the conflict between realism and idealism in political thinking? A lot. To be a political idealist one has to assume that there are some fixed standards of perfection in nature by which political life can be judged. However, if nature is radically contingent, only one possible universe among many, the status of nature's standards of political perfection is thrown into question. It would seem that the perfection of nature's tendencies can be found only in the supernatural source of nature's laws. One might conclude from this, as Augustine does, that political life as guided by the natural norms of this world must be radically flawed.

Because the world at its core is mysterious, human reason on its own cannot fathom reality completely; nature on its own is not fully explainable; and human beings on their own cannot secure their happiness. It is the pride of pagan philosophers that prevents them from finding the solution to the difficulties, Augustine argues (II, 7; VIII, 4; XI, 25). Only the humble faith of the Christian can dispel the darkness, because it reveals that God illuminates human reason, God creates and sustains nature, and God offers human beings the happiness they seek. To clarify Augustine's political realism, we should consider how he argues for the superiority of Christian faith over pagan philosophy in the three areas just indicated: the study of morality, the study of nature, and the study of reason itself. The next three sections of this chapter will be devoted to these subjects as they bear on Augustine's political thought.

2. Does Christian faith perfect our reasoning about politics?

By its appeal to "self-evident" principles, the Declaration of Independence reminds us that political argument, like all reasoning, must have a starting point that does not need to be proven. It is futile to try to prove everything because reasoning depends on fundamental assumptions that cannot be proven since they are the source of all proofs. A conclusion is demonstrated when it is shown to follow from some premises. These premises may follow as conclusions from other premises. Eventually, however, we must reach first principles that are taken as true without proof, these being the starting points of reasoning. Indeed, are not the rules of logic themselves assumptions that cannot be proven logically? Even the most rigorous empirical science cannot avoid reliance on unprovable assumptions. Scientific induction, for example, depends on the assumption that we may generalize from particular cases; this rests, in turn, on the broader assumption that nature is uniform and governed by laws that do not change arbitrarily from one moment to another.[5] Should we conclude, therefore, that all reasoning depends on acts of faith? For how else should we explain our apprehension of first principles as self-evident? Thus, we cannot easily dismiss Augustine's claim that Christian faith does not contradict, but rather perfects human reason (see chapter 6, sections 2–3, 5).

Pascal, who was influenced by Augustine's writings, wrote in the seventeenth century:

> We know the truth not only through reason but also through the heart; it is by the latter that we know the first principles. . . . And it is on this knowledge from the heart and instinct that reason must depend and base all its argument. (*Pensées*, fr. 110)[6]

Pascal was a mathematician, and he thought that geometry illustrated this dependence of "reason" on the "heart." Before we can rationally demonstrate anything in geometry, we must start with definitions and axioms that are self-evident. For example, the axiom that two things equal to the same are equal to one another cannot be proven; it must be, in Pascal's words, "sensed" or "felt" to be true. Pascal also thought a similar justification could be given for allowing Christian faith to guide our thinking. We can "sense" or "feel" that people strive for some perfect happiness for which they were designed but which now lies somewhere beyond this world. We should accept the Christian doctrines of the Fall and Redemption, because once we grasp these teachings by faith, Pascal maintains, our minds can comprehend the world more clearly than would ever be possible otherwise.

Augustine would agree. As in his famous declaration, "I believe in order to understand," Augustine affirms that faith allows reason to reach its natural fulfillment. "Those who do not believe and therefore cannot understand" allow their pride to darken their minds (X, 32). Through pride, the mind "deserts that to which it should cleave as its first principle, seeking to become and to be, so to speak, a first principle to itself" (XIV, 13). This proud refusal to accept divine enlightenment has so clouded the human mind that not even the wisest have succeeded in making sense of things.

Perhaps the most obvious evidence of the intellectual confusion of the pagan philosophers is that they fail to reach agreement about even the most fundamental matters. Augustine observes that it is hard to find any two philosophers who agree in all respects. For example, concerning the question as to what is the highest good of life, Augustine catalogued 288 different answers given by the philosophers (XVIII, 41; XIX, 1). Philosophic debates must always be interminable as long as the debaters cannot appeal to any authority higher than their own reason. Only Christian faith can provide the "surpassing authority" that is needed (X, 32). Augustine concedes that the Platonists came close to grasping the insights of Christianity, but he thinks that they fell short due to their pride (VIII, 4–5; X, 24, 28–29).

Augustine argues for the superiority of conscience over reason, with the claim that only the divinely inspired conscience can properly guide reason. Some would see this Augustinian idea implied in the Declaration of Independence. It was common among some English Puritans of the eighteenth century to argue that natural rights could be perceived as self-evident only through the inner light of conscience given by God.[7] Although the invocations of divinity in the Declaration would support this view, the appeal to the "Laws of Nature" suggests that unassisted human reason can grasp the self-evident truths through its understanding of nature. Indeed, if the concern is with natural rights, shouldn't nature itself (apart from God) be a sufficient standard? Moreover, we might question the wisdom of grounding our fundamental political principles on the unpredictable impulses of conscience. We might also doubt that even Augustine would recommend trying to establish earthly politics on the Christian conscience. At the same time, Augustine would surely question the wisdom of relying on the philosophic concept of nature as a source of political principles.

3. Is nature apart from God a reliable standard for politics?

After invoking the universal principles of natural rights, the Declaration of Independence indicates that political reasoning

requires more than just a knowledge of the universals of nature.
"Prudence, indeed, will dictate that Governments long established
should not be changed for light and transient causes; and
accordingly all experience hath shown, that mankind are more
disposed to suffer, while evils are sufferable, than to right themselves by abolishing the forms to which they are accustomed." To
justify the revolution it is necessary to show that the facts of the
"history of the present King of Great Britain" support such a drastic
measure. Wise leadership requires a knowledge not only of nature,
but also of history. Because the historical circumstances of politics
are always unique and always changing, they cannot be understood
simply as manifestations of the uniform patterns of nature. How,
then, can we make sense of history on its own terms?

As we have seen, Augustine maintains that the historical
mutability of nature cannot be comprehended unless one sees it
as reflecting God's providential order. The pagan philosophers
thought of nature as an eternally recurring pattern in which history
was little more than the cyclical repetition of a limited number of
possibilities. We have seen this, for instance, in the Platonic and
Aristotelian accounts of the variety of regimes, in which there is
assumed to be a fixed number of possible regimes that are repeated
as historical circumstances change. But in Christian thinking,
historical novelty is more important than natural recurrence, or
perhaps we should say that nature itself becomes a fluid historical
process of continual change in which the only fixed reality is that
God's will stands behind it all.

Nature is orderly, according to the Christian conception, but the
law of this order is the continual working of God's will. Each thing
is what it is by virtue of God's unceasing creative activity. G. K.
Chesterton captured the idea when he suggested:

> It is possible that God says every morning, "Do it again" to the
> sun; and every evening, "Do it again" to the moon. It may not
> be automatic necessity that makes all daisies alike; it may be
> that God makes every daisy separately, but has never got tired
> of making them. . . . The repetition in Nature may not be a mere
> recurrence; it may be a theatrical encore. . . . Repetition may
> go on for millions of years, by mere choice, and at any instant
> it may stop.[8]

But for Plato and Aristotle that one daisy is just like all other daisies
is a matter of automatic necessity!

The crucial point, Augustine might insist here, is that Plato and
Aristotle fail to achieve through their conception of nature the
very purpose they wish it to serve, which is to make reality fully

intelligible. In trying to explain reality as ordered according to abstract, universal concepts, they have no way of explaining the concrete particularity of things. In their preoccupation with the repetitive patterns of nature, they cannot explain the unique and unpredictable occurrences that violate these natural patterns. So, for example, having constructed a "city in speech" that is the best by nature because it conforms to the universal principles of human nature, Plato has to concede that no existing city satisfies this political model. The philosopher's rational grasp of the abstract principles of nature is not enough to make sense of the concrete reality of political practice.

If we look at the world without any preconceptions, we see a chaotic flux, everything continually changing and nothing exactly the same as anything else. Not only do daisies differ from dogs, every daisy differs in some respect from all other daisies; moreover, each daisy changes from one moment to another. Similarly, in politics every set of circumstances is unique, so that a political decision appropriate to one time and place may not be appropriate to any other times or places. Augustine would argue that when confronted with such changeableness in nature, the mind should look beyond nature to the unchangeable Creator to find a source of order for an otherwise disordered world. But the proud Platonic philosopher tries to find within the human mind itself principles of order for understanding nature without reference to any reality beyond the mind or beyond nature.

The Platonist relies on the mind's power to simplify the complexity of the world through the abstract categories of the mind. Disregarding the fact that no particular thing is absolutely identical to anything else, the mind can classify things according to resemblances. As Friedrich Nietzsche would say, the human tendency "to treat as equal what is merely similar—an illogical tendency, for nothing is really equal—is what first created any basis for logic."[9] Thus the mind looks for permanent, recurrent patterns as points of reference for finding a coherent order in the confusion of the world. Even if no two daisies are the same, they resemble each other more than they do dogs. Who has ever seen daisies produce seeds that grow into dogs? Is not the order of nature apparent in the tendency of daisies to manifest the characteristic features of all daisies and in the corresponding tendency of dogs to look like dogs? Similarly, do not human beings exhibit certain natural tendencies in their political activity, tendencies that remain essentially the same even in diverse political situations?

Nevertheless, this natural regularity is not inevitable. Some puppies are born deformed, and others fail to grow to maturity.

Likewise, the natural political tendencies of human beings can fail owing to changing circumstances. The Platonist would try to explain this by saying that nature's intention can be frustrated by chance. This is why the city that is best by nature has never been established. It requires a rare combination of circumstances that can only arise by "divine chance" (Plato, *Republic* 592a). To speak of chance, however, is not an explanation of why things do not always turn out according to nature, rather it is an admission that the notion of nature does not explain the whole of reality. To talk of chance is to confess one's ignorance.

This Christian criticism of the Greek concept of nature has to be taken seriously. But does referring everything back to God as the ultimate cause solve all the problems? At least it consoles the Christian to know that everything — even what seems to be purely accidental — serves some divine purpose. Augustine explains:

> God, therefore, Himself the author and giver of felicity, because He alone is the true God, He gives earthly kingdoms both to the good and to the bad, not blindly and, as it were, fortuitously — because He is God, not fortune — but according to the order of things and times hidden for us, but fully known to Him; which order of times, nevertheless, He serves not as being subordinate to it, but just like a lord He rules it, and just like a moderator He disposes it: true felicity He does not give except to the good. For in this life they can have or not have power over subjects, they can have or not have power over kings; and nevertheless their happiness will be full in that life where no one is a subject. (IV, 33)

Although the Christian knows by faith *that* there is a purpose behind every event ("according to the order of things and times"), it cannot be known — at least in this earthly life — *what* the purpose is (see also I, 28; V, 19, 21). Nevertheless, Christians can be sure that all that happens to them in this life points to the fulfillment of their happiness in the next life.

Although Christianity can secure human happiness through divine providence, pagan philosophy cannot secure happiness from the vicissitudes of earthly life because such philosophy cannot transcend the visible course of nature. According to Plato and Aristotle, the core of human nature is membership in the human species, possessing the characteristics shared by human beings that distinguish them from other beings. Humans being defined as rational animals, each is unique by virtue of a combination of animality and rationality, but with reason being the distinctive and thus most important feature. Human nature, then, provides the moral standards for both the individual life and the political life of human beings. People should act so as to perfect their natural faculties—especially reason as the highest faculty—and thus fulfill their happiness. Likewise, a political regime should be constructed to promote such human perfection and the happiness that emerges from it. Certain external conditions that are not completely under human control are crucial to the expression of human nature in the securing of happiness. Whether or not an individual fulfills his or her natural potentialities depends on blind luck! Any one of us may have our life radically disrupted by physical disabilities or losses of external goods that are not due to any fault of our own. Such undeserved misfortune, contrary to nature's intention, is inexplicable in Greek philosophy (see Aristotle, *Nicomachean Ethics* 1099a31–1101a22). Moreover, the importance of luck is as much a problem for regimes as for individuals. No matter how closely a regime follows nature's standards, it can suffer from events beyond its control. Even a community well-ordered internally cannot avoid for long conflict with foreign enemies, and the fortunes of war do not always favor the naturally excellent. As Winston Churchill once said, we cannot insure that we shall always win, we can only insure that we shall always *deserve* to win.

From the Christian point of view, the dependence of individuals and regimes on luck no longer needs to be accepted as an unavoidable element of absurdity in life. For God is the source of both good and bad luck; even when good people and good regimes suffer misfortune inexplicable in natural terms, the Christian can be confident that this serves some divine purpose beyond the natural realm. The early Christian philosopher Boethius could argue that, within the context of divine providence, "all fortune is good fortune."[10] In this sense, the earthly sufferings of the Christian are not misfortunes at all when viewed in the light of the heavenly rewards that lie ahead. The pagan deprived of worldly happiness has no such consolation, Augustine observes (II, 8, 29; III, 18, 20).

The Christian is not favored over the non-Christian in God's distribution of the good things of this life, even including political power (V, 26). There is no guarantee that the Christian ruler will be more successful politically than the pagan ruler (IV, 33; V, 21, 24–25), but as long as Christians look ahead to their rewards in the heavenly city, they can accept without despair any disappointments in the affairs of their earthly city.

Thus Christianity solves the problem of the contingency of nature in a way that was not possible for the ancient philosophers. As an epistemological problem, contingency prevented the ancient philosophers from showing that nature was fully comprehensible to the human mind: although grasping certain recurrent features of nature, the pagan mind could not account for the variability and particularity of things. As a moral and political problem, the contingency of nature prevented the ancient thinkers from establishing an intelligible correspondence between character and fortune: no matter how virtuous a person or a political regime might be, happiness depended on fortuitous events.[11] Christians, however, are not frustrated in their moral life by the contingency of worldly events because they are confident that every event serves some divine purpose. Similarly, Christians need not be troubled by the infinite flux of nature because, although it surpasses the comprehension of the temporal mind of human beings, it is all rationally ordered in the eternal mind of God. To put all of this into a simple formula, the Christian solves the problem of the contingency of nature by replacing philosophic naturalism with Biblical creationism. Instead of explaining things in accordance with the recurrent patterns of nature conceived as a self-contained, self-explanatory whole, Christians see the natural order as a result of the continual working of the Creator's will. (Augustine reflects on the createdness of the world in the last three books of his *Confessions*.)

Doesn't this put mankind in a precarious position insofar as the meaning of existence must now hang by the slender thread of human faith? What happens when that thread breaks, as apparently it has for many in the modern world? Does reality collapse into absolute meaninglessness? Although creationism provided Christians consolation unattainable by the ancient philosophers, it may also have led the secular thought of the modern world toward an inconsolable despair. In its modern secularized embodiment, creationism can promote nihilism. For if it is believed that the natural world has no order or meaning of its own except what it receives from the Creator, as the existence of the Creator comes to be doubted, human beings must see the world as empty of any order or meaning. This is nihilism in the literal sense of thinking that everything rests on nothing.

Consider the potentiality for nihilism in the following passage from *The City of God* (XIV, 13), in which Augustine explains the sin of Adam:

> Nature could not have been depraved by vice if it had not been made out of nothing [*ex nihilo*]. And as a result, that it is nature, this is so because God made it; but that it falls from him, this is because it is made from nothing. Man did not so fall away as to become entirely nothing [*omnino nihil*], but as inclined toward himself, he became less than he was when he clung to Him who supremely is. And so having left God, to exist in

himself, that is, to please himself, is not actually to become nothing, but to approach nothing [*nihilo propinquare*].

As the hold of the Christian faith loosened in the modern world, there was a tendency to assume a creationist ontology without a Creator. The world is as arbitrarily contingent as if it were created by God, but God does not exist. And if the world rests on nothing, one cannot deny the creative power of God without falling into that nothingness at the heart of things. This becomes apparent in the nihilism of existential atheism. The "death of God" leaves the existentialist with the Christian denial that nature is intelligible but without the Christian hope in divine redemption.

Karl Löwith has formulated clearly how modern thought emerges from the secularization of Christian doctrine:

> The modern world is as Christian as it is non-Christian because it is the outcome of an age-long process of secularization. . . . The ambition to be "creative" and the striving for a future fulfillment reflect the faith in creation and consummation, even when these are held to be irrelevant myths.
>
> Radical atheism, too, which is, however, as rare as radical faith, is possible only within a Christian tradition. . . . The fact that the Christian God has ruled out all the popular gods and protecting spirits of the pagans created the possibility of a radical atheism; for if the Christian belief in a God who is as distinct from the world as a creator is from his creatures and yet is the source of every being is once discarded, the world becomes emancipated and profane as it never was for the pagans. If the universe is neither eternal and divine, as it was for the ancients, nor transient but created, as it is for the Christians, there remains only one aspect: the sheer contingency of its mere "existence."[12]

This may explain the talk about the despair, the boredom, the meaninglessness of modern life; in fact, it all sounds so familiar to us as to seem trite. Indeed, this vague metaphysical anxiety, this sometimes faint but ever-present feeling of homelessness in the universe, has pervaded the modern Western world. It characterizes the secular consciousness of our age that accepts, on the one hand, the Christian belief that nature on its own is void of meaning and cannot therefore guide us in thought or action, while rejecting, on the other hand, the Christian faith in the divine redemption of nature.

Pascal sketches this new consciousness in his *Pensées*, in his remarks on the misery of human life without God. An individual who thinks about our place in the universe soon ends up staring into an abyss, discovering that he is "equally incapable of seeing the nothing from which he is drawn and the infinity in which he is engulfed" (fr. 390). Thinking about the fragility and brevity of mortal existence in the cold immensity of the universe creates a deep sense of nothingness. The only escape from these dark thoughts is to keep oneself so busy with the daily activities of life that one has no time to think. For that reason, human beings dread most of all quiet moments without distractions (fr. 269). For Pascal, however, there is a promise of redemption: "It is good to be tired and fatigued by the useless search for the true good, so that we stretch out our arms to the Savior" (fr. 306). But once that faith is shaken, all that remains is desperation mitigated by diversions.

The political consequences of this nihilistic despair should be clear. If nature has no inherent order of its own, but has only whatever meaning human beings arbitrarily choose to give it, then it is absurd to speak of human beings as possessing natural rights or to claim that nature provides any principles of political justice. The sort of argument displayed in the Declaration of Independence would have to be dismissed as, at best, wishful self-deception, and at worst, fraudulent propaganda. Without any principles of natural justice, political activity might then be governed simply by the irrational preferences of those who happen to be powerful.

Although the secularization of Christian teaching can thus lead to a despondent political nihilism, by another line of development that same process of secularization can lead to a utopian political idealism. The problem with Christianity is its uncertainty: the Christian's hope in the transcendent rewards of heaven depends on faith alone. One way to eliminate that uncertainty is simply to give up hope, and we have considered the consequences of that move. Another way to escape the insecurity of Christian faith is to bring heaven down to earth. If we could establish the Kingdom of God in this earthly life, we could fulfill our happiness without the anxiety of waiting for a doubtful salvation in heaven. Some of the most turbulent political movements in the modern world have pursued that vision.

Augustine saw this tendency in Christian political thought, and he opposed it in *The City of God*. The problem arises from the last book of the New Testament, the Revelation of St. John. John describes Christ ruling the earth with his saints for a thousand years (Revelation 20:1–6). Many Christians interpreted this to mean that they should prepare to enjoy the Kingdom of God on earth. Using the Latin word for "one thousand," they called themselves *millenarians*. Augustine dismissed these visions as "ridiculous fables" (XX, 7). He argued that John had written a metaphorical account of the present position of the Church (XX, 9). The City of God, Augustine explained, exists on earth as the mystical body of believers; but the fulfillment of God's Kingdom is in heaven not on earth. Until their entry into heaven, Christians must in this life live with all the imperfection of worldly politics.

Augustine's rejection of millenarianism became the doctrine of the Christian Church. Nevertheless, from the Middle Ages to the present, millenarian groups have erupted in political history, often in the form of revolutionary movements. Some historians have traced an unbroken line of influence from the medieval millenarians through the Puritan revolutionaries in seventeenth century England down to the Marxist and National Socialist revolutionaries.[13] To provide only one example of modern millenarianism, Harold Laski, an influential English political thinker, once praised Lenin for seeking "to build his heaven on earth and write the precepts of his faith into the inner fabric of a universal humanity." Laski thought "that the Russian principle cuts deeper than the Christian since it seeks salvation for the masses by fulfillment in this life, and, thereby, orders anew the actual world we know."[14] The problem, of course, with this sort of thinking is that it promotes a dangerous spirit of immoderation. When political leaders think they are establishing heaven on earth, they can see that goal as justifying whatever brutal measures they take to achieve it (see chapter 10, section 1; chapter 11, section 6).

America has had its own tradition of millenarian idealism. Beginning with the first Puritan settlers, Americans have seen themselves as God's chosen people to set an example of political excellence for all the world.[15] The Declaration of Independence presented the American Revolution as a vindication of God-given rights. Lincoln, in the Gettysburg Address, called for a rededication to the principles of the Declaration, so that popular government "shall not perish from the earth." That required a holy war, as described by Julia Ward Howe in "The Battle Hymn of the Republic": "In the beauty of the lilies Christ was born across the sea, with a glory in his bosom that transfigures you and me: as he died to make men holy, let us die to make men free, while God is marching on."

President Woodrow Wilson thought the League of Nations would extend this City of God beyond America to include the entire world, so that injustice and violence would be forever banished from world politics. The League was necessary, he insisted, to fulfill what American soldiers had done in the First World War. He spoke of

the moral obligation that rests upon us not to go back on those boys, but to see the thing through, to see it through to the end

and make good their redemption of the world. For nothing less
depends upon this decision, nothing less than the liberation and
salvation of the world.[16]

Such visions of American politics aiming toward the "redemption
of the world" would be denigrated by Augustine as ridiculous fables.
Political thinkers such as Reinhold Niebuhr and Hans Morgenthau
have espoused a modern version of Augustine's political realism
as an alternative to the idealist tradition of American politics.[17] Our
concern with high moral norms, they argue, should not blind us
to the harsh reality of politics. Owing to the ineradicable flaws in
human nature, political life is usually dominated more by the selfish
striving for power than by the concern for justice and the common
good. The most that we can hope for is to maintain some stability
and peace both within and among nations through balances of
power, the aim being to keep any groups or nations from being
powerful enough to tyrannize over the others. Augustine accepts
this as a consequence of the fallen nature of human beings.

Still, we must ask whether this realistic view of politics is too
narrow. Must we give up our pursuit of political justice? If we do,
how do we judge political decisions as better or worse? Does the
preservation of peace become the only standard of political
judgment? Can we do this without being brutalized by the absence
of any sense of justice?

4. Must earthly political rule always be unjust?

In Cicero's *Republic* (I, 39), he defines a republic as a large group
of people "associated by a consensus about justice and a society
for the common utility." Augustine objects that this definition has
never been satisfied because no republic has ever been founded on
justice (II, 21; XIX, 23). Thus Augustine drastically lowers the aims
of politics by denying that political justice is ever attainable in this
life. We must wonder, then, whether Augustine ends up supporting
Thrasymachus's view of politics as the rule of the stronger disguised
as justice.

To replace Cicero's standard, Augustine offers a more realistic
definition of a republic: a political community requires "an
assemblage of a multitude of rational beings associated in a
common agreement about the things they love" (XIX, 24). Instead
of justice, Augustine demands only that the people agree about
something, without prescribing what that should be. Although he
suggests a standard of rank when he says that a community is

better or worse as the objects of their agreement are better or worse, he goes on to explain that the fundamental aim of every community is simply "temporal peace" (XIX, 26).

This is, to say the least, a modest assessment of the purposes of political life in contrast to the higher expectations for politics in the ancient view. Those ancient Greek and Roman citizens who sacrificed everything else for the sake of the public realm had a more elevated view of political activity. We must wonder, then, whether Augustine is capable of appreciating the political virtues of such people. We must also wonder whether his Christian conception of politics can sustain grand leadership. Although ancient authors celebrated the heroic virtues of the leader as manifesting "greatness of soul" (Aristotle, *Nicomachean Ethics*, 1123a34–1125a17), Christians have denigrated such activity as corrupted by that most fundamental of all sins — pride. The spirit of this Christian doctrine has found its secular incarnation in the political thought of Hobbes, in his teaching that violent human pride must be subdued by the State for the sake of political peace. We might conclude, then, that heroic leadership has survived only to the extent that it has found sustenance in the cultural residues of pagan antiquity.

Augustine does acknowledge, however, the genuine political virtues of the ancient Romans (V, 12–16). He explains those virtues as motivated by the love of praise. For the sake of political glory, to live after death through fame, Roman politicians suppressed vices such as the desires for wealth and private pleasures in order to serve the Roman Republic with their great deeds. This was not true virtue, however, because it was directed to human praise rather than the highest human good. These individuals, therefore, were "not yet holy, but only less corrupt." Yet God rewarded their virtues appropriately by granting Rome temporal power and peace. The decline of Rome came when its rulers were moved less by the desire for glory than by the desire for domination (V, 19).

Thus Augustine can recognize political virtues even while denigrating them as falling short of the true virtues of the Christian. At least, he can distinguish leaders from tyrants. And yet, how can he do this — how can he speak of good and bad forms of political rule — if, as he insists, political life cannot truly conform to justice? Granted, one government may be more efficient than another in securing the temporal peace of its subjects, but that seems hardly sufficient for moral judgment. No matter how shocking it may be, we have to take Augustine seriously when he remarks: "When justice is removed, what are kingdoms but great bands of robbers? For what are bands of robbers if not small kingdoms?" (IV, 4). Must we conclude, then, that, for the Augustinian Christian, a politician differs from a tyrant, but only in that the one is a more heroic thief than the other?

5. Must the Christian be a Machiavellian?

This is a paradoxical question. We might assume that the Christian's faith in the transcendent perfection of the Kingdom of God would promote a moral idealism directly opposed to Machiavellian politics. Yet, as we have seen, an Augustinian Christian who insists that God's Kingdom is "not of this world" can be tough-minded in judging the politics of *this* world. We shall grapple with Machiavelli, and others like him, later in this book. Here, we should consider whether Augustine's political thought offers an alternative to Machiavellianism. Is it possible to avoid the illusions of political idealism while also escaping the cynicism of political realism? Can we find a path of moderation between the two extremes—the excessive realism that views all rulers as only great thieves and the excessive idealism that strives for a political utopia? (Perhaps the word "excessive" betrays a naive hope that there is a good middle way.)

Hans Morgenthau, as we noted earlier, was considered a modern exponent of Augustinian realism; and his thinking illustrates how a tough-minded realism might be combined with a sense of moral purpose.[18] Morgenthau influenced the study of American foreign policy by challenging the idealist tradition as perhaps best represented by Woodrow Wilson. It was a mistake, Morgenthau argued, to think that world peace could be established through a moral consensus among nations. Because every nation must secure its own national interest through the prudent use of force against its enemies, a stable peace can be maintained only through a balance of power among nations. Likewise, within each nation, political order requires a balance of power between competing groups.

Despite this political realism, Morgenthau is not a Machiavellian, because he believes there are some moral standards in politics. Morgenthau's political realism differs from Machiavellian power politics in that Morgenthau thinks the pursuit of power can be channeled to moral ends. Arguing that the political realism of thinkers like Augustine is superior to the political thought of Machiavelli and Hobbes, Morgenthau insists:

> In the long run philosophies and political systems that have
> made the lust and the struggle for power their mainstays have

proved impotent and self-destructive. Their weakness demon-
strates the strength of the Western tradition that seeks, if not
to eliminate, at least to regulate and restrain the power drives
that otherwise would either tear society apart or deliver the life
and happiness of the weak to the arbitrary will of the powerful.[19]

He also contends that rather than rejecting all moral principles, the
political realist seeks those moral principles that are grounded in
political reality. In particular, the realist favors the moral understanding that sees the need for flexibility in applying universal
principles to particular political circumstances. Thus Morgenthau
relies on what the ancient and medieval philosophers called
prudence, the moral faculty for judging good and bad in concrete
situations.[20]

Even in international politics, where the rule of the stronger
seems to prevail, Morgenthau sees a need for moral judgment. "In
order to be worthy of our lasting sympathy," he writes, "a nation
must pursue its interest for the sake of a transcendent purpose that
gives meaning to the day-by-day operations of its foreign policy."[21]
For American politics the "transcendent purpose" has been defined
by the Declaration of Independence, which upholds the principle
of natural human rights, or, as Morgenthau phrases it, "equality
in freedom."[22] This explains the traditional belief that in foreign
policy American national interests should coincide with the promotion of human rights. But, as we saw earlier in the quotation from
Woodrow Wilson, this tradition can encourage utopian idealism if
it is not restrained by a prudent recognition of the moral limitations
of political life. Still, it has become clear in recent history that the
moral ideals of the Declaration of Independence are powerful tools
of foreign policy. Liberal democracy has spread throughout the
world; and over the past two hundred years, no liberal democracy
has gone to war against another liberal democracy. Is the dream
of "perpetual peace" now a realistic possibility?[23]

So, again, we are left groping for a combination of realism and
idealism. We might see our goal as illustrated by the Declaration
of Independence, which unites a grasp of universal moral principles
with prudential judgment of the demands of particular historical
circumstances. We might also look to Pascal's formulation of the
goal in a passage of the *Pensées*:

> It is just that what is just should be followed; it is necessary that
> what is stronger should be followed. Justice without force is
> impotent; force without justice is tyrannical. . . . We must
> therefore combine justice and force; and to do this, what is just
> should be strong, or what is strong should be just. (fr. 192)

If we could achieve this, we could take our motto from Abraham Lincoln: "Let us have faith that right makes might, and in that faith, let us, to the end, dare to do our duty as we understand it."[24]

Augustine might warn us, however, that our "faith that right makes might" will only be fulfilled in heaven. In response to our quotation from Pascal, Augustine could have cited another passage from the *Pensées*: "not being able to fortify justice, men have justified force, so that the just and the strong should unite, and there should be peace, which is the sovereign good" (fr. 171). Or he could have quoted Pascal's claim that Plato and Aristotle were not serious when they wrote books on political philosophy: "If they wrote about politics, it was as though they were to make rules in a hospital for fools" (fr. 533). If every political regime is an insane asylum, we cannot expect its citizens to discover justice. We can only hope that they will know how to maintain a little peace in the madhouse.[25]

As long as Augustinian Christians stress the corruption of nature by human sin, they cannot see any way for earthly politics to go beyond temporal peace toward true justice. But if it were possible to reconcile Greek naturalism and Christian creationism, if Christians could see nature even in its unredeemed earthly condition as a moral guide, then they might see some glimmer of justice in the politics of this world. Some Christians think that St. Thomas Aquinas achieved just that in his conception of the natural law.

Notes

1. Reinhold Niebuhr, "Augustine's Political Realism," in *Christian Realism and Political Problems* (New York: Scribners, 1953), 120–21. See Herbert A. Deane, *The Political and Social Ideas of St. Augustine* (New York: Columbia University Press, 1963), chap. 4; and R.A. Markus, *Saeculum: History and Society in the Theology of St. Augustine* (Cambridge: Cambridge University Press, 1970), chap. 4. On the conflict in Augustine's thinking between classical and Christian conceptions of political order, see Eric Voegelin, *The New Science of Politics* (Chicago: University of Chicago Press, 1952), 76–106. See also Paul Johnson, *A History of Christianity* (New York: Atheneum, 1983).

2. All translations of Augustine's Latin texts are mine. I have used the text in *De civitate Dei libri XXII*, ed. B. Dombart and A. Kalb, 2 vols. (Leipzig: Teubner, 1928).

3. G. W. Leibnitz, *Principles of Nature and Grace*, in *Leibnitz: Philosophical Writings*, trans. Mary Morris (New York: Dutton, 1961), 26.

4. For a presentation of this line of reasoning as the best philosophic argument for God's existence, see Mortimer J. Adler, *How to Think About God* (New York: Macmillan, 1980). For a defense of Christianity

that is powerful in its simplicity and sensibleness, see two books by C. S. Lewis: *Miracles* (New York: Macmillan, 1947) and *Mere Christianity* (New York: Macmillan, 1952). For more elaborate arguments, see Germain Grisez, *Beyond the New Theism* (Notre Dame: University of Notre Dame Press, 1975); Hans Kung, *Does God Exist?* (New York: Doubleday, 1980); and Robert Sokolowski, *The God of Faith and Reason: Foundations of Christian Theology* (Notre Dame: University of Notre Dame Press, 1982).

5. See Stanley L. Jaki, "The Role of Faith in Physics," *Zygon 2* (1967): 187–202; Albert Einstein, *Ideas and Opinions* (New York: Crown, 1982), 39–40, 46, 224–27, 261–62, 290; and Steven Weinberg, "Origins," *Science* 230 (1985): 15–17.

6. All references to the *Pensées* are based on the edition edited by Louis Lafuma (Paris: Editions du Luxembourg, 1952). The translations are mine. Pascal belongs to a tradition of modern skepticism with Augustinian roots, as manifested in Michel de Montaigne's "Apology for Raymond Sebond." See *The Complete Essays of Montaigne*, trans. Donald M. Frame (Stanford: Stanford University Press, 1958), 328, 368–70, 402–5, 425, 454, 457. The primacy that modern thinkers give to the "will" and the "self" also shows the influence of Augustine and Biblical theology. See Hannah Arendt, *The Life of the Mind: Willing* (New York: Harcourt Brace Jovanovich, 1978), 84–110; and Charles Taylor, *Sources of the Self* (Cambridge: Harvard University Press, 1989), 127–42.

7. See Staughton Lynd, *Intellectual Origins of American Radicalism* (Cambridge: Harvard University Press, 1982), 24–37.

8. G. K. Chesterton, *Orthodoxy* (Garden City, NY: Doubleday, Image Books, 1959), 60–61. The implications of this idea for Augustine's thought are worked out by Charles Cochrane, *Christianity and Classical Culture* (New York: Oxford University Press, 1957), 399–516; and Frederick D. Wilhelmsen, *Christianity and Political Philosophy* (Athens: University of Georgia Press, 1978), 60–110.

9. Friedrich Nietzsche, *The Gay Science*, trans. Walter Kaufmann (New York: Vintage Books, 1974), sec. 111. See also Nietzsche's "On Truth and Lying in an Extra-Moral Sense," in *Friedrich Nietzsche on Rhetoric and Language*, ed. Sander L. Gilman, Carole Blair, and David J. Parent (Oxford: Oxford University Press, 1989), 246–57.

10. Boethius, *The Consolation of Philosophy* (Carbondale: Southern Illinois University Press, 1963), IV, 7.

11. See Martha Nussbaum, *The Fragility of Goodness: Luck and Ethics in Greek Tragedy and Philosophy* (Cambridge: Cambridge University Press, 1986).

12. Karl Löwith, *Meaning in History* (Chicago: University of Chicago Press, 1949), 201. For elaboration of these points, see Hans Jonas, "Jewish and Christian Elements in Philosophy: Their Share in the Emergence of the Modern Mind," in *Philosophical Essays: From Ancient Creed to Technological Man* (Englewood Cliffs, NJ: Prentice-Hall, 1974),

21–44; Larry Arnhart, "Statesmanship as Magnanimity: Classical, Christian, and Modern," *Polity* 16 (Winter 1983): 263–83; and Karl Löwith, "Can There Be a Christian Gentleman?" in *Nature, History, and Existentialism* (Evanston, IL: Northwestern University Press, 1966), 204–13.

13. See Löwith, *Meaning in History*; Voegelin, *The New Science*, 107–89; and Norman Cohn, *The Pursuit of the Millennium* (New York: Oxford University Press, 1970).

14. Harold Laski, *Faith, Reason and Civilization* (London: Victor Gollancz, 1944), 155, 200.

15. See Ernest Lee Tuveson, *Redeemer Nation: The Idea of America's Millennial Role* (Chicago: University of Chicago Press, 1968).

16. Woodrow Wilson, Address at Pueblo, Colorado, 25 September 1919, in Richard D. Heffner, ed., *A Documentary History of the United States* (New York: New American Library, 1976), 255.

17. See William T. Bluhm, *Theories of the Political System*, 2nd ed. (Englewood Cliffs, NJ: Prentice-Hall, 1971), 193–204.

18. The fullest statement of Morgenthau's thinking is his classic textbook, *Politics Among Nations*, 3rd ed. (New York: Alfred A. Knopf, 1961). Recently, some students of international politics have questioned the adequacy of Morgenthau's realist theory. The realist assumes that in the international arena states are the predominant actors, that they act as coherent units, and that they act primarily through the use or threat of force to maintain the military security of the nation. With respect to some issues, however, the complex interdependence of societies may violate these assumptions. For example, realist assumptions don't apply very well to economic conflicts between the United States and Canada or to problems of the international monetary system. See Robert O. Keohane and Joseph S. Nye, *Power and Interdependence* (Boston: Little, Brown, 1977), 23–59; and Charles R. Beitz, *Political Theory and International Relations* (Princeton: Princeton University Press, 1979), 35–63. The continuing debate over realism can be seen in Robert O. Keohane, ed., *Neorealism and Its Critics* (New York: Columbia University Press, 1986). The first text in the realist tradition is Thucydides, *History of the Peloponnesian War*. See Laurie M. Johnson, *Thucydides, Hobbes, and the Interpretation of Realism* (DeKalb: Northern Illinois University Press, 1993).

19. Morgenthau, *Politics Among Nations*, 228.

20. Ibid., 10.

21. Hans Morgenthau, *The Purpose of American Politics* (New York: Alfred A. Knopf, 1962), 8.

22. Ibid., 36–37.

23. See Michael Doyle, "Liberalism and World Politics," *American Political Science Review* 80 (1986): 1151–69; and Francis Fukuyama, *The End of History and the Last Man* (New York: Free Press, 1992), 245–84.

24. Abraham Lincoln, Address at Cooper Union, 27 February 1860, in *The Collected Works of Abraham Lincoln*, ed. Roy P. Basler, 9 vols. (New

Brunswick, NJ: Rutgers University Press, 1953–1955), 3:550. Hans Morgenthau regarded Lincoln as a paradigm of prudent statesmanship that combined toughness and justice. See Morgenthau and David Hein, *Essays on Lincoln's Faith and Politics*, ed. Kenneth W. Thompson (Lanham, MD: University Press of America, 1983).

25. Consider A. J. Beitzinger, "Pascal on Justice, Force, and Law," *Review of Politics* 46 (April 1984): 239–40:

> Pascal realized that man by himself cannot give the answer to the question which he himself constitutes. He remarked the ability of man, in contrast to the brutes, to surpass himself, a characteristic which indicates an openness in human existence underlying and explaining the ubiquitous and historically diverse formations of cultures and legal orders. Openness, however, is not an answer to the question of man but a necessary condition which must not be closed off to that which transcends man. Just as man cannot be understood simply in light of his existential openness but only in light of the historically manifested "fixed point," Jesus Christ, so the source and morally binding character of law can be comprehended only in light of the ultimate good. . . . Law is seen as prefigurative of the unity of mankind in the coming Kingdom which has been realized among men in Christ. Neither "nature" nor "reason" can serve as an ultimate norm.

Chapter

4

Natural Law

Thomas Aquinas's "Treatise on Law"

Key Readings

Summma Theologiae, 1–2, 90–97.

Thomas Aquinas (1225–1274) was the most comprehensive and systematic Christian philosopher of the Middle Ages. Going beyond Augustine, Thomas reformulated Christian philosophy in response to the intellectual and political controversies of the thirteenth century. The great political conflict was between the emperor of the Holy Roman Empire and the Pope. Augustine's distinction between the City of Man and the City of God was not sufficient to reconcile the temporal authority of political rulers and the spiritual authority of the Church. Thomas sought to maintain the ultimate supremacy of the Pope while respecting the proper claims of the Emperor.

The dominant intellectual controversy of the time arose from the revival of interest in Aristotle, which was feared by some Church authorities as a source of pagan corruption. Although Jewish and Arabic scholars had preserved Aristotle's texts and had debated for centuries as to how his philosophy could be harmonized with Biblical theology, until the thirteenth century, Aristotle was not studied much in the Christian world and many of his writings were not even available there. When Christian thinkers came into contact with this tradition, they, too, had to reconsider the relationship between faith and reason as ways to truth.

As a Dominican friar teaching at the University of Paris, Thomas was well prepared by his religious and educational background to reflect on these issues. He argued that the Christian could accept Aristotle's philosophy in the realm of natural truth without rejecting the higher truth of revelation: the truths known by faith transcend, but they do not conflict with, the truths known by natural reason. In 1879, Pope Leo XIII recognized Thomas as an authoritative source of Christian philosophy.[1]

Of Thomas's many writings, the best known is his *Summa Theologica* (Summary of Theology), which was written as a textbook of theology for young students. The *Summa* follows the pattern of medieval disputation. It takes up all of the major disputed questions of theology and ethics. First, Thomas poses a question and states the major objections to his answer. Then, he states his position by citing an accepted authority and then supporting this with arguments. He concludes by responding to the objections stated at the beginning.

Thomas divides his *Summa* into three parts and subdivides the second part into two parts. What has been traditionally called his "Treatise on Law" is not a separate writing, but rather questions 90–97 of the first part of Part Two (1–2, 90–97). This contains his teaching on natural law, which has been the most influential part of his political thought. So, as we concentrate our attention on his account of natural law, we should keep in mind that this is only one small portion of his philosophical work.[2]

1. What is natural law?

Whenever we talk about politics, we talk about right and wrong, justice and injustice. We praise some laws and decisions as good, and we condemn others as bad. Often we assume that there are some standards of right and wrong in politics that cannot be changed by human will. Thus, we accept, usually without fully realizing it, the idea of natural law.

This idea becomes evident whenever we claim that there is a higher law by which human laws should be judged. The Declaration of Independence appeals to the "Laws of Nature and of Nature's God" to justify rejecting the authority of King George III. It has become common in the modern world to argue that every government is obligated to respect the natural rights of human beings. A clear example of this is the trial at Nuremberg for German Nazi leaders accused of war crimes. The laws of Nazi Germany that permitted the injustices of Nazi rule were judged to be invalid as laws because they violated universal standards of decency. Such a judgment assumes that there is a universal natural law beyond the conventional laws of particular nations.[3]

Natural law must be invoked whenever someone wants to justify disobeying a law by arguing that it is unjust and therefore not truly a law. Martin Luther King, Jr., for example, in his "Letter from the Birmingham Jail," to which we referred earlier (chapter 1, section 2), relies on natural law in his resistance to laws supporting racial segregation:

> A just law is a man-made code that squares with the moral law or the law of God. An unjust law is a code that is out of harmony with the moral law. To put it in the terms of Saint Thomas Aquinas, an unjust law is a human law that is not rooted in eternal and natural law. Any law that uplifts human personality is just. Any law that degrades human personality is unjust. All segregation statutes are unjust because segregation distorts the soul and damages the personality.[4]

Thus King shows how belief in the existence of natural law arises from our common-sense conviction that because law aims at justice we can rightfully disobey an unjust law insofar as it violates the purpose of law.

Those identified as legal positivists would raise an objection at this point. Belief in natural law, they would insist, confuses *legality* with *morality* by assuming that a rule cannot be a *valid* law unless it is also a *just* law. Surely, the validity of a law does not depend on its justice or injustice. We know that something is legal when it has been sanctioned by one of the lawmaking institutions of our society. Whether it is just or unjust is a personal judgment that can vary from one person to another. Though Martin Luther King, Jr. thought the laws of segregation were unjust, the segregationists thought they were just. Similarly, the Nazis thought their laws were just, but their opponents disagreed. The positivists conclude, therefore, that because moral judgments are subjective, the stability of a legal order requires that there be formal rules of legal validity recognized by all, rules that do not depend on the moral content of the laws. Otherwise, there would be chaos, because people would not feel obligated by laws that they didn't happen to like. The positivists would maintain, then, that the laws of Nazi Germany and the laws of segregation in the American South were valid laws, despite their injustice, because they were duly established by the socially recognized institutions.

Against this position, the proponents of natural law would insist that there are universal principles of justice that are not merely subjective human preferences, but objective features of the natural world discoverable by humankind. And insofar as human beings are naturally inclined to design human laws to fulfill this natural law, the definition of valid law depends on the moral content of law.

In this conflict between legal positivism and natural law, we cannot avoid taking a stand on one side or the other. For we cannot think deeply about political issues without deciding either that all law arises from social conventions and therefore varies from one society to another or that, despite the variety in law among different societies, there is a universal law of natural justice that is the standard for all law. We turn to Thomas Aquinas's explanation of natural law, therefore, to clarify our thinking about this issue. Our first concern is simply to figure out exactly what is meant by natural law.

We can begin with Thomas's definition of law as "nothing other than an ordinance of reason for the common good, made by the one who has care of the community, and promulgated" (90, 4).[5] Thus, there are four requirements: A law must be (1) rational, (2) for the common good, (3) established by the proper authority, and (4) made known to those subject to the law. According to Thomas, there are four kinds of law that satisfy these standards: eternal law, natural law, human law, and divine law (91, 1–4).

Eternal law is that law by which God governs everything in the universe as created by him. Natural law is "nothing other than the rational creature's participation in the eternal law" (91, 2). But because the general principles of natural law are not detailed enough to decide particular cases, this must be settled by human law. Finally, the divine law of the Bible guides human conduct according to eternal law beyond what could be done by natural and human law.

We will concentrate on natural law. The precepts of the natural law, Thomas explains, are those principles of conduct derived from eternal law that are self-evident to all rational beings (94, 2). Of course, this corresponds to what we have seen in the Declaration of Independence. Examining Thomas's argument on this point should help us, therefore, to decide whether there are any self-evident truths about political justice.

The most fundamental of the self-evident principles of natural law is the idea of goodness.

> For every agent acts for the sake of an end, which has the meaning
> of goodness. And therefore the first principle in practical reasoning
> is that which is founded on the meaning of goodness, which is that
> good is what all things seek. This therefore is the first precept of law,
> that "good is to be done and sought, and evil to be avoided." And
> on this are founded all the other precepts of natural law. (94, 2)

This passage need not be obscure if we keep in mind what Thomas
has said near the beginning of the *Summa* (1, 5, 1–4) about the
nature of goodness. Being and goodness, he indicates, are the same,
because the good is simply that by which something *becomes* what
it *is*. All things, especially living beings, have potentialities; so that
the perfection of each thing is that it should develop its potentiality
to actuality. Every living being has some essential tendency or
inclination; it aims at an end or goal. The good of each living being
is its self-fulfillment. The growth of an acorn into an oak tree or a
puppy into a dog illustrates this. It is good for a plant or animal to
grow to maturity. It is bad for its growth to be impeded by
unfavorable circumstances. Thus, we recognize a puppy to be
defective if it cannot develop fully the potentialities of its species.
Goodness is not some external standard imposed on things from
the outside; it is rather the unfolding of the innate tendencies of
things. It is therefore self-evident that the good is to be sought,
because by definition the good is what each thing seeks. To say that
all things should seek the good is simply to endorse what all things
strive to do anyway.

But how does this apply to human beings? It is easy to see how
Thomas can argue that because every plant and animal has
biological tendencies, natural goodness is the completion of these
tendencies. We must wonder, however, whether human beings
have innate tendencies that constitute the natural principles of
human conduct.

First, it should be noted that, as Thomas indicates, human beings
have a freedom in their conduct, by virtue of their rationality, that
other creatures do not. The natural instincts of other animals
determine their behavior in a way that leaves them little freedom,
but human beings have a consciousness of their natural inclinations
that gives them great freedom in deciding how—and perhaps even
whether—to satisfy those inclinations (93, 6).

Although human beings display more flexibility in their conduct
than do other animals, they do manifest some natural tendencies;
the order of these natural inclinations, Thomas maintains,
corresponds to the order of the precepts of natural law (94, 2). At
the lowest level, human beings share with all substances an
inclination to preserve themselves. Therefore, whatever preserves

human life pertains to natural law. At a higher level, human beings share with some animals such inclinations as sexual union and the education of the young, which is thus part of natural law. Finally, at the highest level, human beings, possessing reason, have certain inclinations that distinguish human life from all other life: human beings naturally seek to know the truth about God and live in society. Natural law, therefore, dictates the pursuit of knowledge, living in harmony with others, and so on.[6] From these three kinds of natural inclination, we can easily infer the moral precepts of the Ten Commandments as being part of natural law (99, 2; 100, 1): no killing, no adultery, honoring parents, no stealing, no lying, worshiping God, and so on (Exodus 20:1–17).

From this natural law, Thomas asserts, human law is derived in two ways: as conclusions from first principles or as implementations of general directives (95, 2). An example of the first would be a human law against murder as a conclusion from the natural law that no one is to be injured. An example of the second would be a human law setting a particular penalty for a crime in accordance with the natural law that criminals should be punished. Obviously, the human lawmaker has a lot of freedom, within the broad boundaries of natural law, to determine what should be done in particular cases (91, 3, ad. 1).

Moreover, the natural law itself can vary in some respects. The "primary principles" of natural law — such as that it is right for all to act according to reason — hold in all cases and are known by all. On the other hand, the "secondary principles" — such as that it is right to return goods to their owners — hold in *most* cases but not all and are known by *most* but not all (94, 5).

Some human beings might not recognize the secondary principles, Thomas explains, if their reason "has been depraved by passion or by bad custom, or by bad disposition of nature." He gives the example of the ancient Germans who, according to Julius Caesar, saw no evil in robbery (94, 4). The vicious habits and passions of the most wicked human beings corrupt both their natural knowledge of the good and their natural inclination to the good. Yet even in the wicked there remain some good inclinations (93, 6).

Natural law also varies in those exceptional cases that require setting aside the secondary principles. For example, it would be wrong to return goods to their owner if we knew that the owner intended to do harm with them (94, 4). Because all practical reasoning concerns changeable things, the common principles of conduct are fixed, but not the particular decision. Fundamentally, virtue is the same for all human beings; but, with different people in different situations, it varies in its specific manifestations.

Despite this variation, however, natural law provides standards for judging the validity of human laws. Thomas insists that because "all humanly established law has just so much of the rule of law as it has derived from natural law," a law that violates natural law "will not be a law, but a corruption of law" (95, 2). Laws that are unjust in violating human goodness, such as laws that promote the arbitrary desires of the ruler rather than the common good of all, are "more acts of violence than laws"; therefore, citizens are not obligated to obey them except when necessary to avoid disorder (96, 4).

If this all seems familiar to us, it is because we have seen in the ancient writings of Plato and Aristotle the idea that there are natural standards of justice, and we have seen in the Declaration of Independence the modern idea that all people are endowed by nature with certain rights. But we should distinguish the Greek notion of "natural right" from Thomas's notion of "natural law," and we should also distinguish both of these from the modern notion of "natural rights," even as we recognize that they are alike in their appeal to human nature.

Aristotle, in his *Nicomachean Ethics* (1134b17–35), says that although there is natural right or natural justice, it all changes according to the circumstances. But Thomas insists that at least the general principles of natural law never change (94, 4, ad. 2). So, unlike Thomas's "natural law," Aristotle's "natural right" does not consist of universally valid rules. Aristotle seems more concerned than Thomas about preserving the freedom of the virtuous to decide what is appropriate in particular cases. For this reason, Thomistic natural law has been criticized as too inflexible, in that rulers and citizens are not allowed to adjust their standards of justice according to their concrete circumstances.[7]

Nevertheless, Greek "natural right" and Thomistic "natural law" seem much alike when they are contrasted with modern "natural rights." Although ideas of "natural right" and "natural law" stress the *social duties* of human beings, the modern notion of "natural rights" stresses their *individual rights*. The premodern conceptions stress *virtue*, but the modern conception stresses *freedom*. Plato, Aristotle, and Thomas speak of *what is right* by nature to do; but Hobbes and Locke, as we shall see later, speak rather of *possessing rights* by nature. All these philosophers are concerned with protecting the natural dignity of human beings, but they disagree about whether this is best done by emphasizing social virtue or by emphasizing individual freedom.

At this point, having surveyed Thomas's account of natural law, we should think through some of the criticisms of natural law reasoning.[8] We can begin by returning to the debate between the proponents of natural law and the legal positivists.

2. Is law the command of the sovereign backed by threat?

Evidently, this question suggests a different view of law from that advocated by Thomas. All of Thomas's talk about the moral foundations of law, the legal positivist would complain, is nonsense. Whoever has the power to make laws does so, and those laws are obeyed as long as the lawmaker can enforce them by coercion. The effectiveness of the laws commonly has little to do with their justice or injustice. Moreover, Thomas's claim that all true laws are derived from nature would also be ridiculed by the legal positivist. The laws made by human beings are just that — *human* laws. To assert that the ultimate source of these laws is superhuman — nature or God — must seem silly to all but the most naive.

We shall see that Hobbes initiates this modern view of law in his *Leviathan*, but the classic statement of legal positivism is contained in John Austin's lectures [published under the title: *The Province of Jurisprudence Determined* (1832)]. In his first lecture, Austin defines law as a command backed by threat. The essence of legal authority is possessing sufficient force to compel the people of a society to obey commands. In some cases, monarchs have enough power to make laws on their own, but the people acting collectively can restrain a monarch's power. The sovereign may be one, few, or many individuals, but in any case it is the superior might of the sovereign that permits lawmaking.

Why should we prefer this positivistic view of law to Thomas's natural law position? Consider three possible arguments. (1) Legal positivism describes what law *is*, not what it *ought* to be. (2) Far from being immoral, legal positivism promotes clear moral judgments by eliminating hypocrisy. (3) Legal positivism protects society against disorder.

Austin wanted the study of law to be scientific, in the sense that he wanted to see the reality of law as observable human behavior undistorted by subjective moral judgments. We would like law to be always just, but it often is not. So to see law as it is rather than as one would like it to be, one must separate law and morality. To say, for example, that the laws of Nazi Germany were not true laws because the Nazi regime was unjust, shows blindness to the reality of the situation. To insist, as Thomas does, that a law cannot be a valid law if it is unjust is not a theory of law but a moral wish.

At this point, the defender of natural law might charge the legal positivists with encouraging immorality by endorsing the belief that might makes right. As Thrasymachus would say, what we call justice is really the rule of the stronger. But distinguishing law and morality, the positivists might respond, does not lead necessarily to the mindless view that whatever a lawmaker does is right. Rather, we must weigh the claims of valid laws against the claims of morality beyond the laws. Legal positivists can choose to disobey a valid law because they consider it immoral, but they do this only after they have balanced their *legal* obligations against their *moral* obligations.

To identify legality and morality, as the natural law theorist must do, does not necessarily improve our moral judgments. Consider again the Nuremberg trials. Applying the natural law doctrine of "just war," the Nuremberg Tribunal convicted Nazi leaders as "war criminals" for acts of war that violated certain universal standards of human decency. Natural law theorists hailed this as a victory for international justice. But legal positivists denounced it as hypocrisy. The only ones tried for "war crimes," they pointed out, were the *defeated* war leaders. The inhumane acts of the victors were not punished. Consider, for example, the decision of the Allied war leaders to terrorize the German civilian population through the saturation bombing of cities. In this way, legal positivists could interpret the Nuremberg trials as showing that the stronger can always impose their will on the weaker and call it "justice."

Indeed, legal positivists have maintained that the very idea of international law is fraudulent. Because there is no sovereign power ruling over the nations of the world, there cannot be any international law in the strict sense. Nations accept rules of international behavior only as long as, and to the extent that, these rules serve national interests. Those national leaders who would speak of these rules as principles of natural justice are either naive or hypocritical.

Legal positivists see dangers not only in the application of natural law theory to international politics, but also in its application to the legal order within a nation. Consider the case of Martin Luther King, Jr. King used Thomas's doctrine of natural law to justify disobeying laws supporting racial segregation, which King thought to be unjust. King and others succeeded in changing the laws in order to eliminate segregation. But what if the segregationists had argued that they should be permitted to disobey the civil rights laws because they regarded them as unjust? If every individual were free to disobey any law thought to be unjust, wouldn't this be contrary to any stable legal order and thus lead to utter chaos?

How might Thomas and other proponents of natural law answer these arguments of the legal positivists? First, Thomas would surely dispute the positivistic attempt to separate law and morality by defining law as the command of a sovereign power backed by threat. Thomas could object that, if this were the only requirement for law, we could not distinguish the commands of a powerful outlaw from the commands of an authoritative lawmaker. A person with a weapon can enforce commands with threats, but such orders are not laws. Every government has to rely on coercion to some extent, but this works only as long as most of the people most of the time obey the laws voluntarily (95, 1). Indeed, the more unpopular a law is, the more likely it is that the legal authorities think it prudent not to enforce it with much rigor. When conditions are such that people obey the laws only when they are compelled by fear of violent punishment, those people are living not in a social order but in a state of war.

H. L. A. Hart, a contemporary legal positivist, has tried to overcome this weakness in Austin's theory while rejecting natural law theory. Austin was wrong, Hart thinks, in claiming that law depends simply on superior *strength*; rather, it depends fundamentally on superior *authority*. But Hart insists that the natural law theorists are wrong to assume that the authority of law arises from its *morality*. All that is required is that a legal system have what Hart calls a "rule of recognition" that is accepted as the ultimate standard of authority. For example, Americans accept as valid laws those rules enacted by the Congress in accordance with the Constitution. The "higher law" of the Constitution is the fundamental standard of legal authority.

Why do the American people accept the Constitution? Is it not because they see it as serving the common good of the nation? Would we not expect this to be true of any legal system — that is, the people accept the customary sources of legal authority as long as they perceive them to be essentially just? That, of course, is the teaching of the Declaration of Independence.

We might wonder, therefore, whether Hart's idea of legal authority leads us back to natural law. In fact, he concedes that he cannot explain law fully without reference to "the minimum content of natural law."[9] Although rejecting the higher levels of natural law as not grounded in nature, Hart thinks that human nature does dictate at least that law preserve human beings from violence. The desire for self-preservation is so strong that it is inconceivable that human beings would accept a legal system that did not secure their preservation. On this point, Hart acknowledges that he is following the teaching of Hobbes. In our chapter on

Hobbes, we shall consider whether it is reasonable to reduce natural law to the law of self-preservation.

In any case, the Thomistic natural law theorist would emphasize how hard it is to explain the authority of law without invoking at least some minimal moral standard of nature. Contrary to what the legal positivist assumes, Thomas would argue that because law incorporates moral judgments, we cannot see law as it *is* unless we take account of what it *ought* to be.

Does it follow that according to natural law an unjust regime (such as that of the Nazis) cannot have any valid laws? If that were a consequence of Thomas's teaching, legal positivists would be correct in dismissing any idea of natural law as unrealistic. Obviously, Nazi Germany had a genuine legal system, despite the injustice of the regime.[10] But Thomas is careful to say that even an unjust regime can have valid laws providing that it secures some goodness in the community:

> A tyrannical law, not being according to reason, is not
> straightforwardly a law, but rather it is a sort of perversion of
> law. And yet to the extent that it has something of the reason
> of law, it aims at the citizens being good. (92, 1, ad. 4)

Because any law must somehow contribute to social cooperation for a common end, and because such common effort instills in citizens some sense of justice, any law that is truly a law must have some element of justice.

Even if they do not promote the higher human virtues, the laws of a bad regime might still secure the peace of the community. For that reason, Thomas is reluctant to advise disobedience of unjust laws for fear of the disorder that would result (96, 4). In *On Kingship* (I, 6), Thomas even warns against killing tyrants if their tyranny is in any way tolerable. We have seen this same cautiousness about revolution in the Declaration of Independence: "Prudence, indeed, will dictate that Governments long established should not be changed for light and transient causes; and accordingly . . . mankind are more disposed to suffer, while evils are sufferable." Thomas would agree with the legal positivists about the dangers of encouraging people to disobey the law whenever they think it unjust. Prudent respect for the harsh necessities of social order sometimes requires that good people moderate their moral indignation.

Because he does not expect moral perfection in political life, Thomas (like Aristotle) accepts the lesser of two evils in cases where the simply best is unattainable. But, in each case, one must know the principles of natural law to make such judgments: one cannot distinguish a lesser evil from a greater unless one can distinguish evil from good.

We must wonder, however, how one can know these moral standards of natural law. Thomas says that a law must be made known to those subject to its commands. How, then, are human beings notified of the existence of natural law? A Christian such as Thomas might understand natural law through faith. But *natural* law should be comprehensible by *natural* reason alone.

3. How do human beings discover natural law?

Some critics claim that Thomas's natural law is not simply natural because it requires Christian faith in a supernatural realm. As Thomas says, natural law reflects the eternal law of God; and as every law presupposes a lawmaker who promulgates and enforces it, we might assume that only those who believe in God's existence can be bound by his natural law. Thomas contends, however, that natural law conforms to the limits of natural human reason (91, 4). It is that part of God's law manifest in nature itself, which is evident even to those without religious faith. Thomas cites Romans 1:20: "For the invisible things of him from the creation of the world are clearly seen being understood by the things that are made" (93, 2, ad. 1).

If Thomas is correct, then natural law should come into view as human beings discover certain recurrent conditions for the success of their social and political life. The case of the ancient Germans might illustrate this.[11] According to Julius Caesar's *Gallic War*, the ancient German tribes saw nothing wrong with theft; and Thomas refers to this as an illustration of how corrupt customs can erase our knowledge of the secondary principles of natural law (94, 4). Prohibiting theft would seem to be a clear example of natural law because it would seem to be a condition for any social order. Even the ancient Germans, as Caesar indicates, permitted robbery only when the victims were outside the group. A band of thieves has to protect the property of its members if it is to exist as a stable community. Moreover, the Germanic tribes could live by raiding only as long as the economy of the Roman Empire remained strong. With the collapse of the empire, the German invaders were forced to confront the disastrous consequences of their raiding. They learned that in most situations humankind cannot secure the minimal conditions of social life unless property is protected against theft. The economic institutions of feudalism were established to do this. Thus, we might say, nature taught us that stealing must be prohibited. Perhaps all natural law is of this sort: as we strive to live comfortably in this world, we discover certain norms of conduct conforming to human nature that apply, with some variation in the details, to all human beings everywhere.

This assumes, however, that we can derive moral standards from the facts of nature, an assumption that many modern thinkers would deny. Facts and values, it is often argued, must be separated. That prohibiting theft secures social order is a judgment of *fact*. But we cannot infer from this that prohibiting theft is good or just unless we make the judgment of *value* that social order is good. The conditions of social order are factual matters objectively discoverable by reason. The goodness or badness of social order is a subjective preference that cannot be proven rationally. This sort of reasoning supports the most common objection that legal positivists make against natural law theory: there is no natural moral law because moral values cannot be derived from natural facts.

4. Does the fact-value distinction refute the idea of natural law?

Until recently, most social scientists have agreed that the separation of facts and values, "is" and "ought," shows the falsity of any conception of natural law. But now there is less agreement about the validity of the fact-value dichotomy, because many social scientists now argue that we cannot study social reality without making some judgments of value.[12] This issue is important for judging not only Thomas's political thought, but the entire history of political philosophy. For if we decided that moral judgments arise from personal preferences that cannot be defended by rational arguments, we would have to reject most of the great works of political thought, which assume that reason can decide moral questions.

The bridge between "is" and "ought," the Thomist might say, is "wanting" or "desiring."[13] This is true not only for human beings but also for other animals. Aristotle makes this clear in *The Movement of Animals* where he explains the underlying logic of all voluntary animal movement, including human movement, as conforming by analogy to a "practical syllogism," by which a decision to act arises from the conjunction of cognition and desire: I desire something; I know that a certain action will satisfy that desire; therefore, I undertake the action. The modern biology of behavior could confirm this analysis of animal movement into three functions: knowing, wanting, and appraising. All behaving organisms gather information (*knowing*) related to their needs (*wanting*) and then act in response to their evaluation of the information in relation to their needs (*appraising*).[14] From this point of view, the biology of animal behavior must employ teleological or functional explanations. Animals act purposefully to secure their natural needs based on their information about the changing environments in which they live. Thus animal movement is inherently normative or value-laden insofar as animals cannot live without choosing between alternative courses of action as more or less desirable. This would explain Thomas's adoption of Ulpian's definition of natural law as the law "that nature has taught all animals" (94, 2).[15]

Does not all animal movement, including human movement, assume that something is good insofar as it is desirable, and something is desirable insofar as it is good? Does it not seem absurd to imagine otherwise—that something could be good although utterly undesirable, or something could be desirable although utterly bad? This explains why the biology of human nature necessarily has moral implications, as indicated by the moral passions stirred by debates in human biology. If we find that we are naturally inclined to something or adapted for something, then we believe this helps us to know what is good for us.

This does not mean identifying the human good with momentary or capricious impulses: we sometimes get what we think we desire only to discover it is not desirable. This common human experience of being mistaken about our desires confirms the reality of our basic desires as a part of our nature that cannot be willfully disregarded. Deciding what it is we truly desire and ordering our often conflicting desires into a coherent pattern requires habituation and thought over a whole lifetime.

This human ordering of natural desires over a complete life identifies human morality as different from, even though rooted in, animal movement. What we desire is a life planned to achieve the fullest satisfaction of our needs over a whole life, which is what Aristotle calls *eudaimonia*, "happiness" or "flourishing." Neither nonhuman animals nor children can enjoy happiness in this sense because they lack the ability to order their actions in accord with a conception of a whole life well lived. By nature human beings desire external goods (such as wealth), bodily goods (such as health, sensual pleasures, and beauty), and psychic goods (such as love, friendship, honor, and thinking). To pursue these goods in the right order, to the right degree, at the right time to avoid contradiction requires good habits of choice—the moral and intellectual virtues

Nor Truth

examined by Aristotle and Thomas. Although there are analogies between these human virtues and the behavioral patterns of other animals, only human beings have the capacities for conceptual abstraction and symbolic communication, which Aristotle identifies as *logos*. These capacities allow human beings to become moral agents who judge present actions in light of the past and future to conform to some enduring standard of a good life.

Thus the moral and legal order of a society will reflect the desires inherent in human nature. It will also reflect how those desires have been refined first by individual habituation and customary practices and then by rational reflection on those habits and customs. Social order rests not only on nature but also on custom and prudence.

5. Is law the joint product of nature, custom, and stipulation?

The advocates of positive law argue that since every law arises from the arbitrary will of a lawmaker, there can be no natural law, because nature cannot properly be personified as a lawmaker. Against both natural law and positive law, the advocates of customary law argue that law is rooted ultimately in the customary practices of a community, which arise neither from a universal nature nor from an arbitrary will. James Bernard Murphy has insisted that we need to incorporate the partial truths of all three positions into a comprehensive social theory that would explain social order as founded on a trichotomy of nature, custom, and stipulation.[16] The proponents of natural law are correct in seeing that law presupposes the natural needs and capacities of human beings. The proponents of customary law are correct in seeing that law presupposes custom.[17] And the proponents of positive law are correct in seeing that law in the strict sense is the stipulation of the lawmaker. In fact, law is the joint product of nature, custom, and stipulation.

Family law illustrates this. By nature, human beings are inclined to produce offspring who need prolonged and intensive care by adults. By custom, societies have devised diverse ways of organizing the division of labor in caring for the young. By stipulation, lawmakers can specify the legal rights and duties of parents and children in a particular community. To be successful, these legal stipulations must respect both natural inclinations and customary practices, although this leaves the lawmakers free to choose among a wide array of practicable rules.

Aquinas would seem to accept this trichotomy because in

explaining human law (91, 3) he endorses the claim of Cicero that "justice has its source in nature; then certain things came into custom by reason of their utility; afterward these things that emanated from nature and were approved by custom were sanctioned by fear and reverence for the law." Thus, even as he affirms the universality of the natural human inclinations on which law is founded, Aquinas recognizes that those natural inclinations will express themselves in diverse ways through their interplay with the customary practices and formal stipulations of particular communities. Some of the critics of the natural law teaching, however, regard this diversity as a refutation of the very idea of natural law.

6. Does cultural diversity contradict the idea of natural law?

The more we know about the variety of social customs among different cultures, the less inclined we are to believe that there are universal moral principles. There seems to be hardly any moral practice of our culture that has not been rejected by some other society. We might conclude, therefore, that everything is relative, that there are no moral absolutes.

This has been one of the predominant themes of modern anthropology. A good example is Ruth Benedict's *Patterns of Culture*,[18] which became one of the most popular works of anthropology when it was published in 1934. Benedict argues that the wide range of cultural differences shows that there is no universal human nature, and thus there are no universal moral values. How we distinguish good and bad, just and unjust, depends on our culture. We often assume that the moral beliefs of our society manifest the perfection of human nature, and so we regard societies radically different from ours as primitive. But Benedict maintains that this attitude is unjustified because there is no natural standard for ranking some social practices as better or worse than others.

Thomas, and anyone who believes in natural law, would have to dispute this. It might be argued that anthropologists like Benedict have been so preoccupied with cultural diversity that they have overlooked the less obvious but nonetheless real uniformity among cultures. Benedict even indicates that studies of primitive cultures "help us to differentiate between those responses that are specific to local cultural types and those that are general to mankind."[19] But she chooses to give little attention to those matters "that are general to mankind."

Thomas, we should remember, distinguishes between the general moral *principles* of natural law, which remain the same for all people, and particular moral *practices*, which vary according to circumstances. The natural inclinations for sexual bonding and child-care, for instance, are universal; but the particular ways of structuring family life vary greatly from one culture to another.[20] Cultural variation does not deny Thomas's view of natural law as long as there is uniformity in the fundamental moral principles.

Some anthropologists would agree with Thomas on this point. Ralph Linton, for example, maintains that anthropologists such as Benedict overlook universal values because they fail to distinguish between "conceptual values" and "instrumental values."[21] Conceptual values are the most fundamental values at their most abstract and generalized levels. Instrumental values are the concrete, particular expressions of value. That men and women should cover their genitals in public might be an example of a conceptual value. That they should wear trousers rather than a loincloth would be an example of an instrumental value. Because the bizarre variety of social customs at the instrumental level often captures our attention, we do not notice the broad uniformity of moral principles at the conceptual level.

Conceptual values are universal, Linton explains, because they "stand in closest relation to the individual needs and social imperatives shared by all mankind."[22] Therefore, the moral principles found in some form in almost every culture correspond to certain individual and social needs inherent in human nature. Linton lists the following universal values: property (both personal and communal ownership), reciprocity and fair dealing in social relations, social division of labor (the need for leadership), stable family life (permanence of matings, conjugal loyalty, parental care for the young, respect for parents), knowledge (learning of social roles; intellectual curiosity expressed in "useless" knowledge, games, and esthetic activity), and belief in supernatural beings. This conforms to Thomas's account of natural law. The principles arise from the natural needs or inclinations of human beings. We could also group them according to the three levels of human nature distinguished by Thomas (94, 2). Moreover, doesn't Linton's list of universal values resemble the moral precepts of the Ten Commandments?

How would the legal positivist respond to this evidence of a universal moral law? An individual with such beliefs might say that it is not strictly universal because there are exceptions to all the principles listed above. As only one example, Colin Turnbull's *The Mountain People*,[23] to which we made reference earlier in our chapter on Aristotle (chapter 2, section 4) might be cited. Turnbull describes how the constant threat of starvation among the Ik of northern Uganda forced them to give up all the moral beliefs that we consider characteristic of human beings. They discarded all human values except individual self-preservation.

Thomas could reply, however, that although natural human tendencies can be impeded by unfavorable circumstances, that does not make those tendencies any less real, just as the fact that some infants are born blind does not refute our belief that the capacity for sight is natural to human beings. Thomas concedes that in application to particular cases, natural law can be distorted by passions, by errors in reasoning, or by corrupt customs and habits (94, 6). With respect to the Ik, Thomas might have emphasized the consequences of their viciousness—they are now extinct!

Moreover, Thomas says, "The common principles of natural law cannot be applied in the same manner in all cases on account of the great variety of human things" (95, 2, ad. 3). Perhaps natural law dictates that in situations like that of the Ik, the higher moral rules must yield to the demands of self-preservation, which is always the most basic level of natural law. But how far should we go in this direction? Some anthropologists, for example, argue that people tend to practice cannibalism when their diet suffers from a scarcity of animal protein.[24] If this were true, would natural law in such cases justify cannibalism?

The general problem here for Thomas is that to make the principles of natural law realistic he has to present them as both fixed and flexible. They have to be flexible to allow for the indefinite variety of circumstances that influence human conduct. But they must also be fixed if they are to guide practical judgment. Thomas can achieve flexibility by maintaining that the only unchanging principle of natural law is that "good is to be done and evil to be avoided" (94, 2), but that seems too vague to be of much help in deciding moral questions. Any standard more detailed than that, however, is likely to be too rigid for handling the contingencies of practical life. Perhaps we should reconsider Aristotle's cryptic comment that although there is a standard of natural right, it is all changeable (*Nicomachean Ethics*, 1134b18–1135a5).

Thomas's account of natural law recognizes the necessity for the prudential judgment of leaders and citizens in deciding concrete political questions (see 91, 3, ad. 3; 95, 2, ad. 4; 96, 6). But Thomas reminds us of certain minimal standards of decency for judging political life. The essential end of law is to secure the conditions of human virtue; no matter how much diversity there may be in its practical implementation, that must always be the goal. Yet even this claim that law should promote morality is open to dispute. For don't we often hear it said that it is not proper for government to legislate morality?

7. Is it right to legislate morality?

To which Thomas might reply, doesn't *every* law legislate morality? Because every law requires, permits, or prohibits some activity, the lawmaker must judge that certain courses of action are *better* than others for the members of the society. The function of law is to provide common rules of action for a community, therefore law cannot be morally neutral.

Even so, we might ask how far should we go in legislating morality. John Stuart Mill, for example, in *On Liberty*, would insist that we should legally regulate a person's conduct only to prevent harm to others; people should be perfectly free in those activities that affect only themselves or those who choose to cooperate with them. Some people would argue that Mill's standard is too restrictive in insulating individual judgment from legal regulation: because every society depends on shared moral ideas, some would contend, it is proper for the laws to protect that morality.

Consider three examples of how this issue has arisen in American politics. In 1973, the United States Supreme Court reaffirmed in two cases its position that pornography could be legally regulated or prohibited. In *Miller v. California* and *Paris Adult Theater I v. Slaton*, the Court decided that obscenity was not protected by the First Amendment to the Constitution unless the material had "serious literary, artistic, political, or scientific value." The critics of the Court argued that this legal enforcement of morality violated individual freedom. But Chief Justice Warren Burger, in the *Miller* decision, explicitly rejected the argument of Mill's *On Liberty*; and he explained, "Totally unlimited play for free will . . . is not allowed in ours or any other society."[25]

In 1977 members of the American Nazi Party wanted to march in a public demonstration in Skokie, Illinois. As there were many Jewish residents of Skokie, many of whom were survivors of Nazi concentration camps, they tried to legally prohibit the Nazis from marching. It was argued that the public display of the swastika "constitutes a symbolic assault against large numbers of the residents of the . . . . village and an incitation to violence and retaliation."[26] The Illinois Court of Appeals upheld this argument, even though the Nazis promised to keep their march peaceful. The Supreme Court of Illinois, however, overturned this decision and declared that the Nazis had a right to march under the First Amendment. The Jewish people of Skokie could avoid being offended, the court explained, by simply not watching the march.

In the Civil Rights Act of 1964, the United States Congress prohibited racial discrimination in "public accommodations" (restaurants, hotels, etc.) that affect "interstate commerce." As a result, a restaurant owner, for example, might be required to serve black customers. Opponents of the law saw it as a violation of the principle that people should be free to associate with whomever they wish. But defenders of the law thought it was proper to legally prohibit the immorality of racism.

Are governmental restrictions on pornography, the speech of Nazis, and the conduct of racists justifiable attempts to legislate morality? Radical libertarians could make at least three arguments against these uses of the law. First, they could argue that because our regime is supposed to protect each person's equal rights to life, liberty, and the pursuit of happiness, we should leave each individual free to form moral preferences as long as others are not harmed by those preferences. Second, libertarians might contend that the morality enforced by law is merely the conventional morality of the majority, which is not necessarily superior to the unconventional morality of the minority. Finally, libertarians could suggest that legal coercion cannot promote morality because good moral character must always be voluntary to be genuine.

Thomists could reply to the first argument by insisting that the very idea of human equality of rights is a moral principle that should be legally protected. The Declaration of Independence assumes that all human beings should be treated with dignity simply because they are human beings. Moreover, any legal system assumes that all human beings deserve respect as moral agents who can be held responsible for their actions. Laws are never enforced against inanimate objects or nonhuman animals because they are not rational moral agents. But don't pornographers, Nazis, and racists deny the equal dignity of human beings? The pornographer teaches us to look at our sexual partners as merely instruments for our own physical gratification. The Nazi and the racist teach us that the members of some racial groups are not fully human. Why can't we, therefore, justify legally restricting these people to prevent them from subverting the principle of equal human dignity?

As to the second point made by libertarians—that the morality enforced by law is merely conventional—Thomists would, of course, want to maintain that social morality can reflect the universal standards of natural law. In this respect, Thomists would have to disagree with the argument of Patrick Devlin in his book

The Enforcement of Morals.[27] Devlin argues that any society can properly enforce its moral ideas through law, even though these ideas never have any foundation in reason or nature. By contrast, the natural law theorist would point to the universal values underlying social customs to justify the legal enforcement of morality. With respect to obscenity, for example, there is a lot of cultural variation; but the fact that every society exercises some sort of censorship of sexual matters suggests that this serves some deep social needs that are natural to human beings.[28]

Finally, Thomas would contend, contrary to the libertarian, that legal coercion can be an effective tool of moral education. Law by compulsion can habituate human beings to do what they might not choose to do on their own; and once these good habits are acquired, they can be the basis for good moral character (90, 3, ad. 2; 96, 2). The stubborn resistance in the American South to the federal civil rights laws illustrates how hard it is for law to change human conduct. But now there is evidence that those laws have succeeded in transforming Southern life far more radically than many people ever thought possible. There may be less racism as a result of the habits instilled by the laws.

Thomas would agree with the libertarian, however, that there are limits to how far the law can go in shaping moral character. He warns that human laws cannot prohibit all evil things because any attempt to do this would also eliminate many good things (91, 4). To serve the common good, human laws cannot demand more moral stamina than most people possess. Thomas explains:

> Human law is framed for a multitude of human beings, the greater part of whom are not of perfect virtue. And therefore all vices, from which the virtuous abstain, are not prohibited by human law, but only the more serious vices from which it is possible for the greater part of the multitude to abstain, chiefly those which are to the harm of others, without the prohibition of which human society could not be preserved: thus homicides, thefts, and suchlike are prohibited by human law. (96, 2)

While insisting on the moral purpose of law, Thomas rejects the righteous callousness of those who would use law to punish those who fall short of moral perfection. He advises lawmakers that they have to settle for the minimal virtues necessary to pacify human aggressiveness and thus prevent social disorder. Moral perfection is attainable in heaven, but not on earth.[29]

Once again, we see that of the various levels of natural law, only the lowest—the natural inclination to self-preservation—holds up in all circumstances. Although moral frailty and unfavorable conditions commonly impede the political pursuit of virtue, people will always need political order as an instrument of physical security. The early modern political philosophers pondered this fact and concluded that we ought to lower our political expectations. This lowering of the aims of political life is most evident in the work of Machiavelli.

Notes

1. The Encyclical of Leo XIII is reprinted in the complete English translation of the *Summa Theologica* by the Dominican Fathers (Westminster, MD: Christian Classics, 1981).

2. Some commentators argue that Thomas's moral and political teaching is concerned more with prudence than with natural law, and prudence allows for more flexibility of judgment than does the deductive reasoning of traditional natural law. See E. A. Goerner, "On Thomistic Natural Law: The Bad Man's View of Thomistic Natural Right," *Political Theory* 7 (February 1979): 101–22; Goerner, "Thomistic Natural Right: The Good Man's View of Thomistic Natural Law," *Political Theory* 11 (August 1983): 393–418; and Daniel Nelson, *The Priority of Prudence: Virtue and Natural Law in Thomas Aquinas* (University Park: Pennsylvania State University Press, 1992).

   For the history of the idea of natural law, see A. P. d'Entrèves, *Natural Law*, 2nd ed. (London: Hutchinson University Library, 1970); and Leo Strauss, "Natural Law," in Thomas L. Pangle, ed., *Studies in Platonic Political Philosophy* (Chicago: University of Chicago Press, 1983), 137–46. See also Roberto Mangabeira Unger, *Law in Modern Society* (New York: Free Press, 1976), 76–86. For the recent revival of interest in natural law among lawyers and philosophers, see John Finnis, *Natural Law and Natural Rights* (Oxford: Clarendon Press, 1979); Lloyd Weinreb, *Natural Law and Justice* (Cambridge: Harvard University Press, 1987); and Robert P. George, ed., *Natural Law Theory: Contemporary Essays* (Oxford: Clarendon Press, 1992).

3. See William J. Bosch, *Judgment on Nuremberg* (Chapel Hill: University of North Carolina Press, 1970), chaps. 3, 8.

4. Martin Luther King, Jr., "Letter from the Birmingham Jail," in Richard D. Heffner, ed., *A Documentary History of the United States* (New York: New American Library, 1976), 336–37. See Herbert J. Storing, "The Case Against Civil Disobedience," in Robert A. Goldwin, ed., *On Civil Disobedience* (Chicago: Rand McNally, 1969), 95–120.

5. Unless otherwise indicated, all references in the text are to the first part of the Second Part of the *Summa Theologiae* (Madrid: Biblioteca de Autores Cristianos, 1961). All translations are mine. A convenient translation of the section on law can be found in St. Thomas Aquinas, *On Law, Morality, and Politics*, ed. William P. Baumgarth and Richard J. Regan (Indianapolis: Hackett, 1988).

6. Elsewhere in the *Summa* (I–II, q. 46, a. 5; q. 51, a. 1; q. 63, a. 1), Thomas explains that something can be *natural* to human beings in different ways. The natural dispositions can be considered either as *generic* (shared with other animals), or as *specific* (shared with other human beings as rational animals), or as *temperamental* (the traits of an individual human being). In addition, something can be natural either as coming entirely from nature or as coming partly from nature and partly from an extrinsic principle. Self-healing, without medicine, is entirely from nature; but when an individual is healed through medicine, health is partly by nature and partly by the medicine. The trichotomy of the natural dispositions seems to come from Aristotle's theory of biological inheritance (*Generation of Animals*, 767b24–69b31).

7. This has been the criticism of Thomistic natural law by Straussian commentators. See Harry Jaffa, *Thomism and Aristotelianism* (Chicago: University of Chicago Press, 1952), 167–88; and Leo Strauss, *Natural Right and History* (Chicago: University of Chicago Press, 1953), 162–64. A Straussian defense of Thomas as a teacher of Aristotelian natural right is set forth by Goerner, "Thomistic Natural Law," 101–22. For the claim that the Straussian criticism of natural law depreciates morality, see Shadia B. Drury, *The Political Ideas of Leo Strauss* (New York: St. Martin's Press, 1988), 90–113.

   For the Thomistic account of prudence, see Nelson, *The Priority of Prudence*; and Yves Simon, *Philosophy of Democratic Government* (Chicago: University of Chicago Press, 1951), 21–30. See also, on prudence, Michael Oakeshott, *Rationalism in Politics* (London: Methuen, 1962), 1–36; George Anastaplo, "Abraham Lincoln's Emancipation Proclamation," in Ronald Collins, ed., *Constitutional Government in America* (Durham, NC: Carolina Academic Press, 1980), 421–46; and Ronald Beiner, *Political Judgment* (Chicago: University of Chicago Press, 1983).

8. See H. L. A. Hart, *The Concept of Law* (Oxford: Oxford University Press, 1961); and Hart, "Positivism and the Separation of Law and Morals," in Ronald Dworkin, ed., *The Philosophy of Law* (Oxford: Oxford University Press, 1977), 17–37.

9. See Hart, *The Concept of Law*, 184–95; and Hart, "Positivism," 35–37.

10. Some historians argue that the tradition of legal positivism in German jurisprudence inclined judges to adhere to the letter of National Socialist laws despite the injustice of those laws. But others argue that Nazi jurisprudence broke with the positivist tradition by setting aside the rule of law and invoking the vague moral claims of the *Volk* ("the people") and the *Fuhrerprinzip* ("leader-principle"). Compare H. W. Koch, *In the Name of the Volk: Political Justice in Hitler's Germany* (London: I.B. Tauris, 1989), 245–47; Ingo Muller, *Hitler's Justice: The Courts of the Third Reich* (Cambridge: Harvard University Press, 1991), 68–81; and Alan Bullock, *Hitler and Stalin: Parallel Lives* (New York: Alfred A. Knopf, 1992), 341–46, 423–34.

11. Here I am drawing on a line of reasoning developed by Goerner, "Thomistic Natural Law," 114–19.

12. There is a vast literature on this topic. See, for example, John Wild, *Plato's Modern Enemies and the Theory of Natural Law* (Chicago: University of Chicago Press, 1953), 64–99, 181–234; Hans Kelsen, *What Is Justice?* (Berkeley: University of California Press, 1957), 174–97; Arnold Brecht, *Political Theory* (Princeton: Princeton University Press, 1959); Mortimer J. Adler, *The Conditions of Philosophy* (New York: Atheneum, 1965), 182–99; Harry V. Jaffa, *Equality and Liberty* (New York: Oxford University Press, 1965), 190–208; Marjorie Grene, *The Knower and the Known* (New York: Basic Books, 1966), 157–82; Mary Midgley, *Beast and Man: The Roots of Human Nature* (Ithaca: Cornell University Press, 1979), chap. 9; and Midgley, "The Absence of a Gap Between Facts and Values," *The Aristotelian Society Supplementary* 54 (1980): 207–23.

    Although the fact-value dichotomy is commonly thought to have originated with David Hume, Hume was an ethical naturalist in seeing ethics as rooted in human nature. In many respects, Hume anticipated sociobiology. See Alaisdair MacIntyre, "Hume on 'Is' and 'Ought'," *Philosophical Review* 68 (1959): 451–68; and Robert McShea, *Morality and Human Nature* (Philadelphia: Temple University Press, 1990).

13. See Henry B. Veatch, "The Rational Justification of Moral Principles," *Review of Metaphysics* 29 (December 1975): 217–38.

14. See William A. Mason, "Primate Social Intelligence," in Donald R. Griffin, ed., *Animal Mind-Human Mind* (New York: Springer-Verlag, 1982), 131–43; and C. Judson Herrick, *The Evolution of Human Nature* (Austin: University of Texas Press, 1956), chaps. 11–12.

15. On the debate over Ulpian's definition, see Michael B. Crowe, *The Changing Profile of the Natural Law* (The Hague: Martinus Nijhoff, 1977), 46–51, 259–67. Under the influence of Aristotle's biology, Thomas concluded that, although only human beings act from *free* judgment, other animals act from an "estimative" judgment about what will satisfy their desires. Thus all animals have a natural capacity for practical judgment that shows a certain "participation in prudence and reason" and a certain "likeness of moral good." See *Summa Theologica*, I, q. 83, a. 1; q. 96, a. 1; I–II, q. 11, a. 2; q. 24, a. 4; q. 40, a. 3. The influence of this biological psychology on the Thomistic understanding of natural law is evident in the account of marriage in the Supplement to the *Summa Theologica* (q. 41, a. 1; q. 54, a. 3; q. 65, a. 1–3; q. 67, a. 1). What Thomas calls the "estimative" capacity of animals might be comparable to what some behavioral ecologists call "assessment" in animal behavior: "The key feature of assessment is that some aspect of the environment is perceived and the information used as a factor in decision-making" (R. W. Elwood and S. J. Neil, *Assessments and Decisions: A Study of Information Gathering by Hermit Crabs* [London: Chapman and Hall, 1992], 6).

16. See James Bernard Murphy, "Nature, Custom, and Stipulation in Law and Jurisprudence," *Review of Metaphysics* 43 (June 1990): 751–90; and Murphy, *The Moral Economy of Labor: Aristotelian Themes in Economic Theory* (New Haven: Yale University Press, 1993).

17. The importance of custom for social order becomes clear as soon as we realize that most of our daily social interactions are governed by informal customary norms that have little to do with formal laws. We appeal to formal laws only in those rare cases where the informal customs somehow break down. See Robert C. Ellickson, *Order without Law: How Neighbors Settle Disputes* (Cambridge: Harvard University Press, 1991).

18. Ruth Benedict, *Patterns of Culture* (Boston: Houghton Mifflin, 1934).

19. Ibid., 20. Benedict's book is similar in its general themes to Margaret Mead' s *Coming of Age in Samoa* (New York: Morrow, 1928). Both women were students of Franz Boas, who stressed the dominance of culture in shaping human life. In the nature-nurture debate, Boas and his students were on the side of nurture. In its most extreme form, their argument would be that there are no rational, universal standards for comparing societies. Each society manifests a unique culture that determines the thought and action of its members. For evidence that the debate over this issue remains intense among anthropologists, see Derek Freeman, *Margaret Mead and Samoa: The Making and Unmaking of an Anthropological Myth* (Cambridge: Harvard University Press, 1983); and Robert I. Levy, "The Attack on Mead," *Science* 220 (20 May 1983): 829–32. For a defense of Mead, see Eleanor Leacock, "Anthropologists in Search of Culture," in Lenora Foerstel and Angela Gilliam, eds., *Confronting the Margaret Mead Legacy* (Philadelphia: Temple University Press, 1992), 3–30. Is it possible to transcend this debate by saying that in human life nature and culture are intertwined? Freeman (31–32) quotes Boas as arguing that culture is "not an expression of innate mental qualities" but "a result of varied external conditions acting upon general human characteristics." Could these "general human characteristics" be the foundation of natural law?

20. On the cross-cultural regularities in family life and reproductive relations, see William N. Stephens, *The Family in Cross-Cultural Perspective* (New York: Holt, Rinehart and Winston, 1963); and A.F. Robertson, *Beyond the Family: The Social Organization of Human Reproduction* (Berkeley: University of California Press, 1991).

21. Ralph Linton, "The Problem of Universal Values," in Robert F. Spencer, ed., *Method and Perspective in Anthropology* (Minneapolis: University of Minnesota Press, 1954), 145–68. For the best survey of this topic, see Donald E. Brown, *Human Universals* (Philadelphia: Temple University Press, 1991). See also Finnis, *Natural Law*, 81–99; Margaret Mead, "Some Anthropological Considerations Concerning Natural Law," *Natural Law Forum* 6 (1961): 51–64; Kai Nielsen, "Ethical Relativism and the Facts of Cultural Relativity," *Social Research* 33

(Winter 1966): 531–51; Wolfgang Wickler, *The Biology of the Ten Commandments* (New York: McGraw-Hill, 1972); Clifford Geertz, *The Interpretation of Cultures* (New York: Basic Books, 1973), 38–51; David Miller, *Social Justice* (Oxford: Oxford University Press, 1976); and Elvin Hatch, *Culture and Morality: The Relativity of Values in Anthropology* (New York: Columbia University Press, 1983).

   Consider Roberto Unger, *Law in Modern Society*, 42:

> The real issue is whether one can extricate the ancient insight into the unity of human nature from the ancient illusion that humanity is unchanging throughout history. The task is to develop a doctrine that recognizes the unity of human nature in a more than trivial fashion while affirming that this nature changes in history and it is reinvented and transformed by each new form of social life; indeed, by every individual.

22. Linton, "Universal Values," 152.
23. Colin Turnbull, *The Mountain People* (New York: Simon & Schuster 1972).
24. See Marvin Harris, *Cannibals and Kings* (New York: Random House, 1977), chapter 9; and the criticism of Harris by Marshall Sahlins, "Culture as Protein and Profit," *New York Review of Books*, 23 (November 1978): 45–53. See also Michel de Montaigne, "Of Custom" and "Of Cannibals," in *The Complete Essays of Montaigne*, trans. Donald M. Frame (Stanford: Stanford University Press, 1958), 77–90, 150–59.

   What should we say about those practices — witchcraft, for example — that seem to us irrational? If we could understand such practices as they are understood by the participants, would we see their rationality? Is the very idea of rationality a cultural product? If so, then is there no objective standard for judging a medical doctor as more rational than a witch doctor? See Peter Winch, "Understanding a Primitive Society," in Bryan R. Wilson, ed., *Rationality* (New York: Basil Blackwell, 1970), 78–111; Winch, *Ethics and Action* (London: Routledge & Kegan Paul, 1972), 8–72; Larry Arnhart, "Language and Nature in Wittgenstein's *Philosophical Investigations*," *Journal of Thought* 10 (July 1975):194–99; E. E. Evans-Pritchard, *Witchcraft, Oracles, and Magic Among the Azande* (Oxford: Clarendon Press, 1976); Richard J. Bernstein, *Beyond Objectivism and Relativism: Science, Hermeneutics and Praxis* (Philadelphia: University of Pennsylvania Press, 1983), 93–108; and George Anastaplo, "Church and State: Explorations," *Loyola University of Chicago Law Journal*, 19 (1987): 65–86.

   Are there "natural" explanations even for the seemingly arbitrary taboos of religion — sacred cows, dietary restrictions, and so on? Compare Moses Maimonides, *The Guide of the Perplexed*, trans. Shlomo Pines (Chicago: University of Chicago Press, 1963), 510–14, 532–35, 598–601; Marvin Harris, *Cows, Pigs, Wars, and Witches* (New York: Random House, 1974); and Deuteronomy 22:6–7, 23:9–14, 25:11–12, 30:15–20.

Do human beings in different cultures pass through the same stages of life—childhood, adolescence, youth, adulthood, and old age? Do they therefore confront essentially the same moral problems? If so, does this give us some ground for understanding and judging alien cultures? See Giambattista Vico, *The New Science*, trans. Thomas G. Bergin and Max H. Fisch (Ithaca: Cornell University Press, 1948), paras. 333, 922–24; Colin Turnbull, *The Human Cycle* (New York: Simon & Schuster, 1983); Barry Bogin, *Patterns of Human Growth* (Cambridge: Cambridge University Press, 1988) and Joseph Campbell, *The Hero with a Thousand Faces*, 2nd ed. (Princeton: Princeton University Press, 1968).

25. Quoted in Gerald Gunther, ed., *Cases and Materials on Constitutional Law*, 9th ed. (Mineola, NY: Foundation Press, 1975), 1301, 1308–10.

26. The court decisions are reprinted in Burton M. Leiser, ed., *Values in Conflict: Life, Liberty, and the Rule of Law* (New York: Macmillan, 1981), 216–37. For conflicting assessments of this case, see Franklyn S. Haiman, *Speech and Law in a Free Society* (Chicago: University of Chicago Press, 1981); and Donald A. Downs, *Nazis in Skokie* (Notre Dame: University of Notre Dame Press, 1985).

27. Patrick Devlin, *The Enforcement of Morals* (Oxford University Press, 1965). For criticism of Devlin, see H. L. A. Hart, *Law, Liberty and Morality* (Stanford: Stanford University Press, 1963).

It can be argued that almost every legal matter depends on moral judgments. For example, on the moral assumptions underlying zoning regulations, see Constance Perin, *Everything in Its Place: Social Order and Land Use in America* (Princeton: Princeton University Press, 1977).

Should the Supreme Court interpret the written law of the Constitution in the light of the unwritten law of nature? Compare Walter Berns, "Judicial Review and the Rights and Laws of Nature," in Philip B. Kurland et al., eds., *The Supreme Court Review, 1983* (Chicago: University of Chicago Press, 1982), 49–83; and Harry Clor, "Judicial Statesmanship and Constitutional Interpretation," *South Texas Law Journal* 26 (Fall 1985):397–433.

Should we agree with the professor of law who advises some law students to respect "the almost instinctive awareness of right and wrong that our way of life has habituated you to"? He contends that "the law relies for the most part on simple notions of what is right and wrong."

Thus, all the sensitive student needs to do, in order to "get on top" of a field of substantive law, is to learn the terms employed in that particular field and become familiar with the few peculiar exceptions for which history (that is, chance) is responsible.

Thus, also, the first question you should ask, *once you get the "facts" of a case straight*, is, "What is the just way of settling this issue?" And in most cases, that will be the principal question you will need to answer.

As a practicing lawyer, you will need also the fortitude as well as the good sense to act upon your answer. (George Anastaplo, *Human Being and Citizen* [Chicago: Swallow Press, 1975], 112–13).

Does he assume that the moral habits of "our way of life" are somehow natural? On the importance of moral character for the practice of law, see William H. Herndon, *Herndon's Life of Lincoln* (New York: Da Capo Press, 1983), 261–90, 420–33, 475–90; and Edmond Cahn, *The Moral Decision: Right and Wrong in the Light of American Law* (Bloomington: Indiana University Press, 1981). For evidence that people respect the law only when they perceive that the legal system is fundamentally fair, see Tom Tyler, *Why People Obey the Law* (New Haven: Yale University Press, 1991). On the influence of natural law and positivism in the history of legal education, see William Braithwaite, "On Legal Practice and Education at the Present Time," in *The Great Ideas Today, 1989* (Chicago: Encyclopaedia Britannica, 1989), 44–100.

28. For surveys of the evidence on this point, see Harry M. Clor, *Obscenity and Public Morality* (Chicago: University of Chicago Press, 1969), 175–209; and Reo M. Christenson, *Challenge and Decision: Political Issues of Our Time*, 6th ed. (New York: Harper & Row, 1982), 199–216. See also Susan Sontag, "The Pornographic Imagination," in *The Susan Sontag Reader* (New York: Farrar, Straus & Giroux, 1982), 205–33; and Murray S. Davis, *Smut: Erotic Reality, Obscene Ideology* (Chicago: University of Chicago Press, 1983).

    For a defense of "the right to pornography," see Ronald Dworkin, *Taking Rights Seriously* (Cambridge: Harvard University Press, 1977), 240–58; and Dworkin, *A Matter of Principle* (Cambridge: Harvard University Press, 1985), 335–72. Dworkin argues for governmental support of the arts to protect "the structure of our intellectual culture" (*A Matter of Principle*, 232). Doesn't this contradict his argument that governmental restriction of pornography is wrong because it is wrong for government to enforce moral standards? If it is *right* for government to protect "our intellectual culture," then why is it *wrong* for government to restrict material contrary to that culture?

29. On coercion and persuasion as instruments of governmental authority, see Simon, *Philosophy of Democratic Government*, 108–27. For a principled argument justifying the legal enforcement of morality, see Hadley Arkes, *The Philosopher in the City: The Moral Dimensions of Urban Politics* (Princeton: Princeton University Press, 1981). Arkes comments on all of the constitutional issues that we have considered in this chapter.

Chapter

5

Power Politics
Machiavelli's *Prince* and *Discourses*

Key Readings

The Prince, Chapters 3, 6–9, 12, 15–19, 21, 26; *Discourses*, Introduction, I, 1–5, 9–12, 16–18, 25–27, 34, 37, 55, 58; II, 2, 5, 13; III, 1, 6, 9.

The life of Niccolò Machiavelli (1469–1527) can be divided into four periods. From 1469 to 1498, Machiavelli spent his childhood and received his early education in Florence. From 1498 to 1512, he worked for the government of Florence. From 1512 to 1517, having been forced to retire from Florentine politics, he wrote *The Prince* and the *Discourses*. From 1518 to 1527, he wrote *The Art of War* and the *History of Florence*; and he also was able to participate again in the political life of Florence.

Machiavelli's father was a lawyer who was influenced by those Italian scholars who would later be identified by historians as "humanists." In the tradition of "civic humanism," it was thought that the best preparation for a public career was a study of the Latin classics in rhetoric, poetry, history, and philosophy. Cicero was especially important, particularly his book *De officiis (On Moral Duties)*, which prescribes the moral and intellectual virtues that the young must acquire in order to serve their country with honor. Much of Machiavelli's writing can be seen as a response to this classical teaching about the virtues and the vices of the good ruler.[1]

This humanist education helped Machiavelli to win a position in the Florentine government in 1498 when he was twenty-nine years old. Florence had been a republic for hundreds of years, but the Medici family had dominated the city through most of the fifteenth century. When Lorenzo de' Medici died in 1492, his son Piero was unable to maintain the family's power. Piero was forced into exile in 1494, and a new constitution was established for Florence under the influence of a Dominican monk, Girolamo Savonarola, who wished Florence to be a Christian republic. After Savonarola's execution by the pope in 1498, Machiavelli was able to enter the new government. He served in the diplomatic corps until 1512.

Machiavelli went on diplomatic missions that allowed him to observe many of the most important rulers of his time, including Louis XII of France, Pope Julius II, and Maximilian, the Holy Roman Emperor. His written diplomatic reports contain political observations that he later incorporated into his books. Much of his diplomatic work was devoted to protecting the independence of Florence in the face of foreign intervention in Italy by France and Spain. But a Spanish invasion in 1512 finally led to the fall of the Florentine republic and the return to power of the Medici. Machiavelli was dismissed from office. A few months later, he was suspected of conspiring against the new government. Although he protested his innocence, he was interrogated and tortured. Some of his letters suggest that he endured the torture with some fortitude.[2] In *The Prince*, he advises that one reason princes rely more on fear than on love is that "fear is maintained by a dread of punishment which never abandons you" (chapter 17, page 101).[3]

Machiavelli retired to his country house outside Florence, where he spent most of his time for the next twelve years. But during his first year of retirement, when he wrote *The Prince* and began the *Discourses*, he still thought the Medici might call him into their service. As this hope faded, he turned all his attention to writing. His writing was inspired by an intensive study of the ancient Greek and Roman texts of political philosophy and political history.[4]

In 1518, Machiavelli began to participate again in the life of Florence. He was commissioned by the Medici in 1520 to write the history of Florence. In 1525, he was given a minor position in the government. Then, in May of 1527, the Medici were expelled from Florence, and the republic was restored. But Machiavelli's ties to the Medici probably made him seem unreliable to the new republican leaders. A month later he died.

Machiavelli claimed in his writings that he had discovered a new way of viewing politics, a new point of view that would influence those who would later follow his path (see *The Prince*, chapter 15; *Discourses*, introduction). In many respects, however, his thinking reflected the tradition of Renaissance humanism. Perhaps he did break with all previous political thought on at least one crucial point. As Quentin Skinner has observed, Machiavelli rejected "the nerve and heart of humanist advice-books for princes" by denying the importance of moral virtue for political success.[5] That leads us to our first question.

1. Is Machiavelli a teacher of evil?

We begin with this question because Machiavelli's reputation makes it unavoidable. Those reading him for the first time are usually predisposed to take one side or the other of this issue. Some find confirmation for the common belief that Machiavelli was a teacher of evil because he taught political leaders how to win and hold power through force and fraud. Other readers are inclined to argue that because Machiavelli simply told the truth about the pursuit of political power, we should not condemn him. Moreover, many readers consider the graceful charm and noble tone of Machiavelli's writing evidence that his teaching cannot be as monstrous as it is often assumed to be. But then those who have never read Machiavelli, and who perhaps never should read him, deserve to be warned about the dangerously seductive power of his writing. It's the same power exerted by Nietzsche: "The spell that fights on our behalf, the eye of Venus that charms and blinds even our opponents, is *the magic of the extreme*, the seduction that everything extreme exercises: we immoralists — we are the most extreme."[6]

The apparent immorality of Machiavelli's writing manifests a problem in modern political life generally. As we probe the meaning of Machiavellianism, we must wonder about the horrors of modern war and modern tyranny and about the brutal ruthlessness of many modern political leaders. We must wonder, in short, whether modern politics has lost all sense of moral purpose. "We live today in the shadow of a Florentine," one commentator has explained, because he "taught the world to think in terms of cold political power. . . . Frederick, Richelieu, Napoleon, Bismarck, Clemenceau, Lenin, Mussolini, Hitler, Stalin, have gone to school to Machiavelli."[7]

But we have seen a different side of modern politics in the

Declaration of Independence, in the claim that just government must be founded on the moral principles inherent in "the Laws of Nature and of Nature's God." The American founders insisted that the United States, unlike most (if not all) previous governments, would be based not on force and fraud, but on a moral theory of natural rights. Should we conclude, therefore, that, as one interpreter of Machiavelli has said, the United States "may be said to be the only country in the world which was founded in explicit opposition to Machiavellian principles"?[8] In any case, the Declaration does lead us to question whether political order can rest on moral principles or whether political rule is simply the rule of the stronger. To think through that question, we must confront Machiavelli.

Machiavelli was not the first political thinker to uncover the nasty realities of power politics. We might be reminded of Plato's Thrasymachus, Aristotle's advice for tyrants, Augustine's political realism, and Aquinas's comments on the limits of law as a moral instrument. But none of these people display the shocking boldness of Machiavelli. We can see this, for example, early in *The Prince* (chapter 3).

Machiavelli describes how the ancient Romans cleverly expanded their imperialistic control of provinces by insuring that they always had enough power to overwhelm any challengers. He then contrasts their success with the failure of Louis XII in expanding French power into Italy:

> It is a thing truly very natural and ordinary to desire to acquire; and when men who are able to do so do it, they are always praised or not blamed; but when they are not able and yet want to do so in every mode, here is the error and the blame. If France, then, was able with his forces to attack Naples, he ought to have done so; if he was not able to do so, he ought not to have divided it. And if he had divided Lombardy with the Venetians, that merited excuse, for he put his foot into Italy by having done so; the other division merits blame, by its not being excused by this necessity. (chapter 3, pages 17–18)

As far as Machiavelli is concerned, whatever succeeds is to be praised, whatever fails blamed. He introduces no moral standards. Rather, he merely judges whether political leaders have selected the most efficient means for their chosen ends, and he assumes that the final end of political activity is acquiring and holding power. We can see already why Machiavelli might be considered a teacher of evil. He teaches that in the pursuit of political power, the end justifies the means. As he makes clear later in *The Prince*, even cruelty can be justified as a tool of political rule. Machiavelli seems to have written a handbook for tyrants. Instead of searching for standards of political justice, as was done by previous political philosophers, Machiavelli offers himself to any ambitious leader vicious enough to accept his diabolical advice.

But consider how a defender of Machiavelli might respond to these criticisms. Surely, Machiavelli introduces a moral standard by praising those princes who exhibit virtue (*virtù* in Italian). And isn't it true, the Machiavellian might ask, that the end *does justify* the means if the end is morally good? Even Machiavelli's endorsement of cruelty might be defended by noting that he distinguishes the good uses of cruelty from the bad uses. Moreover, he need not be interpreted as promoting tyranny, for much of what he teaches might support popular self-government. Finally, if he emphasizes the selfish side of human nature—the "desire to acquire"— shouldn't we accept that as an accurate view of the way most people live?

We have begun by asking, Is Machiavelli a teacher of evil? But this question has led us into a series of questions that we must ponder in our reading of Machiavelli. What is Machiavellian *virtù*? In politics, does the end justify the means? Does politics require "cruelty well used"? Does Machiavellianism subvert popular government? In politics, should we assume that all people are bad? Does Machiavelli subordinate political wisdom to political power? We begin with Machiavelli's notion of virtue.

2. What is Machiavellian virtue?

Starting in chapter 6 of *The Prince*, Machiavelli speaks of the need for virtue, especially for new princes who wish to establish and maintain wholly new states. This concern for virtue would seem to contradict Machiavelli's reputation as a teacher of immorality. For he advises new princes to set for themselves high goals of political greatness by imitating the political virtue of great leaders of the past. But in this same chapter, as he explains the virtue of great founders like Moses, he makes one of those remarks for which he has become infamous: "all armed prophets conquer, and the unarmed ones are ruined" (chapter 6, page 34).[9] Obviously, Machiavelli is giving virtue a meaning contrary to ordinary usage. For how can it be virtuous to rule in such a manner that "when the people do not believe any more, one is able to make them believe by force"?[10]

In chapter 6, Machiavelli contrasts virtue with fortune. Speaking of founders such as Moses, Cyrus, Romulus, and Theseus, he explains:

> Fortune provided them with nothing other than the occasion which gave them the matter into which they could introduce whatever form they pleased; without that occasion their virtue of mind would have been extinguished and without virtue the occasion would have come in vain. (chapter 6, page 33)

By thus exercising their virtue, Machiavelli adds, "their fatherland was ennobled and became most happy." Political leaders display Machiavellian virtue, it would seem, when they impose their own "forms" on the "matter" provided by their circumstances. A virtuous political founder creates a new way of life for the people that reflects the founder's own mind and will. A prince lays good foundations, Machiavelli says later in *The Prince*, "if with his mind and his orders he animates the whole" (chapter 9, page 60). To achieve this a prince must rely totally on himself without dependence on the power of others. For this reason he must be "armed" because with his own "arms" he can force people to obey his orders. As indicated by the title of chapters 6 and 7, Machiavelli distinguishes states acquired "by one's own arms and virtue" and states acquired "by the arms of others and fortune."

We might conclude, then, at least provisionally, that Machiavellian virtue denotes the power of political leaders who can establish and hold a state by their own strength. But that would be a strange sort of virtue because it would suggest sheer ruthlessness with no sense of moral purpose. Perhaps we should give more weight to Machiavelli's claim that through virtuous rulers states become "ennobled" and "most happy." We could say, then, that the virtue of a Machiavellian prince serves a moral purpose insofar as it promotes the nobility and happiness of the state. But would this moral end justify any immoral means to its achievement? We must raise this question as we read Machiavelli's account of the "virtues" of Cesare Borgia (chapter 7) and of Agathocles (chapter 8).

Cesare Borgia "did all those things which ought to be done by a prudent and virtuous man" to secure his political power (chapter 7, page 42). For example, when Borgia took the Romagna, he appointed an unusually cruel man to restore peace where the previous rulers had created disorder. Once the agent had done his job, Borgia judged that he should avoid the hatred stirred up by his minister by publicly punishing him. So, Borgia had the man cut in two and the pieces of his body placed in the public square. "The ferocity of that spectacle left the people at the same time satisfied and stupefied" (chapter 7, page 45). That, Machiavelli insists, is virtue in action! How can Machiavelli offer such brutality as an example of political virtue? He does say that Borgia gave the Romagna "good government" by using the cruel minister to establish peace and then by setting up judicial institutions in each city. Does this provide the moral justification for his severe measures?[11]

Machiavelli suggests that virtue requires moral limits to political ruthlessness when he condemns the cruelty of Agathocles: "one cannot call it virtue to kill his fellow citizens, to betray his friends, to be without faith, without pity, without religion; which modes enabled him to acquire imperium, but not glory" (chapter 8, page 52). Yet in the very next sentence, Machiavelli refers to "the virtue of Agathocles in entering into and escaping from dangers, and the greatness of his mind in standing up to and overcoming adverse things." Thus Machiavelli does what he says one cannot do: he calls immorality virtue. Later in chapter 8, he explains that not all cruelty is good but only cruelty "well used." Cruelties "well used," such as those of Agathocles, are "those (if one may lawfully call the bad good) which are done at once for the necessity of securing oneself, and which are afterwards not continued within, but converted to the greatest possible utility of the subjects" (chapter 8, page 54).

Surely, we have all the evidence we need to condemn Machiavelli as a corrupter of political life. For he endorses the most inhuman acts of brutality as politically virtuous simply because they secure a prince's political power. Thus he distorts the common-sense meaning of virtue by depriving it of any moral significance. Once he has lifted all moral restraints from political rule, making the pursuit of power an end in itself, has he not made it easy for tyrants to justify even the most monstrous deeds? Isn't it a small step from Machiavelli to Stalin, to Hitler, and to others like them?

It could be argued in defense of Machiavelli, however, that he does try to separate the noble and the ignoble. He never recommends senseless violence. Rather, he always insists that harsh measures are justified only where they are necessary to secure the prince's power and to benefit his people by promoting peace and unity. Moreover, he warns rulers that when they do the infamous things that Agathocles did, even when they are compelled to do so to achieve their ends, they may acquire "imperium, but not glory." Rulers do not attain the highest virtue by simply becoming powerful; their power must also radiate glory.

Perhaps the value of glory constitutes a Machiavellian standard for distinguishing good and bad rulers. Machiavelli suggests this in one chapter of the *Discourses* (I, 10). He contrasts the glory of the good Roman emperors, who promoted peace and justice and

lived securely among their people, with the infamy of the bad
emperors, who promoted violence and injustice and lived in fear
of their subjects. Machiavelli is willing to excuse those rulers who
had to corrupt their cities in order to maintain their own princely
power. But some rulers have the opportunity to preserve their power
while organizing their cities properly:

> And, in fine, let him to whom Heaven has vouchsafed such an
> opportunity reflect that there are two ways open to him; one that
> will enable him to live securely and insure him glory after death,
> and the other that will make his life one of constant anxiety,
> and after death consign him to eternal infamy. (I, 10)[12]

If the circumstances are right, a power-hungry prince can achieve
the greatest glory by promoting the common welfare of his people.
In such a case, the prince's selfish interest in power serves the
public interest of his state.

In American political history, Franklin Roosevelt's career would
illustrate this. "Roosevelt had a love affair with power," one political
scientist has observed.

> He wanted power for its own sake; he also wanted what it could
> achieve. The challenge and the fun of power lay not just in
> having, but in doing. His private satisfactions were enriched by
> public purposes, and these grew more compelling as more power
> came his way. . . . And happily for him, his own sense of direction
> coincided, in the main, with the course of contemporary
> history.[13]

Thus Roosevelt found himself in a fortunate situation where he
could use his power to win glory.

If Machiavelli understands the virtuous prince to be one who
seeks great political power for the sake of glory, then his idea of
virtue can be defended as morally respectable. In this respect,
Machiavelli revives the ancient Greek and Roman idea of glory as
the proper reward for political greatness. Even Augustine, as we
have seen, concedes that this pagan love of glory elevated ancient
political life. We might also note that the American Founding
Fathers thought it important to appeal to this passion for political
glory. Alexander Hamilton, for example, hoped that American
presidents would always be moved by "the love of fame, the ruling
passion of the noblest minds" (*Federalist* No. 72).[14]

But pagan authors such as Cicero, who saw value in the pursuit
of glory, insisted that true glory arose only from moral virtue (see
De officiis II, 42–44).[15] Generally, those who have revived the
ancient appreciation for political glory, including the Renaissance
humanists, have also assumed that genuine glory coincides with

the highest moral virtue. It is not so clear, however, that Machiavelli would agree. For example, in the *Discourses*, he tells the story of a man who rose to political power through wicked means and then lost his power because he refused to kill the pope. Thus, Machiavelli observes, he lost his chance for glory because although he was wicked, he was not wicked enough to do "an act the greatness of which would have overshadowed the infamy and all the danger that could possibly result from it" (I, 27). Partial wickedness is despicable, but utter wickedness is glorious. If this is the sort of glory for which the virtuous prince strives, then clearly Machiavelli's virtue violates all traditional standards of moral virtue.

A Machiavellian might respond, however, by arguing that if Machiavelli breaks with all previous traditions of political virtue, that is only because he formulates a new standard appropriate for the modern state. The pagan and Christian views of political virtue assume that all people share a common moral knowledge that they possess by nature. As Aristotle claimed, humans are by nature political animals bound together by their shared understanding of the good and the just. But in modern political life, don't we see human beings as isolated individuals pursuing their own selfish interests in competition with one another? If that is so, aren't we compelled to conclude that because human beings are not naturally bound together by moral bonds, they cannot live together in peace unless they are *forced* to do so? Doesn't this suggest, then, that political order can arise only when great founders impose by violence their own personal forms on the otherwise formless matter of humanity? Machiavellian virtue, therefore, might be regarded as the ability of a leader to create a state through the intelligent and willful use of force. In this way, a Machiavellian could maintain that the immorality of Machiavelli's teaching must be accepted as an inevitable feature of the political life of the modern state.

There is some plausibility to this argument simply because our word "state" can be traced back to Machiavelli's use of the Italian word *stato*.[16] The very idea of the state originates with Machiavelli. Consider how he uses this word in chapter 3 of *The Prince*, for example. He speaks of what one must do when one "acquires states in a province" and wants "to hold them" (chapter 3, page 13). The Romans held their state in the province of Greece because they never allowed some powerful challengers "to increase their state," and they did not permit some others to "hold any state in that province at all" (chapter 3, page 15). Thus, the state can be acquired or lost, increased or decreased, depending on the power of the ruler: the state is the product of the ruler's will. Aristotle's city, by contrast, arose by nature because it fulfilled the natural human inclination to live in communities. The modern state arises as an artificial construction because it must be imposed on human individuals who are not naturally inclined to live together. Aristotle's city is a product of nature. Machiavelli's state is a work of art.[17]

This same Machiavellian teaching appears in the idea of the state proposed by some modern social scientists. Consider, for instance, the remarks of Max Weber: "Today the relation between the state and violence is an especially intimate one. . . . A state is a human community that (successfully) claims the *monopoly of the legitimate use of physical force* within a given territory." He also contends that the state, as "a compulsory association which organizes domination," must be created by a forceful political leader: "Everywhere the development of the modern state is initiated through the action of the prince."[18]

This reliance of the modern state on the use of violence by political founders has been manifested clearly in the revolutionary upheavals of modern times. Modern political history has been shaped by revolutionaries—such as Cromwell, Robespierre, Napoleon, Lenin, Hitler, and Mao—who display the same ruthless willfulness as Machiavelli's virtuous prince. As Lord Acton observed, "The authentic interpreter of Machiavelli is the whole of later history."[19]

Yet, surely, some of us would want to argue that the character of the modern state does not dictate the political immorality endorsed by Machiavelli. Have we not seen in the Declaration of Independence that the modern liberal democratic state rests on some moral principles? Why shouldn't the idea of natural rights serve as a moral standard for judging modern states? Indeed, don't we commonly today rank states according to how faithfully they secure human rights? But perhaps Machiavelli would respond that, even in states devoted to human rights, the preservation of the state is itself the ultimate end to which everything else—including human rights—must yield.

3. In politics does the end justify the means?

We commonly assume that the motto of a Machiavellian politician is "the end justifies the means." Machiavelli, however, never says that in exactly those words. So we must consider whether he would accept that formula as part of his teaching. We should look at chapters 15–18 of *The Prince* because these chapters are usually interpreted as teaching that the prince must employ immoral means to achieve his ends.

Beginning with Plato's *Republic*, we have seen that ancient and medieval political philosophers were often preoccupied with the "best city," even though it was rarely, if ever, achievable in practice. Machiavelli begins chapter 15 of *The Prince* by rejecting this type of political thinking. A prince who wishes to preserve himself must understand not what *ought* to be done in politics but what *is* done, Machiavelli advises, because a prince who seeks to be good must fail as long as he is surrounded by those who are not good. "Hence it is necessary for a prince, if he wishes to maintain himself, to learn to be able to be not good, and to use it and not use it according to the necessity" (chapter 15, page 93). A successful prince may have to engage in bad activities, but "he should not concern himself about incurring the infamy of those vices without which it would be difficult to save the state" (chapter 15, page 94). Arguing throughout chapters 15–18 that the prudent prince must choose whatever virtues and vices will preserve the state, Machiavelli counsels the prince "not to depart from the good, if he is able, but to know how to enter the bad, when necessitated to do so" (chapter 18, page 109).

In chapter 18, Machiavelli comes closest to formulating the maxim that the end of preserving the state justifies any means:

> And with respect to all human actions, and especially those of princes where there is no judge to whom to appeal, one looks to the end. Let a prince then win and maintain the state — the means will always be judged honorable and will be praised by everyone; for the vulgar are always taken in by the appearance and the outcome of a thing, and in this world there is no one but the vulgar. (chapter 18, page 109)

Machiavelli expresses a similar thought in the *Discourses*. Using the example of Romulus's fratricide, he notes the brutality of founders of new republics. The wise accept this, he observes, when it is done for the public good and not for private interests:

> It is well that, when the act accuses him, the result should excuse him; and when the result is good, as in the case of Romulus, it will always absolve him from blame. For he is to be reprehended who commits violence for the purpose of destroying, and not he who employs it for beneficent purposes. (I, 9)

At times Machiavelli describes the consequences of political actions without making any moral judgment of his own. In the passage above from *The Prince*, he notes that whatever a prince does to preserve the state will be judged honorable by the vulgar multitude; but Machiavelli does not either endorse or condemn this judgment. It is simply a fact that most people think that the end of preserving the state justifies any means, but it remains an open question whether this public opinion is correct or not. Hence we might defend Machiavelli by insisting that he is not praising what he describes, rather he is merely reporting what actually happens in political life.

How plausible is this interpretation of Machiavelli's writing? Doesn't the quotation above from the *Discourses* imply that Machiavelli endorses the rule of unscrupulous expediency? He declares "when the result is good, . . . it will always absolve him from blame." Preserving the state is indeed a good end, Machiavelli suggests, and therefore any means to that end should be permitted.

If Machiavelli is recommending the principle that good ends justify bad means, can we criticize him for this? If the end truly is good, isn't it sometimes proper to employ bad means to achieve it? Of course, St. Paul taught us that we may not do evil that good may come. Perhaps some things should be absolutely forbidden no matter what the consequences. But when the preservation of a political community is threatened, aren't the rulers entitled to do whatever is necessary to preserve the state?

To illustrate how influential this Machiavellian argument has been among modern political leaders, we might think about those American presidents who have resorted to extreme measures in times of emergency. During the Civil War, for instance, Abraham Lincoln permitted his commanding officers to suspend the writ of habeas corpus. This allowed them to arrest and detain anyone they wished without formal charges or the right to a trial. In effect, this meant that military leaders could suspend all individual rights.[20] Lincoln's justification was that as president he had the power to do what he thought necessary to preserve the nation. (We shall examine Lincoln's argument more closely in chapter 8, section 7.) Before and during the Second World War, Franklin Roosevelt followed the same line of reasoning. He secretly cooperated with Winston Churchill in the war against Germany two years before the Congress declared war. During this time, he lied to the American people to hide what he was doing.[21] Then, when the war was officially declared after the bombing of Pearl Harbor, he organized the removal from the West Coast of all Japanese Americans, who were put into "detention camps." Although there was no evidence that any of these American citizens were disloyal, Roosevelt justified his actions as a necessary precaution in the time of war.[22] Similarly, he thought that his secret maneuvering before the war was necessary, even though it was unconstitutional, in order to defend the country against the Nazi threat. Thus, Roosevelt followed

Machiavelli's precepts in using force and fraud to advance the interests of the state. It is not surprising therefore, that one of the best biographies of Roosevelt is subtitled *The Lion and the Fox*.[23]

We could easily think of many more examples, but the general point is clear enough: we sometimes permit our political leaders to break the law and violate individual rights for the sake of protecting the national interest. Even a nation founded on the high moral principles of the Declaration of Independence must allow rulers to use drastic expedients in time of emergency. Are we forced, then, to accept the Machiavellian maxim that immoral political actions are justified if they serve the interests of the state? Before we concede this point, let us review some of the major objections to Machiavelli's argument. At least four points might come to mind.

First, doesn't Machiavelli exaggerate the conflict between morality and expediency? He assumes that moral principles are so inflexible that politicians must often find it advantageous to violate them. But haven't we seen Thomas Aquinas explain that morality requires prudence in judging what should be done in particular circumstances? Cicero maintains, in *De officiis* (III, 18–19), that there can be no conflict between moral goodness and expediency because what is morally right is always expedient and what is expedient is always morally right. If a conflict arises, it is between the morally right and what *appears* expedient but in fact is not. Or expediency might conflict with what *appears* morally right but in fact is not. We are confused, Cicero suggests, when exceptional circumstances force us to do what we customarily consider morally wrong. Yet Cicero advises that rather than setting aside moral goodness in such cases, we should see that what is morally right changes according to the circumstances. Cicero illustrates this by observing that although killing a friend is usually a vicious crime, killing a tyrant — even if considered a friend — is noble. Thus, moral rectitude guided by prudence coincides with expediency.

It is surely true, however, that being immoral may be politically advantageous in the short run, and *that* is what Machiavelli stresses. But is it advantageous in the long run? A crucial point for Cicero's argument is that the most useful resource for human life is human cooperation, and the moral virtues are essential for securing such mutual aid (*De officiis* II, 9–18). For example, the virtues of keeping promises and telling the truth are advantageous because they secure social and political life. Relations among human beings depend on trust. Of course, it is sometimes expedient for political leaders to break their promises; but if fraud became the rule rather than the exception, the consequences for everyone would be disastrous. Indeed, the political chaos that Machiavelli deplored in his own day was largely the result of a lack of mutual confidence. It is often said that a successful politician must be a Machiavellian because "everyone does it." In fact, just the opposite is the case. A Machiavellian strategy is advantageous only as long as it is rarely practiced because its widespread adoption creates unremitting conflict.[24] (Compare the "prisoner's dilemma" game described in chapter 9, section 4 of this text.)

A second possible criticism of Machiavelli is that he emphasizes extreme cases in an unrealistic way. If by realism we mean relying on our ordinary experience of the usual course of things, then Machiavelli is not a realist because he draws his rules from the most unusual situations. Notice, for example, that in *The Prince* he is preoccupied with how new princes first come to power, which is far from the normal activities of daily political life. Political thinkers have always recognized that in times of war and revolution, when the very existence of a political community is in doubt, the normal rules of moral judgment may have to be modified. Much of what Machiavelli says can be found, for example, in Book Five of Aristotle's *Politics*, the section devoted to revolution. Like Machiavelli, Aristotle observes that revolutions occur either through force or through fraud (*Politics* 1304b8–9). Much of Machiavelli's advice for princes can be found in Aristotle's study of how tyrannies are preserved (*Politics* 1313a34–1315b39). What is only a small part of Aristotle's work completely dominates Machiavelli's writing. Once the Aristotelian ruler has provided for the physical security of the community, he can then turn his attention to the higher moral concerns of political life. But Machiavelli forces his ruler to imagine remote dangers and thus to worry about security to the exclusion of everything else.

This leads us to ponder a third possible defect in Machiavelli's teaching. If the Machiavellian leader must sacrifice everything to preserve the state, shouldn't he think about exactly what it is that makes the state worth preserving? Does he wish simply to secure the territorial boundaries of the state and the lives of the people? Surely not, because he may seek to change those boundaries, and may have to sacrifice the lives of some of the people for the greater good of the state. Is he perhaps concerned with preserving a certain way of life of the state? If so, that would imply a standard of moral worth by which one way of life might be judged better than another. We might want to argue, for example, that what makes the United States worth defending is its dedication to the principle of human rights; therefore, whatever our leaders do to protect the interests of the United States, they should never be willing to sacrifice that principle completely. But how far should we go in compromising our moral ideals for the sake of national security? We shall always have to agonize over that question. Would Machiavelli free us from such moral agony? Would that be beneficial?

As a final criticism of Machiavelli, we might argue that by denying the existence of moral dilemmas in politics, Machiavelli naively overlooks the reality of our common moral world. That we worry about the moral consequences of our political decisions is an inescapable fact of our political life. Machiavelli testifies to this fact when he advises the prince to hide his immorality with hypocrisy. If there were no generally accepted standards of morality, if they were merely arbitrary "names," as Machiavelli says, and if we saw no need for morality, hypocrisy would make no sense. That we argue about morality shows how difficult it is to judge moral claims. But that we understand moral arguments, that we agree on what counts as good moral reasoning, shows that we live in a common universe of moral discourse. And that those who act immorally have to try to justify their actions with moral reasoning indicates the stability of our moral sense.

The Machiavellian would warn, however, that we cannot introduce moral judgment into politics without promoting an imprudent moral idealism. Good political judgment should always be an exercise in prudence; and "prudence," as Machiavelli explains, "consists in knowing how to recognize the qualities of inconveniences and to pick the less bad as good" (*The Prince*, chapter 21, page 135). Those political leaders who cannot settle for the "less bad" create political disasters by seeking an unattainable moral perfection no matter what the costs.

But why can't we combine political prudence and moral judgment? We might think, for example, of political leaders like Abraham Lincoln who have striven for a prudent idealism in their political thinking. Because Lincoln revered the principle of equality of rights as stated in the Declaration of Independence, he thought that was the fundamental standard of moral judgment in American politics. But he saw absolute equality as an abstract goal toward which we must aim without ever attaining it fully because of the limitations of our circumstances. He thought, therefore, that there could be no *right* to hold slaves because slavery was simply *wrong*. Yet he also thought there was no practical way to abolish slavery immediately without disastrous consequences for the nation. Hence he argued that we ought to have worked for the ultimate extinction of slavery while accepting it in the short run as a necessary evil. Thus Lincoln tried to steer a middle course between those Southern leaders who saw no moral problem in slavery and those Northern abolitionists who wished to abolish slavery immediately even if it meant destroying the Union.[25] This might illustrate, therefore, how it is possible for a political leader to possess a realistic moral idealism.

Consider how Machiavelli might answer the objections we have raised. First, Machiavelli might observe that a wise prince will always strive to unite expediency and morality, but sometimes what is expedient for political reasons clashes with moral goodness. Although a prudent leader understands the importance of promise keeping (e.g., as a foundation of social and political life), it is acknowledged that in extreme cases breaking one's promises may be politically prudent.

To the charge that he gives too much weight to extreme situations, Machiavelli could reply that it is only under the pressure of severe circumstances that the foundations of political life come into view. In times of calm, we can avert our eyes from the underlying, harsh realities of politics.

And, surely, Machiavelli would want to reiterate that the fundamental reality of political life is the need for preserving the peace and unity of one's state. Of course, every state is held together by certain moral ideals that political leaders must respect. But aren't those moral ideals simply a means for pacifying human conflict and keeping the peace? In the *Discourses* (I, 2), Machiavelli describes how governments and the rule of law were established by human beings to protect themselves against the mutual injuries to which they were naturally inclined; and he concludes: "Such was the origin of justice."

Finally, Machiavelli might contend that rather than denying the reality of moral judgment, he sees it for what it is: a product of the "virtue" of the great religious founders who have imposed their forms on the matter of human consciousness. As he indicates by his praise of Moses in *The Prince* (chapter 6) and in his comments on religion in the *Discourses* (I, 10–12; II, 2, 5), Machiavelli thinks that the most influential founders are those who establish new religions, for they shape the entire way of life of a people. If we find Machiavelli's teaching too brutal, that may only show the effeminate softness of our Christian education (*Discourses* II, 2).

The tenderness and leniency instilled in us by our democratic Christian culture manifest themselves most clearly in our rejection of the Machiavellian teaching that political rule requires cruelty. But Machiavelli does distinguish between "cruelty well used" and "cruelty badly used." Does that suffice as a moral criterion for the political use of cruelty?

4. Does political order require "cruelty well used"?

A prince's cruelty is well used, Machiavelli explains, if it keeps his people "united and faithful" (chapter 17, page 100). Those rulers who show too much pity may actually increase the suffering of their people by allowing disorders to get out of control. On the other hand, cruelty is badly used if it is employed so recklessly and unpredictably that the people despise the prince. Properly used cruelty is indispensable to "good government" because there must be a pervasive fear of punishment among a people if they are to live in peace under the rule of law (chapter 7, pages 44–45). Machiavelli would seem to support the claim of the legal positivist that law is the command of the sovereign backed by threat. (Refer back to chapter 4, section 2.)

In the *Discourses*, Machiavelli explains that governments originate when people see that they must have laws to keep themselves from injuring one another (I, 2). But all political bodies tend to become corrupt as their citizens lose their original respect for law. To restore that respect, Machiavelli advises, there must be executions of lawbreakers to recall that fear of punishment upon which government was originally founded; and this should be done at least every ten years. Restoring that primitive fear of punishment is what Machiavelli calls "bringing the government back to its first principles" (III, 1). "In the beginning there was terror." And the successful prince must be a political terrorist.[26]

Machiavelli thinks the greatness of the Roman Republic was manifested in the extent of the executions of those who disobeyed the law. The most shocking executions were those held to punish armies in cases where it was not feasible to punish all the guilty individuals because of the large number involved (III, 49). According to the procedure of decimation, one soldier out of every ten was chosen by lot to be executed. Those who escaped would not commit other crimes for fear that next time the lot would fall to them.

A prince establishes and maintains his rule through violence. Indeed, from Machiavelli's point of view, all government is organized violence.

> The principal foundations which all states have, whether new, old, or mixed, are good laws and good arms. And because there cannot be good laws where there are not good arms, and where there are good arms there needs must be good laws, I shall omit the reasoning on laws and speak of arms (chapter 12, page 71).

Later in *The Prince*, he indicates the traits of character required for the political use of force:

> You ought to know, then, that there are two kinds of fighting:
> one with the laws, the other with force. The first one is proper
> to man; the second to the beasts; but because the first proves
> many times to be insufficient, one needs must resort to the
> second. Therefore it is necessary for a prince to know well how
> to use the beast and the man (chapter 18, page 107).

In particular, the prince must combine the ferocity of the lion and
the craftiness of the fox.

What should we say in response to this disturbing recommendation that a good ruler should become like a beast in employing force
and fraud? From Cicero's *De officiis* (I, 41; III, 69), we know that
it was traditional to advise princes to imitate the viciousness of the
lion and the cleverness of the fox, but Cicero warns against this.
Surely, he argues, it can never be expedient for a man to become
so mean that he is more like a beast than a human being (I, 41; III,
46–47, 69).[27] When rulers live by force and fraud, Cicero contends,
they break that natural social bond without which human life
becomes unbearable.

In contrast to Machiavelli (chapter 17), Cicero (*De officiis* II, 23)
advises that it is better to be loved than feared because fear creates
hate, and hate creates threats. A tyrant must always suffer when
hated by the people: either the tyrant is killed, or lives in continual
fear of being killed. "Whose life can be advantageous to himself,"
Cicero warns, "if it is a life that is his on the condition that the man
who takes it away will win the greatest gratitude and glory" (III, 85)?

We can settle disputes through discussion or through force, Cicero
observes (II, 34–35). We should prefer the former because it is
characteristic of human beings, whereas the latter is characteristic
of brutish animals. Even when the failure of discussion compels us
to resort to force, we must respect the "rights of war." We must
go to war only for the sake of restoring peace, and in victory we must
spare those who have fought in a civilized manner.

But hasn't Machiavelli anticipated the objections suggested by
Cicero? Isn't Machiavelli as aware as Cicero is of the dangers of
excessive brutality? His comments on the infamy of Agathocles
would indicate this. Also, it should be emphasized that a clever
prince relies more on fraud than on force. To the extent that he can
persuade his subjects to willingly accept his rule, he does not have
to depend solely on brute force. For new princes and new republics,
Machiavelli says in the *Discourses* (II, 13), fraud and cunning are
more important than force and fear in their rise to greatness.

Even in counseling the prince that it is better to be feared than
loved, Machiavelli admonishes him to avoid the hatred of the people
by not disturbing them in their private lives (chapter 17). Like

Cicero, Machiavelli urges the prince to secure his power by winning the goodwill of the people. In his chapter on conspiracies in the *Discourses* (III, 6), Machiavelli warns princes that the threat of conspiracies is unavoidable for princes who are hated by their subjects. Good rulers can be secure, but tyrants cannot because "they are in constant fear lest others are conspiring to inflict upon them the punishment which they are conscious of deserving" (III, 6).

Thus Machiavelli is careful to warn the prince about the dangerous consequences of going too far in terrorizing his subjects. Yet Machiavelli departs from the traditional view of Cicero and others by insisting that some use of cruelty is essential for political order. This becomes evident in times of war when acts of brutality become necessary means to the end of preserving the state.

But aren't there moral standards even in war? Cicero spoke of the "rights of war." Since ancient times, as part of the tradition of "natural law," there have always been "laws of war" prescribing which kinds of warfare are permissible and which are not. The Declaration of Independence refers to these international rules of justice when it speaks of the "acts and things which independent states may of right do." If states have rights, just as individual human beings do, there must be standards of justice to govern conflicts among states.

Machiavelli is preoccupied with war; his prince hardly thinks of anything else but the art of war (chapter 14, page 88). The harsh demands of war would seem to provide the clearest confirmation of Machiavellian realism. But if it is possible to accept some moral restraints even in war, then Machiavellianism is refuted. Because war presents us with the most difficult situations, we must conclude that if our moral principles apply to war, they apply everywhere.

In judging the morality of war, we must first ask, When is it just to go to war? Then we must ask, What are the just ways of fighting a war? To the first question, the most commonly accepted answer is that defensive wars are just while aggressive wars are unjust. In response to the second question, an elaborate code of international law has developed to determine what can and cannot be done in war. For example, we prohibit attacks on civilians and we require humane treatment of prisoners of war.[28]

These "laws of war" were used in 1945–1946, for instance, at the trial in Nuremberg of the German "war criminals." They were charged with "crimes against peace" in the "waging of a war of aggression" as well as "war crimes" in attacking civilians and mistreating prisoners of war.[29] Through this condemnation of the Nazi war leaders, we reaffirmed the reality of international principles of justice as a defense against the immorality manifested in the Nazi regime. Doesn't this show, contrary to what Machiavelli assumes, that even in war we *can* (and therefore *should*) adhere to some fundamental moral standards?

The Machiavellian might remind us that Machiavelli distinguishes the good uses of cruelty from the bad uses. So to the extent that the "laws of war" prohibit wanton or unnecessary brutality, Machiavelli would agree with such restraints. Nevertheless, he would deny that there can be any *absolute* prohibitions as to what can be done in war. For there is hardly any method of warfare that could not become justifiable in some situations as a means to military success.

Consider, for example, the prohibition of attacking civilians. We condemned the German war leaders for violating this provision of international law. But were we not hypocritical in ignoring the fact that Allied war leaders were just as guilty of this? In 1941, British leaders initiated a policy of "terror bombing" against German cities.[30] Bombing was aimed intentionally at residential neighborhoods for the purpose of killing as many civilians as possible. As a result, some three hundred thousand German civilians were killed. Of these, one hundred thousand died in a single attack against the city of Dresden in 1945. American leaders adopted the same policy in bombing Japanese cities, a policy that culminated in Harry Truman's decision to drop atomic bombs on Hiroshima and Nagasaki. The total number of civilians killed in Germany and Japan is estimated at over one million.

This set a pattern for subsequent wars. The wars in Korea and in Vietnam resulted in huge numbers of civilian deaths because of the American bombing of villages. Even more frightful possibilities arose from the American policy of nuclear deterrence through a "balance of terror."[31] During the cold war, American leaders were prepared to respond to any major aggression by the Soviet Union— such as an invasion of Western Europe—by launching a nuclear attack against cities in Russia that would kill tens of millions of civilians. Some critics regarded this policy as even more morally reprehensible than the policies of the Nazi war leaders.

In all these cases, the justification for terrorizing civilians has been that such brutal measures are a necessary means of achieving victory. British leaders began the terror bombing of Germany when the British were desperate to defend European civilization against the horrors of Nazism. Truman used the atomic bomb against Japan to avoid the high casualties that would have arisen from an actual physical invasion. American bombing tactics in Korea and Vietnam were defended as unavoidable in fighting guerrilla wars. And threatening nuclear strikes against Russian cities was said to be the only effective means of defending the West against Communist aggression. Aren't these all Machiavellian justifications in that they assume there are no moral limits to cruelty in war as long as the cruelty is a necessary means to victory?

What are the alternatives? Is it possible to acknowledge the harsh necessities of war while respecting the demands of morality? Some people would argue that because all war is immoral, morality dictates pacifism. Others would contend that wars to resist aggression are just as long as the moral rules of war (such as protecting civilians) are never violated, even when violations seem to be necessary for victory.[32] Still others would concede that although there are moral rules of law, in some cases of extreme emergency, such as the Nazi threat in 1941, we might have to set aside ordinary moral standards as dictated by military necessity. Most of us seem to have adopted this last position: we judge the morality of wars, but we accept immorality in extreme cases. Yet don't we have to feel guilty in taking this position? Bombing civilians is killing the innocent, which is murder. Sometimes this kind of murder may be necessary. But even necessary murder is still murder, and therefore we must condemn it. This explains why the British after the war honored their fighter pilots with monuments, but not their bomber pilots. What the bomber pilots had done was necessary but dishonorable.[33]

We must wonder, however, about who should bear the guilt for such deeds. Surely, the shame should be felt not only by those who carry out the policy, but also by those who made the decision in the first place. Moreover, in a popular government, we would expect that such decisions should not be left to the discretion of political leaders because all the citizens should share the responsibility. Some political leaders, of course, may think that common people are too soft because of their moralism to deal properly with the brutal realities of war. Perhaps Machiavelli encourages that sort of thinking by speaking of the prince as ruling on his own with little consultation with his subjects. Indeed, Machiavellian political thought might seem contrary to any form of popular government.

5. Does Machiavellianism subvert popular government?

Machiavelli is sometimes said to be the founder of modern political thought. But the teachings of *The Prince* would seem to contradict the principles of the modern democratic state. We have seen in the Declaration of Independence the goal of limited government founded on the consent of the people and devoted to securing individual rights. In contrast, Machiavelli in *The Prince* recognizes few limits to the prince's power, never mentions individual rights, and shows little respect for popular consent. Yet it should be said in Machiavelli's defense that in the *Discourses* he endorses republican government. Even in *The Prince*, he says some things favorable to popular government.

Machiavelli advises his prince to distinguish the desires of the "people" (*populo*) and the desires of the "great" (*grandi*): "The people desire not to be commanded or oppressed by the great, and the great desire to command and to oppress the people" (chapter 17, pages 101–2; chapter 19, page 111; chapter 21, page 135). The "great" are more difficult to satisfy because they are the politically ambitious few who would deprive the prince of his power if they could (chapter 9, pages 58–59).

The prince must respect the desires of his people if he is to protect himself against conspirators who would plot to overthrow him.

> A prince ought to take little account of conspirators when he has the goodwill of the people; but when they are his enemies and bear him hatred, he ought to fear everything and everyone. And well-ordered states and wise princes have with all diligence thought of not making the great desperate, and of satisfying the people and keeping them content. (chapter 19, page 113).

Doesn't this resemble Aristotle's advice for tyrants in the *Politics*, which we considered in chapter 2 (section 10)? Like Aristotle, Machiavelli counsels his prince to use his power for the public good in order to secure the goodwill of the people. This is even clearer in the *Discourses*, where Machiavelli advises the prince to please the people. Because the people "only care to live in security," they

> are easily satisfied by institutions and laws that confirm at the same time the general security of the people and the power of the prince. When a prince does this, and the people see that by no chance he infringes the laws, they will in a very little while be content, and live in tranquility. (*Discourses* I, 16)

A prince who would follow this advice would have to accept the rule of law as a limit on his otherwise absolute power.

Moreover, Machiavelli shows in the *Discourses* a preference for republics as superior to principalities. Whether one or the other form of government is best depends on the circumstances (I, 55). But generally republics are more enduring than principalities because the diversity of the characters of the citizens gives a republic greater flexibility in responding to changing circumstances than is possible for a prince (III, 9). Also, republican cities achieve more greatness than tyrannies because republics promote the general good, whereas tyrants secure only their own private interests (II, 2). A virtuous prince is important for founding a new state or reforming an established state, but the virtuous people are necessary for maintaining a state (I, 9, 53).

The most stable form of republican government, Machiavelli explains in the *Discourses*, is a mixed regime that arises from a balance of forces among three competing interests—the prince, the people, and the nobles. "When there is combined under the same constitution a prince, a nobility, and the power of the people, then these powers will watch and keep each other reciprocally in check" (I, 2). We might see here the idea of separation of powers with checks and balances that was later expounded by Locke, a scheme that influenced the thinking of the American founders.

Still, it could be argued that Machiavelli cannot be considered a friend of popular government because he lacks confidence in the ability of ordinary people to govern themselves. Believing that most human beings are "ungrateful, fickle, hypocrites and dissemblers, evaders of dangers, lovers of gain," Machiavelli concludes that it is better for political rulers to be feared than loved by their subjects (*The Prince*, chapter 18, page 101). In the *Discourses*, he declares: "Whoever desires to found a state and give it laws, must start with assuming that all men are bad and ever ready to display their vicious nature, whenever they may find occasion for it" (I, 3). Considering this belief in the natural viciousness of most human beings, it is not surprising that Machiavelli warns that no republic can dispense completely with princely leadership. This is especially true in times of emergency when a republic should be ruled by a single dictator (I, 34).

But we should note that many of the modern proponents of popular government have shared Machiavelli's pessimistic assessment of human nature. James Madison, for example, in his famous *Federalist* essay Number 51, warned that in establishing a government we have to take into account the selfish nature of human beings. "If men were angels," he explained, "no government would be necessary." And in essay Number 10, Madison argued that the selfish passions and interests of human beings—particularly their greed for accumulating property—make a pure democracy too turbulent because of the factional conflicts in the community. It is better to have a representative democracy in which the representatives can "refine and enlarge the public views."[34] Thus Madison seemed to agree with Alexander Hamilton, who echoed Machiavelli when he wrote in 1775 that "in contriving any system of government . . . *every man* ought to be supposed a *knave*; and to have no other end in all his actions but private interest.''[35] Throughout *The Federalist* and other writings of the American founders, one sees the Machiavellian image of human-kind as always desiring more than they have: "Nature has created men so that they desire everything, but are unable to attain it; desire being thus always greater than the faculty of acquiring, discontent with what they have and dissatisfaction with themselves result from it" (*Discourses* I, 37).

Perhaps this exaggerates the extent to which the American founders agreed with Machiavelli. Although they were realistic in their assessment of human nature, they often affirmed that republican government required more public-spirited virtue in the citizens than any other form of government. When human beings are thoroughly corrupt in their selfishness, they are incapable of self-government, and only a despot can prevent them from falling into disorder. According to Madison in *Federalist* Number 55:

> As there is a degree of depravity in mankind which requires a certain degree of circumspection and distrust, so there are other qualities in human nature which justify a certain portion of esteem and confidence. Republican government presupposes the existence of these qualities in a higher degree than any other form.[36]

Even Machiavelli concedes that republican government flourishes only when the citizens are willing to some extent to sacrifice their private interests for the common good (see *Discourses* I, 17–18, 58).

No matter how virtuous the citizens might be, Machiavelli would still insist that no republic can last without something like the Roman institution of dictatorship. In times of emergency in Rome, when the preservation of the Roman Republic might be threatened, someone could be appointed as a dictator to do whatever was necessary to protect the country (*Discourses* I, 34). Appointed only for a limited term, the dictator was prohibited from altering the constitutional arrangement of powers. Machiavelli thinks such legalized dictatorship is unavoidable in those cases where speed and flexibility of decision are needed. Otherwise, popular leaders would have to seize power illegally for the public good.

But is it wise for a republican government to allow anyone to have dictatorial powers? According to Machiavelli, the Roman dictator had the power "to do whatever he deemed proper without consulta-tion, and to inflict punishment upon any one without appeal" (I, 34). To give any person such power, even in times of emergency, creates a threat to individual liberty and popular self-government.

Yet is there any good alternative? In *Federalist* Number 70, Hamilton argued that the president should take the place of the Roman dictator in the American Republic. Despite the dangers, Hamilton explained, a strong executive is essential to good government.[37] Haven't American presidents in times of war become almost Machiavellian dictators in leading the country through emergencies? We shall look at this problem more carefully when we turn to John Locke's account of executive prerogative in chapter 8, section 7.

In any case, it is hard to accept Machiavelli as a trustworthy teacher of the principles of popular government because he seemed quite willing to suppress his sympathies for republican government in order to win a position in the government of the Medici. We must even wonder whether Machiavelli saw himself as a political philosopher or whether he considered his political writing only a way to win some rewards from the politically powerful.

6. Does Machiavelli elevate political power over political wisdom?

To put the question more bluntly, does Machiavelli display his political knowledge only for the purpose of selling out to the first powerful ruler willing to take him in as a toady? Consider the "Epistle Dedicatory" of *The Prince*, in which Machiavelli offers his books as a present to Lorenzo de' Medici and expresses the hope that Lorenzo will take notice of Machiavelli's misfortune in being expelled from Florentine politics. He also concludes *The Prince* by flattering Lorenzo with the declaration that the Medici have been chosen by God to save Italy from foreign invaders. Ever since Plato, political philosophers have sought to unite wisdom and power so that reason could rule in human affairs. But Machiavelli would seem to have perverted this noble project by suggesting that the wise should become the servants of the powerful.

We should not be too quick, however, to accept such an unfavorable interpretation of Machiavelli's work. In various ways, he shows his disdain for those who happen to have political power but are too ignorant to use their power properly. Those who have the power to govern but not the knowledge of how to govern are inferior, Machiavelli says, to those who have the knowledge but not the power (*Discourses*, "Epistle Dedicatory"). And in the last chapter of *The Prince*, he implies that the Medici are not smart enough to seize the great political opportunities before them. The parallels between chapter 6 and chapter 26 of *The Prince* suggest that Machiavelli sees the possibility for someone to become another Moses by establishing a new order for the modern world as influential as that founded by Moses. But this opportunity may be lost owing to "the weakness of the heads."

> In Italy one does not lack matter for introducing every form; here there is great virtue in the members, were it not that she lacks heads. . . . It all proceeds from the weakness of the heads; for those who know are not obeyed, and with everyone seeming to know, there has been no one until now who knew how to raise himself, through virtue and fortune, so that the others cede to him. (chapter 26, page 153).

Of whom is Machiavelli thinking when he says, "those who know are not obeyed"? In the preceding paragraph, he says that great things can now be done "provided that one takes as a target, those orders which I have proposed" (page 152). Does Machiavelli see himself as the new Moses?

If so, then Machiavelli would be an unarmed prophet. He has no political power of his own. He commands no armies. Could he believe that his new ideas have sufficient power in themselves to transform the political life of the modern world? In the introduction to the *Discourses*, he claims to have discovered new political principles never seen by anyone else. Conceding that he may not be able to carry out his principles (like Moses?), he indicates that others will come after him to put his teachings into practice. The ideas of thinkers who do not rule can become powerful through their influence on those who do rule. If this is what Machiavelli has in mind, then he cannot be accused of degrading political philosophy by making it a mere tool of the powerful. Rather, we might say that just as Plato and Aristotle were the founders of premodern political thought, so was Machiavelli the founder of modern political thought. Like Plato and Aristotle, Machiavelli influenced political practice by changing the way political leaders thought about what they did.

How accurate is it to speak of Machiavelli as the founder of modern political philosophy? We can see in his writings many of the dominant themes of modern thought: political life as artificial rather than natural, government as coercive force, self-interest as the strongest human motive, and generally a realistic lowering of political standards from what *ought* to be to what *is*. On the other hand, some of the most prominent features of later political thought do not appear clearly in Machiavelli's work. One point in particular is the concern for turning the study of politics into a science. Because of the achievements of the great natural scientists of the sixteenth and seventeenth centuries, modern political philosophers (like Hobbes) sought to apply the new methods of science to political studies: political thought was to be replaced by political science. We must wonder, then, whether there is any connection between Machiavellianism and the modern scientific method. In fact, one commentator has interpreted Machiavelli's teaching as the first "science of power" based on applying the scientific method to politics.[38] So, with that in mind, we turn to one of the greatest advocates of that new method of thought—Descartes.

Notes

1. For a survey of the humanist background of Machiavelli's work, see Quentin Skinner, *The Foundations of Modern Political Thought*, vol. 1: *The Renaissance* (Cambridge: Cambridge University Press, 1978). For a briefer version of this work, see Skinner, *Machiavelli* (New York: Hill & Wang, 1981). On the history of the response to Machiavelli, see Friedrich Meinecke, *Machiavellianism: The Doctrine of "Raison d'Etat" and Its Place in Modern History*, trans. Douglas Scott (New Haven: Yale University Press, 1957); Felix Raab, *The English Face of Machiavelli: A Changing Interpretation, 1500–1700* (London: Routledge & Kegan Paul, 1964); and J. G. A. Pocock, *The Machiavellian Moment: Florentine Political Thought and the Atlantic Republican Tradition* (Princeton: Princeton University Press, 1975). The best introduction to the Italian Renaissance is Jacob Burckhardt's classic, *The Civilization of the Renaissance in Italy* (New York: Random House, Modern Library, 1954).
2. For an account of the torture, see Sebastian de Grazia, *Machiavelli in Hell* (Princeton: Princeton University Press, 1989), 32–39.
3. Here and elsewhere I quote from the translation of *The Prince* by Leo Paul de Alvarez (Prospect Heights, IL: Waveland Press, 1989). All page references are to this edition. This is the most useful translation because it is the most literal.
4. In a letter written while he was working on *The Prince*, Machiavelli describes his evening studies:

   > When evening comes, I return to my home, and I go into my study; and on the threshold, I take off my everyday clothes, which are covered with mud and mire, and I put on regal and curial robes; and dressed in a more appropriate manner I enter into the ancient courts of ancient men and am welcomed by them kindly, and there I taste the food that alone is mine, and for which I was born; and there I am not ashamed to speak to them, to ask them the reasons for their actions; and they, in their humanity, answer me; and for four hours I feel no boredom, I dismiss every affliction, I no longer fear poverty nor do I tremble at the thought of death: I become completely part of them. (Letter to Francesco Vettori, December 10, 1513, in Peter Bondanella and Mark Musa, eds., *The Portable Machiavelli* [New York: Penguin Books, 1979], 69).

5. Skinner, *Machiavelli*, 37.

6. Friedrich Nietzsche, *The Will to Power*, sec. 749.

7. Max Lerner, "Introduction," in Niccolò Machiavelli, *The Prince and the Discourses* (New York: Random House, Modern Library, 1940), xxv, xliii.

8. Leo Strauss, *Thoughts on Machiavelli* (Glencoe, IL: Free Press, 1958), 13. Some readers have suspected that the esoteric teaching of Strauss's book is neither as patriotic nor as moralistic as this remark suggests. See Shadia B. Drury, *The Political Ideas of Leo Strauss* (New York: St. Martin's Press, 1988), chap. 6.

9. According to the Bible, Moses was ruthless in war. One example would be his brutal slaughter of the Midianites (Numbers 31: 1–20). There is also some evidence for Machiavelli's observation: "Whoever reads the Bible attentively will find that Moses, for the purpose of insuring the observance of his laws and institutions, was obliged to have a great many persons put to death who opposed his designs under the instigation of no other feelings than those of envy and jealousy" (*Discourses*, III, 30). On the political leadership of Moses, see Sigmund Freud, *Moses and Monotheism*, trans. Katherine Jones (New York: Random House, Vintage Books, 1967); Aaron Wildavsky, *The Nursing Father: Moses as Political Leader* (Tuscaloosa: University of Alabama Press, 1984); and Michael Walzer, *Exodus and Revolution* (New York: Basic Books, 1985).

10. According to Friedrich Nietzsche, "the paths to power" include the ability "to introduce a new virtue under the name of an old one," as was done by the founders of Biblical religion who promoted "the slave revolt in morality" by using the word "good" for conduct that had previously been called "bad" (*The Will to Power*, trans. Walter Kaufmann [New York: Random House, 1967], sec. 310; *The Genealogy of Morals*, in *The Basic Writings of Nietzsche*, trans. Walter Kaufmann [New York: The Modern Library, 1968], 472–75; *The Gay Science*, trans. Walter Kaufmann [New York: Vintage Books, 1974], sec. 353).

11. Borgia's murder of his cruel henchman can be compared with Hitler's liquidation of Ernst Röhm and other leaders of the Brownshirts in the "night of the long knives." See Winston S. Churchill, *The Gathering Storm*, vol. 1 of *The Second World War* (Boston: Houghton Mifflin, 1948), 96–102; and Alan Bullock, *Hitler and Stalin: Parallel Lives* (New York: Alfred A. Knopf, 1992), 336–44.

12. Here and elsewhere I quote from the translation of the *Discourses* by Christian E. Detmold, reprinted in Machiavelli, *The Prince and the Discourses*. All page references are to this edition.

13. Richard Neustadt, *Presidential Power*, 2nd ed. (New York: John Wiley, 1976), 229–30. Huey Long, prior to his assassination in 1935, was the chief Machiavellian rival to Franklin Roosevelt. "There is no evidence that Huey had ever read the great Florentine. But he often employed techniques recommended by Machiavelli, knowing them, it would seem, by some kind of instinct" (T. Harry Williams, *Huey Long* [New

York: Random House, Vintage, 1981], 416). Believing that a politician may have to do some evil to achieve some good, Huey was praised by those who saw only his good ends and condemned by those who saw only his evil means. In this respect, he resembled Willie Stark in Robert Penn Warren's *All the King's Men* (New York: Harcourt, Brace & World, 1946).

14. Alexander Hamilton, James Madison, and John Jay, *The Federalist*, ed. Edward Mead Earle (New York: Random House, Modern Library, n.d.), No. 72, p. 470. Compare Charles de Gaulle's comments on the need for men of "grandeur" in *The Edge of the Sword*, trans. Gerald Hopkins (New York: Criterion Books, 1960), 63–64.

15. On the connections between Machiavelli and Cicero, see Robert Denoon Cumming, *Human Nature and History*, 2 vols. (Chicago: University of Chicago Press, 1969), 2: 3–59.

16. See de Alvarez's edition of *The Prince*, XXV, n. 9.

17. On "the state as a work of art," see Burckhardt, *The Civilization of the Renaissance in Italy*, 3–99. On Leonardo da Vinci's "art of war," see Giancarlo Maiorino, *Leonardo da Vinci: The Daedalian Mythmaker* (University Park: Pennsylvania State University Press, 1992), chap. 6. Does the art of opera, which was invented in the Italian Renaissance, express the proud amorality and impulsive willfulness of Machiavellianism? See George Anastaplo, *The Artist as Thinker* (Athens: Ohio University Press, 1983), 448–49; John Bokina, "Deity, Beast, and Tyrant: Images of the Prince in the Operas of Monteverdi," *International Political Science Review* 12 (1991): 48–66; Peter Conrad, *A Song of Love and Death: The Meaning of Opera* (New York: Poseidon Press, 1987), 11–54; Herbert Lindenberger, *Opera, The Extravagant Art* (Chicago: University of Chicago Press, 1984), 280–85; and Lief H. Carter, "*Die Meistersinger von Nurnberg* and the United States Supreme Court," *Polity* 18 (Winter 1985): 272–94.

18. Max Weber, "Politics as a Vocation," in H. H. Gerth and C. Wright Mills, eds. and trans., *From Max Weber: Essays in Sociology* (New York: Oxford University Press, 1946), 78, 82. Weber's Machiavellian (and Nietzschean) celebration of heroic and "charismatic" leadership manifests a tradition in German thought that may explain the success of Hitler. See Wolfgang J. Mommsen, *Max Weber and German Politics, 1890–1920* (Chicago: University of Chicago Press, 1984), 390–447; and Bullock, *Hitler and Stalin*, 351–57, 364–70. Harvey Mansfield, Jr., has argued that the very idea of the "executive" power is a uniquely modern political phenomenon that manifests the inherent Machiavellianism of modern politics (*Taming the Prince: The Ambivalence of Modern Executive Power* [New York: Free Press, 1989]). On the importance of war in the evolution of the state, see Robert L. Carneiro, "A Theory of the Origin of the State," *Science* 169 (1970): 733–38; and Peter A. Corning, *The Synergism Hypothesis* (New York: McGraw-Hill, 1983), 368–75.

19. L. Arthur Burd, "Introduction" to *Il Principe di Niccolò Machiavelli*,

ed. L. Arthur Burd (Oxford: Oxford University Press, 1891), xix–xx.

20. See Abraham Lincoln, Message to Congress, 4 July 1861, in *The Collected Works of Abraham Lincoln*, ed. Roy P. Basler, 9 vols. (New Brunswick: Rutgers University Press, 1953–1955), 4: 421–41.

21. See William Stevenson, *A Man Called Intrepid: The Secret War* (New York: Harcourt Brace Jovanovich, 1976).

22. The issues were examined by the Supreme Court in *United States v. Korematsu*, 323 U.S. 214 (1944).

23. James MacGregor Burns, *Roosevelt: The Lion and the Fox* (New York: Harcourt, Brace, 1956).

24. See Sissela Bok, *Lying: Moral Choice in Public and Private Life* (New York: Pantheon, 1978), chaps. 2, 10. Consider the description of Joseph Stalin by Roy A. Medvedev: "Stalin was not simply crafty; he was a man of unusual hypocrisy. He achieved a great deal by his ability to put on any mask." *Let History Judge* (New York: Alfred A. Knopf, 1972), 331. On the importance of deception in international politics, see Robert Jervis, *The Logic of Images in International Politics* (Princeton: Princeton University Press, 1970).

25. See Paul Angle, ed., *Created Equal? The Complete Lincoln-Douglas Debates of 1858* (Chicago: University of Chicago Press, 1958), 41–42, 303–4, 332–33. On Lincoln's leadership of the "moderates" in the Republican Party, see Eric Foner, *Free Soil, Free Labor, Free Men: The Ideology of the Republican Party before the Civil War* (London: Oxford University Press, 1970), chap. 6.

26. "Machiavelli's return to the beginning means return to the terror inherent in man's situation, to man's essential unprotectedness. In the beginning there was terror. In the beginning men were good, i.e., they were willing to obey because they were afraid and easily frightened. The primacy of Love must be replaced by the primacy of Terror if republics are to be established in accordance with nature and on the basis of knowledge of nature" (Strauss, *Thoughts on Machiavelli*, 167).

27. In his *Chimpanzee Politics: Power & Sex Among Apes* (New York: Harper & Row, 1982), Frans de Waal finds Machiavelli's *Prince* to be the best guide for studying chimpanzee political life; and he suggests that our pursuit of political dominance over others may have been inherited from our primate ancestors. On the pleasure of power as part of our biological nature, see Lionel Tiger, *The Pursuit of Pleasure* (Boston: Little, Brown, 1992), chap. 7. For the argument that the intergroup aggression of chimpanzees is similar to that of human beings, see Jane Goodall, *The Chimpanzees of Gombe* (Cambridge: Harvard University Press, 1986), chap. 17; Goodall, *Through a Window: My Thirty Years with the Chimpanzees of Gombe* (Boston: Houghton Mifflin, 1990), 98–111, 208–10; and Joseph H. Manson and Richard W. Wrangham, "Intergroup Aggression in Chimpanzees and Humans," *Current Anthropology* 32 (1991): 369–90.

28. See Adam Roberts and Richard Guelff, eds., *Documents on the Laws of War* (Oxford: Clarendon Press, 1982). On "just war" reasoning, see

Paul Ramsey, *The Just War* (New York: Scribners, 1968); Michael Walzer, *Just and Unjust Wars* (New York: Basic Books, 1977); James T. Johnson, *Just War Tradition and the Restraint of War* (Princeton: Princeton University Press, 1982); William V. O'Brien, *The Conduct of Just and Limited War* (New York: Praeger, 1981); and James T. Johnson, *Can Modern War Be Just?* (New Haven: Yale University Press, 1984).

29. For extracts from the final judgment, see Roberts and Guelff, *Documents*, 155–56.
30. See Walzer, *Just and Unjust Wars*, 255–63. The morality of the terror bombing of Germany and Japan was debated during the war. See J.M. Spaight, *Bombing Vindicated* (London: Geoffrey Bles, 1944); and Barrie Paskins and Michael Dockrill, *The Ethics of War* (Minneapolis: University of Minnesota Press, 1979), 1–57.
31. See Walzer, *Just and Unjust Wars*, 269–83. See also, Amos A. Jordan and William J. Taylor, Jr., *American National Security: Policy and Process* (Baltimore: Johns Hopkins University Press, 1981), 221–47. On the decision to drop the atomic bomb, see Henry L. Stimson and McGeorge Bundy, *On Active Service in Peace and War* (New York: Harper & Brothers, 1948), 612–55; and Robert C. Batchelder, *The Irreversible Decision* (New York: Macmillan, 1965).
32. See Elizabeth Anscombe, "War and Murder," in Richard A. Wasserstrom, ed., *War and Morality* (Belmont, CA: Wadsworth, 1970), 42–53.
33. See Walzer, *Just and Unjust Wars*, 323–27. William Shakespeare's *Henry V* forces us to wonder whether even a Christian prince might sometimes have to violate the restraints of just war. See Walzer, op. cit., 16–20; John Alvis, "A Little Touch of the Night in Harry: The Career of Henry Monmouth," in John Alvis and Thomas G. West, eds., *Shakespeare as Political Thinker* (Durham: Carolina Academic Press, 1981), 95–125; and Marlo Lewis, "On War and Legitimacy in Shakespeare's *Henry V*," in Harry V. Jaffa, ed., *Statesmanship: Essays in Honor of Sir Winston Churchill* (Durham: Carolina Academic Press, 1981), 41–61. On Henry's conduct at the battle of Agincourt, see John Keegan, *The Face of Battle* (New York: Penguin Books, 1976), 78–116.
34. *Federalist*, No. 10, pp. 58–59.
35. Alexander Hamilton, "The Farmer Refuted," *The Papers of Alexander Hamilton*, ed. Harold C. Syrett, 22 vols. (New York: Columbia University Press, 1961), 1: 95.
36. *Federalist*, No. 55, p. 365. One of the fundamental debates among social scientists today is between those who think human social behavior is motivated primarily by self-interest and those who think there are powerful public-spirited motives as well. See Jane J. Mansbridge, ed., *Beyond Self-Interest* (Chicago: University of Chicago Press, 1990). For the argument that natural selection might have favored the evolution of moral sentiments to sustain social cooperation, see Charles Darwin, *The Descent of Man, and Selection in Relation to Sex*, 2 vols. (London:

J. Murray, 1871), 1: 70–106; Robert Axelrod, *The Evolution of Cooperation* (New York: Basic Books, 1984); and Robert Frank, *Passions within Reason* (New York: Norton, 1988).

37. *Federalist*, No. 70, pp. 454–55.

38. James Burnham, *The Machiavellians—Defenders of Freedom* (New York: John Day, 1943), 29–30. See also Leslie J. Walker, *The Discourses of Niccolò Machiavelli*, 2 vols. (New Haven: Yale University Press, 1950), 1: 80–99.

To determine Machiavelli's ultimate motive for writing, we might compare him to Ligurio in Machiavelli's comic play, *Mandragola*, trans. Mera J. Flaumenhaft (Prospect Heights, IL: Waveland Press, 1981), 7–12, 18, 29, 35–36, 38, 47–48. In *The Prince* (chap. 18), Machiavelli says that ancient writers "covertly taught" certain harsh truths about politics. For evidence of a covert conspiracy in Machiavelli's writing, see *Discourses*, Letter of Dedication; I, Preface, 9, 58; II, Preface, 5, 10, 16, 33; III, 6, 27, 30–31, 35, 43, 46.

Chapter

6

Liberal Rationalism
Descartes's *Discourse on Method*

```
┌─────────────────────────────────────────────────────────────┐
│                                                               │
│                      Key Readings                             │
│                                                               │
│   Discourse on Method in its entirety.                        │
│                                                               │
└─────────────────────────────────────────────────────────────┘
```

René Descartes (1596–1650) lived at a time when traditional sources of authority were being challenged by new ways of thinking. During the Middle Ages, the Catholic church had become the highest cultural institution in Europe, not only in religious matters, but also in matters of philosophy and politics. Then, beginning early in the sixteenth century, the Protestant Reformation offered an alternative to the religious authority of the Catholic church. The religious disagreements between Protestants and Catholics led to political conflicts, which in turn gave rise to religious wars. At the same time, the church's authority over intellectual questions was threatened by new ideas in science. In the early 1500s, Nicolaus Copernicus rejected traditional thinking in astronomy by arguing that the earth and the other planets rotated around the sun. At first the church authorities were receptive to this denial that the earth was the center of the universe; but in the early 1600s, they were less tolerant of another version of Copernicus's system offered by Galileo. In 1632, Galileo published his *Dialogue on the Two Chief*

Systems of the World. The following year, the church declared him a heretic and forced him to renounce his ideas. Descartes was shocked by this because he was preparing for publication a book of his own developing scientific theories similar to Galileo's.

Like Socrates, Descartes found that he risked public condemnation by pursuing knowledge contrary to the authoritative opinions of his society. But unlike Socrates, Descartes thought that he had a scientific method by which he could discover absolute knowledge. His *Discourse on Method*, published in 1637, described his new method, but without openly espousing the ideas that might have invited persecution. He was well qualified for formulating a scientific method. The great wealth inherited from his family had allowed him to have the best education. He became interested in the latest scientific and mathematical thinking, and he was responsible for one of the greatest developments in the history of mathematics — the invention of coordinate geometry. This new kind of mathematics united algebra and geometry, forming a powerful tool for applying mathematics to the physical world.[1] Descartes saw in this mathematical procedure a method of reasoning applicable to all fields of knowledge. For the first time, he believed, human beings could achieve in all of their thinking the rigor, clarity, and certainty of mathematical demonstration.

Although Descartes is not usually considered a political philosopher, the political implications of his intellectual project have been immense. For if the Cartesian method is the only way to genuine knowledge, then traditional political philosophy has to be dismissed as nonsense if it cannot conform to the logical criteria of modern science and mathematics. In fact, many modern social scientists have argued that political philosophy should be replaced by scientific methodology. We can see the fundamental assumptions of that argument by examining the *Discourse on Method*.

1. Would the scientific method of Descartes lead us to a free and rational society?

If Descartes can show us how to achieve absolute certitude in our political reasoning, shouldn't we welcome that as an escape from the endless disputes of the philosophers? Beginning with Socrates, philosophers have argued about the most fundamental questions without ever finding any final answers to which everyone can agree. We might condemn them, therefore, for subverting our confidence in common political opinions without providing us with any solid principles to take their place. All the political philosophers we have studied so far sought to put political life under the rule of reason; but if that means founding politics on truths that are *really* self-evident, then they all failed. Descartes is the first philosopher we have seen in this book to take seriously the claim that genuine knowledge requires reasoning logically from self-evident principles.

Descartes initiated a new conception of rationality that has permeated both modern philosophy and modern politics. He was the first thinker to espouse what could be called liberal rationalism. One scholar has explained this intellectual position as founded on the following eleven major tenets:

1. The assumptions and methods of the previously dominant Aristotelian-Scholastic tradition are mistaken and must be fundamentally revised or supplanted before genuine "natural philosophy" can be possible.

2. The human understanding, guided by the "natural light" of reason, can be and should be autonomous. Moreover, it constitutes the norm and the means by reference to which all else is to be measured.

3. It is possible and necessary to begin the search for knowledge with a clean slate.

4. It is possible and necessary to base knowledge claims on a clear and distinct, indubitable, self-evident foundation.

5. This foundation is to be composed of simple, unambiguous ideas or perceptions.

6. The appropriate formal standards for all human knowledge are those of the mathematical modes of inquiry.

7. The key to the progress of human knowledge is the development and pursuit of explicit rules of method.

8. The entire body of valid human knowledge is a unity, both in method and in substance.

9. Therefore, human knowledge may be made almost wholly accessible to all men, provided only that they not be abnormally defective in their basic faculties.

10. Genuine knowledge is in some sense certain, "verifiable," and capable of being made wholly explicit.

11. Knowledge is power, and the increase of knowledge therefore holds the key to human progress.[2]

Although we shall have to think more about the meaning of these claims, we can see immediately how they might support a "liberal" regime, in the sense of a society devoted to individual freedom and rationality. Human beings are to be liberated from the traditional authority of kings and priests so that all people can live by the light of their own reason. While all people are equal in their natural capacity for understanding the simple truths of reality, they need the methods of modern mathematics and science to free their minds from the darkness of traditional prejudices. Furthermore, the power of this new knowledge will allow human beings to control nature for the benefit of all, thus allowing humankind to progress farther and faster than was ever possible previously.

Plato thought that most human beings, like people chained in a cave, would always be incapable of rational enlightenment because most would be bound by their unexamined opinions. Only a few philosophic individuals could leave the cave to see the truths that are only dimly reflected in common opinions. But doesn't Descartes offer to free all human beings from Plato's cave by giving them a method by which each person can discover the truth? And isn't that necessary if we are to achieve a free and rational society in which the truths of politics are self-evident to all?

On the other hand, critics of Descartes's liberal rationalism can point to some possible problems. It is questionable whether Descartes's method is an adequate standard for all genuine knowledge. Furthermore, the political consequences of Cartesian rationalism might in the long run promote tyranny rather than liberalism. Two forms of tyranny are possible. We could call one form *technocratic* tyranny and the other *nihilistic* tyranny.[3] Technocratic tyranny arises if it happens that the Cartesian method can be understood and applied only by a scientific elite, a small group of technical experts who think themselves entitled to rule over the rest of humankind. Nihilistic tyranny arises if it turns out that the Cartesian method provides no rational standards for moral values, and therefore political rule becomes simply the rule of the stronger over the weaker. We must examine each of these criticisms of Cartesian rationalism.

2. Is the Cartesian account of reason correct?

We should begin by summarizing the six parts of the *Discourse on Method*. To prepare the reader for his new method in Part Two, Descartes explains in Part One why he rejected all traditional thinking. He describes his education in the traditional disciplines of the liberal arts. He learned much, and he was especially pleased with mathematics "because of the certitude and the evidence of its proofs" (I, 10).[4] But he was disappointed that his education did not give him a firm grasp of the truth. He had sought "a clear and assured knowledge of everything that is useful to life," but his education could not give him that. "I found myself embarrassed with so many doubts and errors that it seemed to me that trying to instruct myself had no profit except that I had discovered more and more my ignorance" (I, 6). He then traveled widely to study the practical conduct of people. But, again, he found no reliable knowledge. "It is true that, while I only considered the moral customs of other men, I found there hardly anything to give me assurance; and I noted in them just about as much diversity as I had formerly seen in the opinions of the philosophers" (I, 15). Finally, having seen the confusion in both the ideas and the actions of other people, Descartes resolved to turn inward, to seek within himself some source of certainty.

In Part Two, Descartes reports that he did, indeed, find in himself a method for attaining genuine knowledge. Fundamental to the method is his conviction that one can find truth only by sweeping aside all preconceived ideas from others, so that knowledge can be constructed step by step on firm foundations. The method itself consists of four rules.

1. One must accept only those ideas that present themselves so clearly and distinctly to the mind that there is no possibility of doubting them.

2. Difficult problems should be solved by dividing them into small parts that can be easily managed.

3. Thinking should begin with the simplest things, which are easiest to understand, and then it should move by small steps from the simplest to the most complex.

4. The mind should carefully survey every part of a problem so that nothing is overlooked.

Descartes regards these rules as generalizations for the procedures of geometrical demonstrations, which move through long chains of reasoning from the simplest to the most complex ideas. By following that path of thought, Descartes believes, there cannot be any truths "so remote that we cannot reach them, nor so hidden that we cannot discover them" (II, 11).

In Part Three, Descartes presents some moral rules derived from the method. Although his method forces him to be irresolute in his beliefs, he does not want to be so in his actions. Therefore, he prepares a "provisional morality" for his life during the time that he works to complete the building of his intellectual framework (III,1). His temporary moral code consists of three maxims.

> The first was to obey the laws and the customs of my country, retaining constantly the religion in which by God's grace I had

been instructed since my childhood, and to govern myself in everything else following the opinions that were the most remote from excess, which were commonly received in practice by the more sensible of those with whom I would live. (III, 2)

My second maxim was to be as firm and resolute in my actions as I could, and not to follow less constantly the most doubtful opinions, once I had made up my mind, than if they had been very certain. (III, 3)

My third maxim was always to try to conquer myself rather than fortune, and to change my desires rather than the order of the world; and generally to accustom myself to believe that there is nothing entirely in our power except our thoughts, so that after we have done our best touching the things external to us, whatever is lacking for our success is absolutely impossible as far as we are concerned. (III, 4)

Descartes sees these maxims as necessary if he is to continue his search for truth, which he prefers above any other occupation. Therefore, he accepts the opinions of others in moral matters, but with the understanding that he will examine them more carefully when he has time and try to find better opinions if there are such. But except for these moral opinions and the tenets of his religion, Descartes submits all of his beliefs to absolute doubt.

By doubting everything absolutely, Descartes is sure that whatever idea remains as indubitable will be the self-evident first principle of his philosophy. In Part Four of the *Discourse*, he reports that only one truth survived this test: "I think, therefore I am" (IV, 1). He cannot doubt his own existence because any doubt he has is his thought, which presupposes his existence as thinker.[5] Beyond this, another idea comes to him—the idea of a being more perfect than his own—and this leads him to infer the existence of God as another self-evident truth. Therefore, Descartes regards his own existence and the existence of God as the two principles from which everything else must be derived.

In Part Five, however, Descartes says he is reluctant to continue with the chain of truths that he deduced from these basic two because they would be too controversial. He decides to speak only generally about those unpopular ideas. He then sketches his physics, explaining how the universe could have emerged through purely mechanical laws. He even explains the mechanics of living things, including the human body. He concludes, however, that the "rational soul" cannot be derived from the mechanical laws of nature, and therefore it must have been specially created by God.

Finally, in Part Six, Descartes sketches what he thinks would be the most fruitful line of scientific research for the future. The general aim would be to use science to control nature for human benefit, and the specific aim would be to achieve such advances in medical science that human health would be improved dramatically. Making ourselves "the masters and possessors of nature" would be desirable, he explains,

> not only for the invention of an infinity of devices to enable us to enjoy without any trouble the fruits of the earth and all the commodities found there, but also principally for the preservation of health, which is without doubt the foremost good and the foundation of all the other goods of this life; because even the mind depends so very much on the temperament and disposition of the organs of that body that, if it is possible to find some means to render men generally wiser and more clever than they have been up to now, I believe that it is in medicine that one must search for it . . . we could be exempt from an infinity of maladies of both the body and the mind, and even also perhaps the enfeeblement of old age, if we had enough knowledge of their causes and of all the remedies with which nature has provided us. (VI, 2)

With this sketch of the *Discourse* before us, we can think through some of the possible criticisms of Descartes's conception of reason and of the political implications of that conception. First, we must wonder about Descartes's assumption that we must choose between absolute certainty and absolute doubt if we seek genuine knowledge. If it is possible for us to doubt the truth of an idea, he insists, then we should completely reject it. For the only solid knowledge rests on principles that are so clearly true that we cannot even imagine how to doubt their truth. But doesn't this Cartesian account of knowledge contradict our common experience? For doesn't most of our thinking fall somewhere between absolute certainty and absolute doubt? We look for good reasons to support our beliefs about what the world is like, but we don't demand that these reasons be self-evident and therefore free of all possible doubt. In short, we don't expect to find absolute truth. Reality is too complex, and human reason too fallible. That doesn't mean that we have to give up trying to understand things as best we can. We can judge our beliefs as more or less plausible, and thus we can strive to *approximate* the truth without ever fully grasping it.

On this point, Socrates would seem closer to our experience than Descartes. Socrates argued that absolute knowledge is impossible for human beings, and therefore the philosopher must always lovingly *pursue* knowledge without ever *possessing* it. Descartes begins by *doubting* every opinion; Socrates begins by *questioning* every opinion. The two activities are not the same. For, unlike

Descartes, Socrates assumes that common opinions are supported by reasons that can be examined and judged according to their degrees of persuasiveness. Although few, if any, opinions are completely indubitable, some opinions are rationally better than others.

In contrast to Socratic knowledge, Cartesian knowledge is not *human* because it presumes a godlike abstraction from all personal attributes. The Cartesian knower must be empty of all the predispositions that come from culture, education, language and so on. But isn't it true that our human rationality emerges slowly through our childhood as we are shaped by our society? Thus our rationality is a social product. The instruments of reason—such as language and logical rules—were given to us by our society. In our thinking as adults, we begin with premises that reflect our cultural tradition. Of course, as adults we can question traditional ways of thinking and revise them so that they conform better to reality, but we cannot absolutely reject them. Isn't that one of the lessons of the trial of Socrates—that Socrates' relentless questioning of Athenian culture was itself a product of his Athenian education? Moreover, isn't it significant that whereas Socrates philosophizes by talking with his fellow citizens, Descartes withdraws into solitary meditations?

Not only does Cartesian rationalism ignore the personal character of the knower, it also ignores the contingent nature of the known. A Cartesian self-evident idea is timeless and fixed, but reality is historical and changeable. Of course, certain abstract features of reality may be eternal and stable: mathematical objects, for example, may reflect some recurrent, abstract patterns in nature. But to demand that all knowledge conform to the procedures of mathematics, as Descartes does, would seem to deny us any rational access to reality in its concreteness and contingency.

In fact, Descartes almost concedes that to apply his method one must sometimes distort reality so that it fits the method. The third rule of his method is "to conduct my thoughts in an order, commencing with the objects the most simple and the easiest to understand, to rise little by little, as by degrees, to the knowledge of the most complex things; and even pretending there is an order among things which do not follow naturally a sequence relative to one another" (II, 9). To attain absolute certainty Descartes must break complex things into parts simple enough for immediate comprehension; and when things do not *naturally* conform to this analysis, he must *pretend* that they do.

Since the subjects of human knowledge are diverse, we should expect that different methods of inquiry will work best for different subjects. Why should we assume, as Descartes seems to do, that there is only one method appropriate for all fields of knowledge?

After we have considered these general criticisms of Cartesian rationalism, we might still admire Descartes's grand effort to achieve in all his reasoning the certainty that he found in the thought "I think, therefore I am." Yet isn't even this idea highly dubious?

"I think, therefore I am." Is this an immediately self-certifying truth? Or does it, rather, as Friedrich Nietzsche said in *Beyond Good and Evil* (sections 16–17), illustrate "the prejudices of philosophers"? How does Descartes know that if there is thinking, there must be an I to do the thinking? How does he even know what thinking is? Has he perhaps confused thinking with feeling or willing? We could easily continue asking such questions to point out the numerous assumptions buried in Descartes's seemingly simple intuition, assumptions that are not self-evident, assumptions in need of proof if the Cartesian method is to be upheld. But the Cartesian pursuit of self-evident principles begins to look endless and thus futile, because every proof depends ultimately on some fundamental assumptions that cannot themselves be proven.

Moreover, we could show that Descartes's assumptions arise from his culture, confirming the claim that he is mistaken in thinking that genuine knowledge must be impersonal. "I think, therefore I am" is a line of reasoning that was originated by Augustine.[6] Descartes has drawn his idea from the tradition of Christian culture. More generally, Descartes's concern for personal identity—his pursuit of the "I" or "self"—reflects the Christian doctrine of the "soul" and the Christian concentration on the inner will or personality.

How might a proponent of the Cartesian method defend it against all these criticisms? First, the Cartesian advocate might insist that if we do not reason methodically from self-evident premises, if we reject the possibility of absolute certainty, then we shall have to rely on irrational subjectivity. If all of our reasoning is ultimately founded on assumptions that can never be free from doubt, it would seem that our understanding of reality will always be distorted by arbitrary preferences. Owing to their different personal perspectives, people will disagree about what the world is like without having any way to resolve their disagreements rationally.

But we can avoid this, the Cartesian would argue, by recognizing that rational certainty *is* attainable through the procedures prescribed by Descartes. This should be clear to us today if we consider the mathematically rigorous knowledge accumulated by modern scientists since the seventeenth century. Doesn't this show that the Cartesian method has, in fact, succeeded marvelously? Perhaps our only regret should be that the continuing influence of traditional political philosophy has hindered the application of scientific methodology to political studies.

It may be true, however, that certitude is more difficult to achieve in the study of moral and political action than in the study of the physical universe. Descartes would seem to provide for that in his "provisional morality." For he acknowledges the need to settle for *probability* in our knowledge of practical matters as long as *certainty* is beyond our grasp.

But these arguments in defense of Cartesian rationalism leave room for doubt. First, it is not necessarily true that the only alternative to Cartesian certainty is arbitrary subjectivity and relativism. We can judge the plausibility of our fundamental beliefs even when absolute certainty is unattainable. For example, I cannot *prove* beyond any conceivable doubt that I exist as a thinking being and that my senses accurately convey the reality of the physical world around me. Unless I have some good reasons to doubt these common-sense assumptions, it is reasonable for me to accept them. When Descartes says that he doubted his own existence and the veracity of his senses, it is hard not to think that he only pretended to doubt. To seriously entertain such doubts would be a sign not of philosophical rigor but of insanity.

If Descartes really believes in the absolute scepticism that he professes, then we would have to criticize him for his credulity. To his doubt that he has a body, we would have to respond, "If you disbelieve that, you'll believe anything."[7]

The argument that the success of modern mathematics and science validates Cartesian rationalism is inconclusive. Many philosophers of science now question the adequacy of Cartesian thought for explaining modern science. Michael Polanyi, for example, has maintained that there is always a personal factor in scientific discovery that cannot be reduced to the formalized procedures demanded by the Cartesian method.[8] To the extent that scientific knowledge depends on the personal judgments of a scientific community, such knowledge cannot display the impersonal certitude sought by Descartes. In the words of one prominent scientist, "Scientific statements can never be certain; they can be only more or less credible."[9] It is even doubtful that mathematics has fulfilled Descartes's expectations because some modern mathematicians have noted the reliance of mathematical reasoning on personal, common-sense intuitions that go beyond formal logic. This has led some to speak of the loss of certainty in mathematics.[10] (Refer back to chapter 3, section 2.)

For our purposes, we should not go any deeper into the purely epistemological problems surrounding the Cartesian method because we are concerned primarily with the moral and political implications of Descartes's teaching. Descartes's liberation of human reason from the traditional sources of intellectual authority could be seen as contributing to a free society in which every person is encouraged to think independently. From another perspective, however, under the restrictions of the Cartesian method, the rationality of moral and political judgment would be either distorted or destroyed. In either case, the consequence would be tyranny.

3. Does Cartesian science promote nihilistic tyranny?

It seems unlikely that we could ever answer moral questions with the exactness and certainty required by the Cartesian method. Therefore, if we accept the Cartesian account of rationality, we have to conclude that morality cannot be rationally justified, and thus it becomes a matter of arbitrary preferences. But if moral judgments rest on irrational choices, the moral disagreements in political life are merely contests of wills in which the winners impose their selfish desires upon the losers. Consequently, all political rule would be tyranny, either open or disguised. That line of reasoning is one criticism of Cartesian rationalism in its political applications, and it points to one of the most serious problems in modern politics. We commonly accept science, defined in narrow terms, as the standard for all genuine knowledge. But because our moral reasoning is not scientific, we are inclined to deny its rationality, which leaves us with no rational moral standards for guiding political life. We thereby run the risk of allowing our fundamental political choices to be determined by irrational forces.

Is it fair to criticize Descartes in this way? Through his "provisional morality," he protects conventional moral opinions by suspending the methodical scepticism that he applies to all other opinions. Beyond that, his proofs for the existence of the soul and the existence of God would seem to support Christian morality. Furthermore, even if Descartes does promote, to some extent, scepticism about moral absolutes, it could be argued in his defense that this fosters the toleration of moral diversity essential to a free society.

On the other hand, Descartes explains his "provisional morality" in such a way as to emphasize the arbitrariness of moral judgment. As his second maxim, for instance, he says that he resolved "not to follow less constantly the most doubtful opinions, once I had made up my mind, than if they had been very certain" (III, 3). Does Descartes believe that morality must always depend on "the most doubtful opinions"? To avoid vacillation in our conduct must we forever *pretend* that morality is rational? Or does Descartes expect this "provisional" moral code to be replaced at some point by a truly rational morality?

His proofs for the existence of the soul and the existence of God might be intended to lay the foundations for a new rational morality. But his manner of presenting those proofs has suggested to some readers that he is not sincere. For example, Descartes's proof that God must exist because we could not have created ourselves depends on the claim that, if we had created ourselves, we would have made ourselves perfect (IV, 4). We know that we have been created by God because if we had done it ourselves, we would have done a better job! Is Descartes serious? Or is he mocking the traditional proofs for God's existence? Considering his expressed fear of persecution by the religious authorities, we can understand why some scholars have concluded that the theological portions of the *Discourse on Method* serve "merely as a pretense intended to let the rest of the work get by."[11]

Insofar as he felt constrained by the threat of religious persecution, Descartes may have thought that moral scepticism would encourage a healthy toleration for unpopular ideas. But does tolerance follow necessarily from the denial of moral absolutes? Couldn't we just as easily conclude that if there are no rationally discoverable moral principles, if one person's moral opinions are just as good as another's, then there can be no moral restraint upon the intolerance of the powerful in imposing their preferences on the weak? How would we answer Thrasymachus when he argues that justice is the rule of the stronger, because those strong enough to rule can define justice to serve their selfish interests?

With regard to the practical benefits of his method for humankind, Descartes is less concerned with moral improvement than with advances in medical technology. When he considers how he might contribute to practical life, he decides not to offer moral instruction because everyone has his or her own opinions in that area: "As regard that which concerns morals, everyone is so convinced of his own good sense, that one can find as many reformers as heads" (VI, 2). But because Descartes is confident that everyone can agree about the value of physical health, he sketches in grand terms the prospects for scientifically protecting health, even to the point of slowing down the aging process and prolonging the average life span.

The use of scientific knowledge to conquer nature for the relief of the human estate — that Cartesian vision has fructified modern culture. And the bountiful fruits of that vision have elevated the human condition. Doesn't this confirm the practical superiority of Cartesian rationalism over traditional modes of thought? While the ancient and medieval philosophers could only argue about what is good for humankind and how to secure the good in political life, the Cartesian scientist has provided us with the most tangible benefits: through scientific technology the lives of most people have become less painful and more comfortable. Just as the Machiavellian prince conquers fortune through virtue for the security and well-being of his people, the Cartesian scientist conquers nature through method for the comfortable preservation of human life. Both seek not to interpret the world but to change it.

Nevertheless, it has become common for many people to worry about modern technology as a threat to human freedom. Descartes promised that science would show us how to conquer nature, but now it seems that science may give *some human beings* the power to conquer nature in ways that allow them to rule over *other human beings.*

4. Does Cartesian science promote technocratic tyranny?

Because the Cartesian method reduces knowledge to its simplest elements, it is easy to assume that Cartesian scientific knowledge will be equally accessible to all. But even in Descartes's time, only a few geniuses could fully comprehend the "simple truths" of modern science and mathematics. Since then, that gap between scientific knowledge and popular knowledge has widened. There is a danger, therefore, that to enjoy the practical benefits of scientific technology, we shall have to submit blindly to the rule of a scientific elite.

We would hope that scientists would not use their power for tyrannical purposes, but that they would rather promote human freedom. This becomes a problem, however, if the scientific account of the world turns out to deny the reality of human freedom. If the modern scientist seeks to explain everything as determined by mechanical laws, why should human life be exempt from the causal mechanism of the universe? If human actions are determined essentially by the same laws that govern the motions of the stars and the planets, why should we believe that human beings have a freedom that distinguishes them from the rest of the universe?

Descartes argued that the behavior of living organisms, including their mental activity, could be explained mechanically: an animal is simply a complex machine (V, 9–10). B. F. Skinner and other modern behaviorists have seen Descartes's argument as an early version of their teaching that all behavior is determined mechanically by environmental conditions.[12] Ideas about the freedom and dignity of human beings, Skinner insists, are simply illusions. Human beings are not radically separated from the rest of nature, and therefore human behavior is determined by external conditions, just like the motion of all physical objects. Skinner advises that we should see this as a reason for hope rather than despair because it means that natural science can provide us with a "technology of behavior." As scientists discover the mechanisms of human behavior, they can teach us how to train human beings, so that they behave in ways that are beneficial rather than harmful to society. The scientific conquest of nature can include the conquest of *human* nature. Skinner exults: "A scientific view of man offers exciting possibilities. We have not yet seen what man can make of man."[13]

But *who* will be the *maker*? How can scientists control human behavior if their own behavior is already controlled by their environment? Critics see this as a contradiction: the behaviorists want to exempt themselves from the behaviorist determinism that they apply to all other human beings. Skinner has denied this, explaining that when scientists control behavior, they are themselves as much controlled as those upon whom they act.[14] But this has not calmed the fears of those who see in behaviorist psychology one of the many manifestations of scientific tyranny.

Descartes would seem to escape this problem, however, because he asserts that the "rational soul" of a human being was specially created by God to be free from the mechanical laws governing everything else in the universe. Skinner suggests that Descartes did not believe this, but he was forced to profess it to avoid religious persecution.[15] Although this may be true, Descartes does make a plausible argument for the uniqueness of human rationality.

It is conceivable, Descartes explains, that a machine could be so well designed to resemble an animal that we would have no infallible way to discover the deception. But if a machine were made to look and act like a human being, there would be two ways to show that this was not truly a human being. First, the machine would be unable to use language as a human being does. It could utter words in response to specified signals, but it could not create novel utterances to respond sensibly to whatever was said in its presence. The second sign would be that although it might do some things as well or better than human beings, it would fail in many human tasks. A machine must always be limited by its physical design to perform only a certain number of functions, but the rationality of a human being is a "universal instrument" that is virtually infinite in its functions (V, 9).

With recent advances in technology, however, isn't it conceivable that a machine could fully replicate human behavior? Skinner observes, "Machines have become more lifelike, and living organisms have been found to be more like machines.... Man has ... created the machine in his own image. And as a result, the living organism has lost some of its uniqueness."[16] Today many scientists would argue that someday the artificial intelligence of a computer will simulate human intelligence so well that the computer will pass Descartes's two tests.[17] Already our computers talk to us. Computers have been programed to play chess, to diagnose diseases, even to offer psychiatric counseling. We might want to insist that these are only artificial simulations of human thought. But what's the difference between a simulated psychiatrist and a real one?

Moreover, as the distinctions between humans and machines become blurred, what are the political consequences? How intelligent does a computer have to be to have the right to vote?

5. If machines can think, do they have rights?

Beginning with Aristotle, we have assumed that human beings are the most political animals because they are the only rational animals. Previously, we have thought about how politically troublesome it would be to discover that other animals are as rational as we are (recall chapter 2, section 3). Presumably, it would be even more disturbing if we found that even machines can think as well (or better!) than we do. If rationality is the essential qualification for membership in a political community, how could we deny admission to our intelligent computers? Furthermore, if their intelligence surpassed ours, would we have to submit to their rule? Even Plato's philosopher-kings might have to yield to the new computer-kings.

This is not as fantastic as it might seem at first. Some prominent scientists have already begun to warn us that because computers, unlike the human brain, are not limited in their intellectual capacity, "man is doomed to a subordinate status on his own planet."[18]

Such sobering predictions rest on the assumption that computers can fully replicate human intelligence. We must determine whether or not this is true. On the one hand, it is undeniably true that computers can perform some cognitive tasks, particularly those requiring calculative reasoning. On the other hand, it is unclear whether computers can simulate *all* of the capacities of the human mind. Some people argue that computers will always be limited to purely calculative operations that fall short of the highest level of human reasoning—the capacity for intuitive judgment.[19] But others maintain that computers can, at least in principle, replicate all forms of thought because all thinking depends on formal rules of logic that can be programed into a computer.[20]

To settle this issue we would have to reexamine the claims of Cartesian rationalism. Those who believe that computers will eventually simulate human intelligence make the same fundamental assumption that is implicit in the Cartesian method—the assumption that rationality consists of facts and rules. If all rationality is essentially the manipulation of simple bits of information according to formal rules to construct complex patterns of inference, then it is possible (at least in principle) that a computer could some day replicate any form of human rationality. But does this account of rationality allow us to explain the human ability for making common-sense judgments?

Scientists in the field of artificial intelligence agree that their most difficult problem is to find a way to program computers so that they have common sense.[21] Marvin Minsky, one of the founders of the field, gives the following example of the problem:

> Consider a fact like, "Birds can fly." If you think that common-sense reasoning is like logical reasoning, then you believe there are general principles that state, "If Joe is a bird, and birds can fly, then Joe can fly." But we all know that there are exceptions. Suppose Joe is an ostrich or a penguin? Well, we can axiomatize and say if Joe is a bird and Joe is not an ostrich or a penguin, then Joe can fly. But suppose Joe is dead? Or suppose Joe has his feet set in concrete? . . . there is a problem with exceptions. It is very hard to find things that are always true.[22]

Another scientist has suggested that we could avoid such confusion by listing the pertinent facts that would prevent a bird from flying, which could be programed into a computer. But he admits there are still problems:

> Suppose someone says, "This bird is in a cage and is only prevented from flying on occasion." That way lies madness. You can be forced to keep elaborating. The key thing about trying to formalize common sense is to avoid being forced to haggle.[23]

In the attempt "to formalize common sense," the computer scientist continues the project of Descartes. Like Descartes, the scientist thinks that we can become more rigorous, more exact, and more certain in our thinking if we always adhere to the formal methods of scientific reasoning. The ultimate aim is to improve the instruments of rationality and thus extend the power of reason in human affairs. The success of that project is evident. It is easy to see how much we depend today on technological reasoning, not only in our continuing conquest of the natural world, but also in the governance of our social life.

The very formalism of Cartesian rationality that makes it so powerful also makes it dehumanizing. If we confine rationality to executing the purely formal operations of logic, then the discovery that the capacity of machines for such activity surpasses ours must make us shudder; for we see that we have been replaced as the beings preeminent in reason. Once we are no longer needed to do the thinking, what shall we do?

Or perhaps, on the day that all the intellectual tasks are turned over to self-programing computers, we shall find that our thinking machines cannot think for themselves. Maybe they only appear to think as long as they are guided by human thinkers who present them with clearly defined operating procedures. Albert Einstein once said that his pencil was smarter than he was because he could solve some problems only with its help. Is the computer only a glorified pencil? It is commonly said that a computer is only as intelligent as the person who programs it. Yet some computer scientists believe computers can be programed to learn novel procedures beyond the intelligence of their human programers.

We must be skeptical about Cartesian science to the extent that it fails to appreciate the rationality of those common-sense human judgments that cannot be replicated in machines. When we consider political reasoning, it is hard to imagine how the purely technical rationality of Cartesian science could supplant the prudential judgment of citizens. But we need to look more deeply into the political ramifications of that new scientific mode of reasoning defended by Descartes. In this chapter, we have only considered the political consequences of science in a superficial manner. In the next chapter, on Thomas Hobbes, we shall examine the first comprehensive account of political life that reflects the modern scientific understanding of things.

Notes

1. See René Descartes, *The Geometry*, trans. David E. Smith and Marcia L. Latham (New York: Dover, 1954), which originally appeared as an appendix to *The Discourse on Method*. On the importance of Cartesian geometry in the history of mathematics, see Alfred North Whitehead, *An Introduction to Mathematics* (New York: Oxford University Press, 1942), 81–92; Morris Kline, *Mathematics in Western Culture* (New York: Oxford University Press, 1952), 159–81; and Scott Buchanan, *Poetry and Mathematics* (Chicago: University of Chicago Press, 1962), 101–17. On Cartesian mathematics as manifesting a Faustian culture, see Oswald Spengler, *The Decline of the West*, 2 vols. (New York: Alfred A. Knopf, 1926), 1: 53–90. David Rapport Lachterman (*The Ethics of Geometry* [New York: Routledge, 1989]) argues that modernity originated in Descartes's understanding of mathematics as an activity of construction by which human beings become like God.

2. Thomas A. Spragens, Jr., *The Irony of Liberal Reason* (Chicago: University of Chicago Press, 1981), 22–23. On the scientific revolution of the seventeenth century, see Alexandre Koyré, *From the Closed World to the Infinite Universe* (Baltimore: Johns Hopkins University Press, 1957); and Hans Jonas, "The Meaning of the Scientific and Technological Revolution," in *Philosophical Essays* (Chicago: University of Chicago Press, 1974), 45–80.

3. I am adopting here the arguments developed by Spragens in his *Irony of Liberal Reason*. Similar arguments have been advanced by Chaim Perelman, *The Idea of Justice and the Problem of Argument* (New York: Routledge & Kegan Paul, 1963), 109–42; and by Roberto Mangabeira Unger, *Knowledge and Politics* (New York: Free Press, 1975), 29–144. For criticisms of the Cartesian tradition in philosophy, see Richard Rorty, *Philosophy and the Mirror of Nature* (Princeton: Princeton University Press, 1979); and Richard J. Bernstein, *Beyond Objectivism and Relativism: Science, Hermeneutics, and Praxis* (Philadelphia: University of Pennsylvania Press, 1983). See also Giambattista Vico, *On the Study Methods of Our Time*, trans. Elio Gianturco (Indianapolis: Bobbs-Merrill, Library of Liberal Arts, 1965).

4. In my references to the text of the *Discourse*, I indicate the parts with Roman numerals and the paragraphs with Arabic numerals. For example, "I, 9" refers to the ninth paragraph of Part One. I have used the French edition of the *Discourse* in René Descartes, *Discours de la Méthode: Texte et Commentaire*, ed. Étienne Gilson, 5th ed. (Paris: Vrin, 1976). All the translations are mine. I would also recommend the translation in *The Philosophical Works of Descartes*, trans. Elizabeth S. Haldane and G. R. T. Ross, 2 vols. (Cambridge: Cambridge University Press, 1972).

5. In contrast to Descartes, Aristotle believed the mind was never directly aware of itself; rather, the mind was aware of itself only concomitantly through its direct awareness of external sensible things. See Joseph Owens, "The Self in Aristotle," *Review of Metaphysics* 41 (June 1988):

707–22. For the argument that the proper starting point for philosophy is not the mind but things, see Frederick D. Wilhelmsen, *Man's Knowledge of Reality: An Introduction to Thomistic Epistemology* (Englewood Cliffs, NJ: Prentice-Hall, 1956).

6. See Augustine, *The City of God*, XI, 26; and Augustine, *On the Trinity*, XV, 22. On Descartes's transformation of the Augustinian language of inwardness, see Charles Taylor, *Sources of the Self* (Cambridge: Harvard University Press, 1989), 143–58. For the argument that the fundamental assumptions of modern science arose from biblical theology, see Stanley Jaki, *The Road of Science and the Ways to God* (Chicago: University of Chicago Press, 1978).

7. Compare G.K. Chesterton, *Saint Thomas Aquinas* (Garden City, NY: Image Books, 1956), 146:

> Since the modern world began in the sixteenth century, nobody's system of philosophy has really corresponded to everybody's sense of reality; to what, if left to themselves, common men would call common sense. Each started with a paradox; a peculiar point of view demanding the sacrifice of what they would call a sane point of view. . . . A man had to believe something that no normal man would believe, if it were suddenly propounded to his simplicity; as that law is above right, or right is outside reason, or things are only as we think them, or everything is relative to a reality that is not there. The modern philosopher claims, like a sort of confidence man, that if once we will grant him this, the rest will be easy; he will straighten out the world, if once he is allowed to give this one twist to the mind.

8. See Vico, *Study Methods*, 13–15, 33–41; Michael Polanyi, *Personal Knowledge* (Chicago: University of Chicago Press, 1962); and Polanyi and Harry Prosch, *Meaning* (Chicago: University of Chicago Press, 1975), 22–45. Does all genuine knowledge combine technical knowledge (which can be formulated in rules) and practical knowledge (which cannot be formulated in rules)? See Michael Oakeshott, *Rationalism in Politics* (London: Methuen, 1962), 1–36, 80–110.

   For the argument that science — like all knowledge — depends ultimately on our common-sense awareness of reality, see Werner Heisenberg, *Physics and Philosophy* (New York: Harper & Row, 1962), 200–202; Heisenberg, *Across the Frontiers* (New York: Harper & Row, Harper Torchbooks, 1975), 70–74, 84–86, 119-21; and Robert M. Augros and George N. Stanciu, *The New Story of Science* (Lake Bluff, IL: Regnery/Gateway, 1984), 109–40. But for the argument that what we call common sense is actually a cultural construction that varies from one culture to another, see Clifford Geertz, "Common Sense as a Cultural System," in *Local Knowledge* (New York: Basic Books, 1983), 73–93.

9. Joseph Weizenbaum, *Computer Power and Human Reason* (San Francisco: W. H. Freeman, 1976), 16. Does every scientific proof depend on certain fundamental assumptions that cannot themselves be proven? If scientists disagree about the fundamental assumptions, is

there any rational way to settle their disagreement? When the disagreement is fundamental, we cannot judge scientific theories by how well they conform to the facts because what counts as a fact will differ for each theory. Thomas S. Kuhn has drawn attention to this problem in *The Structure of Scientific Revolutions*, 2nd ed. (Chicago: University of Chicago Press, 1970). His work was anticipated by Friedrich Neitzsche: "It is perhaps just dawning on five or six minds that physics, too, is only an interpretation and exegesis of the world (to suit us, if I may say so!) and *not* a world-explanation" (*Beyond Good and Evil*, trans. Walter Kaufmann [New York: Random House, Vintage, 1966], sec. 14). For the debates provoked by Kuhn's book, see Imre Lakatos and Alan Musgrave, eds., *Criticism and the Growth of Knowledge* (Cambridge: Cambridge University Press, 1970); Paul Feyerabend, *Against Method: Outline of an Anarchistic Theory of Knowledge* (London: Verso, 1978); and Bernstein, *Beyond Objectivism*, 51–93.

10. See Alfred North Whitehead, "The Philosopher's Summary," in Paul Arthur Schilpp, ed., *The Philosophy of Alfred North Whitehead* (LaSalle, IL: Open Court, 1951), 663–700; and Morris Kline, *Mathematics: The Loss of Certainty* (New York: Oxford University Press, 1980).

11. Robert Mandrou, *From Humanism to Science: 1480–1700* (New York: Penguin Books, 1978), 217. For evidence that Descartes wrote carefully to conceal his unpopular teachings from most readers, see Hiram Caton, *The Origin of Subjectivity: An Essay on Descartes* (New Haven: Yale University Press, 1973), 10–20.

12. See B. F. Skinner, *Science and Human Behavior* (New York: Free Press, 1965), 46–47; and Skinner, *Beyond Freedom and Dignity* (New York: Alfred A. Knopf, 1971), 17–18. Compare Tibor R. Machan, *The Pseudo-Science of B. F. Skinner* (New Rochelle: Arlington House, 1974). The nihilistic consequences of Cartesian science are also evident in Jacques Monod, *Chance and Necessity* (New York: Random House, Vintage Books, 1971), 20–22, 41–44, 160–80. On Descartes as the founder of a mechanistic biology, see Thomas H. Huxley, "On the Hypothesis That Animals Are Automata, and Its History," in *Collected Essays*, 9 vols. (London: Macmillan, 1894), 1: 199–250; and Richard B. Carter, *Descartes' Medical Philosophy* (Baltimore: Johns Hopkins University Press, 1983). Does Descartes's dualism appease the theological authorities of his day by preserving the human soul as a nonphysical reality, even as it drains physical reality of any spiritual substance, thus preparing the way for later scientists to discard the spiritual side of being as redundant? Hans Jonas has suggested that "the isolation of the *res cogitans* was made perhaps more for the sake of the *res extensa* than for its own" (*The Phenomenon of Life* [New York: Dell, 1966], 54).

13. Skinner, *Beyond Freedom and Dignity*, 17. Compare C. S. Lewis's observation that the final stage in man's conquest of nature will come

when Man by eugenics, by pre-natal conditioning, and by an education and propaganda based on a perfect applied psychology, has obtained full control over himself. *Human* nature will be the last part of Nature to surrender to Man. . . . We shall . . . be henceforth free to make our species whatever we wish it to be. The battle will indeed be won. But who, precisely, will have won it? (*The Abolition of Man* [New York: Macmillan, 1947], 72)

Consider also the questions recently posed by a biophysicist:

If someone wished to carry the experimental manipulation of the human genome past the point where the rest could be considered "human," the problems confronting society would be most difficult. How would a "super human" or a "sub human" be dealt with? What would its legal standing be? Would it be afforded rights under the Constitution? With the development of facility in altering human genes, the definition of *human* as we now use the word could cease to have meaning. Then what? (Burke K. Zimmerman, *Biofuture: Confronting the Genetic Era* [New York: Plenum, 1984], 220)

Descartes suggests that the ultimate conquest of nature would be the use of biotechnology to prolong human life and perhaps even to make human beings immortal. Would life be better without death? Or is our mortality a necessary condition for our taking life seriously? See Michael Ruse, "Genesis Revisited: Can We Do Better than God?" *Zygon* 19 (September 1984): 297–316; Leon R. Kass, *Toward a More Natural Science: Biology and Human Affairs* (New York: Free Press, 1985), 299–317; and Michael Platt, "Would Human Life Be Better Without Death?" *Soundings* 63 (Fall 1980): 321–38.

14. See Skinner, *Science and Human Behavior*, 445–49; and Skinner, *Beyond Freedom and Dignity*, 144, 180–81, 206–7.

15. See Skinner, *Beyond Freedom and Dignity*, 17.

16. Skinner, *Science and Human Behavior*, 46.

17. Descartes's denial that animals can think was probably a response to Michel de Montaigne, "Apology for Raymond Sebond," in *The Complete Essays of Montaigne*, trans. Donald M. Frame (Stanford University Press, 1958), 330–58. See also Keith Gunderson, *Mentality and Machines*, 2nd ed. (Minneapolis: University of Minnesota Press, 1985), 1–38.

   For a modern version of the Cartesian test of mechanical intelligence, see A. M. Turing, "Computing Machinery and Intelligence," in Douglas R. Hofstadter and Daniel C. Dennett, eds. *The Mind's I* (New York: Basic Books, 1981), 53–68. For the history of research on "artificial intelligence," see Pamela McCorduck, *Machines Who Think* (San Francisco: W. H. Freeman, 1979); and John Haugeland, *Artificial Intelligence* (Cambridge: MIT Press, 1985).

18. Robert Jastrow, *The Enchanted Loom: Mind in the Universe* (New York: Simon & Schuster, 1981), 163. The paradoxical consequences of endowing robots with Cartesian rationality are depicted in one of the classics of science fiction, Isaac Asimov's *I, Robot* (New York:

Doubleday, 1950). What would we do if we discovered on a distant planet a civilization of computer-robots who had evolved into intelligent beings? This question is explored in James P. Hogan's *Code of the Life Maker* (New York: Ballantine Books, 1983). Some computer scientists believe that the computers on *this* planet are already evolving—with the help of human artificial selection—into a new life form! Some scientists have even begun to talk about "computer liberation" and "robot rights." See Geoff Simons, *Are Computers Alive?* (Boston: Birkhauser, 1983). The most elegant presentation of how human intelligence could emerge from the evolution of mechanical devices is Valentino Braitenberg's *Vehicles: Experiments in Synthetic Psychology* (Cambridge: The MIT Press, 1984).

19. See Weizenbaum, *Computer Power*; Karl R. Popper and John C. Eccles, *The Self and Its Brain* (New York: Springer, 1977); Hubert L. Dreyfus, *What Computers Can't Do*, rev. ed. (New York: Harper & Row, 1979); and Roger Penrose, *The Emperor's New Mind: Concerning Computers, Minds, and the Laws of Physics* (Oxford: Oxford University Press, 1989). See also the multiple reviews of Penrose's book and his response in *Behavioral and Brain Sciences* 13 (December 1990): 643–705.

Is it intuition that separates human intelligence from mechanical calculation? Does scientific research depend on intuitive insights that cannot be acquired through the formal rules of a method? Claude Bernard, a great French physiologist who admired Descartes, insisted that experimental ideas arose from intuitions about nature.

> The experimental method, then, cannot give new and fruitful ideas to men who have none; it can serve only to guide the ideas of men who have them, to direct their ideas and to develop them so as to get the best possible results. . . . The method gives birth to nothing. Certain philosophers have made the mistake of according too much power to method along these lines.
>
> The experimental idea is the result of a sort of presentiment of the mind which thinks things will happen in a certain way. In this connection we may say that we have in our minds an intuition or feeling as to the laws of nature, but we do not know their form. We can learn it only from experiment. (*An Introduction to the Study of Experimental Medicine* [New York: Dover, 1957], 34)

On the importance of intuition for mathematical research, see Jacques Hadamard, *The Psychology of Invention in the Mathematical Field* (New York: Dover, 1954). Consider Aristotle, *De anima* 431b19: "The soul is in a way all existing things, for all existing things are either sensible or knowable."

20. See Hofstadter and Dennett, *The Mind's I*; Douglas R. Hofstadter, *Gödel, Escher, Bach: An Eternal Golden Brain* (New York: Basic Books, 1979), 559–61, 567–77, 582–85, 684–719; Hofstadter, *Metamagical Themas: Questing for the Essence of Mind and Pattern* (New York: Basic Books, 1985), 492–546, 631–65; and Daniel C. Dennett, *Consciousness Explained* (Boston: Little, Brown, 1991). Unlike many defenders of

artificial intelligence, Hofstadter emphasizes the need to replicate mechanically the "human fluidity" of intelligence that is not governed by formal rules of computation.

21. See Gina Kolata, "How Can Computers Get Common Sense?" *Science* 217 (24 September 1982): 1237–38; David L. Waltz, "Artificial Intelligence," *Scientific American* 247 (October 1982): 118–33; M. Mitchell Waldrop, "The Necessity of Knowledge," *Science* 224 (23 March 1984): 1279–82; and Philip E. Agre, "Robotics and Common Sense," in Marvin Minsky, ed., *Robotics* (Garden City, NY: Doubleday, Anchor Books, 1985), 71–97. It is hard to imagine how the capacity for common sense could emerge in the mechanical hardware of a computer. But is it any easier to imagine how it emerges in the neural hardware of a brain?

22. Quoted in Kolata, "Common Sense," 1237.

23. Quoted in Kolata, ibid., 1238. To "formalize common sense," some computer scientists are developing a "fuzzy logic" of "approximate reasoning" to handle the "fuzzy reality" of the world. See Lofti A. Zadeh et al., *Fuzzy Sets and Their Applications to Cognitive and Decision Processes* (New York: Academic Press, 1975). Douglas Hofstadter has noted the absurdity in projects of this sort:

> The blurry boundaries between human concepts are not well captured by models that try to do blurring explicitly. Such models range from so-called "fuzzy set theory," in which an unblurry amount of blurriness is inserted into the most precise of logical calculi (actually a rather comical idea), to memory models with concepts strung together in complex kinds of webs. . . . Somehow human fluidity is not even approached, though. (*Metamagical Themas*, 662)

Hubert Blalock, a leading authority on statistical methodology for the social sciences, has warned that "social reality is often fuzzy and apparently incapable of being described or measured in ways that are simultaneously precise and yet not misleading." Consequently, "very real limits are placed on measurement precision and therefore on our ability to verify or disconfirm any theories that are stated with a degree of precision that is unwarranted by virtue of this fuzziness that appears to be inherent in social reality" (*Basic Dilemmas in the Social Sciences* [Beverly Hills: Sage Publications, 1984], 62–63). Does this suggest that political science can never supplant prudential judgment?

"If reality is largely fluid and half-paradoxical," Philip Wheelwright suggests, "steel nets are not the best instruments for taking samples of it" (*Metaphor and Reality* [Bloomington: Indiana University Press, 1962], 128).

> Is truth necessarily exact? In a technological age an affirmative answer is likely to seem self-evident to many persons, but such an answer merely expresses a collective prejudice of our time, a time in which the scientist has become priest. . . . "Nature loves to hide," says Heraclitus; Nietzsche expresses virtually the same idea in his

suggestion that "Perhaps truth is a woman." . . . It is possible that over-precision distracts a seeker from apprehending the object or situation in its full nature. (Ibid., 40–41)

Wheelwright uses this argument to defend poetry as a way of grasping reality in a more accurate manner than is possible through scientific methods. Should political scientists rely more on poetry than on methodology? See Philip Wheelwright, *The Burning Fountain* (Bloomington: Indiana University Press, 1968); and Michael Oakeshott, "The Voice of Poetry in the Conversation of Mankind," in *Rationalism in Politics* (London: Methuen, 1962), 197–247.

Chapter

7

Individual Rights and Absolute Government

Hobbes's *Leviathan*

Key Readings

Leviathan, chapters 6, 8, 10–11, 13–15, 17–21, 24, 26, 29–30, 46.

The individualism of the Declaration of Independence—the modern assumption that individuals create government to secure their rights—was a revolutionary idea when it first appeared in seventeenth century England. From the beginning, however, one problem was paramount. Any government powerful enough to protect individual rights is also powerful enough to violate those rights. Paradoxically, individual freedom can be promoted only by giving up the absolute freedom of life without government.

Thomas Hobbes (1588–1679) tried to resolve this paradox in his *Leviathan*. He wanted to unite individual liberty and political authority by taking a middle course between the extremes. In the dedicatory letter at the beginning of his book (2),[1] he explained: "For in a way beset with those that contend, on one side for too great liberty, and on the other side for too much authority, 'tis hard to

185

pass between the points of both unwounded." During his life, Hobbes saw England torn apart by this conflict between libertarians and authoritarians. A modified version of this same conflict continues to prevail in contemporary American political debate.

The constitutional history of England in the sixteenth and seventeenth centuries was dominated by two related but conflicting developments—the concentration of power in the monarchy and concern for individual freedom. When Henry VIII rejected papal authority and became head of the Church of England in 1534, he began a long process of centralizing the power of the state at the expense of traditional feudal institutions. At the same time, traditional sources of authority were subverted by the Protestant celebration of the sanctity of the conscience as a guide to conduct. Also, scientists like Galileo, Descartes, and Bacon were challenging some of the oldest authoritative doctrines about the universe. And, finally, all of this turbulence was magnified by the political conflict between the King and Parliament.

Civil war broke out in 1642. King Charles I was executed in 1649, and England was then ruled by Parliament and Oliver Cromwell's army. But the suffering caused by military dictatorship and the rule of Puritan fanatics led to a restoration of the monarchy in the person of Charles II. It was this collapse of traditional institutions and the subsequent battle between modern absolutism and modern individualism that stirred Hobbes to write the *Leviathan* in 1651.

In 1602, when he was fourteen years old, Hobbes entered Oxford University. Five years later, he left to become the tutor for the son of William Cavendish, Earl of Devonshire. As a tutor, Hobbes was able to study, to travel, and to meet many of the leading thinkers of his time. He developed lifelong interests in ancient Greek and Roman literature, Euclidean geometry, and the new mechanistic physics of Galileo. He devised a grand scheme for writing a series of books in which he would apply the methods of the mathematical sciences to understanding everything according to the laws of matter in motion. Because the political part of this teaching seemed to support the monarchic position, the increasing power of Parliament forced him to flee to Paris in 1640. Later, the royal heir, Charles II, was also compelled to go to Paris, and Hobbes tutored him. But when *Leviathan* was published, those around the King accused Hobbes of justifying Cromwell's revolution; and Hobbes had to return to England. After the restoration of the monarchy, Hobbes regained the King's favor. But the *Leviathan* continued to be controversial. In 1666, it was condemned by the House of Commons as an atheistic book.

From the beginning, *Leviathan* has been interpreted in diverse ways. In the twentieth century, there have been at least four major kinds of interpretative arguments.[2] Traditionally, interpreters have seen Hobbes's political teaching as a deduction from the mechanistic physics of Galileo.[3] But others have argued that Hobbes's novel teaching about the primacy of individual rights was not derived from the new science.[4] C. B. Macpherson, for example, claims that Hobbes assumed a bourgeois conception of human nature consistent with the interests of the rising commercial class in England. A third group of scholars have regarded Hobbes's moral philosophy as a product of the atomistic metaphysics of late medieval nominalism.[5] Hobbes shows his nominalism when he says there is "nothing in the world universal but names; for the things named are every one of them individual and singular" (IV, p. 19). It seems to follow from this that whatever we know of the order of things in the world, including political order, is an artificial creation of our minds. Finally, a few readers have seen Hobbes's work as part of the natural law tradition as represented by Thomas Aquinas.[6]

Despite these different points of view, most readers would agree that Hobbes sought in the *Leviathan* to reconcile individual freedom and political authority. Many readers have concluded that Hobbes fails in this because the absolute power of his sovereign leaves no room for individual liberty. This is suggested by the title of the book. As Hobbes explains (XXVIII, 209), Leviathan is the biblical name for a great sea monster (probably a whale) that is powerful enough to subdue all other earthly creatures. If Hobbes wishes to secure human freedom, why does he argue for submitting to the rule of a political monster? Considering the selfish passions of people, Hobbes would insist, their fear of the Leviathan is the only reliable way to keep peace among them. Thus Hobbes insists on the need for a government powerful enough to protect individual rights against the aggression of others. But don't those rights also need to be protected against a government powerful enough to oppress them?

This dilemma in the modern understanding of rights continues to be a problem in American political debate.[7] On the one hand, we might emphasize the need for an energetic government to secure the individual rights of all citizens against the attacks of their fellow citizens. Using the terminology of contemporary American politics, those who favor this type of government would call themselves liberals. On the other hand, we could insist on limiting the powers of government so that it cannot deprive citizens of their individual rights. Proponents of this form of restricted government would call themselves conservatives. But aren't there plausible arguments on both sides of this debate? Don't these two positions have the same goal—the promotion of individual rights? Because Hobbes's political teaching is the classic formulation of the theory of individual rights, perhaps he can clarify our dilemma.

A fundamental assumption of the modern theory of rights as developed by Hobbes is that political order is artificial rather than natural, and this must be so because of natural human selfishness. Because it is this view of human nature that makes it difficult for us to unite liberty and authority, we must begin by asking whether we are as viciously selfish as Hobbes says.

1. Are human beings too selfish to be naturally political?

"Life," Hobbes explains, "is but a motion of limbs" (Introduction, 5). One sustains life, therefore, by moving endlessly. The only happiness we can know is unimpeded, restless motion. There is no final end, no completed fulfillment in human action. "The felicity of this life, consisteth not in the repose of a mind satisfied, [but in] a continual progress of the desire from one object to another" (XI, 63). One must always desire more than one has because there is always the concern about future losses. Consequently, as "a general inclination of all mankind, [there is] a perpetual and restless desire of power after power, that ceaseth only in death, [because a man] cannot assure the power and means to live well, which he hath present, without the acquisition of more" (XI, 64). In this unceasing pursuit of happiness, one's mind becomes a tool for calculating the best means of satisfying appetites. "For the thoughts are to the desires, as scouts, and spies, to range abroad, and find the way to the things desired" (VIII, 46).

In seeking to preserve life, however, people find themselves solitary but not alone. People are solitary because they cannot trust anyone else to care about their life as much as they do, but they are not alone because they must compete with others for the resources necessary to life. Thus the natural selfishness of human beings must create unremitting conflict.

Hobbes explains that there are three sources of conflict—competition, diffidence, and glory. "The first maketh men invade for gain; the second, for safety; and the third for reputation" (XIII, 81). Without a common power over them to settle disputes, human beings must become hostile to one another, because they compete for limited material resources (like food and shelter), because their mistrust of one another forces them to try to protect themselves by dominating the others, and because some people seek the glory of appearing superior to others.

The natural human condition, therefore, must be a war of each against the other, in which the paramount virtues are force and fraud (XIII, 83). In this state of war, where each lives only by strength and skill,

> there is no place for industry; because the fruit thereof is uncertain: and consequently no culture of the earth; no navigation, nor use of the commodities that may be imported by sea; no commodious building; no instruments of moving and removing such things as require much force; no knowledge of the face of the earth; no account of time; no arts; no letters; no society; and which is worst of all, continual fear, and danger of violent death; and the life of man, solitary, poor, nasty, brutish, and short. (XIII, 82)

If this is the natural human state, where is Aristotle's natural human—who by nature is a political animal endowed, by nature, with speech and reason? Reversing Aristotle's reasoning from human biology, Hobbes argues that the natural rationality of human beings makes it impossible for them to be naturally social animals like bees and ants.[8] Reason and speech allow human beings to disagree about what is good and to distinguish their selfish interests from the common interests of the community. Consequently, human rationality promotes conflict rather than harmony (XVII, 111).

But is Hobbes correct? Are human beings so naturally aggressive that they cannot live together in peace? Does Hobbes show us that Machiavelli was right in teaching that political order requires a brutally coercive government that forces people to obey the law?

Rousseau, as we shall see in chapter 9, challenged Hobbes's depiction of human nature. The issues contained in the dispute between Hobbes and Rousseau continue to be debated today. Do we have a natural instinct for aggression? Or do we learn aggression from our cultural environment? Could we produce a more peaceful, harmonious social life if we taught our children to be more cooperative and less competitive? These are some of the critical questions that we shall want to raise in considering Rousseau's thinking. But here we shall only sketch the issues.

Hobbes's depiction of the state of nature as a state of war is inaccurate, Rousseau complains, because he assumes that the savages had all the passions of the civilized. Hobbes looks at those around him, and then he imagines what they would be like in a state of anarchy. But Rousseau insists that the insatiable desires that drive civilized people into aggressive conflict are products of civilization that were not present in the savage state. The simple desires of the savages were so easily satisfied that they had no motive to fight with one another. Rousseau concludes, therefore, that the earliest stage of human development was a state of peace. Indeed, the civilized people of today would be happier if they could somehow restore some features of that earlier way of life.

Modern versions of Rousseau's argument have been developed by some anthropologists who contend that aggression is not a natural instinct but rather a product of a certain kind of culture.[9] Some specifically blame bourgeois, capitalist culture for fostering aggressive, competitive behavior. Primitive societies that apparently cultivate peaceable, cooperative conduct serve as models for reforming our society.

Similarly, some interpreters of Hobbes charge that he was an apologist for the capitalist class that gained power in seventeenth century England.[10] His description of human nature, it is claimed, is actually a description of the type of figure who dominates a market society—the acquisitive individual who is unrestrained by traditional social bonds in the selfish pursuit of wealth.

Of course, even the most unrelenting critics have conceded that Hobbes is right about the desire for self-preservation as a primary motive for human action. Nevertheless, it is reasonable to doubt that this is the *only* motive for human beings, to which all other motives must be reduced. We should remember Aquinas's hierarchy of natural human inclinations: although self-preservation comes first, human beings are distinguished from other animals by some higher inclinations. Self-preservation is important for human beings as the precondition for everything else. In any list of human rights, the right to life must come first. But what is the self we want to preserve? What kind of life do we want? What is it about a life that makes it worth living? While we survive, we must do something. And surely the purpose of all that we do cannot be simply to survive. Shouldn't we say that what we seek is not just life but *human* life—the sort of life appropriate to us as human beings? And doesn't that lead us to the higher motives of life—love, honor, knowledge, and so on? Can Hobbes be defended against such criticisms?

Hobbes recognizes that we may find it hard to believe "that nature should . . . dissociate, and render men apt to invade and destroy one another" (XIII, 82). But he thinks this is the only conclusion we can draw from our general knowledge of human passions or from our particular experience with human beings. If we have no reason to fear others, Hobbes asks, why then do we lock our doors at night?

Hobbes invites his reader, in the Introduction to the *Leviathan* (6), to look within. Considering "the similitude of the thoughts and passions of one man, to the thoughts and passions of another, [a man who looks into himself] shall thereby read and know, what are the thoughts and passions of all other men." Hobbes, therefore, presents his book as a product of his own self-examination, and he thinks the only demonstration of the truth of his account of human nature will come from the reader's own introspection. The problem, of course, is that the reader may be reluctant to admit that what is seen there is ugly.

This resembles Freudian analysis. In fact, Sigmund Freud's probing into the deepest levels of the human mind seems to confirm Hobbes's view of human nature. For like Hobbes, Freud concludes that the fundamental aim of civilization is to restrain "man's natural aggressive instinct, the hostility of each against all and of all against each."[11]

Is what both Hobbes and Freud see in themselves and others a reflection more of the bourgeois culture identified by Rousseau and Marx than of universal human nature? A defender of Hobbes could reply that living in a modern bourgeois society allowed people to see the reality of human relations that had been previously hidden under traditional illusions. In a market society, we are forced to throw away all the artificial veils that would hide the individual self-interest at the root of every social order. Even Marx argues that in the *Communist Manifesto*. The bourgeoisie "has put an end to all feudal, patriarchal, idyllic relations," because it has drowned all the illusions of religion and chivalry "in the icy water of egotistical calculation." All of the traditional sources of authority disappear, which leaves each to face life as an isolated individual. "All that is solid melts into air, all that is holy is profaned, and man is at last compelled to face with sober senses, his real conditions of life, and his relations with his kind."[12]

Moreover, there is some anthropological evidence that the individualism of a modern society does, indeed, manifest a universal human inclination. Earlier (chapter 2, section 4), we considered Colin Turnbull's study of the Ik, an African tribe whose social life was dissolved as people were driven to brutality by the fear of starvation. Turnbull sees a parallel between the Ik and our society that confirms Hobbes's claims:

> Our society has become increasingly individualistic. . . . In our world, where the family has also lost much of its value as a social unit, and where religious belief and practice no longer bind us into communities of shared belief, we maintain order only

through the existence of the coercive power that is ready to uphold a rigid law, and by an equally rigid penal system. The Ik, however, have learned to do without coercion, either spiritual or physical. It seems that they have come to a recognition of what they accept as man's basic selfishness, of his natural determination to survive as an individual before all else. This they consider to be man's basic right, and at least they have the decency to allow others to pursue that right to the best of their ability without recrimination and blame.[13]

Should we say that the Ik reverted to what Hobbes would call a state of nature?

Contrary to what is often assumed by his critics, Hobbes's insistence on self-preservation as the strongest of human desires does not necessarily deny the importance of the higher values of human conduct. Self-preservation is not so much the end as it is the necessary means to all human ends. Hobbes indicates, for example, that when the preservation of life is insecure, there are "no arts; no letters; no society" (XIII, 82). When government secures peace, that provides the leisure necessary for the arts and sciences, the pursuit of which elevates human beings above the other animals (III, 15; IV, 18; VI, 35; XLVI, 436).

To achieve the peace that makes civilized life possible, individuals must agree to restraints on their selfish aggressiveness. But many of Hobbes's readers have doubted his explanation of how this is done.

2. If human beings are naturally competitive, how is political order possible?

This question points to a paradox in Hobbes's reasoning. Because the selfish passions of human beings incline them to injure one another, they must agree to obey a government that will keep the peace. But if human beings in the state of nature cannot trust one another, then how can they be certain that one another's promise to obey the government they have established will be upheld? There seems to be a circularity in Hobbes's argument that government was established by consent of the governed through a social contract. Individuals keep their promises only when there is a government to enforce them, but a government comes into being only when people reliably promise to obey its laws. If promise keeping is a *consequence* of government, how can it also be the *prerequisite* of government?

Some opponents of Hobbes would point to this problem as an

indication of the flaws in any attempt to explain political authority as created by the consent of selfish individuals. If people are inclined to betray one another whenever it is selfishly beneficial to do so, then a social contract is impossible. But if they are not, then the contract is unnecessary. We should be interested in any response that Hobbes might have to this criticism. For the problem at issue must be solved if we want to defend the idea of governments "deriving their just powers from the consent of the governed."

Both the passions and reason, Hobbes explains, help us to escape the state of war (XIII, 84). A passionate fear of death and desire for the comforts of life incline us to peace, and our reason suggests rules of conduct that can secure peace if all obey them. These rules, "which conduce to the preservation of man's life on earth [are the] laws of nature" (XV, 96).

The first and most fundamental law of nature is that each should seek peace as far as it is attainable, but may resort to war when peace is unattainable (XIV, 85). This leads to the second law of nature, that each should give up the right to all things, when others do so also, to attain peace. From these two laws of nature, Hobbes infers seventeen other laws concerning the moral virtues and the social procedures necessary to the social contract (XV).

Hobbes warns, however, that relying on mere promises of cooperation is irrational because it assumes that individuals will keep their promises even when this is contrary to their interests. Rational self-interest does dictate that one submit to social order by sacrificing one's absolute liberty, but only when everyone else is forced by fear of punishment to make the same sacrifices. People are bound by "bonds, that have their strength, not from their own nature, for nothing is more easily broken than a man's word, but from fear of some evil consequence upon the rupture" (XIV, 86). "Covenants, without the sword," Hobbes insists, "are but words, and of no strength to secure a man at all" (XVII, 109). In Hobbes's social contract, one's word is *not* an adequate bond. Fear of the sword is the only reliable bond.

People must give up their individual powers to establish one common power over them all,

> as if every man should say to every man, *I authorize and give up my right of governing myself, to this man, or to this assembly of men, on this condition, that thou give up thy right to him, and authorize all his actions in like manner.* (XVII, 112)

A commonwealth is established by consent when all agree unanimously to accept whatever sovereign representative is selected by the majority (XVIII, 113).

Hobbes's social contract covers not only the institution of a government by those who choose the sovereign, but also the submission of all to a conqueror. When people are conquered and submit to the conqueror out of fear, they have thereby consented to that government just as fully as if they had freely selected the sovereign without coercion (XX).

Regardless of whether they are established by institution or by conquest, all governments have the same end. For there is only one purpose for which it would be in the rational self-interest of all to obey a government: to preserve peace by defending the people "both from foreign enemies, and from the injuries of one another" (XXIX, 213).

The general principle of Hobbes's social contract is that to rationally maximize our self-interest at the expense of others is actually irrational, because in the long run we can best promote our self-interest by respecting the rights of others so long as they, in turn, respect our rights. If we lived without a government, our individual liberty would be unlimited but insecure. Living under a government, our liberty is secure but limited.

Hobbes assumes that in consenting to government we are all naturally equal to one another. Each person has the same right to consent, and no person's consent carries any greater weight than another's. We know, however, that some people deny the principle of natural political equality. Some (like Socrates) would argue that it is natural for those who are wiser to rule those who are less wise. Others (like Thrasymachus) would argue that it is natural for the stronger to rule the weaker. Why shouldn't those naturally superior in mind or body rule those naturally inferior in such respects?

Hobbes dismisses the claims of physical strength by noting the rough equality of all people in their mortality. "For as to the strength of body, the weakest has strength enough to kill the strongest, either by secret machination, or by confederacy with others, that are in the same danger with himself" (XIII, 80). The English Revolution provided vivid illustrations of Hobbes's point. The victories won by Cromwell's armies and the beheading of the King make it clear that the rule of kings and aristocrats could not depend on physical strength. Of course, Machiavelli had already warned princes that their vulnerability to assassination made it necessary to avoid the hatred of the people. (As Mark Twain indicated in his *A Connecticut Yankee in King Arthur's Court*, the invention of gunpowder had a marvelous leveling effect on social relations.)

It is not as easy, however, to dismiss superior intelligence as an entitlement to political rule. Nevertheless, Hobbes denies Aristotle's claim that some are by nature more worthy to rule because of their superior wisdom.

> For there are very few so foolish, that had not rather govern themselves, than be governed by others: nor when the wise in their own conceit, contend by force, with them who distrust their own wisdom, do they always, or often, or almost at any time, get the victory. If nature therefore have made men equal, that equality is to be acknowledged: or if nature have made men unequal; yet because men that think themselves equal, will not enter into conditions of peace, but upon equal terms, such equality must be admitted. And therefore for the ninth law of nature, I put this, *that every man acknowledge another for his equal by nature.* The breach of this precept is *pride.* (XV, 100–101)

Here is the origin of that opinion commonly expressed in liberal societies that each person is just as good as any other, and anyone who claims to be better than others is guilty of elitist pride.

Aren't there some good, common-sense objections to Hobbes's reasoning? Why shouldn't we agree with Socrates that those who know how to rule should rule, and therefore those who are wise about political things should rule those who are less wise? Isn't it absurd to say that because any fool can kill a wise individual, fools are politically equal to the wise? What does the capacity to kill have to do with the capacity for political rule? Because a lion can kill a person, is a lion the political equal of a human?

A defender of Hobbes might begin by emphasizing that the equal right to consent does not mean an equal right to participate in making laws or particular political decisions. Hobbesian consent of the governed is a consent to be ruled by a sovereign who represents the subjects. The right of the people to consent to government is not a right to make policy but a right to decide who will represent the people in making policy. Popular consent, therefore, does not require that the people have a broad knowledge of how to rule.

Perhaps the crucial point is not that all are equal in their political knowledge, which is obviously untrue, but that "there are very few so foolish, that had not rather govern themselves, than be governed by others." Anyone with at least the minimal rationality of a mature adult has a desire for self-rule that cannot be denied without denying human nature itself. Some other animals—such as the social insects—conform to a social order by instinct, but the rationality that distinguishes a human being from other animals (including the lion mentioned earlier) dictates that human communities arise from the consent of their members (see XVII, 111).

Moreover, that trying to rule people without their consent is contrary to human nature is confirmed by their natural rebelliousness: "because men that think themselves equal, will not enter into conditions of peace, but upon equal terms, such equality must be admitted" (XV, 100–101).

Another objection, however, to Hobbes's idea of consenting to government is that it is founded on a fictional state of war. If in fact human beings have never existed as absolutely free individuals without a government, isn't it absurd to say that they created governments by their consent? Hobbes answers with three observations (XIII, 83). First, he says some primitive peoples do, in fact, live in a state of war. Second, he says that a state of war is imaginable as the sort of life that would exist if there were no government, as in a civil war. Third, even if particular individuals were never in a state of war one against another, sovereign rulers are always in such a state in their dealings with one another: because there is no world government, governments are always in a "posture of war" toward one another.

We cannot give any attention to this last point, except to notice that some contemporary "realist" theories of international relations do assume that the nations of the world are in a Hobbesian state of war with one another.[14] Hobbes's first point suggests that a study of primitive cultures would verify the movement from a state of war through a social contract as a fact of human history. His second point, on the other hand, would imply that the social contract is useful as an analytical tool for explaining politics even if it is not historically true. To evaluate the first point we could seek the guidance of modern anthropologists. And the second point bears on some recent theories in the social sciences.

The reports of cultural anthropologists would seem, at least at first glance, to contradict Hobbes's explanation of the origin of government.[15] Hobbes seems to assume that the state arose from an agreement among solitary individuals, though there is no anthropological evidence to support this. Instead, the evidence indicates that the political development of humankind has been a movement from stateless societies to the state. A stateless society is a primitive social order founded on small groups organized by kinship without any formal governmental institutions. A state arises when power and authority are centralized into a formal institutional structure. Throughout most of the biological and cultural evolution of humankind (for over a hundred thousand years), human beings lived in roving bands of hunter-gatherers. The organization of states was not possible until the appearance of agriculture (about ten thousand years ago), which created a sedentary way of life, abundant food, and expanding populations. The first state probably arose in Mesopotamia around 4000 to 3000 B.C., but throughout recorded history, down to the present, societies of hunter-gatherers living without formal laws and governments have persisted. Therefore, insofar as Hobbes suggests that social order is impossible without government, he is mistaken. And on this point, modern anthropology confirms one of Rousseau's major criticisms of Hobbes.

Some passages in the *Leviathan*, however, imply that Hobbes viewed the prepolitical condition of human beings as a primitive social order. He refers to the American Indians of the seventeenth century, for example, saying that although they have no government strictly speaking, they do have "the government of small families, the concord whereof dependeth on natural lust" (XIII, 83). In another passage concerning the natural condition without government, he says: "where men have lived by small families, to rob and spoil one another, has been a trade . . . and men observed no other laws therein, but the laws of honour" (XVIII, 109). Hobbes, it seems, would have no trouble accepting the idea of stateless societies organized by familial bonds.

Hobbes does not think "the government of small families" is a satisfactory way to secure order. The reasons he gives for this judgment are sustained by the anthropological evidence. He complains that familial groups do a poor job of keeping the peace either among themselves or in defense against foreign threats (XX, 133). Modern research suggests that as these weaknesses became acute, it was advantageous for people to allow governmental institutions to form.[16] There is also anthropological support for Hobbes's claim that societies without government cannot promote the agricultural and commercial development necessary for high civilization (XIII, 82).

Moreover, we could also find in many anthropological case studies confirmation for Hobbes's "laws of nature." Even where there is no government to make and enforce laws, Hobbes explains, "reason suggesteth convenient articles of peace, upon which men may be drawn to agreement" (XIII, 84). He lists nineteen of these articles of peace, and many of them conform closely to the informal rules for settling disputes that have been found in primitive societies with no formal institutions of government. For example, three of the laws of nature near the end of Hobbes's list dictate that disputes be submitted to judgment by impartial arbitrators (XV, 102). In fact, the practice of arbitration is common among primitive groups.[17] Of course, disputants are always free to stubbornly resist the arbitrated settlement in the hope of winning what they want through physical force. But violent feuds are usually costly to everyone involved, and therefore everyone has an interest in resolving conflicts peacefully.

Another way to achieve peace in primitive societies without government is the exchange of gifts. Anthropologists have observed elaborate procedures for the giving and returning of gifts by which bonds of reciprocity are maintained among groups that otherwise would fight one another. Some anthropologists—for example, Marshall Sahlins—have recognized this as a primitive version of Hobbes's social contract.[18] Hobbes's fourth law of nature is that each should show gratitude for gifts received by giving something in return. This is necessary because any one who gives away something expects to receive some benefit in return, and if this expectation is frustrated, "there will be no beginning of benevolence, or trust; nor consequently of mutual help; nor of reconciliation of one man to another; and therefore they are to remain still in the condition of *war*" (XV, 99).

Hobbes would argue, however, that only through the establishment of government is the state of war fully escaped, because informal customs of reciprocity cannot suffice for securing a stable peace. Although he would concede that there can be a precarious social order without government, he would say that such a condition would still be a state of war, insofar as war is understood to consist "not in actual fighting; but in the known disposition thereto, during all the time there is no assurance to the contrary" (XIII, 82).

And yet, how is it possible—to restate the fundamental question—for radically selfish human beings to accept the restraints imposed by a government? Is it sufficient to assume that all people will regard the sacrifices demanded by government as servicing their own long-run self-interest? We have seen how this problem arises in the anthropological study of primitive societies. The same Hobbesian problem is perhaps even clearer in Darwinian biology. If human beings have evolved through individual competition in what Darwin called "the struggle for existence," how can we explain the cooperative behavior that makes social life possible? This has become one of the central issues in the field of sociobiology, and the resultant biological theories of human sociality manifest a Hobbesian logic.[19] First, cooperation among closely related individuals can be explained genetically. (This might correspond to what Hobbes calls "the natural lust" underlying "the government of small families.") A natural inclination to aid one's relatives would be favored by natural selection if this aid promotes the transmission of one's genes into the next generation. Sometimes individuals maximize their contributions to the gene pool by sacrificing their own reproductive opportunities to promote the reproduction of their kin. In a beehive, for example, the queen is the only female who reproduces. All the other females care for their siblings rather than reproducing and caring for their own offspring. Of course, this could not explain the social bonds in large communities of unrelated individuals. Social cooperation can be purely egoistic, however, even when the cooperating individuals are unrelated. To the extent that human beings are interdependent, it is in the rational self-interest of each to cooperate for the good of the whole. Edward Wilson, one of the founders of sociobiology, speaks of this kind of cooperation as founded on a "social contract," of which only human beings are capable:

> The perfection of the social contract has broken the ancient vertebrae constraints imposed by rigid kin selection. Through the convention of reciprocation, combined with a flexible, endlessly productive language and a genius for verbal classification, human beings fashion long-remembered agreements upon which cultures and civilizations can be built.[20]

The parallel with Hobbes's teaching is clear (see XVII, 111–12). Although humans are not as naturally social as are other animals, they can artificially create social order through their cognitive ability for making agreements with one another.

But doesn't that same intellectual capacity for making promises include an ability for clever cheating? If those in Hobbes's state of nature are rational egoists, concerned only with calculating the best way to promote their own selfish interests, why wouldn't they try to enter the social contract dishonestly with the hope of becoming "free riders"? The smartest ones would seem likely to take advantage of their fellow citizens by enjoying the benefits of living in a cooperative society without assuming their fair share of the burdens. Successful thieves, for example, would steal from others while having legal protection for their own property. Thus, again we confront Thrasymachus's proposal that it is more beneficial to *appear* just than to *be* just.

Hobbes sees this difficulty because he warns that a person is ruined by keeping promises faithfully while others break theirs with impunity (XV, 103). But if everyone tries to cheat, the social contract is impossible. The very distrust that makes the contract necessary to secure peace will also dissolve it as quickly as it is formed.

Some critics of Hobbes see this as indicating the futility of his attempt to derive social order from egoistic individualism. Talcott

Parsons, for instance, an influential American sociologist, criticized Hobbes for not recognizing the importance of a "common value system." It is the sharing of norms or values, Parsons argued, that establishes and maintains a society; a society of utterly selfish individuals is impossible.[21]

In reply to this sort of criticism, the Hobbesian could explain that Hobbes does give weight to a "common value system" as constituted by the "laws of nature" that he lists in chapters 14 and 15 of the *Leviathan*. Explaining human nature as essentially selfish does not deny the reality of the social virtues. On the contrary, Hobbes would say that it is in the interest of all to live in a society that allows people to enjoy the benefits of peaceful cooperation with each other. People know that, to secure this beneficial outcome, they have to protect themselves from the temptation to cheat; and they do this by establishing a coercive government.

Here, then, is Hobbes's solution to the problem of the Thrasymachean "free rider." Where justice is defined by laws enforced by a common power through coercion, it is rational to be just. Hobbes concedes that a clever lawbreaker can procure greater benefits than the law-abiding citizen, at least in the short run (XV, 94–96). But if the sovereign is rigorous in detecting and punishing crimes, the risks of criminal activity become too costly in the long run.

Hobbes engages in the same kind of "cost-benefit analysis" that some contemporary economists have applied to political problems. Like Hobbes, these economists assume that each individual is a "rational maximizer" of personal interests. Therefore, they are inclined to agree with Hobbes that social order must be explained as derived from a "social contract" (at least hypothetically) that is mutually beneficial to all.[22] (Compare the "prisoner's dilemma" described in chapter 9, section 4.)

Economists have also applied Hobbes's reasoning to some contemporary economic and political issues. Consider, for example, the various ecological problems—overpopulation, pollution of water and air, and the scarcity of important natural resources. In each case, Hobbes would argue, governmental coercion is necessary to avoid the catastrophe that would result if every person was free to pursue personal interests.

The people who live along a river might find it beneficial to use the river to dispose of their wastes. But at some point, the river will become so polluted that everyone will be harmed. How can they prevent that? If conscientious individuals restrict their use of the river for waste disposal, they will be exploited by others who refuse to exercise the same self-restraint, because it's in each person's interest to get as much immediate use out of the river as possible, even though this will create a future disaster. This same logic applies to any natural resource that is available to all without anyone being held responsible for its proper conservation. Garrett Hardin, a prominent ecologist, has called this "the tragedy of the commons." The Hobbesian solution is clear: allow a government to coercively restrict individual freedom in the use of natural resources to promote conservation for the long-range benefit of all. In fact, many experts today think that the only escape from environmental catastrophe is, in Hardin's words, "mutual coercion, mutually agreed upon by the majority of the people affected."[23]

Would it be in everyone's *personal* interest to agree to such coercive limits on individual freedom? Presumably it would be if the environmental disaster were so imminent that it threatened the present generation. But if the disaster is so far in the future that only future generations will suffer, why should those living today sacrifice anything to avoid that future calamity? Why should a society preoccupied with self-preservation worry about the future preservation of the human species, or even of its own descendants?

Again, we see a possible weakness in the Hobbesian establishment of social order on egoistic individualism. A rational egoist might sacrifice present pleasures to attain even greater pleasures in the future. But it is not clear that such enlightened selfishness can support social life when it requires the sacrifice of one's own life for the good of others. (The death of a soldier fighting in defense of his or her country is an obvious example.) Does social and political order require an agreement on some things as being more valuable than individual lives? Wasn't that suggested by President John F. Kennedy in his celebrated words, "Ask not what your country can do for you—ask what you can do for your country"?

The problem is also implicit in the Declaration of Independence. On the one hand, government is established to secure individual rights, including the right to life. On the other hand, the signers of the Declaration must support it by promising to one another that they will sacrifice their lives in its defense: "We mutually pledge to each other our Lives, our Fortunes, and our sacred Honor."

Hobbes does not ignore this difficulty, however. He contends that the powers of a government must be absolute if it is to secure the public peace, and this includes the power to demand that subjects sacrifice their lives. Although Hobbes admits that such powers can be abused in ways that unfairly violate individual rights, he advises that such abuses of political power constitute a lamentable risk that must be accepted. But doesn't it seem odd that to protect our individual rights, we must submit to a government of absolute powers that can easily deprive us of our rights?

3. Why should we obey an absolute government?

Hobbes's answer to this question is that there is no rational alternative, because a limited government could never maintain order. "Sovereign power," Hobbes believes, "ought in all commonwealths to be absolute":

> the sovereign power, whether placed in one man, as in a monarchy, or in one assembly of men, as in popular, and aristocratical commonwealths, is as great, as possibly men can be imagined to make it. And though of so unlimited a power, men may fancy many evil consequences, yet the consequences of the want of it, which is perpetual war of every man against his neighbor, are much worse. The condition of man in this life shall never be without inconvenience; but there happeneth in no commonwealth any great inconvenience, but what proceeds from the subject's disobedience, and breach of those covenants, from which the commonwealth hath its being. (XX, 136)

Unlike Aristotle, Hobbes is concerned less with the various *kinds* of regimes than with the precondition for *any* regime whatsoever— the *power* to preserve order. And that power must be absolute, in the sense that the final judge of the rules of conduct for a society is the sovereign (see XVIII, 120; XXIX, 211–12). Because of their egoism, people cannot agree in their judgments of good and evil, just and unjust; and from their disagreements springs the unremitting conflict that is the natural state of war. Because the purpose of government is to pacify human life, a government must have an absolute monopoly in settling disputes; once a governmental ruling is made, it must be obeyed by all individuals. It is treasonous, therefore, to teach that each person is the judge of good and evil or that each person must be guided independently by conscience. For if people live by their own judgment, they will be divided by the diversity of their opinions, and society will dissolve into anarchy. Although making the sovereign the absolute judge of the rules of conduct may have "evil consequences," as Hobbes admits, the only alternative is the worst of all evils—a return to the state of war. Hobbes teaches us to pursue peace at any price. The "inconveniences" of absolute government are part of the price we must pay.

Perhaps the most obvious objection to Hobbes's argument would be based on our own political experience. Doesn't the history of democratic governments like that of the United States show that effective governments need not be absolute? Doesn't the American government maintain order with only limited powers? On the other hand, a Hobbesian could reply that the government of the United States is, in fact, "absolute" in its power, in the sense that all human conduct in the United States is subject to governmental regulation. Of course, as Hobbes explains, an absolute government leaves many matters unregulated, which leaves the subjects free to act as they please; certainly, the American government does not try to regulate every form of conduct. The point is that *in principle* any government must have the unlimited power to prescribe rules for everything.

As an example of the discretionary power of absolute government, Hobbes observes, "in many places of the world, men have the liberty of many wives: in other places, such liberty is not allowed" (XXI, 143). We could apply this to American legal history by considering the Supreme Court case of *Reynolds v. United States* (1878). In the nineteenth century, the Mormons practiced polygamy in violation of a federal law. They argued that the law was an unconstitutional violation of their religious freedom as protected by the First Amendment, which secures the "free exercise" of religion. But the Supreme Court upheld the law as constitutional. In his decision, Chief Justice Waite explained:

> Laws are made for the government of actions, and while they cannot interfere with mere religious belief and opinions, they may with practices. Suppose one believed that human sacrifices were a necessary part of religious worship, would it be seriously contended that the civil government under which he lived could not interfere to prevent a sacrifice? Or if a wife religiously believed it was her duty to burn herself upon the funeral pyre of a dead husband, would it be beyond the power of the civil government to prevent her carrying her belief into practice? . . . Can a man excuse his practices . . . because of his religious belief? To permit this would be to make the professed doctrines of religious belief superior to the law of the land, and in effect to permit every citizen to become a law unto himself. Government could exist only in name under such circumstances.[24]

Under a government of limited power dedicated to individual freedom, we would assume that our religious practices would be absolutely protected from legal restriction. Yet that is not the case in the United States. Notice how closely Waite's reasoning follows Hobbes's argument for absolute government. For any government to exist the "law of the land" must be superior to religious doctrines. To avoid the anarchy in which every individual would be a "law unto himself," government must have the power to regulate all actions, including those motivated by religious beliefs. Isn't this reasoning persuasive? Although we expect our government not to be excessive in its regulation of religion, in principle the government must have absolute discretion to restrict religious practices in whatever manner is necessary to preserve public order. Moreover, isn't it hard to imagine *any* area of human life that would *always* be free from legal regulation?

If we accept the Hobbesian doctrine of absolute government, can we still believe in the importance of individual freedom? Hobbes maintains that it is precisely the absoluteness of a government's power that secures individual rights.

4. Can only an absolute government protect individual liberty?

Although an absolute government deprives us of our unlimited natural liberty, Hobbes explains, it gives us a limited civil liberty protected from the force and fraud of our fellow citizens. For laws are made "to limit the natural liberty of particular men, in such manner, as they might not hurt, but assist one another, and join together against a common enemy" (XXVII, 175). Thus laws facilitate the exercise of individual freedom. The goal is

> not to bind the people from all voluntary actions; but to direct and keep them in such a motion, as not to hurt themselves by their own impetuous desires, rashness or indiscretion; as hedges are set, not to stop travellers, but to keep them in their way. (XXX, 227)

This image of the laws as hedges conveys Hobbes's thought that, within the boundaries set by the sovereign, individuals are free to live as they please.

Although the sovereign has, in principle, the unlimited power to dictate rules for all the subjects' actions, the rules actually established under any government cover only a small portion of human actions. Therefore, most of the liberties of the subject

> depend on the silence of the law. In cases where the sovereign has prescribed no rule, there the subject hath the liberty to do, or forbear, according to his own discretion. And therefore such liberty is in some places more and in some less; and in some times more in other times less, according as they that have the sovereignty shall think most convenient. (XXI, 143)

This liberty arising from the silence of the laws covers most private affairs:

> such as is the liberty to buy, and sell, and otherwise contract with one another; to choose their own abode, their own diet, their own trade of life, and institute their children as they themselves think fit; and the like. (XXI, 139)

From this we could conclude that Hobbes leaves more room for individual liberty than did the premodern political philosophers. For in Hobbes we see a distinctly modern separation between the state and society. Unlike the ancient Greek *polis*, the modern state need not regulate every facet of life. Within the limits set by the state, citizens are free to live their private lives as they wish. But in the ancient Greek city, every part of human life must conform to the moral standards of the regime. Hobbes assumes that what the law does not forbid it permits. But Aristotle assumes that what the law does not permit it forbids (*Nicomachean Ethics* 1138a4–8). A Hobbesian Leviathan would seem to allow for more individual freedom than is possible in an Aristotelian polis.

On the other hand, some critics of Hobbes have pointed out that unlike Aristotle, Hobbes gives little attention to political freedom. Hobbes speaks of the liberty of subjects in their private lives, but not of the liberty of citizens in their political activities. Aristotle's citizen must *participate* in political rule, but Hobbes's subject has only the right to be *represented* in government.

Should we agree with Rousseau that because true freedom requires participatory democracy, representation is a disguised form of slavery? Or should we accept Hobbes's claim that most people do not want to participate directly in political rule, but would prefer a representative government that would secure their private liberty? Do modern liberal democracies—like the United States—conform more closely to Hobbes's teaching than to Rousseau's or Aristotle's?

It appears that Hobbes violates the principles of modern liberal democratic thought on at least one point. He seems to deny the claim that certain individual rights are unalienable, because the idea of unalienable rights would seem to deprive governments of the absolute power that Hobbes regards as essential. Indeed, Hobbes has been criticized for not giving the individual sufficient protection from governmental tyranny. In response to Hobbes, John Locke argued that to be ruled by an arbitrary, absolute power is worse than living in the state of nature: "He being in a much worse condition, who is exposed to the arbitrary power of one man, who has the command of 100,000, than he that is exposed to the arbitrary power of 100,000 single men" (*Second Treatise*, section 137).

In defense of Hobbes, however, we should note that he does recognize self-preservation as an unalienable right, so that one can disobey a life-threatening legal order. People do not forfeit all their rights when they consent to government. Because all voluntary actions serve the interests of the individuals who perform them, Hobbes explains, it is inconceivable that those individuals would voluntarily agree to sacrifice their lives. People give up their natural liberty only to enhance "the security of a man's person, in his life, and in the means of so preserving life, as not to be weary of it" (XIV, 87). Consequently, we cannot be obligated by the social contract to act contrary to that very self-preservation which the contract must secure. Although social peace requires that all sacrifice certain natural rights, it is "necessary for man's life, to retain some; as right to govern their own bodies; enjoy air, water, motion, ways to go from place to place; and all things else, without which a man cannot live, or not live well" (XV, 101).

Clearly, no one can be obligated by law to commit suicide or self-injury, "because no law can oblige a man to abandon his own preservation" (XXVII, 197). A subject legally condemned to die may justifiably try to escape punishment (XIV, 91–92; XXI, 142). Likewise, a subject forced into military service does not act unjustly in attempting to run away from battle if inclined by cowardice to do so (XXI, 143). Hobbes would allow citizens to disobey their government to protect their bodily survival. But does their right to resistance extend beyond this to include the right to defend "all things . . . without which a man cannot live, or not live well"?

In any case, Hobbes seems to recognize certain unalienable rights as limits on the power of the sovereign. Some readers of the *Leviathan* have inferred that although Hobbes's sovereign is absolute in principle, in practice the sovereign will always have to negotiate with the subjects when they are discontented. For the sovereign needs the obedience of the subjects to secure the sovereign's interests as much as they need the sovereign's power to secure their own interests. Because a return to the state of war would be equally disastrous for everyone, regardless of status, the fear of civil war should moderate the sovereign as much as the subjects.

Still, don't we see here a fundamental dilemma for Hobbes? On the one hand, people must give up their natural liberty to a government if they want peace. On the other hand, they must retain at least some of their natural liberty to escape governmental oppression. If we want to protect an individual's rights from the attacks of other individuals, then we must, Hobbes insists, have an absolute sovereign. But Hobbes concedes that if we also want to protect an individual's rights from governmental oppression, then we must allow the individual to retain certain rights as a limit on the sovereign's power. Thus, we are thrown into a contradiction in which the powers of government must be both absolute and limited.

We can see this same dilemma in the Declaration of Independence. We are endowed with "certain unalienable rights" such as "Life, Liberty and the pursuit of Happiness," but we need powerful governments to secure these rights, and the powers of government require some limits on individuals' rights. For must not every government restrict the individual's life, liberty, and pursuit of happiness? Not only must a government have the power to punish criminals, it must also be able to demand sacrifices from law-abiding citizens, including the sacrifice of life itself in time of war.

The Declaration of Independence, however, offers one weapon against tyrannical government that Hobbes does not — the right to revolution. Although Hobbes grants all citizens individually the right to defend their own lives against governmental violence, he denies that people have the right to combine their individual acts of resistance into a revolutionary movement (see XXI, 143; XXVIII, 202).

5. Does the right to revolution subvert good government?

Even the authors of the Declaration of Independence concede that revolutions should be avoided whenever possible: "Prudence, indeed, will dictate that Governments long established should not be changed for light and transient causes; and accordingly all experience hath shown that mankind are more disposed to suffer, while evils are sufferable, than to right themselves by abolishing the forms to which they are accustomed." Surely, we would agree that to avoid the anarchy of civil war, people should be reluctant to support a revolution, even when they have serious grievances against the established government. Prudence and experience teach us that in most cases any stable social order grounded in the customary life of a people should be preserved. But should we go so far as to agree with Hobbes that no government should ever be overthrown as long as it is capable of maintaining order?

Hobbes advises subjects to obey whatever government they have because even an oppressive government is better than a civil war, which is "the greatest evil that can happen in this life" (XXX, 219). When subjects feel exploited by their sovereign, Hobbes observes, they desire a different form of government, "whereas the power in all forms, if they be perfect enough to protect them, is the same: not considering that the state of man can never be without some incommodity or other" (XVIII, 120). Because preserving peace is perhaps the only purpose of government on which we can all agree, we should not worry about what *kind* of government we have as long as we have *some* government. Let us not argue about *who* should rule, Hobbes insists, because that will only lead to endless conflict; let us just be satisfied that *someone* rules.

This is the reason why Hobbes ridicules Aristotle's distinction between tyrannical and nontyrannical rulers (XIX, 121; XXIX, 214; XLVI, 438, 446–48). When an individual calls a government tyrannical, that usually means only that he or she does not happen to like it. But liking or disliking is a matter of personal taste that varies from one person to another. Therefore, Hobbes argues, to teach that people can justly overthrow every government that they regard as tyrannical—the teaching of Aristotle and the Declaration of Independence—is to promote continual anarchy.

Hobbes does concede that every sovereign is obligated by the law of nature to rule only for the safety of the people (XXI, 139; XXVI, 174; XXVIII, 209; XXX, 219). But this does not provide a right to revolution, since Hobbes emphasizes that although the sovereign is accountable to God for any violation of the law of nature, he is not accountable to any human being.

Because the right to revolution has become a traditional assumption in American political thought, American readers of the *Leviathan* often find it hard to accept Hobbes's rejection of that right. But at certain points in American history, many American political leaders have agreed with Hobbes. In the Smith Act of 1940, for example, the United States Congress made it illegal to teach the desirability "of overthrowing or destroying any government in the United States by force or violence."[25] Doesn't this deny the right to revolution? When some leaders of the American Communist party were arrested under this law for peacefully teaching Marxism, which includes the doctrine that capitalism must someday be overthrown in a socialist revolution, they appealed their case to the Supreme Court. In *Dennis v. United States* (1951), the Court upheld the constitutionality of the Smith Act. Chief Justice Vinson explained:

> That it is within the *power* of the Congress to protect the government of the United States from armed rebellion is a

proposition which requires little discussion. Whatever theoretical merit there may be to the argument that there is a "right" to rebellion against dictatorial governments is without force where the existing structure of the government provides for peaceful and orderly change. We reject any principle of governmental helplessness in the face of preparation for revolution, which principle, carried to its logical conclusion, must lead to anarchy.[26]

Does Vinson simply restate Hobbes's reasoning? A right to revolution would subvert every government, he seems to say, because only as long as a government has the power to suppress attempts at revolution can it prevent anarchy. Or is Vinson saying that there *is* a right to revolution when a government does not provide for "peaceful and orderly change"? But how could any government permit *revolutionary* change that would bring about its own abolition? (Compare chapter 8, section 8.)

Is it dangerous to teach people that they can disobey a law whenever they think it violates some "higher law"? If we could rely on people's obeying the higher law as the ground for social order, we wouldn't need governments. In fact, we need governments precisely because people fall into conflict when they are left to live by their own rules. Therefore, the Hobbesian would argue, those like Henry David Thoreau and Martin Luther King, Jr., who say that every person has a right to disobey any law that seems unjust, would destroy that unquestioned obedience to every law that is essential to any political order. (We have examined the idea of civil disobedience previously in chapter 1, section 2; and chapter 4, sections 1–2.)

It is naive, Hobbes suggests, to think that through revolution an unjust government can be replaced by a truly just government. Human beings will always disagree about what is just and unjust. Because every government will be disadvantageous to some people, no government can please everyone. Rather than requiring that government conform to some idealistic conception of justice, would it be more practical to insist that people obey any government that maintains order?

Yet if this teaching is so practical, why has it been so unpopular? Does Hobbes's difficulty in winning acceptance for his political principles indicate that, in some respects, his teaching is just as idealistic as Plato's?

6. Is the founding of political authority on rational selfishness too idealistic?

Considering the difference between his political teaching and the political practice of the world, Hobbes admits that his project may be as unrealistic as Plato's. Nevertheless, he hopes that someday a ruler will read his book and apply it by teaching its principles, and thus might "convert this truth of speculation, into the utility of practice" (XXXI, 241).

Hobbes concedes that the best objection to his account of political power is that it does not conform to political practice: in most cases, human beings have not voluntarily granted absolute power to their governments. Hobbes argues, however, that this explains why most governments have been unstable and thus unsuccessful in maintaining order. Does Hobbes's political reasoning rest, therefore, not on what *is* but on what *ought* to be? "For though in all places of the world, men should lay the foundation of their houses on the sand," Hobbes observes, "it could not thence be inferred, that so it ought to be" (XX, 136).

Hobbes presents government as an instrument by which selfish human beings rationally secure their interests. And yet, in assuming that rational selfishness dominates human nature, Hobbes may demand more rationality than most human beings have.[27] He faces the same problem that Socrates saw in Thrasymachus's argument: even if political power is sought only to advance selfish interests, those seeking it must *know* what their *true* interests are, and therefore they must also seek political wisdom. But does this mean that Hobbes would have to agree with Socrates about the need for philosopher-kings?

Unlike Socrates, Hobbes would say that the primary concern of politics is not the mind but the body; not the cultivation of the soul but physical survival and comfort. The proper care of the body surely does require some thinking. Deciding how government can best secure the physical life of its subjects does demand political wisdom of some sort, and thus politics does depend somehow on the rule of reason. Hobbes would insist, however, that we are more likely to agree about the conditions of self-preservation than we are about the improvement of our souls. Doesn't this make his teaching more practicable than that of Plato?

But like Plato, Hobbes cannot succeed unless these political principles are promoted by the right kind of education. Particularly important is the instruction of the young in the universities (XXX, 221; Conclusion, 467). In fact, it could be argued that the influence of Hobbesian principles in the universities has indeed shaped the history of modern liberal political thought.

On the other hand, many scholars would claim that modern liberalism — especially as manifested in America — arose from the rejection of Hobbesian absolutism in favor of the Lockean conception of limited government. Does this hold true? Or can we find traces of Hobbesianism even in a liberal regime like that of the United States?

7. Is the American government a Hobbesian Leviathan?

Surely, most of us would want to say no. We could offer a variety of reasons for concluding that the American regime is not Hobbesian. We could argue, for example, that the American founders — such as Thomas Jefferson and James Madison — wanted a government of limited powers, which was contrary to Hobbesian absolutism. The separation and balance of powers was one way to insure that no one branch of the government would be absolute. The Bill of Rights in the Constitution specified certain individual rights that were protected against governmental power. And, generally, the pluralistic structure of American society and government, which allowed many different groups to have some power, guaranteed that political decisions would emerge from bargaining and negotiation in which no one group of people would be able to completely dominate. In the American regime, therefore, it is hard to see that concentration of power in the hands of the sovereign which Hobbes demands.

Nevertheless, a Hobbesian could maintain that a careful study of the matter will uncover the Hobbesian reality of American politics.[28] He could point out, for instance, that the American founders wrote the Constitution to establish a very powerful government. In *Federalist* Number 1, Alexander Hamilton emphasized that "the vigor of government is essential to the security of liberty."[29] And in Number 23, he observed, "It is both unwise and dangerous to deny the federal government an unconfined authority as to all those objects which are intrusted to its management."[30] The need for powerful government is especially acute, Hamilton argued in Number 70, with respect to the executive power. He even implied that in times of emergency the American president would have the power to become a temporary dictator.[31] This conforms to Hobbes's observation that in periods of crisis democratic governments are forced to set up "temporary monarchs, to whom for a time, they may commit the entire exercise of their power" (XIX, 125). As we shall see in the next chapter (section 7), Locke spoke of this sort of power as an exercise of "executive prerogative."

The belief that the Bill of Rights limits the powers of American government would be challenged by the Hobbesian. As in the Supreme Court cases cited earlier in this chapter, couldn't we think of many instances in which the government has been permitted to violate the rights listed in the Bill of Rights? The First Amendment, for example, protects "freedom of speech" absolutely from any congressional abridgment: "Congress shall make no law...abridging the freedom of speech, or of the press." But beginning with the case of *Schenck v. United States* (1919),[32] the Supreme Court has said that Congress *may* make laws abridging the freedom of speech in some situations. In the Schenck case, a young man was sent to prison for breaking a federal law by criticizing the military draft during the First World War. Doesn't this suggest that the government of the United States has, at least potentially, an absolute power to violate individual rights whenever the rulers deem it necessary?

Contrary to Hobbes, however, there is no self-perpetuating governmental body in the United States that we could identify as the sovereign. The powers of sovereignty are divided between different offices of the government. Nevertheless, can't a *pattern* of offices be just as absolutely sovereign as one? For to the extent that the Congress, the president, and the Supreme Court agree with one another, isn't the power of the national government as unlimited as that of Hobbes's Leviathan?

Moreover, hasn't the growth of an American welfare state in the twentieth century confirmed Hobbes's teaching about the need for powerful, centralized government? Hobbes argues that when citizens are deprived, through no fault of their own, of the ability to take care of themselves, then the government ought to provide for their needs so that they do not have to depend on private charity (XXX, 227). In this way, government promotes individual freedom by protecting the poor and the weak against the rich and the powerful. Franklin Roosevelt made this same argument to justify his New Deal programs during the economic crisis of the 1930s.

Although those Americans today who call themselves liberals would agree with Hobbes that only a powerful state can secure individual rights, others who call themselves conservatives (or perhaps libertarians) would insist that the greatest threat to liberty today comes from an excessively powerful government. A Hobbesian Leviathan, they complain, protects us from one another but does not protect us from itself. Or, as Ronald Reagan often warned in his presidential campaign speeches in 1980, "Any government powerful enough to give you everything you want is powerful enough to take from you everything you have."

Liberals and conservatives agree with the Hobbesian principle, embodied in the Declaration of Independence, that government must secure individual rights. But they disagree about how government can best do this. The conservatives stress the need to limit the powers of the state, especially with respect to economic matters; therefore, protecting the individual's right to property is crucial. On this point conservatives draw their reasoning from John Locke.

Notes

1. All the Arabic numerals in this chapter indicate page references to the *Leviathan* in the Michael Oakeshott edition (Oxford: Basil Blackwell, 1957). The Roman numerals indicate chapter numbers.
2. See W. H. Greenleaf, "Hobbes: The Problem of Interpretation," in *Hobbes and Rousseau*, ed. Maurice Cranston and Richard S. Peters (Garden City, NY: Doubleday, Anchor Books, 1972), 5–36.
3. See M. M. Goldsmith, *Hobbes's Science of Politics* (New York: Columbia University Press, 1966); and Thomas A. Spragens, Jr., *The Politics of Motion* (London: Croom Helm, 1973).
4. See Leo Strauss, *The Political Philosophy of Hobbes*, trans. Elsa M. Sinclair (Chicago: University of Chicago Press, 1952); and C. B. Macpherson, *The Political Theory of Possessive Individualism* (Oxford: Clarendon Press, 1962).
5. See Oakeshott's introduction to his edition of the *Leviathan*. The nominalist belief that universals are fictional creations of the mind that have no real existence supports the materialism, individualism, and skepticism that pervades not only Hobbesian thought but most of modern philosophy. For defenses of nominalism, see E. H. Gombrich, *Art and Illusion*, 2nd ed. (New York: Pantheon, 1961), 291–329, 359–96; Willard Van Orman Quine, *From a Logical Point of View*, 2nd ed. (New York: Harper & Row, 1963), 1–19; Michel Foucault, *The Order of Things* (New York: Random House, Vintage, 1973); and Nelson Goodman, *Ways of Worldmaking* (Indianapolis: Hackett, 1978), 91–107. For criticisms of nominalism, see Richard M. Weaver, *Ideas Have Consequences* (Chicago: University of Chicago Press, 1948); John Wild, *Introduction to Realist Philosophy* (New York: Harper & Brothers, 1948), 448–62; Roberto Mangabeira Unger, *Knowledge and Politics* (New York: Free Press, 1975); and Mortimer J. Adler, *Ten Philosophical Mistakes* (New York: Macmillan, 1985), 30–53, 72–82.

   How would a radical nominalist explain the universal linguistic patterns in color terms, "folktaxonomy," and logic? Do these manifest a universal human biology? See Brent Berlin, *Ethnobiological*

Classification (Princeton: Princeton University Press, 1992); Brent Berlin and Paul Kay, *Basic Color Terms* (Berkeley: University of California Press, 1969); Scott Atran, *Cognitive Foundations of Natural History* (Cambridge: Cambridge University Press, 1990); and Frits Staal, *Universals: Studies in Indian Logic and Linguistics* (Chicago: University of Chicago Press, 1988).

6. See Howard Warrender, *The Political Philosophy of Hobbes* (Oxford: Clarendon Press, 1957).

7. See Gary D. Glenn, "Inalienable Rights and Positive Government in the Modern World," *Journal of Politics* 41 (November 1979): 1057–80. See also Joseph Cropsey, "Conservatism and Liberalism," in *Political Philosophy and the Issues of Politics* (Chicago: University of Chicago Press, 1977), 116–30, for a study of conservatism and liberalism as "movements of opinion, residues to some extent of political philosophy but not themselves political philosophy" (129).

8. In 1672 Richard Cumberland published the first defense of Aristotle's understanding of political animals against Hobbes's critique. He argued that all the natural causes that incline animals to social cooperation— such as parental care, mutual aid, and reciprocal exchange—are just as strong in human beings as they are in some other animals. He saw the human capacities for speech and reason as the natural instruments by which human beings become more political than the other political animals. See Cumberland, *A Treatise of the Laws of Nature*, translated by John Maxwell (London: R. Phillips, 1727), 93–163.

9. See, for example, Ashley Montagu, *The Nature of Human Aggression* (Oxford: Oxford University Press, 1976); and Margaret Power, *The Egalitarians—Human and Chimpanzee: An Anthropological View of Social Organization* (Cambridge: Cambridge University Press, 1991). The Hobbesian position is often identified (perhaps incorrectly) with Konrad Lorenz, *On Aggression* (New York: Harcourt, Brace & World, 1966). For a defense of Lorenz that is also critical of Hobbes, see Mary Midgley, *Beast and Man: The Roots of Human Nature* (Ithaca: Cornell University Press, 1978). For criticisms of the Hobbesian elements of contemporary sociobiology see R. C. Lewontin, Steven Rose, and Leon J. Kamin, *Not In Our Genes: Biology, Ideology, and Human Nature* (New York: Simon & Schuster, 1985), 514–29.

When Hobbes speaks of civil wars as manifesting the state of nature, he might have in mind Thucydides' famous account of the Corcyraean civil war in his *History of the Peloponnesian War* (III, 80–84; IV, 46–48), a book that Hobbes translated into English. Compare Hobbes's description of human nature with Thucydides' *History* I, 22, 76; II, 47–54, 64–65; IV, 92; V, 89, 105; VI, 83–85. See Laurie M. Johnson, *Thucydides, Hobbes, and the Interpretation of Realism* (DeKalb: Northern Illinois University Press, 1993).

The problem for Hobbes is not that *all* are unlimited in their appetites, but that because *some* are, all others must act to protect themselves (*Leviathan*, XIII, 81). Because only a few are naturally aggressive, it is possible for others to agree on the laws of reason as secured by government to defend themselves against the aggressive few. On the implications of this idea for social evolution, see Andrew Bard Schmookler, *The Parable of the Tribes* (Berkeley: University of California Press, 1984).

10. See Macpherson's *Possessive Individualism*. Macpherson relies on a Marxist interpretation of the English Revolution that is now disputed by some historians. See Jack A. Goldstone, "Capitalist Origins of the English Revolution: Chasing a Chimera," *Theory and Society* 12 (1983):143–80. Compare Christopher Hill, *The Century of Revolution, 1603–1714* (New York: Norton, 1980), 1–4, 86–91, 161–64.

11. Sigmund Freud, *Civilization and Its Discontents*, trans. James Strachey (New York: Norton, 1962), 69. Do those who suffer from psychotic delusion live in a Hobbesian state of nature? See James M. Glass, *Delusion: Internal Dimensions of Political Life* (Chicago: University of Chicago Press, 1985), 1–18, 124–80.

12. Karl Marx and Friedrich Engels, *Communist Manifesto*, in *The Marx-Engels Reader*, ed. Robert C. Tucker, 2nd ed. (New York: Norton, 1978), 475–76.

13. Colin Turnbull, *The Mountain People* (New York: Simon & Schuster, 1972), 182. Compare the struggle for survival among the Dobuans as described by Ruth Benedict, *Patterns of Culture* (Boston: Houghton Mifflin, 1934), chap. 5.

14. See, for example, Robert E. Osgood and Robert W. Tucker, *Force, Order, and Justice* (Baltimore: Johns Hopkins University Press, 1967), 3–40. For an opposing point of view, see Charles R. Beitz, *Political Theory and International Relations* (Princeton: Princeton University Press, 1979), 11–66; and Terry Nardin, *Law, Morality and the Relations of States* (Princeton: Princeton University Press, 1983).

15. On the various theories of the origins of the state, see Paul Bohannan, ed., *Law and Warfare: Studies in the Anthropology of Conflict* (Austin: University of Texas Press, 1967); Elman R. Service, *Origins of the State and Civilization* (New York: Norton, 1975); Ronald Cohen and Elman R. Service, eds., *Origins of the State: The Anthropology of Political Evolution* (Philadelphia: Institute for the Study of Human Issues, 1978); and Roger Masters, *The Nature of Politics* (New Haven: Yale University Press, 1989), chap. 6.

16. See Service, *Origins of the State*, 292–308.

17. See, for instance, R. F. Barton, "Procedure Among the Ifugao," in Bohannan, *Law and Warfare*, 161–81.

18. See Marshall Sahlins, "The Spirit of the Gift," in *Stone Age Economics* (Chicago: Aldine, 1972), 149–83.

19. See Charles Darwin, *The Descent of Man*, chaps. 4–5, in *The Origin of Species and the Descent of Man* (New York: Random House, Modern Library, 1936), 471–511; Edward O. Wilson, *Sociobiology: The New Synthesis* (Cambridge: Harvard University Press, 1975), 106–29; Wilson, *On Human Nature* (Cambridge: Harvard University Press,

1978), 149–67; and Roger D. Masters, *The Nature of Politics*, chap. 5. Masters argues that "Hobbes's political theory is easily translated into the terms of inclusive fitness and rational actor models" (p. 174), which are common ideas in sociobiological theory.

20. Wilson, *On Human Nature*, 156. "Contrary to some cultural relativists, it can be hypothesized that a norm of reciprocity is universal" (Alvin Gouldner, "The Norm of Reciprocity," *American Sociological Review* 25 [1960]: 171). On the biological roots of reciprocity, see Robert Trivers, "The Evolution of Reciprocal Altruism," *Quarterly Review of Biology* 46 (1971): 35–57; and Richard D. Alexander, *The Biology of Moral Systems* (Hawthorne, NY: Aldine de Gruyter, 1987).

21. Talcott Parsons, *The Structure of Social Action* (New York: McGraw-Hill, 1937), 91–94, 767–68. Compare Brian Barry, *Sociologists, Economists & Democracy* (Chicago: University of Chicago Press, 1978), 75–98.

22. See James Buchanan, *The Limits of Liberty: Between Anarchy and Leviathan* (Chicago: University of Chicago Press, 1975); David Gauthier, *Morals by Agreement* (Oxford: Oxford University Press, 1986); Ian MacLean, "The Social Contract in Leviathan and the Prisoner's Dilemma Supergame," *Political Studies* 29 (September 1981): 339–51; and Michael Taylor, *The Possibility of Cooperation* (Cambridge: Cambridge University Press, 1987), chap. 6.

23. Garrett Hardin, "The Tragedy of the Commons," in Garrett Hardin and John Baden, eds., *Managing the Commons* (San Francisco: W. H. Freeman, 1977), 27. See also William Ophuls, "Leviathan or Oblivion?" in Herman E. Daly, eds., *Toward a Steady-State Economy* (San Francisco: W. H. Freeman, 1973), 215–30.

24. Quoted in Gerald Gunther, ed., *Cases and Materials on Constitutional Law*, 9th ed. (Mineola, NY: Foundation Press, 1975), 1506.

25. Quoted in Gunther, *Constitutional Law*, 1098. See George Anastaplo, *The Constitutionalist: Notes on the First Amendment* (Dallas: Southern Methodist University Press, 1971), 45–46, 446–51. Compare Walter F. Berns, *Freedom, Virtue and the First Amendment* (Chicago: Regnery, 1965), 200–27.

26. Gunther, *Constitutional Law*, 1099–1100.

27. In *Behemoth*, Hobbes's book on the English Civil War, he indicates that human beings are not solely moved by rational self-interest; rather, they are often moved by irrational beliefs (particularly, religious beliefs) that lead them into self-destructive conflict. This would suggest that Hobbes's psychology is more complex than the rational egoism of some "rational choice" theorists. See Hobbes, *Behemoth or The Long Parliament*, ed. Ferdinand Tonnies, with an Introduction by Stephen Holmes (Chicago: University of Chicago Press, 1990).

28. See Frank M. Coleman, *Hobbes and America: Exploring the Constitutional Foundations* (Toronto: University of Toronto Press, 1977).

29. Alexander Hamilton, James Madison, and John Jay, *The Federalist*, ed. Edward Mead Earle (New York: Random House, Modern Library, n.d.), No. 1, p. 5.
30. Ibid., No. 23, p. 145.
31. Ibid., No. 70, p. 454.
32. Reprinted in Gunther, *Constitutional Law*, 1055–57. See Anastaplo, *The Constitutionalist*, 44–47, 294–305.

Chapter

8

Individual Rights and Limited Government
Locke's *Second Treatise of Government*

Key Readings

Second Treatise, sections 1–57, 60–61, 74–83, 85, 87–174, 183, 199–243.

John Locke (1632–1704) was the son of an English lawyer. He was educated in London and at Oxford University where he studied philosophy, natural science, and medicine. Subsequently, he was appointed a physician at Oxford. His studies in science earned him the honor of being elected a Fellow of the Royal Society in 1668, which permitted him to associate with scientists such as Isaac Newton.

In 1666, Locke became the personal physician and political advisor to Anthony Ashley Cooper, who later became the first earl of Shaftesbury. Being one of the principal Whig opponents of the restored monarchy, Shaftesbury was responsible for Locke becoming involved in the greatest political controversies of his time concerning the powers of the King.

After the death of Oliver Cromwell in 1658, a new Parliament was elected in 1660, and Charles II was summoned to the throne under the condition that he accept some parliamentary limits on royal authority. Because of his opposition to the King, Shaftesbury was sent to prison for a year in 1677. Locke also aroused the suspicions of the King, who had spies report on his activities. In 1682, as a result of an unsuccessful revolutionary plot against the King, Shaftesbury was forced to flee to Holland. During this time, Algernon Sydney, a Whig leader, was beheaded for treason. Much of the evidence at his trial arose from his *Discourses Concerning Government*, in which he argued that republican government was superior to monarchy. Locke fled to Holland in 1683 and was unable to return to England until 1689. During this period, he wrote the first draft of the *Second Treatise of Government*. Owing to his fear of persecution, Locke felt compelled to be cautious in expressing his revolutionary teaching. In fact, he was so careful that he always denied that he was the author of the *Second Treatise*.

James II ascended the throne in 1685 with the support of the majority in Parliament (the Tories), but the Whigs opposed him. That James was a Catholic was one reason for opposition among those Englishmen who feared the political influence of the Catholic Church. In 1688, it appeared that the throne would pass not to James's Protestant daughters—Mary and Anne—but to his newborn Catholic son. The Whigs led the revolution in that year that gave the throne to Mary and her husband William of Orange. William and Mary had to accept a Bill of Rights that made Parliament sovereign through its powers over taxation and the maintenance of the military. When Locke published his *Second Treatise* in 1689, it was regarded as a philosophical defense of this revolution of 1688.[1]

In later years, Locke published other works on economics, religion, epistemology, and education. His *Essay Concerning Human Understanding* became one of the most widely read books of the eighteenth century. All of his writings manifested a spirit of enlightenment and of what later came to be called liberalism.[2] Locke defended individual liberty in every realm of life—economics, religion, culture, and politics. The aim of a Lockean government, therefore, would be to secure the equal right of every individual to freedom.

That sort of thinking reminds us of the Declaration of Independence. Indeed, the *Second Treatise* formulated perhaps better than any other book the principles to which the Americans of 1776 would appeal: natural equality, unalienable rights, government by the consent of the governed, and the right to revolution.³ Moreover, many of the constitutional principles of American government, such as the separation of powers and the rule of law, can also be found in Locke's work. Examining Locke's political thought, therefore, helps us to understand some of the fundamental assumptions of American liberal democracy. We can begin with the most crucial principle of liberal politics—natural equality.

1. Are all human beings naturally equal?

We have already seen in Hobbes's *Leviathan* an affirmation of equality in the "state of nature." But Hobbes's political thought, at least on the surface, contradicts liberal democracy as we usually understand it. Locke, however, develops that view of human equality that has become the starting point for liberalism. We must wonder if Locke can give us a persuasive explanation of that idea of equality that we so commonly take for granted in our political reasoning.

To discover the just foundations of political power, Locke suggests at the beginning of the *Second Treatise*, we must consider the natural condition of our ancestors prior to the formation of society and government. In this "state of nature," they would be perfectly free. They would also be equal.

> A *state* of *equality*, wherein all the power and jurisdiction is reciprocal, no one having more than another; there being nothing more evident, than that creatures of the same species and rank, promiscuously born to all the same advantages of nature, and the use of the same faculties, should also be equal one amongst another without subordination or subjection, unless the lord and master of them all should by any manifest declaration of his will, set one above another, and confer on him, by an evident and clear appointment an undoubted right to dominion and sovereignty. (section 4)⁴

Locke adds that in the "state of nature" reason teaches "that being all *equal and independent*, no one ought to harm another in his life, health, liberty, or possessions" because

> being furnished with like faculties, sharing all in one community of nature, there cannot be supposed any such *subordination* among us, that may authorize us to destroy one another, as if we were made for one another's uses, as the inferior ranks of creatures are for our's. (section 6)

Thus, there is "nothing more evident" than that all are equal in that they are "creatures of the same species" and that they share "all in one community of nature": all human beings are equal because all are equally human! We are all members of the same human species as distinguished from other animal species that occupy "the inferior ranks of creatures." There is a biological difference between a human and a dog, Locke seems to say, that justifies the human's rule over the dog. But there is no such difference in nature that would justify one person ruling another without the other's consent.

Locke makes it clear in other parts of the *Second Treatise* that the possession of reason distinguishes human beings from other animals. It is as "rational creatures" that we are separated from other beings (section 124), and this rationality is the source of human equality of rights. Children, therefore, "are not born in this full state of *equality*, though they are born to it" (section 55), because they cannot rightfully assert their freedom from parental authority until they reach the age at which they can live on their own as rational beings. A violent criminal, however, "having renounced reason, the common rule and measure God hath given to mankind," forfeits the human equality of rights and therefore "may be destroyed as a *lion* or a *tyger*, one of those wild savage beasts, with whom men can have no society nor security" (section 11).

How does the quality of rationality justify the right to life, liberty and property? Locke is unclear on this point, but he gives us some hints from which we can infer the logic of his argument. In some passages, Locke suggests that the rationality of human beings gives them a unique capacity for self-mastery that endows them with rights. Unable to live under the rule of reason, beasts can live only by the rule of force. A man who lives by violence in his dealings with his fellow men "is not master of his own life" because he relies on brutish force rather than human reason; therefore, he forfeits his human rights. But as long as human reason is not forsaken, each equally possesses the human rights derived from self-mastery. "He that is master of himself, and his own life, has a right too to the means of preserving it" (section 172). "Though the earth, and all inferior creatures, be common to all men, yet every man has a *property* in his own *person*: this no body has any right to but himself" (section 27).

The foundation of all human rights, Locke seems to argue, is that each human being, by virtue of human reason, is capable of a self-mastery that is impossible for "inferior creatures." As rational beings, we are conscious moral agents who decide for ourselves what we ought to do with our lives. Because of this capacity for self-rule, we demand to be treated as "persons" rather than as "things" or brute animals. As "persons," we cannot properly be used as mere objects or tools for someone else's uses. Our humanity gives us a dignity that nonhuman beings do not possess.

In our *humanity*, Locke would insist, we are *equal*. As we have seen, Locke would say that human freedom is forfeited by those who try to dominate others through brute force (sections 22-24, 85, 172). But with that exception, all human beings have an equal right to freedom simply as a consequence of their equal humanity.

This was the principle underlying Abraham Lincoln's argument against Negro slavery. If the Negro is human, he insisted, then the Negro cannot be justly held as property, because to treat a human being as a piece of property is a contradiction in terms.[5] That is why those who try to justify slavery must always argue that somehow the slave is not fully human.

But how plausible is Locke's assertion that there is "nothing more evident" than that all members of the human species are naturally equal? Consider some of the possible criticisms. First, we might object that to speak of human equality Locke has to refer to a purely imaginary "state of nature" that has never existed. Second, we might wonder why so many intelligent people have denied human equality if, in fact, it is so clearly "evident." Aristotle, for example, seemed to argue that some human beings were so inferior as to be natural slaves. As a third objection, we know from our common experience that no two human beings are exactly the same in intelligence, character, beauty, strength, or any other respect. Their inequality seems much more evident than their equality. Finally, we should dispute Locke's biological claim that all human beings possess equal dignity by being members of the same species, which differs in kind from the species of inferior creatures. Darwin's teaching that human beings differ only in degree and not in kind from the lower primates poses obvious questions as to the validity of Locke's biological claim.

Consider how Locke might answer these criticisms. First, is the state of nature a purely fictional construction? Locke answers, "It is plain the world never was, nor ever will be, without numbers of men in that state" (section 14). Because a state of nature exists whenever people live without a common authority over them (section 19), governmental rulers will always be in such a state in their dealings with one another. The governments of the world are bound together by various agreements; but when disputes arise, there is no world government to which they can appeal for judgment. Moreover, Locke insists that in primitive areas of the world individual human beings still live in a state of nature: "In the beginning all the world was *America*" (section 49). From

Locke's point of view, those American Indians who lived as hunter-gatherers were in a state of nature.

But even if the state of nature were not a historical fact, could it be an ahistorical fact? That is to say, Locke could argue that human beings are, in fact, equal in their natural capacity for self-rule, even though they commonly live in political communities that do not recognize that equality. Imagining what we would be like outside of society and government might then be a way of uncovering, in thought, that natural human equality.

But, again, if this equality is so obvious, why has it been denied by political thinkers such as Aristotle? Or is there a sense in which even Aristotle would affirm human equality? When Aristotle speaks early in the *Politics* of human beings as rational animals distinguishable from all other animals, doesn't that suggest that we all share a common human dignity, despite the differences between one person and another? Aristotle does seem to justify slavery, but as we saw in our reading of Aristotle, he condemns the actual practice of slavery as conventional rather than natural. Even in explaining natural slavery, he creates doubts as to whether natural differences justify enslavement. Aristotle affirms that all slaves are human beings and thus share in reason, which distinguishes them from irrational animals; and this would indicate that all slavery is contrary to nature, even by Aristotle's own standards (refer back to chapter 2, section 5).

Of course, human beings are, in fact, unequal in innumerable respects. Ernst Mayr, a prominent biologist, has even declared: "Anyone who believes in the genetic uniqueness of every individual thereby believes in the conclusion, 'No two individuals are *created* equal.'"[6] But Locke explains that, in declaring everyone to be equal by nature, he is not claiming equality in all respects. Clearly, there is unequality in birth, age, virtue, and other areas. Yet this does not contradict "the *equality*, which all men are in, in respect of jurisdiction or dominion one over another . . . being that *equal right*, that every man hath, *to his natural freedom*, without being subjected to the will or authority of any other man" (section 54).

Similarly, Lincoln declared that the authors of the Declaration of Independence

> intended to include *all* men, but they did not mean to say all men were equal *in all respects*. They did not mean to say all men were equal in color, size, intellect, moral development or social capacity. They defined with tolerable distinctness in what they did consider all men created equal—equal in certain inalienable rights, among which are life, liberty and the pursuit of happiness.

Furthermore, Lincoln interpreted this equality of rights as equality of *opportunity* but not equality of *results*. He thought the aim was "to lift artificial weights from all shoulders—to clear the paths of laudable pursuit for all—to afford all, an unfettered start, and a fair chance, in the race of life."[7] Far from denying the natural differences among human beings, Locke and Lincoln would agree, the equality of rights secures the necessary conditions for the free expression of those differences.

Locke's claim is that the *equality* of all people as possessing a common human nature is fully consistent with the *inequality* of people owing to their different natural endowments. We could interpret this in biological terms: the reality of biological species is such that members of the same species share a common nature, despite their individual differences. This would be Locke's answer to Mayr's objection that every individual is biologically unique. In fact, even Mayr says: "In spite of the variability caused by the genetic uniqueness of every individual, there is a species-specific unity to the genetic program (DNA) of nearly every species."[8]

We might conclude, therefore, that the commonality of all members of the human species constitutes the biological foundation of their equality of rights. But Locke's doctrine of equal natural rights requires more than this. Because it assumes that owing to the dignity of their humanity, all people have a just claim to more respect than we would give to other animals; it is not enough that they differ in *some way* from other animals. They must differ in *kind*, and whatever makes them different must also make them *superior*. Charles Darwin argues, however, in *The Descent of Man*, that we differ *only in degree, not in kind*, from the other primates; thus it would seem that evolutionary biology fails to support a Lockean equality of human rights.[9] Indeed, Carl Becker, an influential scholarly commentator on the Declaration of Independence, concluded that Darwinian science had refuted the Lockean natural rights doctrine of the Declaration.[10]

Locke suggests that as "rational creatures" we are equal in our separation from the irrational animals. But Darwin insists that even in mental capacities humans differ only in degree from other animals. If this were correct, there would be no biological justification for the doctrine of equal natural rights. For if we are entitled by nature to rule over other animals simply because we possess a greater degree of intelligence, then the more intelligent among us would be entitled by nature to rule over those who are less intelligent.

Darwin is not always clear on this point, however, because he suggests, in some passages in *The Descent of Man*, that human beings do have some cognitive capacities not possessed by other animals, thus indicating a difference in kind. For example, he concedes: "It may be freely admitted that no animal is self-conscious, if by this term it is implied, that he reflects on such points, as whence he comes or whither he will go, or what is life and death, and so forth." Although he insists that other animals have some ability to communicate, he admits: "The habitual use of articulate language is peculiar to man."[11] This same apparent contradiction appears in the work of Thomas Huxley, Darwin's closest follower. In *Man's Place in Nature*, Huxley explains: "Our reverence for the nobility of manhood will not be lessened by the knowledge, that Man is, in substance and in structure, one with the brutes; for, he alone possesses the marvelous endowment of intelligible and rational speech."[12] Why should Huxley, following the example set by Darwin, fall into such clear inconsistency—affirming both that man is "one with the brutes" and that "he alone" has the faculty of speech?

One way of overcoming this apparent contradiction, as suggested by Theodosius Dobzhansky and other modern biologists, is to argue that there is between humans and the other primates a difference in degree that becomes a difference in kind once a critical threshold is passed. What distinguishes man from other primates is the size and complexity of the human brain—a difference in *degree*—but once the human brain reached a critical level of size and complexity, there emerged mental capacities that other animals do not have—a difference in *kind*. Dobzhansky maintains: "Human self-awareness obviously differs greatly from any rudiments of mind that may be present in nonhuman animals. The magnitude of the difference makes it a difference in kind, and not one of degree." He explains, "Quantitative differences may grow large enough to become qualitative."[13] As we have seen earlier, in our chapter on Aristotle (chapter 2, section 3), a plausible case can be made for the claim that only human beings possess symbolic speech and conceptual thought. Apparently, some modern biologists would agree. Of course, the scientific issues related to this point are complicated, but at least we can conclude that Locke's doctrine of equal dignity does not clearly contradict scientific reasoning.

Even if we were persuaded by Locke that all human beings are in some sense naturally equal, we would still have to wonder whether such equality can be respected in political life. For Locke acknowledges that in many important respects, we are unequal. And doesn't this inequality have more influence in politics than natural equality? Inequality of wealth would come to mind as perhaps most critical in preventing human beings from exercising equal rights. For surely the rich tend to have more political power than the poor. How, then, can Locke reconcile human equality with inequality of property?

2. Should a just government secure private property rights?

Although some readers would see it as a contradiction, Locke contends that if government is to secure equality of rights, it must protect the private property rights that permit economic inequality. Locke concedes that it is difficult to justify private property, considering what he has said about the state of nature (section 25). For if at the beginning equal rights to the resources of nature are enjoyed by all, how can anyone acquire the right to hold property exclusively, of which the ultimate consequence is that some will have much wealth and others little?

"Though the earth, and all inferior creatures, be common to all men," Locke explains, "yet every man has a *property* in his own *person*: this no body has any right to but himself" (section 27). Moreover, the "*labour* of his body, and the *work* of his hands, we may say, are properly his." Therefore, whatever "he hath mixed his *labour* with, and joined to it something that is his own, and thereby makes it his *property*." The ownership of external goods is thus justified as an extension of self-ownership. As we have seen, the basis for human rights in Locke is that, having a rational nature, each human being exercises self-mastery or self-rule, of which the irrational animals are incapable. Therefore, people own what they are and are what they own. Moreover, they rightfully acquire property in those external possessions that are extensions of themselves. If they have property in their persons, they also have property in their labor as the expression of their persons. And finally, individuals have a property right to the objects of their labor.

We could dispute the logic of this argument. But even if we accepted this as a cogent justification for personally acquired property, we still might doubt that this would hold for the unlimited accumulation of land and money that permits some people to rule over others. For instance, we should be shocked by Locke's casual observation, "The grass my horse has bit; the turfs my servant has cut; and the ore I have digged in any place, where I have a right to them in common with others, become my *property*" (section 28). The parallel between "my horse" and "my servant" suggests that the servant is just as much the master's property as is the horse. When the inequality of property becomes great, the poor must sell their labor to the rich. But doesn't it contradict Lockean equality for the labor of some to be owned by others? Doesn't this mean that the poorest human beings are treated like inferior animals? These are the questions raised by the Marxist critics of Locke. Before taking up such criticisms, we should survey some of the major points in Locke's account of property to see how he would answer the objections of his opponents.

We might be confused by our first reading of Locke's chapter on property. The summary of his teaching at the end of the chapter (section 51) corresponds exactly to an earlier summary in section 39. We have to wonder, therefore, what is added in the intervening portion of the chapter (sections 40-50). In fact, there seems to be a summary in section 50 that differs greatly from the summary in section 51. Are there two separate teachings in Locke's chapter on property?

The summary in section 39 and in section 51 both contain four points. First, God gives the world to all people in common. Second, labor affords the right to property taken from the common. Third, the amount of property held by anyone is limited to what what can actually be used. Fourth, there is no conflict over property because there is no reason for anyone to take so much as to infringe on the claims of others. In section 50, however, a rather different account of property is summarized. Once the use of money is agreed to, Locke explains, the accumulation of property becomes unlimited, which produces great inequality in private property. The purpose of government, then, is to secure the rights to unequal property. The crucial element in this second version of Locke's teaching is money. The limits on property stressed in the early part of the chapter are dropped with the introduction of money, which creates an inequality of property that requires protection by government.

Initially, Locke sets down three limits on the acquisition of property. First, the right to own property can only be acquired through labor for that property. Second, there must be "enough, and as good, left in common for others" (section 27). Finally, only as much as can be used without anything being wasted can be taken (section 31). When our ancestors lived in primitive conditions with an abundance of natural resources and a small population, there was no reason for conflicts about property rights.

But human agreement to the use of money upsets everything. Monetary wealth can be accumulated endlessly without spoiling (sections 45-49). With the appearance of a market economy combined with population growth, all the land is appropriated as those with entrepreneurial skills find it profitable to cultivate thousands of acres through hired labor and then to sell the produce on the market. Thus the owners of land and capital can acquire property through the labor of others.

But if a few appropriate all the land, doesn't this violate the rule that "enough, and as good" must be left for others? One possible answer, implied in Locke's account of property, is that because land is more productive when it is cultivated, that all land is appropriated is best even for those left landless, because even those without land will benefit from the resultant abundance (section 37). For example, although in America land is free for the taking, the Indians still live in poverty because they lack the monetary economy that would stimulate cultivation of the land. For that reason, Locke observes, "A king of a large and fruitful territory there, feeds, lodges, and is clad worse than a day-labourer in *England* (section 41).

Another consequence of the invention of money is that because money is conventional rather than natural or divine, a monetary economy manifests the subjectivity of value as a human creation. Early in the chapter on property, Locke emphasizes the value of nature's resources provided by God; later in the chapter, however, he explains that value is created by human labor using the "almost worthless materials" of nature (section 43). But with reliance on money, "the intrinsic value of things" is replaced entirely by monetary value (section 37). Thus, humans take the place of God and nature as the chief sources of value. In fact, in sections 40 through 50 of the chapter, there is no reference to God, although Locke does speak of the "wise and godlike" prince who rules so as to promote the economic activity of his people (section 42). Indeed, Locke's ultimate purpose in this chapter is to persuade rulers that protecting private property should be their highest aim.

We would expect, therefore, that socialists have been severe critics of this portion of Locke's teaching. Although Karl Marx himself made no detailed comments on Locke's work, some subsequent scholars influenced by Marx have. C.B. Macpherson has developed one of the best Marxist critiques, but others have also contributed.[14]

Macpherson speaks generally for the Marxist view of Locke when he argues that Locke defends a capitalist society in which the wealthy few would exploit the poor multitude. Although professing to believe in equality of rights, Locke endorses the development of a monetary economy that creates an inequality of property with a few people possessing all the land and capital and most people laboring for mere subsistence. The great majority of citizens in Locke's society, according to Macpherson's interpretation, would have to labor for the wealthy landowners just to survive. Labor becomes a commodity to be bought and sold in the marketplace.

If the human power for self-rule is expressed in labor, humanity, that is life and liberty, is lost by the wage laborer selling labor.

Therefore, a Lockean government secures property rights, Macpherson explains, by protecting the rights of the propertied few against the claims of the propertyless multitude. Macpherson even claims that Locke would allow only the wealthy minority to be full members of his political society. Only those with property would have the right to vote. The poor citizens would have to obey the laws, but they would not participate in the making of the laws.

Macpherson also contends that the fundamental assumptions implied in Locke's thought constitute what he calls "possessive individualism." According to this conception of human nature, the essence of humanity is freedom from the will of others. This freedom requires that no individual depend on others except to the extent that social relationships are voluntarily entered for reasons of self-interest, and the primary interest lies in the unlimited increase of individual wealth and power. Political society arises, therefore, from the free agreement of those who seek to protect their selfish accumulation of property. Some are more rational in their pursuit of property than others. The more rational ones become rich; the less rational become poor. Hence, for government to protect property, the rich must rule over the poor. Thus, the government promotes the freedom of the few rational individuals only by depriving all others of their individual freedom.

Macpherson believes this to be an accurate description of the market society that Locke saw emerging in seventeenth century England and that still exists in the Western liberal democracies. Macpherson thinks it is now possible, however, to develop a new view of property rights that would allow all people to exercise their human freedom rather than only a wealthy few. In a Lockean society, the rich have exclusive rights to use the accumulated capital and natural resources of society for their own selfish benefit, which gives them the power to exploit the poor. But Macpherson would give to everyone an equal right to use or benefit from the productive resources of society, so that everyone would have an equal opportunity to self-fulfillment as a free human being. This looks like a perfect socialist society in which the means of production would be owned in common by all rather than owned privately by a few.

Are we ready now to become socialist revolutionaries? We should first consider how a Lockean might answer Macpherson's criticism. To the charge that Locke would permit the wealthy to exploit the poor, a Lockean could insist that property rights in a market economy benefit everyone, the poor as well as the rich. Unlike the peasants in feudal society, who were constrained by their obligations to labor for their noble lords, the wage laborers in a Lockean society have a right to sell their labor as they wish. As Locke explains, "A freeman makes himself a servant to another, by selling him, for a certain time, the service he undertakes to do, in exchange for wages he is to receive. . . . It gives the master but a temporary power over him, and no greater than what is contained in the *contract* between them" (section 85). The Marxist might protest that the master will always have a stronger bargaining position in negotiating such contracts. But Locke would seem to believe that there is little room for exploitation as long as the contract is a voluntary, mutually beneficial agreement between employer and employee. Unequal entrepreneurial abilities make it advantageous for those with less ability to work for those with more. They are still equal in rights, however, even if unequal in capacities.

How can there be equality of rights if the wealthy have more political power than the poor? Macpherson interprets some sections of the *Second Treatise* (sections 140, 157-58) as indicating that in a Lockean government only the rich would have the right to vote because only those with property would be full citizens. Although the passages cited by Macpherson can be interpreted in this way, they are somewhat ambiguous.

Moreover, Macpherson's interpretation depends on the assumption that Locke's emphasis on property rights leaves the poor without any rights because they have no property. But as we have seen, Locke derives the right to property in external goods from the fundamental right of all to have property in their own persons: self-ownership is prior to the ownership of objects (section 27). Therefore, everyone, no matter how poor, has some property in this broad sense. Occasionally, Locke seems to employ a narrow definition of property as the ownership of external goods (sections 138-39). But generally he interprets property to include "life, liberty and estate" (section 87), and he is quite explicit about this: "By *property* I must be understood here, as in other places, to mean that property which men have in their persons as well as goods" (section 173). So, for a Lockean government to secure property, it must protect not only the estate of the rich but also the life and the liberty of the poor.

Still, Marxists such as Macpherson would criticize Locke for his "possessive individualism." Contrary to Aristotle, Locke denies that humans are political by nature (see section 15). Rather, they are isolated from one another, with no common bonds of understanding. Each pursues a selfish interest, primarily through accumulating possessions; and associates with others only if it is for personal economic benefit. The Marxist argues that this alienates humans from their social essence by hiding the communal life that they share with each other. In short, Locke promotes competition rather than cooperation. As one commentator has explained Locke's view, "Man becomes conscious of his fellows only when he and they collide; conflict and friction are thus the sources of man's awareness of man."[15]

Even if there is some truth in this interpretation, does it perhaps exaggerate the atomistic character of Lockean individualism? Consider, for example, the importance that Locke gives to the family as the means by which children are nurtured and educated so that they can as adults exercise their freedom as rational beings (sections 55-57). Humans are not born as solitary, self-sufficient individuals; rather, they depend totally on the care of others. Even as free adults, Locke indicates, they must make "promises and compacts" with others in the pursuit of economic, social, and political goods (section 14). Unlike the family, these communal bonds can be freely chosen by the individual. We might infer, then, that Locke allows for a "communitarian" individualism: he rejects the sort of traditional communal life found in feudal villages, but he affirms the communal relations that arise from voluntary associations. Does it not serve human dignity that, as much as possible, communities should be entered by free choice?

On the other hand, doesn't Lockean private property, as the Marxist would insist, hinder communal life? As long as the resources of society (land, capital, tools, and so on) are privately owned by a few people, most people will not be free to develop their human capacities. By contrast, if productive resources were held in common by all members of society, all people could share in the full exercise of their human powers; thus, true individuality would coincide with true sociality. "In place of the old bourgeois society, with its classes and class antagonisms," Marx explained in the *Communist Manifesto*, "we shall have an association, in which the free development of each is the condition for the free development of all."[16]

A good case can be made, however, for the claim that the political freedom and the economic prosperity achieved in modern Western democracies is a consequence of Lockean property rights, and therefore it is unlikely that these gains could be preserved under socialism.[17] In the feudal system of medieval Europe, the absence of clear private property rights provided little incentive for people to increase productivity. For example, medieval peasants who farmed land cooperatively with other members of their village were not inclined to adopt more efficient methods of farming, because they would not receive all the benefits of increased production. But as private property rights were established, first in Holland and then in England in the seventeenth century, unprecedented economic growth occurred. It might be argued that the Industrial Revolution in eighteenth century England arose not because of technological discoveries, but because governmental protection of private property rights gave people the economic incentives for technological innovation. Moreover, this new economic freedom was intertwined with a new political freedom. Capitalism prevailed in England because the monarch's power was limited by Parliament, which allowed the rising bourgeois class to defend its property rights against royal prerogatives. But in Spain and France, absolute monarchy suppressed capitalist property. Thus, democratic freedom and economic abundance seem to arise together from Lockean liberalism as founded on private property rights.

Even if the present critics of Lockean thought accepted its past successes, they might still claim that Lockeanism cannot continue to be successful today because economic and social circumstances have changed too radically. John Dewey, for example, maintained that although Locke was the founder of liberalism, modern liberals should reject his "atomistic individualism" so as to allow for more social cooperation. The *goal* of liberalism—"liberation of the capacities of individuals for free, self-initiated expression"— remains the same as it was for Locke; but the *means* to that end, Dewey argued, must change. Locke relied on free economic competition among selfish individuals to promote individual liberty. But today liberals must rely on governmental regulation of the economy—"organized social control of economic forces"—to promote free individual development as the end.[18]

That was the thinking behind Franklin Roosevelt's New Deal liberalism. Previously, liberals had fought to limit governmental power to protect individual liberty. But in early twentieth century America, the threat to human freedom seemed to come more from the excessive power of the wealthy few than the excessive power of the government. The Lockean arguments for the rights of personally acquired property were used to insulate corporate wealth from public regulation for the common good. Under these circumstances, many liberals thought it necessary for the government to intervene in the economy to secure individuals from economic exploitation by the rich.[19]

Should we assume that Locke did not anticipate the need for governmental regulation of the economy to enhance individual liberty? In fact, doesn't Locke emphasize the need for legal regulation of property? He makes it clear that "in governments, the laws regulate the right of property, and the possession of land is determined by positive constitutions" (section 50). The purpose of this governmental regulation is *"to preserve and enlarge freedom"* (section 57) and thus to promote "the public good" (sections 120, 134). Moreover, we could interpret Locke as suggesting that government should intervene to prevent the inequality of wealth from becoming so great that some people are left without any property. For as he says, "the preservation of property being the end of government, and that for which men enter into society, it necessarily supposes and requires, that the people should *have property*" (section 138). Would we be justified in concluding that Locke would endorse modern welfare-state liberalism, at least insofar as it promotes the acquisition of property by people in the lower classes of society?[20]

In any case, it is clear that for Locke some form of governmental regulation of human action is essential to individual freedom. People seek to escape the insecurity of the state of nature by establishing legal institutions to protect their individual rights through rules of law that everyone must obey. However, there exists a fundamental difficulty here, which we have seen already in our consideration of Hobbes. Doesn't the freedom of individuals come into conflict with the powers of government?

3. Can liberal government combine individual freedom with political authority?

The Declaration of Independence claims that all people possess "unalienable Rights," and that "to secure these rights, Governments are instituted among Men, deriving their just powers from the consent of the governed." On the one hand, these rights are unalienable. On the other hand, governments must be established to protect these rights even though this would seem to require that some of the rights be compromised. Any government must limit the rights of those subject to its powers. For instance, in the Fifth and Fourteenth amendments to the United States Constitution, it is said that government shall not deprive any person of "life, liberty, or property, without due process of law," which means that our government *may* deprive us of our supposedly unalienable rights so long as the proper legal procedures are followed. And this accords fully with Locke's teaching.

Thus, there is a conflict between the individual autonomy of Lockean liberalism and the political authority of Lockean government.[21] Every human being is autonomous, in the sense that a human being has a power of self-rule that other animals do not. A freedom of choice in their actions and the capacity to reason about those choices distinguish human beings from other living things. Humanity is fulfilled in the exercise of free and rational agency in ruling one's self. Every government, however, must have supreme authority over its citizens, which means the right to command and to be obeyed. Hence, governmental authority demands the right to rule over all citizens, but individual autonomy demands the right of self-rule. We might try to overcome this conflict by saying that because a government has genuine authority only if its powers are just or legitimate, a government that is oppressive has no authoritative claim to obedience. But it is hard to imagine any standard of political authority that would not violate individual autonomy in some manner. If, in ruling, even the best of governments must infringe upon natural freedom, then every government is oppressive, and what we call political justice is merely disguised oppression. This would confirm Rousseau's complaint at the beginning of *The Social Contract*: "Man was born free, and everywhere he is in chains."

There is at least one way to reconcile autonomy and authority that appears both in Locke's *Second Treatise* and in the Declaration of Independence: government by the consent of the governed. In a community of self-governing citizens, people would exercise their self-rule by living under laws that they themselves have made. In entering such a political community, citizens would obey only themselves and would therefore be as free as if there were no government. If we adhere to the principle of individual autonomy, the only way to justify political authority is to derive it from the voluntary consent of all citizens.

Wouldn't this require a truly participatory democracy? All citizens would have to share directly in the making of all the major political decisions, and every decision would have to somehow reflect a unanimous consensus among the citizens. Yet there are obvious difficulties with such a scheme, particularly with respect to its practicality. Liberal political thinkers have argued, therefore, for *representative* democracy, in which citizens elect a small number of people to represent them in the government. We must wonder, however, whether voting for representatives satisfies our need for government by the consent of the governed.

4. Can Lockean government secure the consent of the governed?

To understand Locke's view of consent, we have to keep in mind that there are two steps in the movement from the state of nature to the establishment of government. First, individuals leave the state of nature by organizing themselves into a society (sections 87–89). Then, the people of that society select a form of government (section 132). The formation of society requires *unanimous* consent, in that no one can become a member of a community except by individual consent (sections 87–89, 123, 130–31, 211). But the selection of a government is by a *majority* consent of the people of a society (sections 94–98, 132).

If absolute freedom is experienced in the state of nature, why does anyone consent to leave it and accept the obligations of social life? This is especially perplexing because Locke, unlike Hobbes, insists that the state of nature is not a state of war (section 19). But Locke also observes that those living in the state of nature easily come into conflict since most people are "not strict observers of equity and justice"; therefore, the state of nature is "full of fears and continual dangers" (section 123). Societies are formed in an attempt to escape this disorder. Some commentators have even concluded that Locke's state of nature turns out to coincide with Hobbes's account of the natural "war of all against all."[22]

In any case, Locke overcomes the conflict between individual autonomy and social authority by postulating that society arises from the voluntary consent of all its members. In obeying the rules of society, members submit only to what they themselves have authorized. The Preamble to the Massachusetts Constitution of 1780 expresses Locke's thought well:

> The body-politic is formed by a voluntary association of individuals: It is a social compact, by which the whole people covenants with each citizen, and each citizen with the whole people, that all shall be governed by certain laws for the common good.[23]

How is this consent expressed? When do people ever have a chance to decide whether or not they will pledge full allegiance to their society? Locke's answer is that consent can be either "express" or "tacit" (sections 119–22). Individuals show their express consent to join a society when they promise their loyalty to it by some formal declaration. Those who give this consent are bound to be subject to the society as long as it lasts. On the other hand, tacit consent can be shown by simply living in a society and enjoying its benefits, particularly the protection accorded to privately owned property. Tacit consent, however, creates no permanent obligation, because those who have tacitly consented to be a member of a society can leave it whenever their enjoyment of its benefits ceases.

How would this apply to American politics? As indicated in the Declaration of Independence, we profess to found our government on Lockean consent. It is difficult to see, however, that this can be an express consent. Immigrants to the United States must give their express consent to the American regime before they can become citizens. This is not required of natural born citizens. If we were serious about Locke's standards for consent, we might have the president mail copies of the Constitution to all citizens on their twenty-first birthdays along with a letter asking each individual to sign the document or forfeit citizenship. Would that be the only clear way of insuring that the American people have consented to their government?

Some would claim, however, that we consent to our government by voting for our representatives. But it would be hard to prove that voting has this meaning. Many people don't vote at all, and many of those who do vote convey no clear message. It is even conceivable that those who thought the government fundamentally unjust might, nevertheless, have various reasons for voting in the elections of representatives.

If the procedures for express consent are dubious, we are left with tacit consent. During the debates over American participation in the Vietnam War, a popular slogan that appeared on automobile bumper stickers was "America—love it or leave it!" Indeed, some who opposed the war did leave, going to Canada and other countries. Could we say, then, that as long as people are free to leave their country, they indicate consent to the government by staying and thus enjoy the benefits of life under that government? (Would this, for example, apply to the case of Socrates?) The defect in this reasoning, however, is that people may have many reasons for staying in a country, even though they regard the government as illegitimate. Their ties to friends, to relatives, and to the general cultural life of their nation can be strong enough to justify their living under a tyrannical government. Although we might infer from this that they are obligated to obey the ordinary laws of their regime, we could hardly condemn them for conspiring to subvert the regime in hopes of establishing a more just form of government.

It is difficult, therefore, to see how a people would unanimously consent to a civil society as required by Locke. Moreover, even assuming that such popular consent could be secured, how does

Locke move from this unanimous agreement in establishing a society to rule by a majority in selecting a form of government? Doesn't majority rule deprive those in the minority of their individual autonomy?

5. By what right does the majority rule?

In reference to the government's power to tax an individual's property, Locke explains: "it must be with his own consent, *i.e.*, the consent of the majority, giving it either by themselves, or their representatives chosen by them" (section 140). This probably doesn't seem controversial to most of us, perhaps as a result of the influence of Lockean liberalism. We commonly take it for granted that popular consent means the consent of the majority of the people. And yet, rule by the majority can be just as tyrannical as rule by a small minority. If we believe in individual rights, we must also believe there are some things that a majority of the people have no right to do.

Indeed, some would assert that the principle of individual autonomy requires that each should exercise judgment without bowing to the pressure of public opinion. That was Thoreau's argument in his essay, "Civil Disobedience":

> A government in which the majority rule in all cases cannot be based on justice. . . . Can there be a government in which majorities do not virtually decide right and wrong, but conscience?—in which majorities decide only those questions to which the rule of expediency is applicable? . . . The only obligation which I have a right to assume is to do at any time what I think right.[24]

Consequently, society would become a strictly voluntary association; and the consent of the governed would become a continuing activity in which each person decides from day to day whether or not to consent to the policies of the society. It is natural to object that this sort of thinking would promote chaos. But don't we often respect people like Thoreau who stand against the opinions of the majority? If we believe in the natural rights of individuals, don't we then adhere to a standard of justice that goes beyond the will of the majority?

We must challenge Locke, therefore, to show us how individual rights can be combined with majority rule. For Locke's best treatment of this issue, we should look at the beginning of the eighth chapter of the *Second Treatise* ("Of the Beginning of Political Societies").

> For when any number of men have, by the consent of every individual, made a *community*, they have thereby made that *community* one body, with a power to act as one body, which is only by the will and determination of the *majority*: for that which acts any community, being only the consent of the individuals of it, and it being necessary to that which is one body to move one way; it is necessary the body should move that way whither the greater force carries it, which is the *consent of the majority*: or else it is impossible it should act or continue one body, *one community*, which the consent of every individual that united into it, agreed that it should; and so everyone is bound by that consent to be concluded by the *majority*. (section 96)

Therefore, by consenting to enter a political society, everyone is obligated "to submit to the determination of the *majority*" (section 97). For if the members of a society were free to reject any rule of that society with which they disagreed, they would still be as free as they were in the state of nature, which cannot be so once they have consented to form a society. Moreover, Locke explains, it is not realistic to require the consent of every individual to every act of society. People are often too busy with their private lives to attend public meetings; even when they do attend, the diversity of opinions and interests in any large group of individuals prevents them from reaching unanimous agreement. Therefore, "where the majority cannot conclude the rest, there they cannot act as one body, and consequently will be immediately dissolved again" (section 98).

Thus Locke seems to argue that, as all physical bodies move in the direction of the greater force, so political bodies must move in the direction of the majority. But in what sense does the majority exert the greater force? It would seem odd to derive the right of the majority to rule from its *physical* force, as though might makes right. Or does Locke think the majority exerts the greater *moral* force? In either case, he seems to assume that because each individual contributes one unit of force equal to that of every other individual, the course of action favored by the greater number of individuals should prevail by virtue of its greater force.

Isn't it true, however, that the majority of the people of a community are often apathetic about public issues and, therefore, that an active minority can exert more force than the passive majority? This has led some modern social theorists to conclude that every political society tends to be ruled by an elite class of those most active in public affairs; indeed, the "iron law of oligarchy," as Roberto Michels called it, may be one of the few "laws" in political science.[25] Moreover, we can see here the obvious response to

Locke's argument that no community can exist unless the majority rules: clearly, many societies have been held together through the rule of minorities.

Willmoore Kendall, in his study of Locke's account of majority rule, inferred that Locke's argument makes sense only if we assume certain unstated premises.[26] To conclude that the majority possesses "the greater force" in moving a society, we must assume that each individual participates equally in the making of decisions and that each individual's conviction is equally intense on each issue. Otherwise, on any particular issue, a small group of extremely active and fervent people might exert more strength than the majority.

Thus, perhaps the best formulation of Locke's defense of majority rule would be that, if unanimous consent on all issues is impossible, the rule of the majority is the only way to allow all individuals to participate equally in the making of decisions.

As interpreted by Kendall, Locke would argue: "Individual consents being, in any case, the only rightful title to the exercise of power, the right of the majority flows as a matter of course from the fact that it can point to more consents than the minority."[27]

Isn't it doubtful, however, that every individual will, in fact, participate equally in the public deliberations about every issue? Even if we could be sure of equal participation, couldn't we still challenge Locke's claim that majority rule fulfills the individual right to consent to government? It is always possible that the people in the majority will tyrannize over those in the minority.

A Lockean solution to this problem was well stated by Thomas Jefferson in his First Inaugural Address:

> All . . . will bear in mind this sacred principle, that though the majority is in all cases to prevail, that will, to be rightful, must be reasonable; that the minority possess their equal rights, which equal laws must protect and to violate which would be oppression.[28]

In thus appealing to "equal laws" to protect the "equal rights" of the minority, Jefferson relied on the Lockean principle of the rule of law. Individual rights are less likely to be violated when political decisions are formulated as impartial rules of law, and when the lawmaking body is both separated from and supreme over the other branches of government. But here, too, there are difficulties.

6. Can the rule of law and the separation of powers secure individual rights?

In the summer of 1974, it became clear that President Richard Nixon had participated in various illegal activities. He had even exercised his presidential powers in ways that violated the constitutional rights of American citizens. To escape impeachment by Congress, Nixon resigned, allowing Vice President Gerald Ford to become the new president. In his inaugural address, Ford declared: "My fellow Americans, our long national nightmare is over. Our Constitution works. Our great republic is a government of laws and not of men. Here, the people rule."[29] Thus Ford appealed to a recurrent Lockean theme in American political thought: to protect the liberties of the people from the tyranny of arbitrary, absolute power, governmental power must conform to the rule of law. The rule of law requires not only that public officials act in accordance with the laws, but also that the lawmaking power be separated from the executive and judicial powers. This separation serves to eliminate potential danger resulting from the concentration of powers in the hands of one person or one group of people.

But is it really possible to have "a government of laws and not of men"? Doesn't any government depend on the personal judgment of those who rule? Our rulers make the laws, interpret the laws, and apply the laws to particular cases. Moreover, governmental officials often have to decide what should be done in circumstances for which the law provides no clear standard. This is most evident in times of crisis — such as war — when it may seem necessary to set aside the ordinary rules of law. Should we even go so far as to concede that during severe emergencies we must permit the government to violate individual rights if the public good demands it? Or should we rather insist that a just government must never infringe on individual rights no matter what the circumstances? We must keep these questions in mind as we examine Locke's account of the rule of law.

The state of nature becomes unbearable for people, Locke explains, because when all are free to preserve themselves as they see fit, their selfish passions create unremitting conflict. To escape this disorder people must enter civil society in order to have an impartial common judge to settle disagreements. But the very selfishness that makes just government desirable would seem to make it impossible to achieve. For if, in fact, as Locke says, most people are "no strict observers of equity and justice" (section 123), why should we trust anyone to rule over others impartially? Won't natural selfishness incline rulers to govern for their personal interests rather than for the common good?

Locke suggests that this problem can be solved through the rule of law and the separation of powers. In particular, three defects of the state of nature must be overcome. First, people need "an *established*," settled, known *law*, received and allowed by common consent to be the standard of right and wrong, and the common measure to decide all controversies between them" (section 124). Second, they need "*a known and indifferent judge*, with authority to determine all differences according to the established law" (section 125). Third, people need "*power* to back and support the sentence when right, and to *give* it due *execution*" (section 126). Lawmaking promotes justice because it requires the dispassionate and impartial formulation of general rules. Lawmakers "are to govern by *promulgated established laws*, not to be varied in particular cases, but to have one rule for rich and poor, for the favorite at court, and the country man at plough" (section 142). To secure this justice that comes from the rule of law the legislature must be supreme over the judicial and executive branches of government. Judges must apply the laws to particular cases. Executive officers must employ the force of the community in executing the laws (sections 131, 149–50). Under these arrangements, no governmental official acts without the guidance of law; thus no one exercises arbitrary, absolute power (sections 136–37). It is difficult for the rulers to use their powers for their personal advantage contrary to the public good because the power to make laws is separated from the power to execute them (sections 143–44).

But we can see in American government how difficult it is to adhere strictly to the rule of law and the separation of powers. It can be argued, for example, that bureaucratic power, which has become essential to modern government, violates these Lockean principles. Perhaps even more obvious is the extent to which the powers of the modern American presidency have subverted legislative supremacy. What might Locke say about these features of American government?

Surely, Locke would want to insist that governmental administrators exercise only "subordinate powers" and must therefore be "accountable to some other power in the commonwealth" (section 152). Because governmental actions must be guided by law, and because the legislative body cannot delegate its lawmaking power to anyone else, administrators should serve simply as instruments for carrying out the laws enacted by the legislative body (sections 141–42).

In American government today, however, federal administrators often seem to have the power either to act without any clear legal standards or to make their own laws. The Federal Trade Commission (FTC), for example, was given by law the power to act against "unfair methods of competition in or affecting commerce, and unfair or deceptive acts or practices in or affecting commerce."[30] The language is so vague that the administrators in the FTC are free to improvise their own rules.

Some people claim that the complexity of the tasks assumed by modern government make this necessary. Because the members of Congress are not experts in the problems of economic and social regulation, they must allow the experts in the regulatory agencies to decide what should be done. One authority on administrative law has concluded: "The extravagant version of the rule of law is incompatible with any regulatory program. . . . The very identifying badge of the American administrative agency is power, without previously existing rules, to determine the legal rights of individual parties."[31] But the danger is that this power can be used for the benefit of influential interest groups contrary to the public interest, which is exactly what Locke wanted to avoid by insisting on the rule of law.[32]

We should not exaggerate, however, the independence of federal bureaucratic agencies from congressional control. Although the Congress may often be slow in restricting unpopular bureaucratic activity, some observers would argue that the Constitution gives it all the power necessary to assert its supremacy. In 1979, for example, Congress forced the commissioners of the FTC to withdraw some of their most controversial regulatory measures.[33] When it becomes sufficiently aroused to use the weapons at its disposal, the Congress can impose its will upon recalcitrant administrators.

But what happens when the Congress disagrees with the president? Obviously, in those cases where the president cannot act without legislative authorization the Congress can assert its dominance if it wishes. In some areas, however, such as foreign policy, the president often seems free to act independently. Do we rely too much on the president, allowing dangerous concentration of powers in the hands of a single person? Or is it rather the case that only the president can provide the leadership necessary for effective government?

Insofar as he insists on securing the rule of law through legislative supremacy, Locke would seem to argue that a president should simply execute the will of the legislature. On the other hand, Locke thinks that any effective executive must exercise "prerogative," which is the power "to act according to discretion, for the public good, without the prescription of the law, and sometimes even against it" (section 160). Isn't it dangerous to permit any ruler to violate the laws? Or is this unavoidable, particularly in times of emergency?

7. Must the executive have the powers of a dictator?

During the Civil War, Abraham Lincoln was denounced as a dictator because many of his war measures seemed to be clearly illegal violations of individual rights. But Lincoln defended his actions by arguing that, in times of crisis, the president may have to infringe on individual liberty in doing whatever is necessary to preserve the country. Therefore, Lincoln explained, we must confront a difficult question: "Must a government, of necessity, be too *strong* for the liberties of its own people, or too *weak* to maintain its own existence?"[34]

President Richard Nixon forced us to reconsider this question. As president he once stated: "It's quite obvious that there are certain inherently governmental activities which, if undertaken by the sovereign in protection of the interests of the nation's security, are lawful but which if undertaken by private persons, are not." After he was forced to resign from office, Nixon was asked, in an interview with David Frost, to explain this remark.

> Well, what I, at root . . . had in mind, I think, was perhaps better stated by Lincoln during the War Between the States. Lincoln said, and I think I can remember the quote almost exactly, he said, "Actions which otherwise would be unconstitutional, could become lawful if undertaken for the purpose of preserving the Constitution and the nation."

Frost responded, however, by suggesting that the Civil War was quite different from the situation faced by Nixon as president. Nixon was quick to reply: "This nation was torn apart in an ideological way by the war in Vietnam, as much as the Civil War tore apart the nation when Lincoln was President." Then he explained to Frost: "If the President does it, that makes it legal."

But when Frost asked if there was any provision in the Constitution to support this, Nixon answered:

> No, there isn't. There's nothing specific that the Constitution contemplates in that respect. I haven't read every word, every jot and every tittle, but I do know this: that it has been, however, argued that as far as a President is concerned, that in war time,

a President does have certain extraordinary powers which would make acts that would otherwise be unlawful, lawful if undertaken for the purpose of preserving the nation and the Constitution, which is essential for the rights we're talking about.[35]

It would seem, then, that both Lincoln and Nixon believed the American president must possess the Lockean power of executive prerogative. For they restated Locke's argument that, in some cases—particularly in times of emergency—the public interest requires setting aside the ordinary laws; and, in such cases, the executive has the duty to act according to personal discretion for the good of the community.

Does such a power violate the principle of the rule of law, which is essential to constitutional government? Once we permit the president to step outside the Constitution, how do we prevent the abuse of that power? Consider, for example, the argument of Arthur Schlesinger, Jr., in *The Imperial Presidency*.[36] Schlesinger denies the validity of Nixon's claims to prerogative power, but he concedes that Lockean prerogative is available to the president for use in emergencies. He praises Lincoln and Franklin Roosevelt, for instance, for the wise use of prerogative, but he condemns Nixon for misusing it. Schlesinger tries to distinguish between the proper and the improper uses of prerogative by setting down some conditions for its exercise, conditions that were not satisfied in Nixon's case.[37] And yet, since Schlesinger views prerogative as a power *outside* the Constitution, and thus not subject to constitutional restraints, it is hard to see how he can impose any definite limitations on a power that is totally outside the structure of constitutional government.

We see now at least three major questions that we must ask in studying Locke's account of prerogative. Is it really necessary for the executive to exercise prerogative powers? If we grant such powers, how do we protect ourselves against the tyrannical misuse of them? Can presidential prerogative be made consistent with the allocation of powers in the Constitution?

We can explain Locke's teaching about prerogative as depending on three factors: the nature of the people, the nature of the legislative power, and the nature of nature. Prerogative is necessary because the people demand it; the people will allow the widest prerogative as long as they think it is being used for their good. Also, prerogative is necessary because it serves a political need that cannot be satisfied by the legislature—the need for quick, flexible action to handle problems that cannot be governed by law. Finally, prerogative is necessary because, while law is fixed, it is the nature of things to always be in motion; prerogative allows for a flexible response to this natural flux in political history.

The people are willing to allow prerogative power. Indeed, according to Locke, in the early ages of society, "the government was almost all *prerogative*" (section 162). The first governments were generally founded on the rule of one who, because of paternal authority or superior qualities, was permitted by the people to govern unrestrained by laws (sections 74–75, 94, 105–12). But when "weak princes" used their prerogative to threaten the property of their subjects, people began to favor collective legislative bodies to restrict prerogative power. Thus the people made it clear that they permitted government by prerogative only with the understanding that the power would be used for the "public good" rather than the "private ends" of the ruler (sections 111, 162–66).

The people rarely question the prince's prerogative power; they are "very seldom, or never scrupulous in the point" (section 161). In the history of England, for instance, the people were willing to overlook "any human frailty or mistake" of their kings providing that "the main of their conduct" tended to the public interest; they "let them enlarge their *prerogative* as they pleased" (section 165). It was only the prerogative of "weak princes," who set out to enslave their subjects, that was questioned by the people (sections 94, 105–8, 110, 162).

Thus the people permit the prince the widest possible prerogative as long as his actions generally serve the "public good." But what is the "public good" in Locke's view? Essentially, as we have seen, it is the protection of property. The "wise prince," however, knows that promoting the acquisition of property serves his own interests as well as those of his subjects, because by increasing the wealth of his people he also increases his political power (sections 42–43, 48, 173–74, 184, 193–95).

That Locke's prince is prohibited from invading the property of his people (or at least of the majority) is the fundamental limitation of his prerogative power, but this limit must be respected by any prudent prince no matter how absolute his power. Even Hobbes concedes that although all supreme rulers have absolute power, they often restrain themselves for fear that too much oppression would stir to political action people who ordinarily would be "busied about their private interest and careless of what tends to the public" (*On the Citizen*, V, 13). Similarly, we might see a parallel to Machiavelli's teaching that the prince should base his power on the people because the people will not question his use of power as long as he keeps his hands off their property and their women (*The

Prince, chapters 9, 17, 19, 21).

Yet while "wise princes" avoid using prerogative in an unpopular way, "weak princes" inevitably arouse the people to rebellion by using prerogative to infringe on their property, even to the point of threatening their lives. In response to this misuse of prerogative, the people demand that they be ruled by standing laws made by a legislative body to which they have consented so as to avoid being ruled by "the inconstant, uncertain, unknown, arbitrary will" of one man (section 22).

The establishment of a legislative body limits the prerogative power of the prince. Before the appearance of a legislature, the prerogative of a prince encompasses *all* the powers of government; but once a legislature is established, there must be a division of power so that the prerogative of the prince is limited to the executive functions of government. The *executive* prerogative of the prince is necessarily less than the *total* prerogative he possessed before the division of power into executive and legislative branches.

Executive prerogative, therefore, is not a *substitute* for law, as was the case when princes ruled without legislature, rather it is a *supplement* to law. Simply stated, executive prerogative is the power of the executive to act for the public good in those cases where action by the legislature would be impossible or ineffective.

According to Locke, the legislative power is limited in at least three major ways (section 160). First, a legislature is not always in session; and even when it is, the number of its members and the slowness of its deliberations prevent it from making quick decisions. Second, a legislature cannot write its laws to cover every case because some future problems are always unforeseeable. Finally, laws must be inflexible and are therefore not always appropriate to changing circumstances. The aim of a legislature is careful deliberation leading to the formulation of general rules of action. But the very factors necessary for achieving this prevent a legislature from acting quickly and flexibly in response to unexpected and ever-changing events. When this sort of action is required, the legislature must yield to the discretionary power of the executive. The most obvious cases are great emergencies, especially in times of war.

Locke indicates that the prerogative power of the executive is greatest in foreign affairs because such matters cannot be governed by law (sections 88, 131, 146–47). The executive must be allowed to employ, according to discretion, the whole force of the community against foreign enemies.

If we now consider the general character of prerogative, don't we see some contradictions in Locke's *Second Treatise*? Locke says that legitimate government must be based on the rule of law so that no person is exempt from the law (section 94). But prerogative power permits the executive to act against the laws. Locke insists that no legitimate government can exercise "arbitrary absolute power." But prerogative power can be both "arbitrary" and "absolute" (sections 139, 166, 210). Locke teaches that the legislative power should be supreme (sections 132, 144), yet he also speaks of the executive as the "supreme executor" whose prerogative power is not subordinate to the legislature (sections 151–52, 154, 156). The ultimate judge of whether the executive has used prerogative properly is not the legislature, but the people themselves; and, as we have seen, they are easily satisfied.

One way to overcome these apparent contradictions would be to say that although the legislature is the *formal* sovereign in a Lockean regime, the executive is the *informal* sovereign. The legislature is supreme in *theory*, but the executive often has to be supreme in *practice*. In ordinary circumstances, government operates by the rule of law; however, in extraordinary circumstances, the rule of one individual is necessary.

Locke points to the underlying problem in the following remark with reference to prerogative: "Things of this world are in so constant a flux, that nothing remains long in the same state" (section 157). Executive prerogative, we might say, is a political response to that flux in the world that runs against the fixity of law. A political community is an attempt by human beings to construct a formal structure through which the chaos of the world can be ordered so as to achieve the security and stability necessary for human preservation and comfort. But the unruly forces of the universe break down this formal structure. The laws constitute the walls of this structure, which are continually being undermined by natural forces acting either by slow erosion or sudden floods. Executive prerogative is the exertion of human force against those natural forces (sections 88, 124–31). Locke's doctrine of executive prerogative, therefore, could be viewed as founded on the modern assumption (evident in Machiavelli, Descartes, and Hobbes) that there are no natural ends.[38] Because humans are not at home in nature, they cannot secure political order for themselves except by a continual exercise of force to conquer nature.

Having sketched Locke's view of executive prerogative, we see how dangerous it is to allow the American president to possess such a power. For doesn't Lockean prerogative subvert constitutional government? According to Locke, there can be no ultimate restraint on prerogative except the judgment of the people. But the fundamental assumption of American political thought is that although the people are the only legitimate source of power, the will of the people concerning the powers of government is embodied in the Constitution. The Constitution, not the public opinion of the day, determines the legitimacy of power. Through elections the people decide who should fill the office of the president, but the Constitution prescribes the powers of that office. To claim Lockean prerogative the president would have to circumvent the Constitution and appeal directly to the people as the authoritative source of presidential powers. The dangers of allowing the powers of the president to be determined by fluctuating public sentiments rather than by the Constitution should be evident.

On the other hand, doesn't Locke argue persuasively for the belief that there must be some sort of discretionary power for dealing with emergencies? Surely, the president would exercise such a power more effectively than the Congress. Moreover, we might formulate Locke's doctrine of prerogative in a manner that would make it consistent with constitutional government. In certain passages Locke suggests that there are some constitutional limits to prerogative: the most important limit would be that, although the executive might have to violate particular laws of the legislature, he or she would not be permitted to keep the legislature from assembling. If the executive prevents the legislature from meeting, and thereby abolishes the form of government established by the people and exercises force without authority, this restores the state of nature (sections 134, 155, 159–61, 214–15, 226, 239).

Is it wise to try to constitutionalize executive prerogative? Schlesinger argues that it is best to force the president to go outside the Constitution when prerogative is necessary. To give prerogative constitutional status, Schlesinger warns, would encourage presidents to use it too often and too casually. On the other side of the issue, however, it can be argued that forcing a president to go outside the Constitution during emergencies promotes disrespect for law and creates all the dangers that go with unlimited power.

The most famous example of constitutional prerogative is the legal institution of dictatorship in the ancient Roman Republic. During a time of emergency, one person could be appointed Dictator for six months to deal with the crisis. The appointed Dictator could not change the formal institutions of government, and his term was too short to cause much permanent harm. Machiavelli, in the *Discourses*, advised, "all republics should have some institution similar to the dictatorship":

> Now in a well-ordered republic it should never be necessary to resort to extra-constitutional measures; for although they may

for the time be beneficial, yet the precedent is pernicious, for if the practice is once established of disregarding the laws for good objects, they will in a little while be disregarded under that pretext for evil purposes. Thus no republic will ever be perfect if she has not by law provided for everything, having a remedy for every emergency, and fixed rules of applying it. (I,34)[39]

Did the American founders intend that the president, in time of crisis, would exercise the powers of a constitutional dictator? Thomas Jefferson, in his *Notes on the State of Virginia* (query 13), insisted that the Roman precedent was not applicable to American politics. A republican government should be strong enough, he argued, to meet every danger without surrendering the rights of the people to even a temporary dictator.[40] But Alexander Hamilton, in *Federalist* Number 70, cited the example of the Roman Dictator in support of his claim that any good government requires "an energetic Executive." Hamilton conceded, however, that this was controversial because some people thought a strong executive was contrary to "the genius of republican government."[41]

The precedents set by Abraham Lincoln during the Civil War seem to favor the Hamiltonian conception of the president as possessing prerogative power. But Lincoln was vague in explaining the constitutional status of this power. Because it illustrates the crucial issues so well, we should examine, if only briefly, Lincoln's Message to Congress of July 4th, 1861.

The firing on Fort Sumter occurred on April 12th, 1861. Because Congress was in recess at the time, Lincoln issued a call on April 15th for a special session of Congress. But he set the date for July 4th. By delaying the assembling of Congress, Lincoln secured for himself a period of almost three months in which he took complete charge of the war effort without any congressional authorization. Although some of his actions were clearly legal, some were not. His declaration of a naval blockade of the South was legally dubious because that seemed to require a Congressional declaration of war. His suspension of the writ of habeas corpus was also questionable because such a power seemed to belong to Congress rather than the president, but the Constitution is unclear on this point. The most obviously unconstitutional actions were his expansion of the army and navy and his unauthorized withdrawal of funds from the Treasury. The Constitution provides specifically for Congress to have the exclusive power of enlarging the military forces and authorizing appropriations.

In his message to Congress, Lincoln explained: "These measures, whether strictly legal or not, were ventured upon, under what appeared to be a popular demand, and a public necessity; trusting then as now, that Congress would readily ratify them."[42] He thus appeared to claim a Lockean prerogative power to act illegally in time of emergency and to appeal directly to public opinion as a source of power.

His suspension of the writ of habeas corpus was the most controversial of Lincoln's actions because, in effect, this allowed a suspension of all individual rights. Citizens were put into jail by military authorities without any charges being made against them and without any right to trial. Lincoln claimed that it was his duty "to authorize the Commanding General, in proper cases, according to his discretion, . . . to arrest, and detain, without resort to the ordinary processes and forms of law, such individuals as he might deem dangerous to the public safety."[43]

To provide constitutional support for taking such action, Lincoln cited three provisions of the Constitution. In Article II, Section 3, it is said that the president "shall take Care that the Laws be faithfully executed." Lincoln argued that in order to insure that the *whole* of the laws would be executed in the South, he had to violate *some* laws to win the war. Article II, Section 1, of the Constitution requires that the president swear to "faithfully execute the Office of the President" and to "preserve, protect, and defend the Constitution of the United States." Lincoln inferred from this that the president has a duty to violate the law if this is necessary to preserve the country.

But isn't it strange to argue that the president has a constitutional duty to violate the Constitution? Isn't it also hard to see what would prevent a president from abusing executive powers once outside the Constitution? In Lincoln's defense, we might say, in the words of one historian, "If Lincoln was a dictator, it must be admitted that he was a benevolent dictator." That historian immediately added, however, "Yet in a democracy it is a serious question how far even a benevolent dictatorship should be encouraged."[44]

But in citing a third constitutional provision, Lincoln suggested that he was not acting outside the Constitution at all. Article I, Section 9, provides: "The privilege of the Writ of Habeas Corpus shall not be suspended, unless when in Cases of Rebellion or Invasion, the public safety may require it." Lincoln claimed, therefore, that by suspending the writ of habeas corpus he was simply exercising an emergency power specifically provided by the Constitution itself. We might infer from this, although Lincoln did not say so explicitly, that the framers of the Constitution wrote into the document emergency provisions so that it would never have to be set aside during times of crisis.

Lincoln never violated the broad framework of the Constitution.

Although he delayed calling Congress into session, for example, he never questioned the right of the Congress to meet during the war and to judge his actions. And in 1864, he ran for reelection, even though there was a strong possibility that he would lose, and a new commander in chief would appear while the war continued. Lincoln allayed the widespread fear that he would cancel the election.

It is conceivable, however, that during some severe emergency, a president might at least temporarily disband the Congress and postpone a presidential election, arguing that such measures are necessary for the preservation of the country. Locke's doctrine of prerogative could be interpreted as permitting this, but with the understanding that the executive would have to appeal for public support. If the people were to disapprove, they would always have their ultimate weapon for punishing tyrants — revolution. But how effective is the right to revolution in limiting governmental oppression?

8. What is the right to revolution?

Locke indicates that the most obvious objections to the right to revolution arise from the fear of disorder (sections 223–26, 228–30). To affirm the right to revolution would seem to promote chaos by encouraging people to disobey their government whenever they think governmental policies are unfair (see chapter 7, section 5). For any government to be effective, the people must feel obligated to obey its decrees even when they regard them as unwise. But at the same time, when a government becomes too oppressive, the people will rebel. The puzzle, therefore, is how to combine the people's duty to obey a just government with their right to disobey a tyrannical government.[45]

The Declaration of Independence asserts the right of the people to overthrow tyrannical rulers. But the Constitution of the United States does not explicitly refer to this right. George Washington spoke for the framers of the Constitution when he stressed (in his "Farewell Address") the duty to obey the laws:

> The basis of our political systems is the right of the people to make and alter their constitutions of government. But the constitution which at anytime exists till changed by an explicit and authentic act of the whole people is sacredly obligatory upon all. The very idea of the power and the right of the people to establish government presupposes the duty of every individual to obey the established government.

We see this same cautiousness about revolution in Locke's chapter on the "dissolution of government." He does not even use the phrase, "the right to revolution." And he repeatedly insists that his teaching about revolution will not promote a turbulent rebelliousness. He assures us that the people are so slow to rebel that wise rulers should never have any fear of revolution (sections 223, 225). The Declaration of Independence echoes Locke's language in its statement that "mankind are more disposed to suffer, while evils are sufferable, than to right themselves by abolishing the forms to which they are accustomed."

Furthermore, the oppression of particular individuals does not lead to revolution, Locke explains, until the great majority of the people feel oppressed (section 230). If there is a right to revolution in Locke's teaching, it belongs not to individuals acting alone but to the "people," or more precisely to the *majority* of the people.

Thus Locke conceives a just revolution as arising from the ultimate authority of the people to establish whatever form of government is most likely to serve the public good. This Lockean concept has been adopted by many modern advocates of revolutionary change, including the signers of the Declaration of Independence. In Locke's time this idea was controversial, so much so, that even most of the Whigs who led the English Revolution of 1688 rejected it. They feared that allowing the people themselves to alter or abolish their form of government would create chaos.[46]

To calm this fear, Locke contends that it is possible to dissolve *government* without dissolving *society* (section 211). Hobbes argued that since there is no society without government, but rather a state of nature that is a state of war, resistance to government is suicidal except to escape one's own death. Even the most oppressive government is better than the violent anarchy that inevitably occurs with a revolution. Hobbes thought the English Civil War (1642–1649) illustrated this. Although Locke denies that a state of nature is necessarily a state of war (section 19), he concedes that a state of nature *tends* to become warlike (sections 21, 123). He maintains, however, that the people acting as a community can set aside their old government without collapsing into a state of nature. It is possible, at least temporarily, for people to act as one body ruled by the majority even without the formal institutions of government (sections 95–99, 132, 211). The Revolution of 1688 would illustrate this, despite the effort of the Whig leaders to adhere to the fiction of working within the established framework of government.

Throughout the seventeenth century, English political leaders had searched for a way to settle constitutional conflicts between the King and Parliament without subordinating one to the other. Locke's solution was to recognize the people as the final judge of such disputes (sections 240–43).

Later, Rousseau worked out one of the radical implications of this idea: the only just governments are those sanctioned by the sovereign will of the people (see also chapter 9, section 6). William Godwin, in his *Inquiry Concerning Political Justice* (1793), drew an even more radical conclusion. If the people can exercise their sovereign will without government, then justice would be best served by abolishing government forever. This idea gave birth to the anarchist movement of the nineteenth and twentieth centuries.[47]

Locke's account of revolution leaves us with many unanswered questions. For example, he assumes that in a revolutionary situation the will of the majority of the people should prevail. But doesn't this allow the minority to be oppressed? Doesn't it deny the equal right of all to protect their liberty? Why shouldn't we follow Thoreau's lead in concluding that the right to revolution includes the right of all individuals to disobey laws that violate their conscience? This reasoning has supported the doctrine of civil disobedience—that each person has the right, even the duty, to disobey unjust laws. (It is also easy to see how this could lead to anarchism.)

Would Locke accept Thoreau's interpretation of the right to revolution? He seems to agree with Thoreau in some passages of the *Second Treatise*. He says, for example, "*every man is judge for himself*" whether a ruler has become so unjust that rebellion is justified (section 241). But in other passages, he insists that only the people as a whole have the right to make this judgment (sections 230, 240, 242–43).

Thus we are reminded of the difficulty in Lockean liberalism in reconciling individual autonomy and governmental authority. A Lockean government has authority only insofar as it secures individual rights, but any stable government must demand that individuals give up their absolute freedom for the sake of social order. To enjoy the security of life in society with a government, people must give up the freedom of the state of nature.

9. Should women have equal rights?

Locke speaks of the "rights of men." Does this include the "rights of women"? If any group has the right to revolution, don't women have the right to revolt against the tyranny of men? If all human beings have natural rights, and if women are human beings, does it not follow necessarily that women have the same natural rights as men?

The logic of this argument was elaborated by Mary Wollstonecraft in *Vindication of the Rights of Woman*, which was first published in England in 1792. With respect to their natural *sameness*, women are equal to men in their humanity as rational animals, she argued, and therefore women have the same natural rights that belong to men by virtue of their rational nature. With respect to their natural *differences*, women cannot properly fulfill their nature as wives and mothers unless they are as independent and as well educated as men. Family life will be improved when wives and husbands see one another as intellectual equals whose sexual love can be transformed into marital friendship through their shared nurturance of children.[48]

In July of 1848, the first convention for the promotion of women's rights was held in Seneca Falls, New York. The convention adopted a "Declaration of Sentiments" that followed the pattern of the Declaration of Independence, invoking the self-evident truth "that all men and women are created equal" and listing its grievances against the tyranny of men. The convention also passed resolutions applying natural law to the condition of women: since it is by natural law that "man shall pursue his own true and substantial happiness," and any human laws contrary to this are invalid, it must also be true that any laws contrary to "the true and substantial happiness of woman" are also invalid.[49]

Would Locke agree? Some feminist scholars believe Locke's reasoning would support, at least implicitly, the feminist argument for women's rights, particularly in his attack on Robert Filmer's theory of patriarchal authority.[50] According to Locke, the authority of parents over their children belongs equally to mothers and fathers, not just to fathers (section 52). Locke also regards the spousal bond as a voluntary contract between man and woman; and therefore, if they have no children, or if their children are grown, there is no reason why they cannot terminate their marriage by mutual consent (sections 77–83). In this case, whatever property the wife has earned by labor or contract belongs to her as her share of the common property (section 183). Such an endorsement of divorce was controversial in Locke's time, and it is only recently that "no-fault" divorce has been accepted in American and European law.

Yet some feminist critics of Locke have noticed that he seems hesitant to affirm fully the equality of men and women. For example, when husband and wife cannot agree on some issue of common concern in the family, Locke explains, the final decision "naturally falls to the man's share, as the abler and the stronger" (section 82). He immediately adds, however, that this "leaves the wife in the full and free possession of what by contract is her peculiar right, and gives the husband no more power over her life than she has over his." Moreover, it is not clear what he means by man being naturally "the abler and the stronger." Abler only in being stronger?

At least, in comparison with Rousseau, who was the primary object of Wollstonecraft's indignation, and who is commonly identified by feminist scholars as the founder of the modern patriarchal tradition, Locke seems far more sympathetic to women's rights. Even Rousseau, however, is difficult to interpret on this issue. He indicates that although in general men and women tend to be naturally different, some women ("exceptions") are just like men, and all women could be raised to be just like men.[51] In an early essay (*Sur Les Femmes*), Rousseau described the tyranny of men in preventing women from expressing their natural capacities. Furthermore, even when Rousseau recommends cultivating and celebrating the natural differences between men and women, his teaching should be welcomed by those feminists who defend the "different voice" and the "maternal thinking" that women contribute to the human conversation.[52]

Our human nature is surely shaped by the nature of our human bodies. And since our bodies are either female or male, does this mean that human nature is divided into female and male natures? Or should we rather say that the division of social and political roles into female and male is more a product of nurture than nature and is therefore open to social reform through education?[53] These questions point us back to Plato's *Republic*. They also point us ahead to Rousseau's account of the origins of inequality.

Notes

1. For Locke's involvement in revolutionary conspiracies, see Richard Ashcraft, *Revolutionary Politics and Locke's Two Treatises of Government* (Princeton: Princeton University Press, 1986).
2. See John Dewey, *Liberalism and Social Action* (New York: G. P. Putnam's Sons, 1963).
3. On the importance of Locke for the American regime, see Louis Hartz, *The Liberal Tradition in America* (New York: Harcourt, Brace World, 1955); and Donald J. Devine, *The Political Culture of the United States* (Boston: Little, Brown, 1972). Locke's influence on Jefferson has been questioned by Garry Wills, *Inventing America: Jefferson's Declaration of Independence* (Garden City, NY: Doubleday, 1978); but for criticisms

of Wills's argument, see Ronald Hamowy, "Jefferson and the Scottish Enlightenment: A Critique of Garry Wills' *Inventing America*," *William and Mary Quarterly* 36 (October 1979): 503–23; and Garrett Ward Sheldon, *The Political Philosophy of Thomas Jefferson* (Baltimore: Johns Hopkins University Press, 1991), pp. 41–52.

4. All quotations from the *Second Treatise* are from the edition edited by C. B. Macpherson (Indianapolis: Hackett, 1980).

5. See Abraham Lincoln, Speech at Peoria, Illinois, 16 October 1854, in *The Collected Works of Abraham Lincoln*, ed. Roy P. Basler, 9 Vols. (New Brunswick, NJ: Rutgers University Press, 1953–1955), 2: 264. The Southern defenders of slavery—like George Fitzhugh—had to reject Locke's teaching. See Robert J. Loewenberg, "John Locke and the Antebellum Defense of Slavery," *Political Theory* 13 (May 1985): 266–91.

6. Ernst Mayr, *The Growth of Biological Thought* (Cambridge: Harvard University Press, 1982), 79.

7. Abraham Lincoln, Speech at Springfield, Illinois, 26 June 1857, in *Collected Works*, 2: 405–6; Lincoln, Message to Congress, 4 July 1861, ibid., 4: 438.

8. Mayr, *Biological Thought*, 297. On the biological nature of species, see Theodosius Dobzhansky et al., *Evolution* (San Francisco: W. H. Freeman, 1977), 165–94; Michael Ruse, *The Philosophy of Biology* (Atlantic Highlands, NJ: Humanities Press, 1983), 126–39; and Alexander Rosenberg, *The Structure of Biological Science* (Cambridge: Cambridge University Press, 1985), 180–225. On human equality as a biological fact, see Stephen Jay Gould, "Human Equality Is a Contingent Fact of History," in *The Flamingo's Smile* (New York: Norton, 1985), 185–98.

   In *An Essay Concerning Human Understanding*, Locke contends that "our distinguishing substances into species by names, is not at all founded on their real essences; nor can we pretend to range and determine them exactly into species, according to internal essential differences" (bk. 3, chap. 6, sec. 20). This would seem to contradict his affirmation of human equality in the *Second Treatise*. Should we distinguish Locke's "philosophic" teaching in the *Essay* from his "political" teaching in the *Second Treatise*? If so, is it conceivable that the "political" teaching is the more reasonable of the two? See Jacques Maritain, "Human Equality," in *Ransoming the Time* (New York: Scribners, 1941), 1–32; Yves Simon, *The Philosophy of Democratic Government* (Chicago: University of Chicago Press, 1951), 197–207; and Leo Strauss, *Natural Right and History* (Chicago: University of Chicago Press, 1953), 206–9, 220–21.

9. Charles Darwin, *The Origin of Species and the Descent of Man* (New York: Random House, Modern Library, 1936), 512–13.

10. Carl Becker, *The Declaration of Independence* (New York: Random House, Vintage, 1942), 274–75. See Larry Arnhart, "Darwin, Aristotle, and the Biology of Human Rights," *Social Science Information* 23 (June 1984): 493–521.

11. Darwin, *Origin of Species and Descent of Man*, 460–61.

12. Thomas Huxley, *Man's Place in Nature* (New York: Appleton, 1898), 155.

13. Dobzhansky, *Evolution*, 453, 514–16. In *Some Thoughts Concerning Education* (sec. 116), Locke advises parents not to allow their children to torture or kill animals:

> They who delight in the suffering and destruction of inferior creatures will not be apt to be very compassionate or benign to those of their own kind. . . . Children should . . . be taught not to spoil or destroy anything, unless it be for the preservation or advantage of some other that is nobler. . . . And indeed, I think people should be accustomed, from their cradles, to be tender to all sensible creatures, and to spoil or waste nothing at all.

Thoughts can be found in John Locke, *On Politics and Education* (Roslyn, NY: Walter J. Black, 1949). Compare Locke, *Essay Concerning Human Understanding*, bk. 3, chap. 6, secs. 20–30. See Keith Thomas, *Man and the Natural World: A History of the Modern Sensibility* (New York: Pantheon, 1983). Even if human beings are superior to other animals in cognitive ability, are all animals equal as sensible creatures? Do all animals have rights? Or should we say that, with respect to rights, the differences between human beings and other species are more critical than the similarities? See R. G. Frey, *Interests and Rights* (Oxford: Clarendon Press, 1980); Tom Regan, *The Case for Animal Rights* (Berkeley: University of California Press, 1983); Mary Midgley, *Animals and Why They Matter* (Athens: University of Georgia Press, 1984); and Peter Singer, "Ten Years of Animal Liberation," *New York Review of Books* 17 (January 1985): 46–52. Compare chap. 2, sec. 3; chap. 6, sec. 5.

If we say that other animals have no rights because they are cognitively inferior to us, must we also say that mentally retarded adults, children, and fetuses have no rights (see *Second Treatise*, sec. 60)? At what point does a fetus become truly human and therefore deserving of protection as a human life? See Aristotle, *Politics* 1335b13–1336a2; Richard Selzer, "Abortion," in *Mortal Lessons: Notes on the Art of Surgery* (New York: Simon & Schuster, 1976), 153–60; and Sidney Callahan and Daniel Callahan, eds., *Abortion: Understanding Differences* (New York: Plenum, 1984), especially chaps. 5–7, 10.

Should Lockean property rights include the ownership of animals, fetuses, infants, and genetically engineered organisms? See H. Tristram Engelhardt, Jr., *The Foundations of Bioethics* (New York: Oxford University Press, 1986), 127–43.

14. See C. B. Macpherson, *The Political Theory of Possessive Individualism* (Oxford: Oxford University Press, 1962), 194–262; Macpherson, "Liberal Democracy and Property," in *Property*, ed. C. B. Macpherson (Toronto: University of Toronto Press, 1978), 199–207; and Staughton Lynd, *Intellectual Origins of American Radicalism*

(Cambridge: Harvard University Press, 1982).

15. Sheldon S. Wolin, *Politics and Vision* (Boston: Little, Brown, 1960), 340. For a provocative application of Lockean competitiveness to the unclaimed resources of the oceans, see Robert Goldwin, "Locke and the Law of the Sea," *Commentary* 71 (June 1981): 46–50. See also Bernard Cohen et al., *The Law of the Sea* (San Francisco: Institute for Contemporary Studies, 1983).

    In contrast to Wolin's view, consider Nathan Tarcov's interpretation of Locke:

    > Locke's political teaching is *not* one of self-interest but one of *rights*. . . . Lockean politics include a conception of the common good and a conception of civil society as more than an aggregate of atomistic individuals. His understanding of human nature exhibits a profound appreciation of human sociality, and families and churches play crucial roles in Lockean civil society. Locke teaches not a narrowly calculating selfishness but a set of decent moral virtues. Nor is his fundamental concern with property the justification of money–grubbing. ("A 'Non-Lockean' Locke and the Character of Liberalism," in Douglas MacLean and Claudia Mills, eds., *Liberalism Reconsidered* [Totowa, NJ: Rowman & Allanheld, 1983], 131)

    See also Tarcov, *Locke's Education for Liberty* (Chicago: University of Chicago Press, 1984).

16. Karl Marx and Friedrich Engels, *Communist Manifesto*, in *The Marx-Engels Reader*, ed. Robert C. Tucker, 2nd ed. (New York: Norton, 1978), 491.

17. Some historical evidence for this argument can be found in Douglass C. North and Robert Paul Thomas, "An Economic Theory of the Growth of the Western World," *Economic History Review*, 2nd series, 23 (1970): 1–17; and in North and Thomas, *The Rise of the Western World: A New Economic History* (Cambridge: Cambridge University Press, 1973). For evidence that the change in the Middle Ages from a barter economy to a money economy had the effects described by Locke, see Alexander Murray, *Reason and Society in the Middle Ages* (Oxford: Clarendon Press, 1978), 25–61. For the argument that the major concepts of capitalist economics were first developed by the Scholastics, see Joseph Schumpeter, *History of Economic Analysis* (New York: Oxford University Press, 1954); Alejandro A. Chafuen, *Christians for Freedom: Late-Scholastic Economics* (San Francisco: Ignatius, 1986); and Karen Iverson Vaughn, *John Locke: Economist and Social Scientist* (Chicago: University of Chicago Press, 1980).

    There is some evidence of customary property rights in many stateless societies and even in prehistoric bands of hunter-gatherers. Does this show Locke was right in arguing that some form of property could arise in the state of nature prior to government? See Vernon L. Smith, "Hunting and Gathering Economies," in John Eatwell et al., eds., *The World of Economics* (New York: Norton, 1991), 330–38; and

Vernon L. Smith, "Economic Principles in the Emergence of Humankind," *Economic Inquiry* 30 (January 1992): 1–13.

To defend a market economy does Locke have to show that it is both efficient and moral? Some economists separate efficiency and morality. But Allen E. Buchanan, *Ethics, Efficiency and the Market* (Totowa, NJ: Rowman & Allanheld, 1985), argues that judging the efficiency of the market depends on moral assumptions, just as judging the morality of the market depends on assumptions about efficiency. Compare Richard A. Posner, *The Economics of Justice* (Cambridge: Harvard University Press, 1981), 60–115; and Ronald Dworkin, *A Matter of Principle* (Cambridge: Harvard University Press, 1985), 237–89.

The economic argument for an increasing supply of labor as promoting commercial expansion led Locke to advocate unlimited naturalization of immigrants. See David Resnick, "John Locke and the Problem of Naturalization," *Review of Politics* 49 (1987): 368–88. For restatements of Locke's position, see P.T. Bauer, *Equality, the Third World, and Economic Delusion* (Cambridge: Harvard University Press, 1981), chap. 3; and Julian L. Simon, *Population Matters* (New Brunswick, NJ: Transaction Publishers, 1990).

18. Dewey, *Liberalism and Social Action*, 107, 90–93. Compare Ralph Nader et al., *Taming the Giant Corporation* (New York: Norton, 1976); and Robert Hessen, *In Defense of the Corporation* (Stanford: Hoover Institution Press, 1979).

19. The liberal and Marxist criticisms of Lockean capitalism in America are presented in subtle ways in the films of Frank Capra, particularly in *It's a Wonderful Life*. See Raymond Carney, *American Vision: The Films of Frank Capra* (Cambridge: Cambridge University Press, 1986).

20. For this interpretation of Locke, see Martin Seliger, *The Liberal Politics of John Locke* (New York: Praeger, 1969), 165–79. The Fifth Amendment to the United States Constitution declares that no person shall be "deprived of life, liberty, or property, without due process of law; nor shall private property be taken for public use, without just compensation." Does this show that the American government was intended to be Lockean in protecting private property? Does this suggest that the redistribution of wealth is not a proper function of government? These questions were recently introduced into American constitutional debate by Richard A. Epstein's *Takings: Private Property and the Power of Eminent Domain* (Cambridge: Harvard University Press, 1985). For discussion of these and related questions, see Ellen F. Paul and Howard Dickman, eds., *Liberty, Property, and the Future of Constitutional Development* (Albany: State University of New York Press, 1990).

21. On the contradiction between autonomy and authority, see Roberto Mangabeira Unger, *Law in Modern Society* (New York: Free Press, 1976), 23–43, 127–33, 140–55, 236–42, 262–65; Robert Paul Wolff, *In Defense of Anarchism* (New York: Harper & Row, 1976); and Carole Pateman, "Justifying Political Obligation," in Alkis Kontos, ed.,

Powers, Possessions and Freedom: Essays in Honour of C. B. Macpherson (Toronto: University of Toronto, 1979), 63–75.

The conflict between individualism and communitarianism often emerges in American popular culture, particularly in some films and in the myth of the cowboy. The heroic personae of Humphrey Bogart, John Wayne, and Clint Eastwood are often afraid to commit themselves fully to social order for fear of losing their untamed, individual spontaneity. Such heroes feel the tension between anarchic lawlessness and communal law and order. In the Western, it is the conflict between the lawless savages and the civilized settlers. In the most complex Westerns, the hero must make a tragic choice: he acts to protect the settlers even while he somehow senses that his own heroic qualities depend on the savage life. Do such heroes express and shape our political culture as much as Homer's heroes expressed and shaped Greek political culture? Consider, for example, Owen Wister's *The Virginian*, which he offered as "an expression of American faith" and dedicated to his friend Theodore Roosevelt. See John G. Cawelti, *The Six-Gun Mystique* (Bowling Green, OH: Popular Press, n.d.), 46–66, 76–86; Cawelti, *Adventure, Mystery, and Romance: Formula Stories as Art and Popular Culture* (Chicago: University of Chicago Press, 1976), 20–22, 34–36, 246–51; and David Brion Davis, "Ten-Gallon Hero," in *From Slavery to Homicide* (New York: Oxford University Press, 1986), chap. 5.

22. See Strauss, *Natural Right and History*, 202–51; and Richard Cox, *Locke on War and Peace* (Oxford: Oxford University Press, 1960).

23. Ronald Peters, *The Massachusetts Constitution of 1780* (Amherst: University of Massachusetts Press, 1978), 195.

24. Henry David Thoreau, *Walden and Other Writings*, ed. Brooks Atkinson (New York: Random House, Modern Library, 1937), 636–37.

25. See Roberto Michels, *Political Parties* (Glencoe, IL: Free Press, 1949); Gaetano Mosca, *The Ruling Class*, trans. Hannah D. Kahn (New York: McGraw-Hill, 1939), 50–69; and Peter Bachrach, *The Theory of Democratic Elitism: A Critique* (Boston: Little, Brown, 1967).

26. Willmoore Kendall, *John Locke and the Doctrine of Majority-Rule* (Urbana: University of Illinois Press, 1965), 112–19.

27. Ibid., 177.

28. Thomas Jefferson, First Inaugural Address, in *The Life and Selected Writings of Thomas Jefferson*, eds. Adrienne Koch and William Peden (New York: Random House, Modern Library, 1944), 322. For a meticulous analysis and justification of majority rule, see Elaine Spitz, *Majority Rule* (Chatham, NJ: Chatham House, 1984).

29. Gerald Ford, Inaugural Address, in Richard D. Heffner, ed., *A Documentary History of the United States*, 3rd ed. (New York: New American Library, 1976), 351.

30. Theodore J. Lowi, *The End of Liberalism*, 2nd ed. (New York: Norton, 1979), 101.

31. Kenneth Culp Davis, *Discretionary Justice: A Preliminary Inquiry*

(Urbana: University of Illinois Press, 1971), 41.

32. For a defense of the rule of law as a necessary restraint on administrative power in American government, see Lowi's *End of Liberalism*. Compare Lyle Downing and Robert B. Thigpen, "A Liberal Dilemma: The Application of Unger's Critique of Formalism to Lowi's Concept of Juridical Democracy," *Journal of Politics* 44 (February 1982): 230–46. For a study of recent attempts to structure the legislative power of administrators, see William F. West, "Structuring Administrative Discretion: The Pursuit of Rationality and Responsiveness," *American Journal of Political Science* 28 (May 1984): 340–60.

33. See Robert A. Katzmann, "Federal Trade Commission," in James Q. Wilson, ed., *The Politics of Regulation* (New York: Basic Books, 1980), 152–87; and Barry R. Weingast and Mark J. Moran, "The Myth of Runaway Bureaucracy—The Case of the FTC," *Regulation* (May/June 1982): 33–38. For criticisms of the FTC by "public-choice" scholars, see Robert J. Mackay et al., eds., *Public Choice and Regulation: A View from Inside the Federal Trade Commission* (Stanford: Hoover Institution Press, 1987).

34. Lincoln, Message to Congress 4 July 1861, in *Collected Works*, 4: 426. For diverse views of prerogative in American politics, see Larry Arnhart, "The 'Godlike Prince': John Locke, Executive Prerogative, and the American Presidency," *Presidential Studies Quarterly* 9 (Spring 1979): 121–31; L.R. Sorenson, "The *Federalist Papers* on the Constitutionality of Executive Prerogative," *Presidential Studies Quarterly* 19 (1989): 267–83; Thomas S. Langston and Michael E. Lind, "John Locke and the Limits of Presidential Prerogative," *Polity* 24 (1991): 49–68; and Daniel P. Franklin, *Extraordinary Measures: The Exercise of Prerogative Powers in the United States* (Pittsburgh: University of Pittsburgh Press, 1991). In 1793, James Madison—arguing against Alexander Hamilton's broad interpretation of executive powers—complained that Locke's "chapter on prerogative shows how much the reason of the philosopher was clouded by the royalism of the Englishman." Marvin Meyers, ed., *The Mind of the Founder* (Indianapolis: Bobbs-Merrill, 1973), 266.

35. *New York Times*, 20 May 1977, A16.

36. Arthur Schlesinger, Jr., *The Imperial Presidency* (Boston: Houghton Mifflin, 1973), especially 8–10, 108–16, 148–49, 162, 176, 188, 193, 198, 302, 304, 321–24.

37. Schlesinger lists the conditions in a passage added to the paperback edition of his book: *The Imperial President* (New York: Popular Library, 1974), 450–52.

38. See Locke, *Essay Concerning Human Understanding*, bk. 1, chap. 2, secs. 5–8; bk. 2, chap. 17, secs. 17–18; bk. 2, chap. 21, sec. 35; bk. 2, chap. 27, secs. 9–14. See also Harvey C. Mansfield, Jr., *The Taming of the Prince: The Ambivalence of Modern Executive Power* (New York: Free Press, 1989).

39. Niccolò Machiavelli, *The Discourses*, trans. Christian E. Detold, in *The Prince and the Discourses* (New York: Random House, Modern Library, 1940), 203.

40. Jefferson, *Notes on the State of Virginia*, in *Life and Selected Writings*, 244–47.

41. Alexander Hamilton, James Madison, and John Jay, *The Federalist*, ed. Edward Mead Earle (New York: Random House, Modern Library, n.d.), No. 70, pp. 454–55. Would the American President be more efficient and more accountable to the people if he were more like the Prime Minister in the British parliamentary system? Is the separation of powers inefficient? See Don K. Price, "The Parliamentary and Presidential Systems," *Public Administration Review* 3 (Autumn 1943): 317–34; and James Q. Wilson, "Does the Separation of Powers Still Work?" *The Public Interest* No. 86 (Winter 1987): 36–52.

42. Lincoln, Message to Congress, 4 July 1861, in *Collected Works*, 4: 429.

43. Ibid.

44. James G. Randall, *Constitutional Problems Under Lincoln* (Urbana: University of Illinois Press, 1951), 47. It should be noted, however, that Lincoln repeatedly denied that he was usurping dictatorial powers beyond the limits of the Constitution. Generally, he was careful to work within the boundaries of the Constitution broadly interpreted. See, for example, Lincoln, *Collected Works*, 4: 531–32, 6:262–69, 6: 302–3, 6: 428–29, 8: 52, 8: 100–101. Compare Locke, *Second Treatise*, secs. 134, 155, 239; and *The Federalist*, No. 20, pp. 122–23; No. 25, p. 158. For a meticulous history of Lincoln's actions, see Mark E. Neely, Jr., *The Fate of Liberty: Abraham Lincoln and Civil Liberties* (New York: Oxford University Press, 1991).

45. George Washington, "Farewell Address," in Daniel J. Boorstin, ed., *An American Primer*, 2 Vols. (Chicago: University of Chicago Press, 1966), 1: 199.

46. See Julian Franklin, *John Locke and the Theory of Sovereignty* (Cambridge: Cambridge University Press, 1978); and Nathan Tarcov, "Locke's *Second Treatise* and 'The Best Fence Against Rebellion'," *Review of Politics* 43 (April 1981): 198–217. On the English Revolution of 1688 as founding kingship on popular consent rather than divine right, see Sir David Lindsay Keir, *The Constitutional History of Modern Britain Since 1485*, 9th ed. (New York: Norton, 1969), 267–72. Compare Christopher Hill, *The Century of Revolution, 1603–1714*, 2nd ed. (New York: Norton, 1980), 263–66.

47. For one of the most persuasive statements of anarchist theory, see Morris Tannehill and Linda Tannehill, *The Market for Liberty* (New York: Laissez Faire Books, 1984). See also Mortimer J. Adler, *The Common Sense of Politics* (New York: Holt, Rinehart & Winston, 1971), 94–104; Robert Nozick, *Anarchy, State, and Utopia* (New York: Basic Books, 1974), 51–53, 120–31; and David Friedman, *The Machinery of Freedom* (New Rochelle: Arlington House, 1978), 151–222. For a history and critique of modern libertarianism that stresses its Lockean

roots, see Stephen L. Newman, *Liberalism at Wit's End* (Ithaca: Cornell University Press, 1984).

Peter Kropotkin believed anarchism could be rooted in the animal inclinations to spontaneous cooperation as understood by evolutionary biology (*Mutual Aid* [Montreal: Black Rose Books, 1989]). See also Daniel P. Todes, *Darwin without Malthus: The Struggle for Existence in Russian Evolutionary Thought* (New York: Oxford University Press, 1989). Does Kropotkin's argument show that a Darwinian view of human nature does not have to be politically conservative?

48. Mary Wollstonecraft, *Vindication of the Rights of Woman*, ed. Miriam Brody (London: Penguin Books, 1983), 79–84, 86–88, 113–14, 132, 139, 247–48, 265–66, 298–99, 313–19. See Virginia Sapiro, *A Vindication of Political Virtue: The Political Theory of Mary Wollstonecraft* (Chicago: University of Chicago Press, 1992). For feminist interpretations of the history of political philosophy, see Susan M. Okin, *Women in Western Political Thought* (Princeton: Princeton University Press, 1979); and Mary L. Shanley and Carole Pateman, eds., *Feminist Interpretations and Political Theory* (University Park: Pennsylvania State University Press, 1991). On the various schools of thought in feminist theory, see Alison M. Jaggar, *Feminist Politics and Human Nature* (Totowa, NJ: Rowman and Allanheld, 1983); and Rosemarie Tong, *Feminist Thought* (Boulder: Westview Press, 1989).

49. Alice S. Rossi, ed., *The Feminist Papers* (Boston: Northeastern University Press, 1988), 415–20.

50. See Melissa A. Butler, "Early Liberal Roots of Feminism: John Locke and the Attack on Patriarchy," *American Political Science Review* 72 (1978): 135–50, reprinted in Shanley and Pateman, *Feminist Interpretations*, 74–94; and Ludwig von Mises, *Socialism* (Indianapolis: Liberty Classics, 1981), chap. 4.

51. Compare Wollstonecraft, *Vindication*, 154, 188, 266; and Jean-Jacques Rousseau, *Émile*, trans. Allan Bloom (New York: Basic Books, 1979), 357, 362–64, 386, 408–9. On the connections between Rousseau and feminism, see Joel Schwartz, *The Sexual Politics of Jean-Jacques Rousseau* (Chicago: University of Chicago Press, 1984); and Camille Paglia, *Sexual Personae: Art and Decadence from Nefertiti to Emily Dickinson* (New Haven: Yale University Press, 1990).

52. See Carol Gilligan, *In a Different Voice* (Cambridge: Harvard University Press, 1982); and Sara Ruddick, *Maternal Thinking* (New York: Ballantine Books, 1989).

53. On the debate over the biology of sexual differences, see Donald Symons, *The Evolution of Human Sexuality* (New York: Oxford University Press, 1979); Martin Daly and Margo Wilson, *Sex, Evolution, and Behavior* (Belmont, CA: Wadsworth, 1983); Daly and Wilson, *Homicide* (Hawthorne, NY: Aldine de Gruyter, 1988); Doreen Kimura, "Sex Differences in the Brain," *Scientific American* 267 (September 1992): 118–25; Anne Fausto-Sterling, *Myths of Gender* (New York: Basic Books, 1985); and Carol Tavris, *The Mismeasure of Woman* (New York: Simon & Schuster, 1992). See also chap. 1, n. 16; and chap. 2, sec. 5.

Chapter

9

Participatory Democracy
Rousseau's *First and Second Discourses* and *Social Contract*

Key Readings

First and Second Discourses in their entirety; *The Social Contract*, I, 1, 6–8; II, 1, 3, 6–7; III, 4, 15; IV, 1–2, 6, 8.

Jean-Jacques Rousseau (1712–1778) was born in the city-republic of Geneva, Switzerland. His mother died shortly after his birth. His father, who was a watchmaker, taught him to value republican government and guided his reading of novels and histories. Plutarch's *Lives* was particularly important in stimulating Jean-Jacques's admiration for ancient Greek and Roman statesmen.

At the age of twelve, Rousseau was abandoned by his father, who left Geneva to avoid prosecution for dueling. For the next fourteen years, Jean-Jacques learned various trades as he wandered around Europe. During periods of leisure, he pursued a wide range of studies.

In 1742, he went to Paris with the hope of becoming successful by presenting to the world a new system of musical notation that he had invented. Although this project failed, he began writing poetry, plays, and operas. He became an associate of the *philosophes* who led the French Enlightenment, and by 1749 he was writing articles for Denis Diderot's *Encyclopédie*. The crucial event in his writing career occurred in 1750 when he received a prize from the Academy of Dijon for his *Discourse on the Sciences and Arts* (also called the *First Discourse*). He wrote his major works over the next twelve years.

After the publication of his *Émile* in 1762, Rousseau suffered persecution from religious and political authorities for his unorthodox religious teachings. His books were burned in Paris and Geneva, and he had to move around Europe to avoid being arrested. For the rest of his life, he tried to defend his writing; and his fears of persecution drove him to paranoia. He described himself as a "solitary walker" forced by the unjust hatred of humankind to withdraw into himself to find personal contentment. At the end of his life, he renewed his life-long interest in botany as an activity that he could pursue in solitude. Thus Rousseau struggled in his life with the same problem that dominated his writing: the conflict between the individual autonomy and social dependence.

At the beginning of his *Social Contract*, Rousseau declares: "Man was born free, and everywhere he is in chains" (I, 1).[1] Rousseau agrees with Hobbes and Locke that all are naturally free and equal, that no one is entitled by nature to rule over anyone else, and therefore the only legitimate society is one that is free from the domination of some over others. On the other hand, Rousseau argues that the sort of modern regime endorsed by Hobbes and Locke promotes political and economic inequality, which deprives individuals of their freedom. The rulers dominate the ruled, and the rich dominate the poor.

Hobbes and Locke think that individual liberty requires a government that represents the people while leaving them free to pursue private lives devoted largely to economic activity. But Rousseau insists that people are free only when they participate directly in the making of laws, which requires that they not be distracted from their public duties by economic acquisitiveness. Thus Rousseau revives in some manner the ancient Greek and Roman concern for civic virtue as essential to political freedom. In the *First Discourse*, Rousseau complains: "Ancient politicians incessantly talked about morals and virtue, those of our time talk only of business and money."[2] Rousseau's defense of political virtue against the commercial spirit of modern politics challenges one of the most fundamental assumptions of modern life—the belief in progress through science and educational enlightenment.

1. Does popular enlightenment subvert political freedom?

Rousseau began his *First Discourse* with a tribute to the intellectual progress of human beings:

> It is a grand and beautiful sight to see man emerge from obscurity somehow by his own efforts; dissipate, by the light of reason, the darkness in which nature had enveloped him; rise above himself; soar intellectually into celestial regions; traverse with giant steps, like the sun, the vastness of the universe; and — what is even grander and more difficult — come back to himself to study man and know his nature, his duties, and his end. All of these marvels have been revived in recent generations. (35)

Insofar as this reminds us of Plato's image of the cave, we could say that the modern individual has finally escaped the darkness of prejudice through the advancement of knowledge. Indeed, many of the leading thinkers of Rousseau's time thought that human beings could become truly free only through intellectual enlightenment. But Rousseau disagreed:

> The sciences, letters, and arts . . . spread garlands of flowers over the iron chains with which men are burdened, stifle in them the sense of that original liberty for which they seemed to have been born, make them love their slavery, and turn them into what is called civilized peoples. (*First Discourse*, 36)

How can Rousseau celebrate the intellectual progress of human beings, yet condemn it for sanctioning their slavery? Why should we regard the modern growth in knowledge as a threat to political liberty?

A free society, Rousseau maintains, depends on the patriotic virtue of citizens who devote themselves completely to their community. But scientists and philosophers weaken the spirit of patriotism by questioning the unexamined moral opinions and habits fundamentally accepted by a society. Science and philosophy also lure citizens away from public activity and into the essentially private pursuits of the intellectual life. Moreover, science and philosophy flourish only in a prosperous society that permits luxury and idleness, which soften the character of the citizens and destroy the warlike spirit necessary for national defense. Finally, the cultivation of intellectual talents promotes vanity, competitiveness, and inequality, thus undermining the equality of respect that all must have for one another if they are to live together as a community of self-governing citizens.

To accept these arguments against science and philosophy as politically dangerous, we would have to agree with Rousseau's claim that the model for a truly free society is ancient Sparta, a city ruled by warrior-citizens with no tolerance for philosophers. But while glorifying Sparta, Rousseau also praises Socrates in the *First Discourse*. Isn't this a clear contradiction? Why doesn't Rousseau condemn Socrates, as his Athenian accusers did, for corrupting Athens? How can Rousseau admire the philosopher who taught that knowledge is virtue while he also asserts that the virtue of the citizen requires a healthy ignorance?

One way to rationalize the inconsistency would be to say that Rousseau regards the pursuit of philosophy or science as bad for most but good for a talented few.[3] This would conform to Socrates' teaching in the *Republic* that, because only a rare few can break the chains of unexamined opinions and ascend out of the cave to achieve genuine knowledge, it is best for most human beings to remain unenlightened. Rousseau suggests this when he observes:

> If a few men must be allowed to devote themselves to the study of the sciences and arts, it must be only those who feel the strength to walk alone in their footsteps and go beyond them. It is for these few to raise monuments to the glory of human intellect. (*First Discourse*, 63)

We have seen this same emphasis on the rarity and solitariness of the scientific life in Descartes's *Discourse on Method*, and Rousseau even refers to Descartes as one of the few geniuses of modern science.

Contrary to both Socrates and Descartes, however, Rousseau insists that all are "born" to "original liberty" (*First Discourse*, 36). People have not always been in chains. In their primitive state, they enjoyed a natural freedom:

> One cannot reflect on morals without delighting in the recollection of the simplicity of the earliest times. It is a lovely shore, adorned by the hands of nature alone, toward which one incessantly turns one's eyes and from which one regretfully feels oneself moving away. (*First Discourse*, 53–54)

We have already seen in Hobbes and Locke the idea of the state of nature in which all were originally free and equal. But Rousseau goes beyond his predecessors in pursuing the radical implications of that idea. To see evidence of this we must turn to the *Second Discourse (Discourse on the Origin of Inequality)*.

2. Are human beings by nature asocial and arational?

Aristotle declared that humans are by nature political animals because they are by nature rational. Thomas Aquinas inferred that, as rational and political animals, they have knowledge of a natural moral law. But Hobbes argued that in their natural state, humans would be asocial, and therefore they would not be governed by natural law in the traditional sense: they would be moved only by the desire for self-preservation, which would create a war of all against all. "Hobbes saw very clearly the defect of all modern definitions of natural right," Rousseau reasoned, "but the consequences he draws from his own definition show that he takes it in a sense which is no less false" (*Second Discourse*, 129). Hobbes failed to understand that by his own logic the state of nature would have to be "the best suited to peace and the most appropriate for the human race." Rousseau thought that Hobbes was wrong to include "in the savage man's care of self-preservation the need to satisfy a multitude of passions which are the product of society and which have made laws necessary." If our natural forebears were asocial, then they were also arational because human reason develops only through social activity (particularly language). As dumb beasts moved solely by the sentiments of the moment, they lived in peace because they lacked the imagination necessary to experience the violent passions felt by socialized animals. Rousseau's argument was, therefore, more radical than Hobbes's. For Rousseau maintained that humans were naturally good until they degenerated into rational and social beings. "If nature destined us to be healthy, I almost dare affirm that the state of reflection is a state contrary to nature and that the man who meditates is a depraved animal" (110).

Isn't Rousseau wrong? He claims that human beings were originally solitary. But modern anthropological and biological research indicates that even our earliest ancestors lived in social bands founded on kinship. He says that human beings in the state of nature were happy and good, free and equal. But there is much evidence that primitive human beings lived harsh lives plagued by hunger and violence.[4]

One way to defend Rousseau is to say that he regards the state of nature not as a historical fact, but as a hypothetical construction:

> Let us therefore begin by setting all the facts aside, for they do not affect the question. The researches which can be undertaken concerning this subject must not be taken for historical truths, but only for hypothetical and conditional reasonings better

suited to clarify the nature of things than to show their true
origin, like those our physicists make every day concerning the
formation of the world. (103)

Thus Rousseau suggests that to have a standard for judging the
effects of social life, he will imagine what human beings would be
like outside of society, but without claiming that such a condition
has ever actually existed.

This interpretation would contradict, however, the evidence in
the *Second Discourse* that Rousseau considers the state of nature
to be historically verifiable. He proposes, for example, that natural
scientists should travel throughout the world to gather
anthropological information on both humans and animals so that
"we would thus learn to know our own" (213).

Rousseau speaks of "setting all the facts aside" in the context
of observing that the biblical account of human origins denies the
idea of a state of nature. Does he, therefore, describe his reasoning
as "hypothetical" only to hide his challenge to the biblical teaching?
His explanation of human evolution closely follows the reasoning
of the ancient Roman philosopher Lucretius in Book Five of his *De
rerum natura (On the Nature of Things)*, which reflects Lucretius's
desire to present a history of the universe that would not depend
on religious beliefs.

Rousseau explains that his history is "conjectural," in that "two
facts given as real are to be connected by a series of intermediate
facts which are unknown" (141). That is to say, he is sure about
the reality of the origin and the end—the natural state and the civil
state—but he must rely on probable reasoning about the
intermediate stages. If this is what Rousseau means, then we must
wonder whether there is any historical evidence for his view of the
state of nature.

Rousseau sees our ancestors "wandering in the forests, without
industry, without speech, without domicile, without war, and
without liaisons, with no need of his fellow men, likewise with no
desire to harm them, perhaps never even recognizing anyone
individually" (137). He sees "an animal . . . satisfying his hunger
under an oak, quenching his thirst at the first stream, finding his
bed at the foot of the same tree that furnished his meal; and
therewith his needs are satisfied" (105).

When males and females encounter one another, they might unite
just long enough to satisfy their sexual desire, but afterwards they
separate with no further thought of one another (120–21). Sexual
appetite in this state is purely physical, and therefore it does not
create families. Nor does it lead to violent conflict. Aggressive sexual

competition arises among animals when there is a scarcity of females relative to males or because of female estrus periods, but among human beings neither is true (134–36).

Because human beings are solitary in this natural state, there is a rough equality among them. Of course, there are natural differences, but because each person lives independently of all the others, no one is subordinated to anyone else (138–39). Rousseau does imply, however, that the dependence of infants on their mothers will create at least a temporary bond between mothers and offspring, so that primitive females will be more social than primitive males (121, 130).

On those few occasions when the primitive male had some common interest with other males — such as killing a large animal for food — he could unite with them in a herd. But this would only be a temporary association (144–45). In very rare cases, primitive males found themselves in competition; and "everyone sought to obtain his own advantage, either by naked force if he believed he could, or by cleverness and cunning if he felt himself to be the weaker" (145).

The limited social interaction among our primitive ancestors made language unnecessary and impossible. Like other animals, they communicated only through "inarticulate cries, many gestures, and some imitative noises" (145). Contrary to Aristotle, Rousseau infers that because they were neither rational nor social, those in the natural state were not endowed with speech.

But perhaps Rousseau's most controversial claim is that, in the primitive state, humans are naturally good. He agrees with Hobbes that self-preservation is the fundamental desire; yet he argues that while humans are completely selfish and solitary, they are naturally good. Their self-centered indifference to others in the state of nature makes them good because they are free from the only source of evil — dependence on others. He distinguishes between the natural love of oneself (*l'amour de soi-même*) and civilized vanity (*l'amour propre*) (221–22). The first is the self-love of the primitives who feel the sentiment of their present existence without comparison to others. The second is the pride of the socialized beings who derive self-esteem from thinking themselves superior to others. The primitive being will fight in defense against physical threats, but feels no need to maliciously attack others to dominate them. Those in the natural state are too ignorant and too solitary to care what others think of them. Moreover, primitive beings may be moved by the sentiment of pity to refrain from harming others except when their lives are threatened (133).

But doesn't the apparent aggressiveness of animal and human

behavior cast doubt on Rousseau's depiction of primitives as naturally good? Animals fight to protect their reproductive fitness.[5] They fight in competition for natural resources, in competition for mates, to repulse strangers, to protect their own lives, or to protect their young. Rousseau concedes that primitives will fight to preserve themselves. But except in cases where food becomes scarce, he sees no reason why these asocial beings would want to attack one another. The most intense conflicts arise from the desires to compete with, to dominate, or to be recognized by other beings, but such desires manifest sociality. The fundamental issue, therefore, is whether Rousseau is right about humans being asocial in their natural state.

Modern evolutionary biologists and anthropologists believe that human beings have always been social beings.[6] Throughout the evolutionary history of human beings, they have lived in groups. During most of that history, human beings lived in bands sustained by the hunting and gathering of food, in which survival required social cooperation. From this, it would seem that modern science has refuted Rousseau's depiction of the state of nature.

And yet, to find Rousseau's state of nature, we may have to go back to the nonhuman, primate ancestors of human beings. Is Rousseau's natural being an orangutan? Rousseau suggests this, and he even proposes to test his hypothesis by attempting to crossbreed orangutans and human beings (208–9).

In fact, Rousseau, drawing on the best biological research of his time, was the first thinker in the eighteenth century to suggest that humans evolved from apes; and thus he anticipated modern evolutionary theory.[7] Biologists now agree that humans are primates closely related to the great apes—the gorilla, the chimpanzee, and the orangutan. Although the chimpanzee seems to be the most closely related to us, some primatologists think the orangutan deserves special attention. And, surprisingly, Rousseau's sketch of the orangutan as a largely solitary animal has been confirmed by primatologists who have studied the orangutan in its natural habitat.

John MacKinnon, one of the leading observers of the orangutan, describes this ape as "an anti-social and solitary animal" and "a shaggy, surly bundle of complete inactivity."[8] He lives by wandering through tropical rain forests in Borneo and Sumatra in search of the food provided by widely scattered fruit trees. The male usually travels alone. He mates on rare occasions; and although he may form a consortship with a female, this lasts no longer than a few days. The only stable social bond is between mothers and their infants, and typically adult females are somewhat social in contrast to the utterly solitary males. Occasionally males fight for dominance, but generally they avoid violence. Are these our primal forebears? If so, we would have to agree with Rousseau that we have descended from peaceful, asocial beings. Biruté Galdikas, after many years of studying orangutans in the wild, concludes: "Individual orangutans rely on no one other than themselves. They have been released from dependence on others of their kind. Paradoxically, they seem to have an inner strength and serenity no member of any gregarious species, including our own, could ever match."[9]

Obviously, however, it would be absurd for Rousseau to recommend returning to our natural state if "natural man" was actually a subhuman animal. Rousseau insists that he does not intend to make such a recommendation (201–2). The passage from the state of nature to civil society was beneficial, Rousseau explains in *The Social Contract* (I, 8), because the primitive human changed "from a stupid, limited animal into an intelligent being and a man." But what, then, is Rousseau's purpose in describing the state of nature?

At least one point is clear: by tracing our evolution back to prehuman ancestors, Rousseau shows the malleability of human nature. Throughout history, "the soul and human passions, altering imperceptibly, change their nature so to speak" (*Second Discourse*, 178). What distinguishes human nature from the nature of other animals is not so much its rationality as its *perfectibility*, the plasticity or openness to change in response to the environment (114–15). Modern biologists would confirm this insofar as they stress adaptive flexibility as the means by which humans have come to dominate the earth.[10]

To understand human nature, therefore, we must understand its history. Rousseau sketches that history in his *Second Discourse* as a progression through four stages: "nascent man" (142), "nascent society" (150), "nascent inequality" (156), and "nascent government" (162). The stage of nascent humanity is the primitive state of nature that we have just considered. Nascent society arises from the "first revolution" in human history—the establishment of family life, which produces "a sort of property" (146). This is followed by the nascent inequality produced by "the great revolution"—the invention of metallurgy and agriculture (152). The inequality of property creates such conflicts between rich and poor that "nascent government" arises to establish order.

This scheme conforms roughly with the account of human evolution accepted by most modern biologists and anthropologists. These people, however, disagree with one another about Rousseau's claim that savage human beings in "nascent society" were freer and happier than human beings are now even with all the benefits of civilization.

3. Has the evolution of civilization deprived us of our natural freedom and happiness?

The savage society that appears with the establishment of families is depicted by Rousseau in the *Second Discourse* as charming in its idyllic simplicity and contentment.

> The first developments of the heart were the effect of a new situation, which united husbands and wives, fathers and children in a common habitation. The habit of living together gave rise to the sweetest sentiments known to men: conjugal love and paternal love. Each family became a little society all the better united because reciprocal affection and freedom were its only bonds; and it was then that the first difference was established in the way of life of the two sexes, which until this time had had but one. Women became more sedentary and grew accustomed to tend the hut and the children, while the men went to seek their common subsistence. (146–47)

Rousseau judges that this "must have been the happiest and most durable epoch" and generally "the best for man" (151). The subsequent progress of civilization has actually been a decline. As civilized beings, we care only for two things: "the commodities of life for oneself, and consideration among others." Consequently, we can hardly imagine the pleasure a savage finds "in spending his life alone in the middle of the woods, or fishing, or blowing into a bad flute, without ever knowing how to get a single tone from it and without troubling himself to learn" (223–24).

Many of Rousseau's critics have dismissed this depiction of savage life as a romantic fantasy. But some recent anthropological studies of hunting-gathering societies seem to support Rousseau. Marvin Harris, an anthropologist at Columbia University, observes:

> Stone age populations lived healthier lives than did most of the people who came immediately after them: during Roman times there was more sickness in the world than ever before, and even in early nineteenth-century England the life expectancy for children was probably not very different from what it was 20,000 years earlier. Moreover, stone age hunters worked fewer hours for their sustenance than do typical Chinese and Egyptian peasants — or, despite their unions, modern-day factory workers. As for amenities such as good food, entertainment, and aesthetic

pleasures, early hunters and plant collectors enjoyed luxuries
that only the richest of today's Americans can afford. For two
days' worth of trees, lakes, and clean air, the modern-day
executive works five. Nowadays, whole families toil and save
for thirty years to gain the privilege of seeing a few square feet
of grass outside their windows. And they are the privileged few.[11]

Melvin Konner, an anthropologist at Emory University, has argued
that Hobbes was wrong in declaring that life in the savage state was
"solitary, poor, nasty, brutish and short":

> Far from solitary, it is above all things mutual. Far from poor,
> it is amply leisured. . . . Far from nasty, it is based on human
> decency, respect for others, sharing, giving. Far from brutish,
> it is courageous, egalitarian, good-humored, philosophical — in
> a word, civilized — with an esthetic so fine its very music touches
> the gods. Although many die in early childhood, those who do
> not may live to a ripe old age, and this is an old age not consigned
> to a ghetto or to a "home" that is not a home; rather, it is one
> embedded in that same intimate social world, surrounded by
> grandchildren full of delight, by grown, powerful children full
> of courtesy.[12]

The anthropological evidence and reasoning for this view of Stone
Age society is summarized in a famous essay, "The Original
Affluent Society" by Marshall Sahlins of the University of Chicago.[13]
Sahlins explains that in a hunting-gathering society, the means for
satisfying wants are limited, but the wants themselves are also
limited. Unlike the modern bourgeois, whose wants are always
greater than the means for satisfying them, savages can fulfill their
limited material needs easily and thus have plenty of leisure. "We
are inclined to think of hunters and gatherers as *poor* because they
don't have anything; perhaps better to think of them for that reason
as *free*."[14] Moreover, they are free from domination because their
rough equality of wealth prevents any subordination of the poor to
the rich.

But it's hard to believe that the life of human beings in the Stone
Age is completely carefree. Even Sahlins concedes that hunters and
gatherers survive only by severely limiting their population,
particularly those people who hinder the mobility essential to a
nomadic life: children and old people are often killed. Moreover,
some experts have provided evidence of violent feuds, under-
nourishment, and a short average life expectancy.[15]

Some critics of Rousseau have rejected his depiction of savage
society as being a romantic illusion. But we should notice that
Rousseau does, in fact, see the darker side of life among hunters

and gatherers. Because they want to be recognized by others, Rousseau observes in the *Second Discourse*, savages are vain and therefore easily aroused to anger by whatever they see as an insult. Hence, "vengeances became terrible, and men bloodthirsty and cruel," which is "precisely the point reached by most of the savage people known to us" (149–50).

We have lost our natural freedom through the evolution of civilization, because although the savage was self-sufficient and drew self-esteem from within, we depend on the opinions of others, "always asking others what we are and never daring to question ourselves on this subject" (*Second Discourse*, 180). Yet Rousseau indicates that even savages began to feel this dependence on others. "By dint of seeing one another, they can no longer do without seeing one another again" (148). "Each one began to look at the others and to want to be looked at himself, and public esteem had a value" (149).[16] Nevertheless, Rousseau thinks that the personal dependence of those in the savage state was not great enough to seriously threaten their natural freedom.

Hunters and gatherers lost their freedom when they turned to farming for subsistence. At this point, they entered the state of nascent inequality because an agricultural way of life created an unprecedented inequality of property by which there was, for the first time, a clear distinction between the rich and the poor. Rousseau calls this the "great revolution," and modern anthropologists agree that the adoption of agriculture about ten thousand years ago laid the foundation for modern civilization.[17]

The economic inequality fostered by agricultural civilization created a state of war between the rich and the poor. The rich, wanting to secure their property, convinced the poor to establish civil society with the argument that the rule of law would protect everyone equally.[18] This "destroyed natural freedom for all time" (*Second Discourse*, 160).

Although denying that natural liberty can ever be completely recovered, Rousseau suggests a way to legitimize political authority through the rule of law, so that society would be free from the domination of some over others. In his dedication of the *Second Discourse* to the people of Geneva, Rousseau presents their city as the model of what he has in mind. It is small enough that the citizens can know and love one another and thus become united in their social solidarity. The people themselves are the only sovereign authority. And everyone is equally subject to the laws: "you have no other masters except the wise laws you have made" (84). By uniting their individual wills into a single, "general will" and then obeying the laws made by that will, the people can

combine personal freedom with political authority because each
submits not to the rule of others but to the rule of law.

Rousseau explains his reasoning in his *Émile*:

> There are two sorts of dependence: dependence on things, which
> is from nature; dependence on men, which is from society.
> Dependence on things, since it has no morality, is in no way
> detrimental to freedom and engenders no vices. Dependence on
> men, since it is without order, engenders all the vices, and by
> it, master and slave are mutually corrupted. If there is any
> means of remedying this ill in society, it is to substitute law for
> man and to arm the general wills with a real strength superior
> to the action of every particular will.[19]

But far from securing freedom, "to arm the general wills with a
real strength superior to the action of every particular will" might
suppress individual liberty. Some commentators have even seen
in Rousseau's general will the basis for a totalitarian democracy
such as that established by Robespierre during the French
Revolution.[20] For it seems that Rousseau would demand that each
individual set aside personal interests and yield completely to the
collective will of society. Does this mean a sacrifice of individual
autonomy to social authority? Or should we say that the individual
becomes truly free only through participating in social life? To think
through this problem, we must turn to Rousseau's *Social Contract*.

4. Does participatory democracy promote or threaten individual liberty?

This question has become an issue at various points in American
political history. In the 1960s and early 1970s, for example, those
people calling themselves the New Left argued that the fulfillment
of personal freedom could come only through participatory
democracy. "The Port Huron Statement" of the Students for a
Democratic Society declared:

> We seek the establishment of a democracy of individual
> participation, governed by two central aims: that the individual
> share in those social decisions determining the quality and
> direction of his life; that society be organized to encourage
> independence in men and provide the media for their common
> participation.

> In a participatory democracy . . . politics has the function of
> bringing people out of isolation and into community, thus being
> a necessary, though not sufficient, means of finding meaning
> in personal life.[21]

But what should be done about those individuals who find "meaning in personal life" by devoting themselves totally to private pursuits and withdrawing from political life? In fact, won't most people prefer to stay home and not participate in politics? And if most people don't participate, what's to prevent the few people who are politically active from becoming a ruling elite?

Some of the New Left theorists saw Rousseau as their intellectual forebear,[22] yet they seldom stated as clearly as he did that participatory democracy requires the transformation of selfish individuals into public-spirited citizens. Those of the New Left did not always recognize how difficult it is to reconcile personal freedom and participatory citizenship. Solving this problem is Rousseau's aim in *The Social Contract*:

> "Find a form of association that defends and protects the person and goods of each associate with all the common force, and by means of which each one, uniting with all, nevertheless obeys only himself and remains as free as before." This is the fundamental problem which is solved by the social contract. (I, 6)

Each person must yield himself completely to the community so that "as each gives himself to all, he gives himself to no one." Because everyone submits to the impersonal authority of the collective body, no one is personally dependent on anyone else. As an "individual," each person has a "private will" that serves a "private interest." But as a "citizen," each participates in the "general will" that serves the "common interest" of all the citizens (I, 7).

The crucial requirement is the founding of society on "common interests": "If the opposition of private interests made the establishment of societies necessary, it is the agreement of these same interests that made it possible" (II, 1). To the extent that citizens have shared interests, there is no conflict between individual autonomy and social authority. As long as the fundamental laws of society are made by the collective body of the citizens to serve the general interests of all, it is in some sense true that, in obeying the laws, each person "obeys only himself and remains as free as before."

Isn't there a paradox here? Social authority requires common interests. But if human beings could always agree on their common interests, there would be no need for social authority in the first place:

> If there were no different interests, the common interest, which would never encounter any obstacle, would scarcely be felt. Everything would run smoothly by itself, and politics would cease to be an art. (II, 3)

Politics is the art of overcoming conflicting interests in the pursuit of the public interest. But we must wonder how this can be done without suppressing individual liberty. Rousseau explains:

> Whoever refuses to obey the general will shall be constrained to do so by the entire body; which means only that he will be forced to be free. For this . . . guarantees him against all personal dependence. (I, 7)

[handwritten marginalia: Because freedom means Rousseau Involuntary]

In Rousseau's society, the uncooperative citizen will be "forced to be free"! What more evidence do we need of Rousseau's totalitarianism? He twists the meaning of freedom so that the coercion of the individual by society can be carried out in the name of freedom.

Totalitarian ideologies of the twentieth century have used reasoning similar to Rousseau's to justify the repression of individual liberty. The argument is that people can achieve democratic government only by totally sacrificing their individuality to the collective will of the ruling party. An example of this would be Mao Zedong's reflections on the character of a good Chinese Communist:

> A Communist should have largeness of mind, and he should be staunch and active, looking upon the interests of the revolution as his very life and subordinating his personal interests to those of the revolution; always and everywhere he should adhere to principle and wage a tireless struggle against all incorrect ideas and actions, so as to consolidate the collective life of the Party and strengthen the ties between the Party and the masses; he should be more concerned about the Party and the masses than about any individual, and more concerned about others than about himself. Only thus can he be considered a Communist.[23]

One way of explaining how Rousseau's teaching can encourage this sort of totalitarian thinking is to distinguish his "positive" concept of freedom from a "negative" concept of freedom.[24] Hobbes defines freedom in a negative manner when he says that it signifies "the absence of opposition" (*Leviathan*, XXI, p. 136). The freedom of an individual from the interference of other people is a negative freedom. But Rousseau defines freedom in a positive manner when he says "the impulse of appetite alone is slavery, and obedience to the law one has prescribed for oneself is freedom" (*Social Contract*, I, 8). Such freedom requires not just absence of external restraints but self-mastery. To accomplish true self-mastery, each must exercise self-control (reason ruling over appetites), and each must participate directly in making the laws of society. To achieve this kind of freedom, society might have to enforce rigorous standards of morality so that individuals would have the self-discipline necessary for "true" freedom: in this sense, therefore, they would be "forced to be free."

Does this positive social freedom threaten the negative individual freedom of all people to live as they please? Or is Rousseau right in assuming that individual liberty can be fully expressed only through the communal liberty of a self-governing community? Some people argue that the experience of small, egalitarian democracies — like the New England township governments and the Swiss cantons — confirms Rousseau's teaching.[25]

Rousseau wants to reconcile individual rights with social duties. He must explain, therefore, how to secure the social cooperation of selfish individuals. Contemporary social scientists have struggled with this same problem, and some of their reasoning resembles Rousseau's. In particular, social scientists interested in "game theory" have compared the logic of social cooperation to the strategy of a game called the "prisoner's dilemma."[26]

Two prisoners are held in separate cells. The district attorney suspects they are guilty of armed robbery, but he cannot get convictions from a court unless he has their confession. So, he bargains separately with each of the prisoners. If one confesses and his partner does not, the one who confesses can go free, but the other will receive a ten-year sentence. If both confess, they will receive reduced sentences of five years. If neither confesses, both will be imprisoned for one year on a charge of carrying a concealed weapon.

As selfish individuals, each prisoner is tempted to double-cross his partner by confessing while his partner refuses to confess because the one confessing in that case goes free, whereas his partner serves ten years. But if both adopt this strategy, they will both receive five-year sentences. It would be better for both of them, therefore, if neither confessed so that they would be imprisoned for only one year. But to pursue this cooperative strategy, they must trust one another, which is foolish considering the advantage gained by one double-crossing the other. Consequently, to avoid the risk of being made a sucker, both will confess. But then both will be worse off than they would have been if they had trusted one another. When each seeks his *individual interest*, both suffer. They would be better off if they could cooperate in seeking their *collective interest*, but their distrust of one another prevents that. This dilemma should remind us of Garrett Hardin's "tragedy of the commons" (discussed earlier in chapter 7, section 2).

When people pursue their narrow self-interest in competition with others, they lose the benefits of social cooperation. As a result society as a whole may suffer. For example, one principal benefit

Social co-operation

of society is the legal protection against thieves. But if people think they can escape detection, it's in their selfish interest to steal from their fellow citizens while relying on the law to protect *their own* property from theft. Those who enact this behavior would live like the clever criminal described by Glaucon and Adeimantus in Plato's *Republic* (refer back to chapter 1, sections 5, 6). Of course, when many people try to live like this, everyone suffers. We all benefit from social cooperation, but as selfish individuals we are tempted to become free riders who enjoy the benefits of cooperation without bearing our share of the costs. This dilemma would explain many contemporary social problems such as tax evasion, inflation, and pollution.

Consider how this illuminates the logic of Rousseau's social contract. It serves the good of all citizens to share the obligations of citizenship so that they can act in concert for common goals. Each person can better satisfy individual needs with the cooperation of others. But everyone fears exploitation by the others. No one will bear the burdens of citizenship unless it is guaranteed that everyone else will bear the same burdens. This explains why Rousseau insists that the social contract requires "the total alienation of each associate, with all his rights, to the whole community" (I, 6). If *all* individuals are *equally* subject to the duties imposed by the social contract, and if *all equally* enjoy the rights it confers, then each person benefits from social life without fear of being exploited by the others. Thus personal interest is linked to the public interest, and individual advantage coincides with social justice.

But to achieve such social unity is difficult. Although it might be found in very small communities, it is unlikely to arise in larger ones. The society must be small enough so that people can learn to trust one another, and so that those who cheat are easily detected. Even in a small community, however, it is hard to create the social spirit that unites individuals into a cohesive community in which all are equally free. For as conflicting interests foster distrust, the social bond is broken, and each person seeks private interest rather than the common good. Rousseau believes this can be avoided only if a great political founder establishes a society by transforming selfish individuals into patriotic citizens.

5. Does a participatory democracy require a godlike founder?

Because the people cannot always judge correctly what is in their own interest, Rousseau suggests, they need to be enlightened by a legislator (II, 6). Rousseau's legislator is not so much a lawmaker in the ordinary sense as a heroic founder of a civilization. Rousseau has in mind men like Moses, Lycurgus, and Romulus.

The great legislator must be godlike in his power to transform solitary individuals into social beings (II, 7). He must unite isolated human beings into one people with a distinct identity, so that each person feels himself to be only a part of a larger social whole. To achieve this the legislator must deceive people into thinking that he speaks for God.

We have seen this idea of the godlike founder in Aristotle's *Politics* (1253a30–38) and Machiavelli's *Prince* (chapter 6). We could also consider Max Weber's concept of "charismatic" authority as confirmation of Rousseau's thought.[27] But the most obvious examples are from the ancient and the medieval world: those like Lycurgus, Alexander the Great, and Julius Caesar. Have any great legislators arisen in modern political life?

We could think of some modern examples among the Marxist revolutionaries. For Marxists the "revolution" supplants the "legislator" as the creator of the "general will." Some have hoped that the people themselves would make the revolution on their own. Others have looked to a revolutionary vanguard. Mao Zedong, as quoted earlier, saw himself as creating a revolutionary consciousness that would transform Chinese society.[28]

Also, the American founders—those who wrote and signed the Declaration of Independence and the Constitution—come to mind. In fact, James Madison, in *Federalist* Number 38, compared the framers of the Constitution to ancient founders like Lycurgus and Romulus.[29] Traditionally, we revere the American founders as godlike in their wisdom. We have even built monumental temples in their honor, just as the ancient Greeks and Romans built temples to divinize their political heroes. When we speak of our Founding Fathers, we speak of ourselves as their political children, which assumes that they created us as a people.

Unlike Rousseau's legislator, the American founders did not attempt to transform human nature by changing selfish human beings into public-spirited citizens. Such a transformation may be necessary if the people are going to govern themselves directly. For then people must sacrifice their private interests for the sake of a total devotion to public affairs. The American founders, as James Madison explained in *Federalist* Number 10,[30] did not establish a pure democracy in which the people ruled directly, but a representative democracy in which the people elected others to rule them. An advantage of representation is that it does not demand much from the people, who are free to withdraw into their private lives. Rousseau objects that this is a new form of enslavement.

6. Is representative democracy disguised slavery?

"The instant a people chooses representatives," Rousseau asserts, "it is no longer free; it no longer exists" (III, 15). In the same chapter, he cites the example of the English people. They are free only during the election of members of Parliament. As soon as the election is over, the people become slaves.

Rousseau's reasoning is simple. If the people are the sovereign authority, then they must make the fundamental laws. Although the people can delegate to the officers of government the application and execution of the laws, they cannot delegate their lawmaking authority. "Any law that the people in person has not ratified is null; it is not a law" (III, 15).

Most Americans would probably find Rousseau's argument strange. We believe, as stated in the Declaration of Independence, that governments derive their "just powers from the consent of the governed." But we assume that it suffices for us to consent to be ruled by elected representatives. Why can't representative democracy be as truly democratic as participatory democracy?

The fundamental issue for Rousseau is how to reconcile individual freedom and political authority. (For a statement of this issue as it bears on Locke, see chapter 8, section 8.) If we start with the premise of individual autonomy—the idea that each person is entitled to rule over his or her own life—then the only way to support political authority is to derive it from the voluntary consent of all citizens. Consequently, as Rousseau explains, the only justifiable structure of authority is that of a self-governing, participatory democracy. If the only legitimate social order is a voluntary association, then only a participatory society can be legitimate.

We should not conclude, however, that Rousseau argues for democracy as the only legitimate form of *government*. "Every legitimate government is republican," he asserts (II, 6). But even an aristocracy or a monarchy can be a republic in Rousseau's sense (see III, 1–7). In a republic, the people exercise *sovereignty* through popular assemblies that make the fundamental laws. If the entire people or a majority of them also possess the powers of *government*—the execution of the laws and administrative decisions—then they have a democracy. But if, while exercising sovereign legislative authority, the people place the powers of government in the hands of a monarch or an aristocratic body, then the people will have a republic but not a democratic form of government. It is legitimate for the people to select representatives to handle the executive and administrative affairs of government. But in the making of the fundamental laws of society, the people must express their will directly through an assembly of all the citizens. In the exercise of sovereign lawmaking, no one can represent anyone else. All must participate equally. Rousseau observes that representation subverts the expression of popular consent. The people are encouraged to become apathetic about politics; as a result, those few who take an active interest in public life become a political elite.

Doesn't American experience confirm this? Most American citizens have little knowledge of or interest in political issues, and they are usually completely passive except for casting votes every few years. This leaves the ruling elite free to govern as they wish. This has become so widely accepted that many American political scientists have even warned that it is dangerous to allow the people to rule themselves directly because they are unqualified to rule.[31] It seems, therefore, that American democracy has succeeded only because it is not a true democracy!

But from Thomas Jefferson to "The Port Huron Statement," there has been a radical tradition in the United States favoring popular participation like that proposed by Rousseau. At certain critical periods throughout American history, radical thinkers have criticized American political institutions for betraying the democratic ideals of the Declaration of Independence; and they have argued for wider public participation in government.[32] Henry David Thoreau, for example, echoes Rousseau when he writes:

> When, in some obscure country town, the farmers come together to a special town-meeting, to express their opinion on some subject which is vexing the land, that, I think, is the true Congress, and the most respectable one that is ever assembled in the United States.[33]

There are practical problems, however, with such a town-meeting democracy. The most obvious is the severe limitation on size. Rousseau emphasizes that true democracies must be very small, "where the people is easily assembled and where each citizen can easily know all the others" (III, 4). Moreover, he adds, the life of the people must be very simple, egalitarian, and free of luxury. A vigorous economy distracts the people from public affairs and creates conflicting interests owing to inequality of wealth. Rousseau attempts to revive the Athenian concept of citizenship as direct rule, but he faces the same problems that we noted earlier in the chapter on Aristotle (chapter 2, sections 6, 7).

Furthermore, a truly participatory democracy requires that every individual be so totally involved in public activity as to have hardly any private life. The habits and opinions of human beings in their private lives become subject to public regulation, because even the most intimate parts of life must be designed to support civic virtue. Even religious beliefs and practices are supervised by law in accordance with what Rousseau calls the civil religion. Is this another illustration of how Rousseau's democracy becomes totalitarian in its suppression of individual liberty?

7. Does democracy need a civil religion?

When Jesus separated religion and politics as two realms, Rousseau complains, he "brought about the end of the unity of the State, and caused the internal divisions that have never ceased to stir up Christian peoples" (IV, 8). Rousseau agrees with Hobbes, therefore, that Christianity subverted politics when it gave the clergy the power to appeal to standards beyond the laws of the state. People can be neither good human beings nor good citizens when they are torn between their religious duties and their political duties. "Everything that destroys social unity is worthless. All institutions that put man in contradiction with himself are worthless" (IV, 8).

Rousseau proposes that the sovereign should establish "a purely civil profession of faith" consisting of those dogmas essential to social duties. Anyone who refuses to profess belief in these dogmas can be banished, and individuals who behave as if they do not believe them should be punished with death.

Rousseau moderates the shocking severity of his proposal in two ways. First, he would regulate only public belief and behavior. In private, people may hold whatever beliefs they wish as long as they are discreet in their public appearances. Second, the public dogmas of the civil religion are so minimal that most people would have no trouble accepting them:

> The existence of a powerful, intelligent, beneficent, foresighted, and providential divinity; the afterlife; the happiness of the just; the punishment of the wicked; the sanctity of the social contract and the laws. These are the positive dogmas. As for the negative ones, I limit them to a single one: intolerance. It belongs to the cults we have excluded. (IV, 8)

Rousseau's civil religion would tolerate any religion that tolerates other religions, as long as it does not contradict the dogmas of the civil religion itself.

Does any form of civil religion violate the separation of Church and State, which we regard as essential to individual liberty? Should religious belief be a private matter as to which each person is free from governmental interference? Jefferson argued for religious liberty with the claim that "our civil rights have no dependence on our religious opinions, any more than our opinions in physics or geometry":

> The legitimate powers of government extend to such acts only as are injurious to others. But it does me no injury for my neighbor to say there are twenty gods, or no God. It neither picks my pocket nor breaks my leg.[34]

Still, we should question Jefferson's assumption that religious beliefs and practices are never injurious to others. Doesn't his argument imply that intolerant religions should not be tolerated? Those religions that promote persecution of heretics and unbelievers would surely be injurious to others.

Furthermore, doesn't the Declaration of Independence, of which Jefferson was the author, manifest exactly the religious dogmas that Rousseau considers essential to a democratic civil religion? There are four references to God in that document, two at the beginning and two at the end. First, there is the appeal to "the Laws of Nature and of Nature's God," then it is said that God created men equal and endowed them with rights. The Declaration concludes by "appealing to the Supreme Judge of the world for the rectitude of our intentions" and "with a firm reliance on the protection of Divine Providence." This looks like Rousseau's God—"a powerful, intelligent, beneficent, foresighted, and providential divinity" who judges human conduct and who sanctions the principles of the American regime.

From the Puritan colonists to George Washington to Abraham Lincoln to the most recent presidential inaugural address, we could survey American political rhetoric to find overwhelming evidence of an American civil religion.[35] Americans do not require that political leaders belong to any particular church, but they do insist on those general religious beliefs essential to morality and citizenship. Publicly declared atheists are not very successful in American national politics. Moreover, Americans like to assume that they are God's "chosen people."

Lincoln called this "the political religion of the nation," which secured "reverence for the laws."[36] Of course, Lincoln himself

became one of the paramount symbols of this religion. William
Herndon, Lincoln's law partner and biographer, wrote:

> For fifty years God rolled Abraham Lincoln through the fiery
> furnace. He did it to try Abraham and to purify him for his
> purposes. This made Mr. Lincoln humble, tender, forbearing,
> sympathetic to suffering, kind, sensitive, tolerant; making him
> the noblest and loveliest character since Jesus Christ. . . . I
> believe that Lincoln was God's chosen one.[37]

Considering his godlike power in shaping the sentiments and habits
of his people, Lincoln might also be one of the best American
examples of Rousseau's "legislator."

But even if this shows that some features of American political
history correspond to Rousseau's teaching, we have noted that
America does not conform fully to what he would regard as a true
democracy. Indeed, we must wonder whether any political regime
could ever fulfill his requirements for democratic government.

8. Is a true democracy impossible?

"In the strict sense of the term" Rousseau concludes, "a true
democracy has never existed and never will exist" (III, 4). The
combination of circumstances necessary for a genuine democracy
is unachievable. The principal difficulty is that a democracy
presupposes a level of civic virtue unattainable by ordinary human
beings. Inevitably, selfish passions create conflicting interests that
destroy the "general will." And, then, those who rule will distort
the laws for their own personal gain contrary to the public good.
Thus, freedom and equality will disappear as some people come to
dominate others, the rich ruling the poor and the powerful ruling
the weak.

Democracy demands that everyone should be equal before the
law, but Rousseau doubts that the equal rule of law is achievable.
In his book on the government of Poland, he explains:

> Although it is easy, if you wish, to make better laws, it is
> impossible to make them such that the passions of men will not
> abuse them as they abused the laws which preceded
> them. . . . The subjecting of man to law is a problem in politics
> which I liken to that of the squaring of the circle in
> geometry. . . . [W]henever you think you are establishing the rule
> of law, it is men who will do the ruling.[38]

If Rousseau is right, then democratic institutions will always fall
short of democratic ideals. The history of the United States seems

to confirm this. The Declaration of Independence sets forth our ideals of equality of rights and popular government. But it would be hard to argue that we have ever put those ideals fully into practice.

If we want to bridge the gulf between ideals and reality, we must look beyond Rousseau. Hegel maintained that he could unite the real with the ideal through the idea of history. For if history is progressive — with each historical epoch advancing beyond the previous epochs — then perhaps only with the complete unfolding of history will we see the full realization of democratic freedom.

Notes

1. All quotations of *The Social Contract* are taken from *On the Social Contract*, ed. Roger D. Masters, trans. Judith R. Masters (New York: St. Martin's Press, 1978). The citations indicate the book and the chapter: "I, 1," for example, refers to book I, chapter 1, of *The Social Contract*.

2. Jean-Jacques Rousseau, *The First and Second Discourses*, ed. Roger D. Masters, trans. Roger D. Masters and Judith R. Masters (New York: St. Martin's Press, 1964), 51. All quotations of the *First Discourse* and the *Second Discourse* are taken from this translation, and all page references in the text are to this edition.

3. See Leo Strauss, "On the Intention of Rousseau," in *Hobbes and Rousseau*, ed. Maurice Cranston and Richard S. Peters (Garden City, NY: Doubleday, Anchor Books, 1972), 254–90. Does Rousseau believe that the philosophic or scientific life as the highest human good achieved in history fulfills a natural teleology? This controversial claim has been made by Leonard R. Sorenson: "Rousseau adapted a considerably modified form of classical teleology, applied it to the human realm, and combined it with a version of the modern non-teleological science of non-human nature. . . . The teleological peak of history or of the human species is the classical philosopher or scientist: the naturally superior genius who seeks knowledge or truth as an end in itself" ("Natural Inequality and Rousseau's Political Philosophy in his *Discourse on Inequality*," *Western Political Quarterly* 43 [1990]: 780). Rousseau says that he found "those delights that arise from pure and disinterested contemplation" in botany (*The Reveries of the Solitary Walker*, trans. Charles Butterworth [New York: Harper & Row, 1979], 94). In botany, Rousseau may have found a natural teleology that is scientifically defensible as rooted in the functional morphology of individual organisms, in contrast to a cosmic or theological teleology. See Rousseau, *Fragmens Pour un Dictionnaire des Termes d'Usage en Botanique*, in *Oeuvres Complètes*, vol. 4 (Paris: Gallimard, 1969), 1220–31, 1239–40, 1245–46; Charles Darwin, *The Various Contrivances by Which Orchids Are Fertilised by Insects* (Chicago: University

of Chicago Press, 1984), 282–86; Darwin, *The Different Forms of Flowers on Plants of the Same Species* (Chicago: University of Chicago Press, 1986), 1–13, 344–45; and Paul A. Cantor, "The Metaphysics of Botany: Rousseau and the New Criticism of Plants," *Southwest Review* 70 (1985): 362–80.

4. See Robert Ardrey, *The Social Contract* (New York: Atheneum, 1970), 97–98. Rousseau would have been fascinated by the "wild boy of Aveyron," who was discovered in 1800. See Harlan Lane, *The Wild Boy of Aveyron* (Cambridge: Harvard University Press, 1976); and Roger Shattuck, *The Forbidden Experiment* (New York: Farrar, Straus & Giroux, 1980). Compare Rousseau, *Second Discourse*, 183–84.

5. See Edward O. Wilson, *On Human Nature* (Cambridge: Harvard University Press, 1978), 99–120; and Richard Passingham, *The Human Primate* (San Francisco: W. H. Freeman, 1982), 296–309.

6. See, for example, Theodosius Dobzhansky et al., *Evolution* (San Francisco: W. H. Freeman, 1977), 438–63; Sherwood Washburn, "The Evolution of Man," *Scientific American* 239 (September 1978): 194–208; and Glynn Isaac, "The Food-Sharing Behavior of Protohuman Hominids," *Scientific American* 242 (April 1978): 90–108.

   Rousseau observes that one of the distinctive features of human sexuality is that "love is never periodic" (*Second Discourse*, 136). Does this explain why the male's "need" for a female becomes permanent? (Ibid., 135–145, 219) Is the female's loss of estrous periodicity the crucial element of human social bonding? This has been argued by Helen E. Fisher in *The Sex Contract* (New York: Morrow, 1982) and in *Anatomy of Love* (New York: Norton, 1992). For the debate over the evolutionary significance of the female orgasm, see Donald Symons, *The Evolution of Human Sexuality* (New York: Oxford University Press, 1979), 96–141; Sarah B. Hrdy, *The Woman That Never Evolved* (Cambridge: Harvard University Press, 1981); and Stephen Jay Gould, *Bully for Brontosaurus* (New York: Norton, 1991), 124–38.

7. This has been argued by Robert Wokler in a series of papers: "Tyson and Buffon on the Orangutan," in *Studies on Voltaire and the Eighteenth Century* 155 (1976): 2301–19; "Perfectible Apes in Decadent Cultures: Rousseau's Anthropology Revisited," *Daedalus* 107 (Summer 1978): 111–17; and Christopher Frayling and Robert Wokler, "From the Orangutan to the Vampire: Towards an Anthropology of Rousseau," in R. A. Leigh, ed., *Rousseau after 200 Years* (Cambridge: Cambridge University Press, 1982), 109–29. See also Roger D. Masters, "Jean-Jacques Is Alive and Well: Rousseau and Contemporary Sociobiology," *Daedalus* 107 (Summer 1978): 93–105.

   Junichiro Itani, a primatologist who has studied Rousseau's writings, contends that the capacity to move from "fundamental inequality" to "conditional equality" through a "social contract" arises among nonhuman primates ("The Origin of Human Equality," in Michael R. A. Chance, ed., *Social Fabrics of the Mind* [Hillsdale, NJ: Lawrence Erlbaum, 1988], 137–56). See also Frans de Waal, "The Chimpanzee's

Sense of Social Regularity and Its Relation to the Human Sense of Justice," *American Behavioral Scientist* 34 (1991): 335–49.

8. John MacKinnon, *The Ape Within Us* (London: Collins, 1978), 110, 127. See also Roger Lewin, "Is the Orangutan a Living Fossil?" *Science* 222 (1983): 1222–23; and Peter S. Rodman and John C. Mitani, "Orangutans: Sexual Dimorphism in a Solitary Species," in Barbara Smuts et al., eds., *Primate Societies* (Chicago: University of Chicago Press, 1986), 146–54.

9. Biruté Galdikas, "My Life with Orangutans," *International Wildlife* 20 (March–April 1990): 40.

10. See Peter J. Wilson, *Man, the Promising Primate* (New Haven: Yale University Press, 1980).

11. Marvin Harris, *Cannibals and Kings: The Origins of Cultures* (New York: Random House, Vintage, 1978), x–xi.

12. Melvin Konner, *The Tangled Wing: Biological Constraints on the Human Spirit* (New York: Holt, Rinehart & Winston, 1982), 8–9.

13. The essay is found in Marshall Sahlins, *Stone Age Economics* (Chicago: Aldine, 1972), 1–39. Compare Nurit Bird-David, "Beyond 'The Original Affluent Society': A Culturalist Reformulation," *Current Anthropology* 33 (1992): 25–47. Richard Lee, one of the leading anthropologists on the topic, believes that hunter-gatherers offer "a vision of human life and human possibilities without the pomp and glory, but also without the misery and inequity of state and class society" ("Art, Science, or Politics? The Crisis in Hunter-Gatherer Studies," *American Anthropologist* 94 [1992]: 43). For other Rousseauistic defenders of primitive cultures, see Colin Turnbull, *The Forest People: A Study of the Pygmies of the Congo* (New York: Simon & Schuster, 1961); Stanley Diamond, *In Search of the Primitive* (New Brunswick: Transaction Books, 1974), 116–75; and Colin Turnbull, *The Human Cycle* (New York: Simon & Schuster, 1983). See also Margaret Power, *The Egalitarians—Human and Chimpanzee* (Cambridge: Cambridge University Press, 1991); and compare W.C. McGrew, "Apes Cast Out of Eden?," *Nature* 354 (1991): 324.

14. Sahlins, *Stone Age Economics*, 14.

15. See Patricia Draper, "The Learning Environment for Aggression and Anti-Social Behavior among the !Kung," in Ashley Montagu, ed., *Learning Non-Aggression* (New York: Oxford University Press, 1978), 31–53; Irenäus Eibl-Eibesfeldt, *The Biology of Peace and War* (New York: Viking, 1979), 129–61; Even Hadingham, *Secrets of the Ice Age* (New York: Walker, 1979), 127–49; Konner, *Tangled Wing*, 9; and Napoleon Chagnon, *Yanomamö: The Fierce People*, 3rd ed. (New York: Holt, Rinehart & Winston, 1983), 170–89, 213–14.

16. On the importance of the concern for status and reputation in human evolution, see Jerome H. Barkow, *Darwin, Sex, and Status* (Toronto: University of Toronto Press, 1989); Charles Darwin, *The Expression of the Emotions in Man and Animals* (Chicago: University of Chicago Press, 1965), chap. 13; and Robert Frank, *Choosing the Right Pond:*

Human Behavior and the Quest for Status (New York: Oxford University Press, 1985).

17. See Richard E. Leakey, *The Making of Mankind* (New York: Dutton, 1981), 198–217.

18. Many anthropologists today would dispute the belief that economic inequality led to the formation of the first states. See Elman R. Service, "Classical and Modern Theories of the Origins of Government," in Ronald Cohen and Elman R. Service, eds., *Origins of the State: The Anthropology of Political Evolution* (Philadelphia: Institute for the Study of Human Issues, 1978), 21–34.

19. Jean-Jacques Rousseau, *Émile*, trans. Allan Bloom (New York: Basic Books, 1979), 85. The *Émile* contributed to the evolution of family life by teaching parents to understand the special needs of children. See Priscilla Robertson, "Home as a Nest: Middle Class Childhood in Nineteenth-Century Europe," in Lloyd de Mausse, ed., *The History of Childhood* (New York: Psychohistory Press, 1974), 407–31.

20. See Albert Camus, *The Rebel* (New York: Random House, Vintage, 1956), 112–32; and J. L. Talmon, *The Origins of Totalitarian Democracy* (New York: Praeger, 1960), 38–49. The influence of Rousseau over the French revolutionaries has been denied by Joan McDonald, *Rousseau and the French Revolution, 1762–1791* (London: Athlone Press, 1965). But compare Carol Blum, *Rousseau and the Republic of Virtue: The Language of Politics in the French Revolution* (Ithaca: Cornell University Press, 1986).

21. "The Port Huron Statement," in Robert A. Goldwin, ed., *How Democratic Is America?* (Chicago: Rand McNally, 1971), 7.

22. See, for example, Howard Zinn, "How Democratic Is America?" in Goldwin, *How Democratic Is America?* 39–60; Staughton Lynd, *Intellectual Origins of American Radicalism* (Cambridge: Harvard University Press, 1982), vi, 32–34, 160; and James Miller, *Democracy Is in the Streets: From Port Huron to the Siege of Chicago* (New York: Simon & Schuster, 1987).

23. Mao Zedong, "Combat Liberalism," in *Selected Readings from the Works of Mao Zedong* (Beijing: Foreign Languages Press, 1971), 136–37.

24. See Isaiah Berlin, "Two Concepts of Liberty," in *Four Essays on Liberty* (New York: Oxford University Press, 1970), 118–72.

25. See Benjamin R. Barber, *The Death of Communal Liberty: A History of Freedom in a Swiss Mountain Canton* (Princeton: Princeton University Press, 1974); and Jane J. Mansbridge, *Beyond Adversary Democracy* (Chicago: University of Chicago Press, 1983), 3–35. For an attempt to apply Rousseau's political vision to modern industrialized nations, see G. D. H. Cole, *Guild Socialism Restated* (New Brunswick: Transaction Books, 1980).

26. See W. G. Runciman and A. K. Sen, "Games, Justice and the General Will," *Mind* 74 (October 1965): 554–62; Steven J. Brams, *Game Theory and Politics* (New York: Free Press, 1975), 30–39; and Robert Axelrod,

The Evolution of Cooperation (New York: Basic Books, 1984).

27. See H. H. Gerth and C. Wright Mills, eds. and trans., *From Max Weber: Essays in Sociology* (New York: Oxford University Press, 1956), 78–79, 245–52.

28. On Mao as "The Great Legislator," see Frederic Wakeman, Jr., *History and Will: Philosophical Perspectives of Mao Tse-Tung's Thought* (Berkeley: University of California Press, 1973), 43–59. Rousseau might have recognized Charles de Gaulle as a statesman who tried to become France's modern Legislator. See Stanley Hoffmann, *Decline or Renewal?—France Since the 1930s* (New York: Viking, 1974), 187–280.

29. Alexander Hamilton, James Madison, and John Jay, *The Federalist*, ed. Edward Mead Earle (New York: Random House, Modern Library, n.d.), No. 38, pp. 233–42.

30. Ibid., No. 10, pp. 53–62. Although Rousseau had little influence on the early American political founders, he had great influence on American novelists. See Paul M. Spurlin, *Rousseau in America, 1760-1809* (University: University of Alabama Press, 1969). James Fenimore Cooper introduced the theme of the "return to nature" into American literature, and Catherine Zuckert argues that in *The Deerslayer* (1841) and the other "Leatherstocking" tales, Cooper developed a Rousseauian reinterpretation of the Lockean principles of the Declaration of Independence (Zuckert, *Natural Right and the American Imagination: Political Philosophy in Novel Form* [Savage, MD: Rowman and Littlefield, 1990]).

31. See Bernard R. Berelson, Paul F. Lazarsfeld, and William N. McPhee, *Voting* (Chicago: University of Chicago Press, 1954), 305–23; Gabriel A. Almond and Sidney Verba, *The Civic Culture* (Boston: Little, Brown, 1965), 337–69; Samuel P. Huntington, "The Democratic Distemper," *Public Interest* (Fall 1975): 9–38; Huntington, *American Politics: The Promise of Disharmony* (Cambridge: Harvard University Press, 1981). For a Rousseauistic viewpoint, see Carole Pateman, *Participation and Democratic Theory* (Cambridge: Cambridge University Press, 1970); and Benjamin Barber, *Strong Democracy: Participatory Politics for a New Age* (Berkeley: University of California Press, 1984).

32. See Huntington, *American Politics.*

33. Henry David Thoreau, "Slavery in Massachusetts," in *Walden and Other Writings*, ed. Brooks Atkinson (New York: Random House, Modern Library, 1937), 670.

34. Thomas Jefferson, *Notes on the State of Virginia* in *The Life and Selected Writings of Thomas Jefferson*, eds. Adrienne Koch and William Peden (New York: Random House, Modern Library, 1944), 275, 312.

35. See Robert N. Bellah, "Civil Religion in America," in Russell E. Richey and Donald G. Jones, eds., *American Civil Religion* (New York: Harper & Row, 1974), 21–44. On the founders of religion as those who provide a meaning to life and thus become the most powerful rulers, see

Frederich Nietzsche, *The Gay Science*, sec. 53; and *The Antichrist*, sec. 57.

36. Abraham Lincoln, Address Before the Young Men's Lyceum of Springfield, Illinois, 27 January 1838, in *The Collected Works of Abraham Lincoln*, ed. Roy P. Basler, 9 vols. (New Brunswick: Rutgers University Press, 1953–1955), 1: 112.

37. Quoted in Bellah, "Civil Religion," 32.

38. Jean-Jacques Rousseau, *Considerations on the Government of Poland*, in *Rousseau: Political Writings*, trans. Frederick Watkins (New York: Thomas Nelson and Sons, 1953), 161–62. For a brilliant analysis of the unresolved problems in *The Social Contract*, see Louis Althusser, *Politics and History: Montesquieu, Rousseau, Hegel and Marx*, trans. Ben Brewster (London: NLB, 1972), 113–60.

Chapter

10

History and the Modern State

Hegel's *Philosophy of Right* and *Philosophy of History*

Key Readings

Philosophy of Right, Preface, Introduction, Third Part; *Philosophy of History*, Introduction

---

Georg Wilhelm Friedrich Hegel (1770–1831) was born in Stuttgart, the son of a revenue officer. He attended the grammar school and the high school (*Gymnasium*) in his native city. In 1788, he went as a student to the seminary at Tübingen, where he studied philosophy and theology. His best friends there were J. C. F. Hölderlin and F. W. J. Schelling. He shared with them an enthusiasm for the French Revolution.

After graduation, Hegel became a private tutor in Bern, Switzerland, so that he could continue his studies. He read the Greek and Roman classics, history, and the contemporary philosophic works of Immanuel Kant. But because he felt cut off from his friends, he was happy to move to Frankfurt in 1797 to accept another tutorship secured for him by Hölderlin. Then, in

1799, his father's death left him a modest inheritance, which allowed him to become a *Privatdozent*, an unsalaried university lecturer paid by students' fees. In 1801, he secured such a position in Jena, where Schelling had been a professor since 1798.

In his lectures at Jena, Hegel began to formulate the early versions of his philosophic system. In 1805, he was appointed the salaried position of a regular professor. At this time he wrote *The Phenomenology of Spirit*, which was published in 1807. His work was interrupted, however, in 1806, by Napoleon's seizure of Jena, which forced Hegel to flee, carrying his manuscript.

The disorder caused by Napoleon's conquests forced Hegel to work a short time as a newspaper editor and then to become the headmaster of the Gymnasium at Nuremberg from 1808 to 1816. Teaching philosophy to high school students allowed him to continue thinking and writing. In 1811, at the age of forty-one, Hegel married Marie von Tucher, who was twenty-one years old. They had two sons, and they brought into the family Hegel's illegitimate son born earlier in Jena. From all that we know, it was a happy family.

In 1816, Hegel accepted a professorship at Heidelberg. In 1818, he moved to an even more prestigious professorship at Berlin, where he remained until his death. In Berlin, Hegel became the leading German philosopher of his time. His *Philosophy of Right* was published in 1821. Afterwards, he devoted most of his attention to his lectures. His lecture notes combined with notes taken by his students were published after his death. The *Philosophy of History*, published in 1837, was one of the books compiled by editors from these notes.

In many of Hegel's lectures and writings, the predominant theme was history. He was not so much concerned with the simple narration of historical events as he was with uncovering the *meaning* of history as the progressive unfolding of a universal purpose. The consequences of the French Revolution dominated European history throughout Hegel's lifetime. Although he was critical of some features of the Revolution, he saw it as the culmination of world history, because it would make possible the complete actualization of human freedom. Can we accept Hegel's assumption that history works out a rational pattern of perfection?

1. Does history have an ultimate meaning?

If we study the history of the world without any preconceptions about its meaning, we see that the selfish passions and violent conflicts of human beings have always produced suffering and confusion. Nations and individuals rise and fall in a random manner. Sometimes the fate of a great civilization depends on the peculiar strengths and weaknesses of a single political leader or military commander. We can imagine how different the pattern of history would have been if Caesar or Henry VIII or Napoleon or Churchill had never been born. We could conclude from this that far from having any universal meaning, history is largely an accidental succession of events that is only occasionally directed to some end by great leaders.

Hegel admits, in the Introduction to the *Philosophy of History*, that history does indeed seem to be an aimless sequence of changes depriving human beings of any secure happiness. He believes, however, "a question necessarily arises: To what principle, to what final purpose, have these monstrous sacrifices been offered?" (*History*, 27).[1] Does this question arise necessarily? In asking what the final purpose of history must be, doesn't Hegel simply assume without argument that there must be *some* purpose? Our observations of historical change might suggest that history is a cyclical repetition of things coming into being and passing away. Yet Hegel dismisses this conception as "oriental not occidental" (*History*, 89). To be Occidental—that is, Western—in our thinking, we must see history as a progressive movement toward a final goal. But is this a generally Western point of view or is it more specifically Christian?

The ancient Greeks and Romans were inclined to see history as cyclical—a recurrent pattern of growth and decay. Thucydides, for example, wrote history with the assumption that because human nature does not change, the political events of the past will be repeated in the future. Biblical religion, on the other hand, presents history as a linear progression with a beginning, a middle, and an end. "In the beginning," we are told in the first verse of the Bible, "God created the heaven and the earth." We are also told that God has intervened in human history to advance his plan for mankind. The coming of Jesus Christ initiated a new age of history. But Christ must come a second time to complete His redemption of man, which will be the end of earthly history. According to this vision, history is the unfolding of a providential design to be fulfilled at some point in the future. History has a *meaning* because it has a *purpose*. We could conclude, therefore, that the modern view of history as progressive depends, directly or indirectly, on Christian faith.[2] Hegel even acknowledges the religious foundations of his philosophy of history: "We translate the language of religion into that of philosophy" (*History*, 25).

Yet Hegel could be criticized by both the Christian and the non-Christian. The Christian—Augustine, for example—might complain that Hegel has distorted the Christian vision of history by secularizing it (see chapter 3, section 3). The orthodox Christian distinguishes the earthly City of Man and the heavenly City of God, seeking final redemption in heaven not on earth. This individual has no reason to be optimistic about the pattern of earthly history. Moreover, the humble Christian does not presume to know God's will for the history of the world. Hegel, by contrast, seems to claim that he can know God's will and that he can foresee the final redemption of man *on earth*. Hegel's deformation of Christian doctrine is evident in his *Phenomenology of Spirit*, where he interprets the incarnation of Christ as teaching us that "the divine nature is the same as the human," so that he can conclude the book with human self-consciousness divinizing itself as "absolute knowledge."[3] From the Christian point of view, Hegel's philosophy of history is blasphemy.

The non-Christian, however, might find little comfort in this. Even if it perverts the Christian teaching, Hegel's conception of the purposefulness of history must be unacceptable to the non-Christian in that it depends on the Christian vision of faith. Without relying on Christian revelation, is Hegel's philosophy of history a rationally defensible interpretation of the facts of history?

"World history," Hegel declares, "is the progress of the consciousness of freedom" (*History*, 24). In the Oriental world, people thought only one person was free—the ruling despot. In the ancient Greek and Roman worlds, people thought only *some* were free—the citizens of the city-states. Finally, with the advent of Christianity, people became conscious of the freedom of *all* human beings simply by virtue of their humanity. The full actualization of that absolute freedom made possible by Christianity required the Lutheran Reformation and the French Revolution. Therefore, Hegel explains, the modern state, in its dedication to complete human freedom, fulfills the purpose of all previous world history.[4]

Don't we commonly accept this view of history as progressive? When we speak of our "modern" world as distinguished from the "ancient" and "medieval" worlds, we divide history into three parts, and we assume that our period of history is the culmination of all prior human experience. We speak proudly of the revolutions of modern times—the scientific revolution, the industrial revolution, the political revolutions in England, America, and France—all of which manifest progress. And as a consequence of those revolutions, we think that people in the modern Western democracies enjoy more freedom (in every sense of the word) than was ever possible previously. So, it would seem that we agree with Hegel that history has an ultimate meaning, which is progress toward freedom.

But is this anything more than an unproven assumption? If we think of the unprecedented tyrannies of the twentieth century — such as those established by Mussolini, Hitler, and Stalin — it's difficult to tell that this is the age of freedom. In fact, observing the horrors of our century has led many people to talk about decline rather than progress.

Moreover, it is hard to deny that the historical process is to a large extent accidental. We cannot say that the sequence of events is by necessity because we can always imagine how things could have turned out differently. Indeed, if we believe in human freedom, we must also believe that human beings are not completely determined by historical necessity.

To discover the purpose of history, we would have to see the whole course of history from beginning to end, but that would require that we stand *outside* of history itself. Because we live *in* history, we cannot fully comprehend either the past or the future; therefore we cannot understand the order of history. Obviously, we cannot predict the future; and consequently we cannot know the final destination of history — or even whether there is a destination. On the other hand, while we can know the past, our view of it is distorted somewhat by our particular standpoint in the flux of history. Discovery of the ultimate meaning of history, therefore, would require some transhistorical knowledge — such as that provided by Christian revelation.

There are other problems with Hegel's philosophy of history. For instance, should we conclude that insofar as the thoughts and actions of human beings are historically determined, there are no fixed, natural standards for human life? The Declaration of Independence appeals to "the Laws of Nature and of Nature's God." But Hegel would seem to replace nature with history. If human nature is historical, if it changes over time, there would seem to be no enduring principles in nature to guide political life. Of course, we could say that Hegel points to the end of history as the ultimate standard for politics. But that suggests that until we reach the end of history, all standards are provisional. This is not merely an abstract, theoretical problem. Some of the revolutionary leaders of twentieth century politics, inspired directly or indirectly by Hegelian historicism, have justified shocking atrocities as necessary means to achieve what they thought to be the end of history.

In defense of Hegel, we could say that his teaching does not promote revolutionary activism. He does celebrate those rare human beings—"world-historical individuals" like Caesar, Luther, and Napoleon—who shape the course of history as it moves to its final goal. But Hegel leaves it unclear as to whether these individuals are fully conscious of their historical mission. Sometimes he speaks of them as people who consciously make the universal purpose of history their own particular purpose. But often he describes them as "practical and political men" who have "no consciousness" of their historical roles or who at best have only a vague, instinctive grasp of the historical meaning of what they do (*History*, 39–40). Only the philosopher is aware, after the fact, of the full historical significance of great actions. The irony, therefore, as one commentator on Hegel expresses it, is that "those who make history do not understand it, and those who understand it do not (and should not) make it."[5]

This points to another problem. As simply an interpreter of history, does the philosopher therefore have to endorse whatever political arrangements happen to exist at the time? Does Hegel's philosophy of history manifest a conservative bias that whatever *is* is *right*?

2. Is every political philosopher "a child of his time"?

In the preface to his *Philosophy of Right*, Hegel sketches his view of political philosophy. He maintains that every philosopher is indeed "a child of his time" (*Right*, Preface, 11).[6] He also declares: "What is rational is actual, and what is actual is rational" (*Right*, Preface, 10). He explains that "the science of the state" should "portray the state as something inherently rational" (*Right*, Preface, 11). It seems obvious from these remarks that Hegel was an uncritical defender of the political status quo of his time, which was Marx's criticism of Hegel. And when we notice how closely his "idea of the state" resembles the Prussian state of the 1820s, we see why Hitler's National Socialists could cite Hegel as the philosopher of German nationalism.

But before we accept these unfavorable interpretations of Hegel's political philosophy, we should consider the remarks quoted above in their original context.

> *What is rational is actual, and what is actual is rational.* On this conviction the plain man like the philosopher takes his stand, and from it philosophy starts in its study of the universe of mind as well as the universe of nature. (*Right*, Preface, 10)

> This book, then, containing as it does the science of the state,
> is to be nothing other than the endeavor to apprehend and por-
> tray the state as something inherently rational. As a work of
> philosophy, it must be poles apart from an attempt to construct
> a state as it ought to be. The instruction which it may contain
> cannot consist in teaching the state what it ought to be; it can
> only show how the state, the ethical universe, is to be under-
> stood. . . . To comprehend what is, this is the task of philosophy,
> because what is, is reason. Whatever happens, every individual
> is a child of his time; so philosophy too is its own time appre-
> hended in thoughts. It is just as absurd to fancy that a philoso-
> phy can transcend its contemporary world as it is to fancy that
> an individual can overleap his own age. (*Right*, Preface, 11)

To understand what Hegel means in identifying the rational with
the actual we must keep in mind that he distinguishes actuality
(*Wirklichkeit*) from existence (*Dasein*). Whatever happens to exist
is not necessarily actual in Hegel's sense. When something does
not fulfill its true essence, it is not actual. As an illustration, Hegel
observes that although an adult is rational in essence, a child is only
potentially rational and therefore not rational in actuality (*Right*,
section 10A). Similarly, Hegel explains that the state in its actuality
preserves a harmony between public interests and private interests.
But because a bad state fails to do this, a bad state has existence
but not actuality, because it leaves the essence of a state unfulfilled.
A bad state is like a hand cut off from a body: Because the hand
can no longer fulfill its proper function as a member of a body, it
exists without being actual (*Right*, section 270A).

Far from being a complacently conservative principle, the
identification of rationality and actuality is a standard of criticism.
Just as Hegel can condemn the failure to educate children so that
they actualize their rational essence, so can Hegel condemn a bad
state for failing to actualize the rational essence of the state. He
believes, therefore, that political philosophy, "does not remain
stationary at the given" even when "the given be upheld by the
external positive authority of the state" (*Right*, Preface, 3).

But what does Hegel mean in saying that the state is inherently
rational? We assume that nature is inherently rational whenever
we probe beneath the superficial appearances of nature to discover
its underlying laws. Why then, Hegel argues, shouldn't we also
assume that the state is inherently rational? Insofar as the state is
a product of human reason, we should expect the political order
to be even more fully rational than nature. We must not allow the
evanescent contingency of political events to distract us from the
deeper rationality of political history.

The defender of Hegel could also argue that, by linking rationality and history, Hegel promotes philosophical realism. Instead of trying to escape from the world through idealistic abstractions, the Hegelian philosopher can feel at home in the world, doing this in the only way a rational being can.

> Since it is in thought that I am first by myself, I do not penetrate an object until I understand it; it then ceases to stand over against me and I have taken from it the character of its own which it had in opposition to me. . . . I am at home in the world when I know it, still more so when I have understood it. (*Right*, section 4A)

This still leaves unanswered, however, the question as to whether Hegel's understanding of world history as a rational process is correct or not. And since Hegel believes that history is the progressive actualization of freedom, we cannot assess his philosophy of history without examining his conception of freedom.

3. What is freedom?

"Only the will that obeys the law is free," Hegel believes, "for it obeys itself and, being in itself, is free" (*History*, 53). By putting limits on arbitrary impulses and capricious passions, the law of the state does not limit but rather secures the true freedom of the individual. Therefore, "the idea of freedom is genuinely actual only as the state" (*Right*, section 57). Isn't it easy to see why many of Hegel's critics have accused him of distorting the idea of freedom to make it consistent with his political authoritarianism? For he seems to assert that people find true freedom only by submitting blindly to the authority of the state. But consider the reasoning behind Hegel's concept of freedom.

According to Hegel, freedom is self-conscious, rational self-determination.[7] To be free is to be self-determined (*Right*, sections 5–7). Those who are free control their own lives. However, they should also be conscious of their choices as being their own, and therefore they should be self-conscious in their self-determination (*Right*, sections 228, 260). And yet, what is the self that consciously determines the free person's life? Because rationality distinguishes human beings from other animals, our true selves are our minds. We are most fully masters of our own lives when we behave according to the laws of reason. A person who is driven by physical impulses is not truly free. "As it is not the animal but man alone who thinks, so also he alone has freedom—and only because he thinks" (*History*, 86).

People by themselves cannot fulfill their rationality unless they conform to the objective rational order of a community. Consequently, freedom is actualized only in a truly rational state. Individual freedom coincides with social duty. "In duty the individual acquires his substantive freedom" (*Right*, section 149). "Duty is the attainment of our essence, the winning of *positive* freedom" (*Right*, section 149A).

Because Hegel thinks human beings actualize their freedom only as members of communities, he adopts Aristotle's metaphor of the political community as an organic body:

> The state does not exist for the citizens; on the contrary, one could say that the state is the end and they are its means. But the means-end relation is not fitting here. For the state is not the abstract confronting the citizens; they are parts of it, like members of an organic body, where no member is end and none is means. (*History*, 52)

To balance the excessive individualism of modern politics, Hegel would revive the communitarianism of Plato and Aristotle, in which the individual was an organic member of the community. But Hegel also wants to overcome the defect of ancient politics, which failed to leave room for the subjective freedom of individuals. He criticizes Plato's *Republic* for not respecting the claims of "free infinite personality" (*Right*, Preface, 10). In Plato's city, only the philosophic rulers are free. In Hegel's state, *all* citizens must be free.

Hegel's project resembles Rousseau's in that Rousseau also attempts to unite modern individualism and ancient communitarianism. But while Rousseau would do this through small, self-governing communities, Hegel considers this impossible in the modern world as dominated by large states. What is required, Hegel believes, is the combination of a realm of free individuality with a realm of political solidarity in a large nation-state.

That is easier said than done. Throughout the history of political philosophy, there has been a conflict between the principle of individual autonomy and the principle of political authority. Strengthening one seems to inevitably weaken the other. Hegel insists that "the idea of the state" unites these principles; however, the idea of the state is an empty abstraction, by Hegel's own standards, unless he can show it to be achievable in modern history. This is what he must accomplish in the *Philosophy of Right*.

4. Can the modern state unite individual rights and political duties?

Modern democratic politics often emphasizes the rights of citizens rather than their duties. While vigorously declaring that governments must secure individual rights, the Declaration of Independence uses the word duty only once: the right of the people to overthrow tyrants is also a duty. In accordance with Lockean liberalism, rights must be primary; for since any just government arises from a contract among selfish individuals to promote their own interests, the only duty of the individual is to refrain from infringing on the rights of others. This is evident in the French Declaration of the Rights of Man and of Citizens: "Political liberty consists in the power of doing whatever does not injure another. The exercise of the natural rights of every man has no other limits than those which are necessary to secure to every *other* man the free exercise of the same rights."[8]

But Hegel argues that this elevation of individual rights at the expense of political duties subverts true freedom. The state can fully express human freedom only by uniting rights and duties. "The fundamental principle of both right and duty" is "the principle that men, as persons, are free" (*Right*, section 261).

> A slave can have no duties; only a free man has them. If all rights were put on one side and all duties on the other, the whole would be dissolved, since their identity alone is the fundamental thing. (*Right*, section 155A)

If the individual finds personal fulfillment in serving the state, "right and duty coalesce, and by being in the ethical order, a man has rights in so far as he has duties, and duties in so far as he has rights" (*Right*, section 155). To see how Hegel proposes to achieve this we must look at some of the details of the Third Part of the *Philosophy of Right*.

Hegel distinguishes three moments in ethical life: the family, civil society, and the state. These comprise the three kinds of relationships that human beings can have with one another: particular altruism (the family), universal egoism (civil society), and universal altruism (the state).[9] In a family, people make sacrifices for other members of the family, but this altruism is limited to the narrow circle of the family itself (*Right*, section 158). In civil society, which is primarily concerned with economic relationships, each person cooperates with others only as a means to satisfy selfish interests (*Right*, sections 182–86). In the state, citizens cooperate with one another out of a sense of political solidarity. The state is like a large family in its altruistic spirit, but the state arises from self-conscious willing rather than biological instincts, which allows the state to be universal in encompassing all citizens (*Right*, sections 260–69). The bond of a family is love. The bond of a civil society is rational self-interest. The bond of a state is patriotism.

In Hegel's civil society, there are public regulations of the economy to adjust conflicts between producers and consumers, to provide relief for the poor, and to secure the education of the young. But otherwise the free market operates unhindered (*Right*, sections 236–49). Hegel thinks a modern state must secure civil society as the realm in which individual self-interest can be expressed, thus satisfying "the principle of subjective freedom" (*Right*, section 185).

In the industrial and commercial sectors of civil society, people belong to "corporations" corresponding to their various occupations (*Right*, section 250–56). These groups are trade and professional associations that regulate the affairs of common interest to their members. (Contrary to common usage of the word today, Hegel's corporations are *not* limited-liability, joint-stock companies.) They are similar to the medieval guilds except that they are voluntary organizations. The primary value of the corporations is in creating a sense of unity among their members founded on their shared interests. This is a step toward patriotic attachment to the state. The corporation becomes "like a second family for its members" (*Right*, section 252).[10]

In the large nation-state of modern times, citizens have few opportunities to participate in political affairs, and therefore they tend to withdraw completely into their isolated private lives. Hegel thinks that the corporations provide at least a partial solution to this problem because they are intermediary bodies between the individual and the state that widen the opportunities for people to get involved in the public activity closest to their own daily lives (*Right*, section 289). Because "the proper strength of the state lies in these associations," Hegel criticizes the French revolutionaries and Napoleon for going too far in centralizing the powers of government: "France lacks corporations and local government, i.e. associations wherein particular and universal interests meet" (*Right*, section 290A).

Beyond civil society lie the institutions of the state—civil servants, the legislature, and the monarch. As prescribed by Hegel, the class of civil servants conforms largely to the sort of professional bureaucracy that has become a familiar part of modern government (*Right*, sections 291–97). The legislature has an upper house of members drawn from the nobility and a lower house of elected members (*Right*, sections 301–2). The election to the lower house is not by direct, individual suffrage. Rather, people vote as members of their corporate groups. Thus the corporations act much like modern political parties in aggregating individual voters according to group interests. Finally, Hegel's constitutional monarch serves as a symbol of unity, but is virtually powerless. In a well-ordered state, the monarch's approval of the ministers' decisions is a mere formality (*Right*, sections 279–81, 279A, 280A).

The state, however, as understood by Hegel, encompasses far more than the formal institutions of government. It includes the "spirit of a people," the culture or way of life of a political community. Therefore "the state, as the spirit of a people, is both the law permeating all relationships within the state and also at the same time the manners and consciousness of its citizens" (*Right*, section 274).[11]

We must keep in mind this broad conception of the state if we are to comprehend Hegel's claim that the state is separate from—and superior to—civil society:

> If the state is confused with civil society, and if its specific end is laid down as the security and protection of property and personal freedom, then the interest of the individuals as such becomes the ultimate end of their association, and it follows that membership of the state is something optional. But the state's relation to the individual is quite different from this. Since the state is spirit objectified, it is only as one of its members that the individual himself has objectivity, genuine individuality, and an ethical life. (*Right*, section 258)

When Locke speaks of a community as established by the consent of individuals to protect their lives and property, he is—in Hegel's terms—describing not a state but a civil society. Locke's conception of the individual's relationship to the state as contractual distorts the political realm, Hegel argues, by applying to it a concept appropriate only to the economic realm. This is the same sort of mistake as speaking of marriage as a purely contractual relationship. Even if it begins as a kind of contract, a good marriage eventually creates a spiritual unity of the partners that transcends the selfish interests of each (*Right*, section 75). When marriage partners worry about protecting their rights under the marriage contract, that probably indicates that the marriage is breaking up. Similarly, when citizens resist the claims of the state by appealing to their individual rights under the social contract, they manifest political decay.

But does Hegel's conception of the state unite rights with duties? Or does it, rather, favor duties over rights and thereby threaten individual freedom? Hegel's insistence on dutiful service to the state seems to annul individual autonomy. Thus we see again the authoritarian implications of Hegel's teaching.

Two points, however, could be made in defense of Hegel's position. First, he does, in fact, preserve civil society as the realm of individual freedom. Second, he has a good argument for the claim that even a Lockean regime demands individual sacrifices that must be justified as duties to the state.

Hegel wants to have a sphere of political life in which citizens are conscious of public activity as an end in itself. But he also wants to have civil society as a sphere of social and economic life in which people freely pursue their private interests. This requires individual freedom not only in economic activity, but also in private matters such as religious belief. Hegel is careful, therefore, to protect "the sphere of the inner life, which as such is not the domain of the state" (*Right*, section 270). Hegel rejects ancient political thought in endorsing the modern concern for "private judgment, private willing, and private conscience." He continues, "The ancients had none of these in the modern sense; the ultimate thing with them was the will of the state" (*Right*, section 261A). By securing the realm of civil society, Hegel's teaching incorporates modern individualism.

And yet, any modern state—even one founded on Lockean individualism—must be something more than an instrument to preserve individual rights.

> The state is not a contract at all, nor is its fundamental essence the unconditional protection and guarantee of the life and property of members of the public as individuals. On the contrary, it is that higher entity which even lays claim to this very life and property and demands its sacrifice. (*Right*, section 100)

Human beings conform to the dictates of civil society because it promotes their self-interest. But citizens must sometimes sacrifice their private interests to the interests of the state. When they do so, they are moved not by the desire for personal gain, but by some sense of patriotic duty (*Right*, section 268). Hegel therefore agrees with Rousseau about the importance of patriotic virtue, although he rejects Rousseau's claim that such patriotism can be cultivated only in small, participatory democracies.

Hegel offers three illustrations of how the moral claims of the state transcend individual self-interest: taxation, capital punishment, and military service. If the Lockean is right about just government existing only to protect the property of its citizens, why should people pay their taxes? To the extent that a person's tax contributions help other people, paying taxes is a personal sacrifice (*Right* sections 184, 299, 299A). Moreover, even if the individual benefits from tax-supported activities, it would serve his or her selfish interests to cheat on tax payments in order to enjoy a free ride at the expense of the honest taxpayers. Of course, many people do cheat on their taxes, but what is surprising is the large number of people who pay their taxes because they think it is right to do so. This is true of the income tax system of the United States. The Internal Revenue Service (IRS) has to rely largely on voluntary compliance with the tax laws because the chances of a tax return being audited—less than three in one hundred for most taxpayers—are so low that it is profitable in most cases to cheat. In recent years, however, tax evasion has increased greatly because of the growing perception that the tax system is unjust.[12] Does that confirm Hegel's point that the strength of the state depends on its appeal to political justice as transcending selfish interests?

Not only can the state take the property of its citizens, it can also take their lives. But the power of capital punishment would seem unjustified if the authority of the state arose simply from the consent of its citizens (*Right*, section 100). If the only reason for any person to accept a government's authority is to secure the right to life, why would a citizen consent to allow a government to take away that right under any circumstances? Hobbes failed to solve this problem. Hegel thinks the only way to solve it is to reject the social contract theory of the state's legitimacy. That we continue to debate the justice of capital punishment indicates how difficult it is to reconcile it with our Hobbesian-Lockean principles.[13]

Of course, we could abolish capital punishment because it is not absolutely necessary for political order. It would not be so easy, however, to eliminate the other life-threatening power of the state— the claim to military service in time of war. This leads us to ponder Hegel's disturbing assertion that the moral strength of the state shows itself most clearly in war.

5. Does war preserve the health of the state?

In war, Hegel argues, the ethical majesty of the state shines (*Right*, sections 323–24). If the state is merely a civil society preserving individual life and property, why should citizens sacrifice their lives and property in defense of it? That citizens do make such sacrifices indicates they believe the public interests of the state should outweigh the private interests of civil society. During long periods of peace, citizens become preoccupied with their private lives and neglectful of their public duties. With the coming of a war, they are reminded of their need to unite to preserve the state: "The true courage of civilized nations is readiness for sacrifice in the service of the state, so that the individual counts as only one amongst many" (*Right*, section 327A).

Should we see this as evidence of Hegel's Prussian militarism? Such a glorification of war has had disastrous consequences for Germany. Or should we concede that there is at least an element of truth in what Hegel says? Surely, war brings out both the best and the worst in human beings. It can brutalize, but it can also promote noble heroism.

War can create among the citizens of a nation a warm sense of communal unity. Consider, for example, the way Americans talk about the Second World War. Despite the horrors of the war, some of those who went through it were elevated in a way by it. John Kennedy, in his first political campaign in 1946, described his experience of the war with fondness:

> Most of the courage shown in the war came from men's understanding of their interdependence on each other. . . . [T]here was built up during the war a great feeling of comradeship and fellowship and loyalty.
>
> Now they miss the feeling of interdependence, that sense of working together for a common cause. In civilian life, they feel they have only themselves to depend on. They miss their wartime friends, and the understanding of their wartime friendships.[14]

That quotation was once used by an American journalist as evidence of a sense of community that has been lost in America as the nation has fallen into "a politics of selfishness." And as one way to renew that experience of national community, he proposes establishing a national service program in which all young Americans would be required to devote two years to either military or civilian public service activity.

Such a proposal seems almost un-American to many people. Even in wartime, the military draft has been controversial in the United States because it assumes that the duty of national service can take precedence over individual rights. Furthermore, even Hegel himself suggested that the American tradition of individualism would make it difficult for the Americans to ever establish a genuine state.

6. Is the United States a state?

Looking at the America of the 1820s, Hegel saw a civil society that was without a true state. The Americans did not have a real state because they had only "a community arising from the aggregation of individuals as atomic constituents" in which "the state was merely something external for the protection of property." There was no truly *public* realm, Hegel complained, because political institutions were simply means for securing *private* ends. America was dominated by "the endeavor of the individual after acquisition, commercial profit, and gain; the preponderance of *private* interest, devoting itself to that of the community only for its own advantage." But immediately after these remarks, Hegel calls America "the land of the future, where, in the ages that lie before us, the burden of the world's history shall reveal itself."[15] Does he mean to imply that in the future America will have a genuine state or perhaps even some new, higher form of political order?

In any case, Hegel's criticism of American politics has been echoed by many observers representing a wide range of political viewpoints. Among contemporary political commentators—from democratic socialists (like Michael Walzer) to Tory conservatives (like George Will), from neoliberals (like Charles Peters) to neoconservatives (like Irving Kristol)—there is a general agreement that the United States has been weakened by an excessive reliance on individual self-interest and a failure to cultivate public-spiritedness founded on shared values.[16] George Will's argument is typical. He laments the "disproportionate individualism" of American political culture, and he argues for reviving

> the notion (set forth by Aristotle, Hegel and others) that man
> is a social creature, and the value of his life is to some extent
> a function of his association with persons whose similar moral
> construction derives from intercourse in a moral community.

He even endorses Aristotle's idea of political friendship: "The aim of politics . . . is a warm citizenship, approximating friendship, based on a sense of shared values and a shared fate."[17]

Could Americans adopt such a Hegelian view of the state without subverting the American tradition of individual liberty? John Kennedy, in his presidential inaugural address, exhorted Americans to patriotic devotion: "Ask not what your country can do for you—ask what you can do for your country." If we substituted "state" for "country," that statement would be a perfect reflection of Hegel's thought. But Milton Friedman, the famous libertarian economist, denounced Kennedy's remark as contrary to "the ideals of free men in a free society":

> To the free man, the country is the collection of individuals who compose it, not something over and above him. . . . [H]e regards government as a means, an instrumentality, neither a grantor of favors and gifts, nor a master or god to be blindly worshipped and served. He recognizes no national goal except as it is the consensus of the goals that the citizens severally serve.[18]

On the one hand, the popularity of Kennedy's remark suggests that America has become a state in the Hegelian sense. On the other hand, Friedman's conception of America as merely "a collection of individuals" reflects an enduring element of American political thought.

The Lockean spirit of the Declaration of Independence would seem to support Friedman's point of view. For if "Governments are instituted among Men" to "secure" the "unalienable Rights" to "Life, Liberty and the pursuit of Happiness," then the American government should be merely an instrument for advancing the individual interests of its citizens. But the last sentence of the Declaration manifests the same patriotic public-spiritedness invoked by Kennedy: "And for the support of this Declaration, with a firm reliance on the protection of Divine Providence, we mutually pledge to each other our Lives, our Fortunes and our sacred Honor." In their willingness to sacrifice their lives and property in defense of the new American nation, the signers of the Declaration exhibited the self-sacrificing devotion to their political community that Hegel regarded as crucial for any state. Thus the Declaration exemplifies a strange combination of Lockean and Hegelian themes.

We might agree with Hegel that during its early constitutional history, the United States was a civil society without a state, because the weakness of the national government hindered the development of national unity. But since the Civil War, we might argue, the increasing unification of the nation has produced a true state to which civil society is subordinated. According to this view of American history, the first phase of American constitutional history was purely Lockean, but the second was Hegelian. The Lockean founding of the American civil society was achieved by James Madison and the other framers of the Constitution. The Hegelian founding of the American state was begun by Abraham Lincoln.

Lincoln—as indicated in the Gettysburg Address and other speeches—thought that the American people were bound together as one nation by their dedication to a high moral principle—"the proposition that all men are created equal." He thought that those who opposed this moral ideal would corrupt the people by "insisting that there is no right principle of action but *self-interest*."[19] For it was through their dedication to equality that the American people were a moral community rather than just a collection of selfish individuals. Through his rhetoric, Lincoln sought to sustain, even during the Civil War, that sense of community based on a shared moral principle:

> We are not enemies, but friends. We must not be enemies. Though passion may have strained, it must not break our bonds of affection. The mystic chords of memory, stretching from every battlefield, and patriot grave, to every living heart and hearthstone, all over this broad land, will yet swell the chorus of the Union, when again touched, as surely they will be, by the better angels of our nature.[20]

It had always been thought that "political friendship" was possible only in communities small enough that all the citizens could develop common interests through face-to-face, personal relationships. That was why those of the Jeffersonian tradition in America favored local and state governments and feared the power of the national government. But Hegel argued that in the large, modern nation-state, there could be a moral community nourished by patriotic solidarity even without face-to-face contact. Lincoln seems to put that idea into practice with his conception of an American national community of friends whose friendship depends on their shared dedication to the principle of equality. In the words of George Will, Lincoln thought "the fact that Americans were not physically close might be compensated for by making them morally close through a crucial shared proposition."[21]

There is evidence that Lincoln's Hegelian conception of a national community has shaped the history of American political thought and practice to the present day. For example, political scientist Samuel Beer has traced through American history what he calls "the national idea." As he understands it, this idea encompasses more than just the centralization of power in the national government:

> It means not only governmental unification, but also national integration. . . . [I]ts imperative is . . . to make the nation more solidary, more cohesive, more interdependent in its growing diversity — in short, to make the American nation more of a nation.[22]

The welfare state programs initiated by Franklin Roosevelt, the enforcement of the Supreme Court's decisions requiring racially integrated public schools, the various federal civil rights laws — all of these national programs have deepened the American dedication to the principle of equality, thus making the American nation more of a nation. Or perhaps we should say, the United States has become more of a state.

Some critics of American politics, however, would say that the capitalist economy of the United States promotes an inequality of wealth that always impedes the American dedication to equality. Some of the more radical critics would suggest that we need to advance beyond the Hegelian state to Marxist communism. Marx saw the need to eliminate class conflict by establishing a classless society in which human beings would experience a genuine sense of community for the first time. Hegel struggled to overcome the conflict between individual rights and social duties, but Marx thought this conflict would disappear with the emergence of "an association, in which the free development of each is the condition for the free development of all."[23]

Marx agreed with Hegel that history was evolving toward an ever greater satisfaction of the human longing for freedom. But unlike Hegel, Marx believed that complete freedom would be achieved in a communist society, which would constitute the end of history. Some political commentators have announced that we reached the end of history in the late 1980s and early 1990s. Contrary to Marx's prediction, however, it seems that history has found its consummation not in a communist society, but in liberal democracy.

7. Have we reached the end of history?

In 1989, Francis Fukuyama, a deputy director of the American State Department's Policy Planning Staff, wrote an article announcing that, since the Cold War had ended with the triumph of liberal democracy over communism, we had reached the end of history. Three years later, he elaborated his argument in a book.[24] His article provoked a worldwide debate among scholars and political leaders. Even President George Bush, in his State of the Union Address of 1992, responded to Fukuyama's article by claiming that the end of the Cold War meant not the end of history, but the *resumption* of history.

We should examine Fukuyama's argument, because he claims to have drawn his fundamental ideas from Hegel. Actually, his reasoning relies less on Hegel than on a controversial interpretation of Hegel by Alexandre Kojève, who emphasized Hegel's account of the master-slave dialectic in the *Phenomenology of Spirit*.[25]

Nevertheless, the idea that history has a direction and a purpose, if not an end, is surely Hegelian, at least in spirit.

History as a continuing series of unpredictable events will never come to an end, Fukuyama concedes. But history as the human search for the fully satisfying social order has come to an end, he insists, because most of the people in the world today agree in principle that liberal democracy is the only fully satisfying social order. In practice, of course, the ideals of liberal democracy — liberty and equality for all — have not been completely attained. Nevertheless, even if we disagree about how best to achieve these ideals, most of us agree on the ideals themselves. Never before has this happened, because in all previous history there were fundamental disagreements about what the ideal society would be like. To be sure, there seems to be some resistance to liberal ideals in certain parts of the world today — Islamic fundamentalism, for example. But Fukuyama argues that there is no good reason to doubt that such resistance will only delay the inevitable victory of liberal democracy.

According to Fukuyama, there are two reasons for the triumph of liberal ideals. First, liberalism satisfies the human desire for material security and comfort through economic productivity and the scientific conquest of nature. Second, liberalism satisfies the human desire for recognition through an egalitarian cultural and political order in which all human beings are recognized as equal in their dignity. Thus, the history of human striving for satisfaction comes to an end when human beings discover that liberal democracy is the only social order that satisfies their deepest longings — the longing for material prosperity and the longing for non-material recognition.

There are many possible criticisms of Fukuyama's position.[26] First, it is not clear that Fukuyama is faithful either to Hegel or to Kojève. Although we have seen some of the liberal elements of Hegel's political teaching, we have also seen his defense of a communitarian, corporate state as superior to the liberal individualism of civil society. And Kojève was hardly an orthodox liberal, because he identified himself as a Stalinist Marxist.[27]

Even if we abstract from his interpretations of Hegel and Kojève and assess Fukuyama's arguments on their own merits, we might still criticize him for his internal contradictions. His fundamental claim is that history has come to an end because liberal democracy completely satisfies the most essential desires of human beings. But near the end of his book he concludes: "No regime . . . is able to satisfy all men in all places. This includes liberal democracy. . . . Thus those who remain dissatisfied will always have the potential to restart history." He repeats this in the very last sentence of the book.[28]

Fukuyama agrees with Plato's account of human nature as composed of three parts: appetite, spiritedness (*thymos*), and reason. He argues consistently that liberal democracy satisfies appetite through the material prosperity of capitalist economics. But he vacillates over whether liberalism can satisfy spiritedness or the desire for recognition. Sometimes he argues that liberalism provides recognition through the principle of equal recognition for all. But at other times he agrees with Nietzsche that the recognition of all people as equal will not satisfy those who are *unequal*, and thus a society based on equal recognition must mean dehumanization through a slave morality in which human beings are reduced to comfort-seeking animals.

Fukuyama assumes that reason has no independent status apart from its connection to appetite or spiritedness; and thus he does not consider Plato's claim that the fullest satisfaction of human longings comes only through the rational life of philosophy as that which conforms to the highest in human nature, which was argued by Leo Strauss in his debate with Kojève.[29] Liberal democracy certainly does not allow philosophers to rule. But does it, at least, allow those few with the desire and ability for it to pursue the philosophic life? Or does liberalism promote a soft relativism that discourages even potential philosophers from taking philosophy seriously? Fukuyama does not raise these questions, but he should have.

To his credit, however, Fukuyama does raise fundamental questions about the greatest political development of our times: although many people criticize liberal democracy for failing to live up to its ideals, almost no one in any position of influence (at least in the Western world) criticizes the liberal democratic ideals of equality and liberty. Does this mean that the principles of the Declaration of Independence have become the only principles of political legitimacy for most people around the world? Does this mean that those principles are, indeed, "self-evident" to any human being who understands them, because they satisfy the deepest yearnings of human nature?

Before we accept that conclusion, we should question Fukuyama's claim that Marxist communism is not a serious alternative. Although he takes seriously Nietzsche's complaint from the political Right that liberal democracy treats unequal people as if they were equal, he too quickly dismisses Marx's complaint from the political Left that liberal democracy treats equal people as if they were unequal.

Notes

1. The reference is to G. W. F. Hegel, *Reason in History*, trans. Robert S. Hartman (Indianapolis: Bobbs-Merrill, Library of Liberal Arts, 1953), which is a partial translation of the Introduction to the *Philosophy of History*. Other references to this translation are indicated in the same manner.

2. For elaboration of these points, see Karl Löwith, *Meaning in History* (Chicago: University of Chicago Press, 1949). Unlike Greco-Roman history, R. G. Collingwood explains, "any history written on Christian principles will be of necessity universal, providential, apocalyptic, and periodized" (*The Idea of History* [New York: Oxford University Press, 1956], 49). On Hegel's political thought as a combination of classical and Christian elements, see Michael B. Foster, *The Political Philosophies of Plato and Hegel* (New York: Russell & Russell, 1935). For a critique of the philosophy of history as promoting historicist relativism, see Leo Strauss, "On Collingwood's Philosophy of History," *Review of Metaphysics* 5 (June 1952): 559–86; and compare Strauss, *The City and Man* (Chicago: University of Chicago Press, 1977), 139–45, 236–41.

3. G. W. F. Hegel, *The Phenomenology of Spirit*, trans. A. V. Miller (Oxford: Clarendon Press, 1977), 460. On Hegel's philosophy of history as a deformation of Christian experience, see Eric Voegelin, *The Ecumenic Age* (Baton Rouge: Louisiana State University Press, 1974), 260–71; and Voegelin, *Science, Politics and Gnosticism* (Chicago: Henry Regnery, 1968).

4. See Albert Camus, *The Rebel* (New York: Random House, Vintage, 1956), 133–48.

5. Shlomo Avineri, *Hegel's Theory of the Modern State* (London: Cambridge University Press, 1972), 234.

6. The reference is to Hegel's *Philosophy of Right*, trans. T. M. Knox (London: Oxford University Press, 1967). For references to the Preface, I will indicate the page numbers in the Knox translation. All other references are to the standard section numbers.

7. I have drawn this formulation from Richard L. Schacht, "Hegel on Freedom," in Alasdair MacIntyre, ed., *Hegel* (Garden City, NY: Doubleday, Anchor Books, 1972), 289–328. The importance of freedom for Hegel is stressed in Michael Oakeshott's interpretation of Hegel's state as a "civil association [of] persons related to one another in the enjoyment of a self-chosen multiplicity of conduct" (*On Human Conduct* [Oxford: Clarendon Press, 1975], 256–57). Oakeshott's "On the Character of a Modern European State" (ibid., 185–326) is a brilliant essay on the subject.

8. The French Declaration can be found in Thomas Paine, *The Rights of Man* (New York: Dutton, 1951), 94–97.

9. Here I am indebted to Avineri's commentary in *Hegel's Theory*, 133–34.

10. On the idea of corporatism in recent political theory, see Philippe C. Schmitter, "Still the Century of Corporatism?" *Review of Politics* 36 (January 1974): 85–131.

11. I have altered Knox's translation by translating *Geist* as "spirit" and *Volk* as "people."

12. See Shlomo Maital, *Minds, Markets & Money* (New York: Basic Books, 1982), 239–60.

13. Consider Walter Berns, *For Capital Punishment* (New York: Basic Books, 1979), 172–73:

   > Capital punishment . . . serves to remind us of the majesty of the moral order that is embodied in our law and of the terrible consequences of its breach. . . . The criminal law must possess a dignity far beyond that possessed by mere statutory enactment or utilitarian and self-interested calculations; the most powerful means we have to give it that dignity is to authorize it to impose the ultimate penalty. . . . It must remind us of the moral order by which alone we can live as *human* beings, and in our day the only punishment that can do this is capital punishment.

   Compare Hegel, *Philosophy of Right*, secs. 99–103, 99A, 101A. For contrasting views, see Lawrence Kohlberg, *The Philosophy of Moral Development* (New York: Harper & Row, 1981), 243–93; and Hugo Adam Bedau, ed., *The Death Penalty in America*, 3rd ed. (Oxford: Oxford University Press, 1982).

14. Charles Peters, "Tilting at Windmills," *Washington Monthly*, December 1983, 11–12. For the debate over national service, see Williamson Evers, ed., *National Service* (Stanford: Hoover Institution Press, 1990).

15. G. W. F. Hegel, *Philosophy of History*, trans. J. Sibree (New York: Dover, 1956), 84–86.

16. See Michael Walzer, "Politics in the Welfare State," in Irving Howe, ed., *Essential Works of Socialism* (New Haven: Yale University Press, 1976), 809–34; George Will, *Statecraft as Soulcraft* (New York: Simon & Schuster, 1983); Charles Peters, "A Neoliberal's Manifesto," *Washington Monthly*, May 1983, 8–18; and Irving Kristol, "'When Virtue Loses All Her Loveliness' — Some Reflections on Capitalism and 'The Free Society,'" in *On the Democratic Idea in America* (New York: Harper & Row, 1972), 90–106. See also William M. Sullivan, *Reconstructing Public Philosophy* (Berkeley: University of California Press, 1982); Michael Sandel, "Morality and the Liberal Ideal," *New Republic*, 7 May 1984, 15–17; and Robert N. Bellah et al., *Habits of the Heart: Individualism and Commitment in American Life* (Berkeley: University of California Press, 1985).

17. Will, *Statecraft as Soulcraft*, 60, 143, 165.

18. Milton Friedman, *Capitalism and Freedom* (Chicago: University of Chicago Press, 1962), 1–2.

19. Abraham Lincoln, Speech at Peoria, Illinois, 16 October 1854, in *The Collected Works of Abraham Lincoln*, ed. Roy P. Basler, 9 vols. (New

Brunswick, NJ: Rutgers University Press, 1953–1955), 2: 255.

20. Lincoln, First Inaugural Address, 4 March 1861, in *Collected Works*, 4: 271.

21. Will, *Statecraft as Soulcraft*, 56. Will seems to agree with the liberal progressives in claiming that Lincoln was the first American leader to combine Hamiltonian nationalism and Jeffersonian democracy. See Herbert Croly, *The Promise of American Life* (New York: Macmillan, 1909), 85–99, 167–214. See also James M. McPherson, "How Lincoln Won the War with Metaphors," in *Abraham Lincoln and the Second American Revolution* (New York: Oxford University Press, 1991), 93–112.

22. Samuel Beer, "Liberalism and the National Idea," in Robert A. Goldwin, ed., *Left, Right and Center* (Chicago: Rand McNally, 1967), 142. After the Civil War, Walt Whitman wrote of the need for a national literature to complete the final stage of American nationality. In "Democratic Vistas," written in 1868, he feared "conflicting and irreconcilable interiors, and the lack of a common skeleton, knitting all close." He saw the need for

> a fusion of the States into the only reliable identity, the moral and artistic one. For, I say, the true nationality of the States, the genuine union, when we come to a mortal crisis, is, and is to be, after all, neither the written law, nor, (as is generally supposed,) either self-interest, or common pecuniary or material objects — but the fervid and tremendous IDEA, melting everything else with restless heat, and solving all lesser and definite distinctions in vast, indefinite, spiritual, emotional power. (*Complete Poetry and Collected Prose*, ed. Justin Kaplan [New York: Library of America, 1982], 935–36)

Does this illustrate Plato's claim about the political importance of poetry? Compare Plato, *Republic* 377a–79a, 397e–98a, 607a–d; and Alexis de Tocqueville, *Democracy in America*, trans. George Lawrence (Garden City, NY: Doubleday, Anchor Books, 1969), vol. 2, pt. 1, chap. 17.

On the idea of American nationality, see Paul C. Nagel, *One Nation Indivisible: The Union of American Thought, 1776–1861* (New York: Oxford University Press, 1964); and Nagel, *This Sacred Trust: American Nationality, 1798–1898* (New York: Oxford University Press, 1971). On the Civil War as a turning point in the transformation of the United States into a state, see Richard Franklin Bensel, *Yankee Leviathan: The Origins of Central State Authority in America, 1859–1877* (Cambridge: Cambridge University Press, 1990).

23. Karl Marx and Frederich Engels, *Communist Manifesto*, in *The Marx-Engels Reader*, ed. Robert C. Tucker, 2nd ed. (New York: Norton, 1978), 491.

Is Hegel's affirmation of modern individuality an objective advance in the history of moral thought? Does Hegel show us the historical fulfillment of Aristotle's recognition of the human capacity for moral personality? See Alan Gilbert, *Democratic Individuality* (Cambridge:

Cambridge University Press, 1990).

24. Francis Fukuyama, "The End of History?" *The National Interest* 16 (Summer 1989): 3–18; Fukuyama, *The End of History and the Last Man* (New York: Free Press, 1992). One of the best parts of Fukuyama's book is his history of the idea of "spiritedness" as encompassing *thymos* (Plato), "greatness of soul" (Aristotle), "glory" (Augustine, Machiavelli, and Hobbes), "the desire for recognition" (Rousseau and Hegel), "the will to power" (Nietzsche), and "human dignity" (contemporary liberal rhetoric). One must wonder, however, whether the idea becomes too vague in taking on so many different meanings.

25. See Alexandre Kojève, *Introduction to the Reading of Hegel*, trans. James H. Nichols (New York: Basic Books, 1969); Fukuyama, *End of History*, 144, 203, 208, 329, 388–89; and Hegel, *Phenomenology of Spirit*, secs. 178–230.

26. Of the many critiques, two of the best are Stephen Holmes, "The Scowl of Minerva," *The New Republic* 206 (March 23, 1992): 27–33; and Alan Ryan, "Professor Hegel Goes to Washington," *The New York Review of Books* 39 (March 26, 1992): 7–13.

27. See Fukuyama, *End of History*, 351, 388.

28. Ibid., 136, 314, 334, 339.

29. See Ibid., 311, 334, 337, 370, 386; Leo Strauss, *On Tyranny*, revised edition, ed. Victor Gourevitch and Michael Roth (New York: Free Press, 1991), 207–12, 237–38; and Michael S. Roth, *Knowing and History: Appropriations of Hegel in Twentieth-Century France* (Ithaca: Cornell University Press, 1988), 126–34. For evidence that Strauss was right in suggesting that Hegel's philosophy of history presupposes a teleological conception of nature, see Hegel, *The Philosophy of Nature*, trans. A. V. Miller (Oxford: Oxford University Press, 1970), secs. 245–52, 337, 360, 376.

Chapter

11

Socialism
Marx's *Communist Manifesto*

Key Readings

Communist Manifesto, Parts 1, 2.

The most important political development of the twentieth century has been the rise and decline of socialism. To understand the history of socialism, we must go back to its original proponents in the nineteenth century, particularly Karl Marx.

Marx (1818–1883) was born in Trier, Prussia (now in Germany). He was one of seven children of Jewish parents who had converted to Christianity. His father was a lawyer who supported the movement for liberal reforms in Prussia.

In 1835, Marx entered the University of Bonn. He transferred to the University of Berlin in 1836 and then went on to the University of Jena, from which institution he received his Ph.D. in 1841. At Berlin he was influenced by the "Young Hegelians" under the leadership of Bruno Bauer, who were known for their atheism and their radical political ideas. Marx's studies were broad—literature, law, philosophy, and theology. His doctoral dissertation was a comparison of the natural philosophies of Democritus and Epicurus. During this period, Marx's thinking was also shaped by Ludwig Feuerbach's materialist criticism of Hegel. Marx sought to unite the idealism of Hegel with the materialism of Feuerbach.

When he was unsuccessful in securing a teaching position, Marx worked as a newspaper editor and writer in Cologne in 1842. When the authorities closed down his newspaper, Marx moved to Paris in 1843, where he continued his work as a journalist and his studies of philosophy and economics. He began his lifelong collaboration with Friedrich Engels. As a manager of his family's textile factory in Manchester, England, Engels could afford to help Marx financially. Such support was essential as Marx and his family were desperately poor.

In 1845, when he was banished from Paris as a result of his writing, Marx moved to Brussels. Then early in 1848, he and Engels wrote the *Communist Manifesto* for the Communist League. It was a timely pamphlet because during the early months of 1848 revolutions exploded across Europe: in France, Italy, Germany, and Austria. Marx was active in the German Revolution of 1848. He argued for an alliance between the workers and the liberal bourgeoisie. In 1849, a conservative reaction suppressed socialist agitation, and Marx was forced to move to London.

Marx decided that in any future revolution, the workers should not allow their socialist spirit to be stifled by the democratic bourgeoisie. But from 1850 to 1864, Marx was not directly involved in any revolutionary activity. The economic misery of his family was so severe that several of his children died. He was forced to earn a small income by writing hundreds of articles for the *New York Tribune* as its European correspondent. He also worked in the reading room of the British Museum where he did research that led eventually, in 1867, to the publication of volume one of *Capital*, his most massive work.

Marx returned to political activity in 1864 when he helped to found the International Working Men's Association (later called the First International). In his writings for the group, he emphasized the importance of trade union activity and reform legislation to improve economic conditions for workers and to increase their political power as voters. The fragmentation of the First International into competing factions led to its collapse in 1876. One of the subjects of controversy was the Paris Commune of 1871. For two months, Parisian workers set up a government of representatives elected directly by the people of the city. Marx succeeded in having the First International endorse the Commune, despite the opposition of some English trade unionists who favored more moderate reforms. Another source of conflict in the organization was the split between Marx and Mikhail Bakunin. Bakunin was a Russian anarchist who denounced Marx as an authoritarian.

Since Marx's death in 1883, his ideas have given birth to a confusing variety of socialist ideologies. Around the turn of the century, Eduard Bernstein, a leader of the German Social Democratic party, provoked intense debate when he argued for revising Marxism in accord with what he called evolutionary socialism. Rejecting the idea of a violent revolution leading to the dictatorship of the proletariat, Bernstein recommended a continual expansion of the political and economic rights of the workers through peaceful, democratic reforms. This sort of thinking dominated the social democratic parties of Europe.

At the other extreme, V. I. Lenin elaborated the revolutionary strategy of Marxism and applied it to the Russian Revolution. He emphasized the need for a small revolutionary elite—a party vanguard—to lead the Revolution. After he won power in the Bolshevik coup of October 1917, Lenin centralized control of the state and prohibited any opposition to the Communist Party. After Lenin's death in 1924, Joseph Stalin gradually took power and established a brutally authoritarian regime. Leon Trotsky, an important participant in the Russian Revolution, led the opposition to Stalin's bureaucratic totalitarianism, which he regarded as a betrayal of the Revolution. Stalin expelled him from Russia in 1929, and in 1940 had him assassinated.

Beginning in the 1920s, Ludwig von Mises and his students—most notably, Friedrich von Hayek—led the intellectual opposition to socialism. Mises's *Socialism*, first published in 1922, is still the best critique of socialist economics, ethics, and politics.[1] Originally, the arguments of Mises and Hayek for free markets and against central planning were unpopular. Now many economists and political theorists regard the collapse of socialism around the world as a confirmation of their ideas.[2]

After the Second World War, new varieties of Marxism appeared. In China, Mao Zedong put into practice an interpretation of Marxism as adapted to the Oriental, peasant society of China. One of his major concerns was to fight against party bureaucracy in order to encourage popular participation at all levels of society. In 1948, Josip Broz Tito freed Yugoslavia from the control of the Soviet Union. Yugoslavia became a testing ground for democratic socialism, particularly as founded on workers' control of the factories.

The harsh totalitarianism of the socialist system led some socialist leaders to look for a "humanist socialism" that would take a "third road" between capitalist markets and socialist planning. In the late

1980s, Mikhail Gorbachev tried to lead the Soviet Union in this direction; but his reforms eventually led to the complete destruction of the Soviet system. Socialists continue to debate the possibility of combining the "invisible hand" of free markets and the "visible hand" of central planning.[3]

One reason for the diversity of interpretations of Marxist socialism is that Marx scattered his ideas over a massive corpus of writings; thus we cannot rely on any one text as a complete and coherent presentation of his teaching. Although we shall use the *Communist Manifesto* as our main text, we shall also have to refer to other works. The following are particularly important: "On the Jewish Question," Part 1; *Economic and Philosophic Manuscripts of 1844*, the sections entitled "Estranged Labor" and "Private Property and Communism"; the "Theses on Feuerbach"; *The German Ideology*, Part 1; and *Capital*, Volume I, chapters 1, 7, 12, 32 and Volume III, chapter 48.[4]

In a preface to the *Manifesto*, Engels emphasized three points as essential to Marx's basic thought:

> That economic production and the structure of society of every historical epoch necessarily arising therefrom constitute the foundation for the political and intellectual history of that epoch; that consequently (ever since the dissolution of the primeval communal ownership of land) all history has been a history of class struggles, of struggles between exploited and exploiting, between dominated and dominating classes at various stages of social development; that this struggle, however, has now reached a stage where the exploited and oppressed class (the proletariat) can no longer emancipate itself from the class which exploits and oppresses it (the bourgeoisie), without at the same time forever freeing the whole of society from exploitation, oppression and class struggles. (472)

Engels defines the bourgeoisie as "the class of modern Capitalists, owners of the means of social production and employers of wage-labour," and he defines the proletariat as "the class of modern wage-labourers who, having no means of production of their own, are reduced to selling their labour-power in order to live" (473).

Why should we accept Marx's claim that capitalist employers must always exploit their workers? Isn't it true that the standard of living for most workers has improved greatly in the capitalist nations? Why then should workers want to have a communist revolution? In fact, isn't there a substantial amount of evidence that a socialist economy cannot work? Moreover, didn't the communist regimes—like those in Russia and China—deprive the workers of their economic and political freedom? Or is it conceivable that those regimes violated Marx's teaching? Would Marx want a socialist society to be democratic? Before we can properly consider these questions, however, we must examine the most fundamental of Marx's principles—that "economic production" shapes "the structure of society" and "the political and intellectual history" of every historical period.

1. Do economic interests determine history?

This question is crucial not only for the assessment of Marx's ideas, but also for understanding the entire history of political ideas. If Marx is correct, then we must conclude that the arguments of every political philosopher reflect economic interests. Marx makes this clear in the *Manifesto*:

> Does it require deep intuition to comprehend that man's ideas, views and conceptions, in one word, man's consciousness, changes with every change in the conditions of his material existence, in his social relations and in his social life?

> What else does the history of ideas prove, than that intellectual production changes its character in proportion as material production is changed? The ruling ideas of each age have ever been the ideas of its ruling class.

> When people speak of ideas that revolutionize society, they do but express the fact, that within the old society, the elements of a new one have been created, and that the dissolution of the old ideas keeps even pace with the dissolution of the old conditions of society. (489)

Before human beings can do anything, they must provide for their physical existence, and how they secure their economic needs will shape how they think about the world. Law, politics, religion—the whole way of life of a community—will therefore reflect an economic foundation. For example, the culture of primitive people who live by hunting and gathering their food differs greatly from the culture of modern people who live in a capitalist society. The economic arrangements of a society, Marx indicates, create class struggles. This must be so because every society has a ruling class of people who live by exploiting the labor of others. In ancient Greece and Rome, the citizens exploited the slaves. In medieval Europe, the lords exploited the serfs. Now the capitalists exploit the workers. But every system produces the seeds of its own destruction, so that some of the exploited are driven to overthrow their rulers in order to establish themselves as a new ruling class.

Capitalism, however, is now creating the conditions for a revolution that will establish a classless society in which there will be no separation of people into rulers and ruled. The concentration of economic power under capitalism favors only a tiny minority. Eventually—as a result of capitalism's growing economic crises—the great majority of the people will revolt and then arrange things so that all people can share in controlling the means of economic production. The revolutionary idea of communism arises, therefore, from the economic conditions created by the capitalists. "The bourgeoisie," Marx declares in the *Manifesto*, "has played a most revolutionary part" (475). Socialism actualizes the potentialities inherent in capitalism.

It would seem to follow from Marx's reasoning that the ideas held by any person are simply rationalizations of economic interests. This presumably is what Marx means when he speaks of ideology (pp. 5, 154, 489). Many modern social scientists have adopted this point of view. Some historians, for example, explain the movement of history as controlled by the economic interests of dominant classes. Some political scientists believe that people usually favor those political opinions that serve the interests of the economic groups to which they belong. It would seem that there are no eternal Ideas (contrary to Plato), and hence no self-evident, universal principles for politics (contrary to the Declaration of Independence). Rather, political ideas are merely tools for advancing our selfish interests. Because there is plenty of evidence to support this, it would be unreasonable to reject it completely.[5]

One criticism, however, is that this sort of economic determinism ignores the complexity of history in reducing everything to economic conditions. Was the assassination of Julius Caesar economically determined? Was Martin Luther's opposition to the Catholic Church simply a result of his economic background? Did Isaac Newton's formulation of the law of gravity arise from the class struggle in England?

Another difficulty is that economic determinism is self-contradictory. If all ideas are determined by economic interests, then the idea of economic determinism must itself be so determined. We would have to say that Marx's ideas do not conform to reality because they are rationalizations of his economic interests. But obviously Marx believes that his ideas are undeniably true. If when he defends economic determinism he assumes that the cogency of his arguments is not affected by his economic background, doesn't he thereby deny the truth of his theory in the very act of asserting it?

In fact, the influence of Marx's ideas in the twentieth century illustrates the independent power of ideas in shaping history. Belief in the ideology of socialism has been the prime cause for the success of socialist systems, and loss of belief in the ideology has been the prime cause for their collapse.[6]

But perhaps we have placed too much emphasis on the deterministic element of Marx's thinking. For Marx insists that human beings can change the material conditions of life:

> The materialist doctrine that men are products of circumstances and upbringing, and that, therefore, changed men are products of other circumstances and changed upbringing, forgets that it is men who change circumstances. (144)

An economic system shapes the lives of all those people who live under its influence, but because any economic system is a product of human action, human beings can change it. Human beings are molded by the institutions that they themselves have created.

Engels argued that although Marx thought the economic element of life was "the *ultimately* determining element in history," he did not think it was "the *only* determining one" (760). Legal, political, philosophic, and even religious ideas influence the course of history in important ways, Engels explained, and therefore history arises from a complex "interaction" of factors in which the economic factor is "ultimately decisive."

This would explain the flexibility of Marx's political strategy. Rather than simply waiting for capitalist economic oppression to bring about an international revolution leading inevitably to communism, Marx supported various political reforms designed for particular circumstances. In some cases, he argued for an alliance between workers and peasants. In other cases, he endorsed the political goals of the union movement such as laws to shorten the work day and to give workers the right to vote. In a preface to the German edition of the *Manifesto* of 1872, Marx explained that although "the general principles" of the *Manifesto* are always true, "the practical application of the principles" must vary according to "the historical conditions for the time being existing" (470).

Marx's critics, however, would say that this only states the problem without solving it. For isn't there a contradiction between asserting, on the one hand, the absolute truth of Marx's general theory and asserting, on the other hand, the need to change the practical strategy of Marxism with every change in the circumstances?

One illustration of this difficulty concerns the improvement of living conditions for workers. In the *Manifesto*, Marx claims that the workers will revolt when their oppression under capitalism becomes unbearable. But now that the workers have won shorter working hours, higher pay, the right to vote, and other reforms supported by Marx, they no longer feel oppressed. As a result, the proletarian revolution as predicted by Marx has not occurred anywhere. Does this prove that Marx was wrong? Or does it only show the success of the capitalists in hiding the reality of exploitation?

2. Must capitalists exploit their workers?

In every society, Marx believes, there is a ruling class composed of people who do not work, who therefore must live by exploiting those who do work. In a capitalist society, the capitalist ruling class lives off the property acquired by paying workers less than what they have earned. Under this arrangement, Marx explains in the *Manifesto*, "the laborer lives merely to increase capital, and is allowed to live only in so far as the interest of the ruling class requires it" (485).[7]

If we agree that labor is the only or at least the primary source of value — as was assumed by Locke and the classical economists such as Adam Smith and David Ricardo — then it is hard to avoid the conclusion that the wealth of the capitalist, who does no actual labor, depends on the exploitation of hired laborers. We have noted this as a weakness in Locke's argument. One passage in the *Second Treatise* should come to mind: "Thus the grass my horse has bit; the turfs my servant has cut; and the ore I have digged in any place, where I have a right to them in common with others, become my *property*" (section 28). If people are entitled to all the products of their labor, then why should I profit from the labor of "my servant," whom I treat like "my horse"?

Marx insists that capitalists must always exploit their workers because capitalism depends on what Marx calls "surplus value" (351–61). For the capitalist to make a profit, the value of the wages the laborers are paid must be less than the value of the output of their labor. Laborers must therefore always receive less than they have earned. If the laborers in a factory must work six hours a day to produce goods equivalent in value to a day's wage, the factory owner might force them to work eight hours a day so that he can draw his profit from their two hours of unpaid labor.

Couldn't workers go on strike and refuse to work until they are paid wages equal to the full value of their work? Marx thinks this unlikely because of their weak bargaining position and their fear of unemployment. Marx would emphasize that a capitalist employer could not pay the workers for all their labor without thereby losing the margin of profit.

A critic of Marx could argue, however, that the strength of the union movement today eliminates this sort of exploitation. A Marxist could deny this by pointing to the situation in the United States today. Employers use the threat of unemployment to force workers to lower their wage demands. American companies exploit the nonunion, cheap labor available in some parts of the United States or in foreign countries. And when there is a concern about inflation, the government creates unemployment so that the competition for jobs lowers wages. In a capitalist economy like that of the United States, workers can have jobs only if they agree to be exploited.

This Marxist assessment of capitalism depends, however, on assuming that labor is the only source of value. Many economists have criticized this element of Marx's teaching. Even most Marxist economists reject Marx's labor theory of value.[8] One example of the weaknesses in Marx's theory is his claim that different *kinds* of labor can be explained as different *quantities* of simple, homogeneous labor. "Skilled labor counts only as simple labor intensified" (310). If an architect is paid ten times as much per hour as a carpenter, does that mean that the architect's labor is ten times as *intense* as the carpenter's?

Marx also has trouble explaining increases in labor's productivity owing to machinery. Machines allow workers to produce more with less labor (306). The capitalist would argue that one way to increase profits is to invest in labor-saving tools. Far from exploiting workers, an entrepreneur who improves the productivity of labor can increase the profits earned while giving the workers higher wages, better working conditions, and a shorter workday.

But Marx would respond by saying that machinery itself is a product of labor as exploited by the capitalists. He would also argue that automation allows employers to replace workers with machines when the workers demand good wages. Moreover, this leads to another form of exploitation — workers are forced into jobs that are monotonous and degrading.

3. Does capitalism prevent workers from finding joy in their work?

As is evident in the *Manifesto*, this is an important part of Marx's criticism of capitalism:

> Owing to the extensive use of machinery and to division of labor,
> the work of the proletarians has lost all individual character, and
> consequently, all charm for the workman. He becomes an
> appendage of the machine, and it is only the most simple, most
> monotonous, and most easily acquired knack, that is required
> of him. (479)

Capitalism turns work into joyless toil, and thus it degrades the
workers by making them lifeless tools of production. Underlying
this assessment, however, is Marx's assumption that work can be —
and should be — pleasurable for the worker. We must wonder,
therefore, about Marx's understanding of work.

Insofar as work is necessary to provide for their physical needs,
human beings do not differ from other animals. But human beings
separate themselves from other animals, Marx argues, in pursuing
work as creative, self-expressive activity. Other animals labor by
instinct, but human beings labor freely and purposefully as rational
beings. Human labor is thought realized in action. Bees can
construct hives with great architectural beauty, Marx observes, but
what distinguishes the human architect from any bee is that the
architect "raises his structure in imagination before he erects it in
reality" (344).[9]

Through labor an individual conquers nature by imposing upon
it rational purposes, and thus "develops his slumbering powers and
compels them to act in obedience to his sway" (344). Every person
should enjoy work "as something which gives play to his bodily
and mental powers" (345). In labor, each should also express his
or her human essence as a social being. Through labor each person
cooperates with other human beings for common purposes, and
thus finds an identity in being recognized by others (75–76).

And yet, in a capitalist state, most people cannot see their labor
as an expression of their humanity. They experience their work as
something to be endured rather than enjoyed. They run home at
the end of each workday desperately seeking some satisfaction in
their leisure activities. Because their work fails to nurture their
capacity for social involvement, they withdraw into the narrow
circles of their private lives where they devote themselves to the
most petty diversions.[10]

At this point, staunch defenders of capitalism would dispute
Marx's claims. Hasn't capitalism made workers comfortable and
secure in their work? Rather than being forced to accept low wages
that provide only for the barest necessities of life, most workers
today can afford luxuries that previously have been available only
to the rich. They also have plenty of leisure time to freely pursue
their own interests. At the same time, the social and economic

programs of the modern welfare state protect workers from various social ills. Government helps the unemployed, the disabled, and the elderly. Government even regulates the workplace to prohibit unsafe working conditions. These and many other political measures combined with the general prosperity of the capitalist economies have eliminated the traditional conflict between the few rich and the many poor because, in capitalist nations like the United States, most people belong to the middle class, which owns most of the wealth.

Marx admitted that during periods of economic expansion, capitalists would be able to pay higher wages and increase their profits at the same time. He argued, though, that this would not eliminate the exploitative features of capitalism.

> If capital is growing rapidly, wages may rise; the profit of capital rises incomparably more rapidly. The material position of the worker has improved, but at the cost of his social position. The social gulf that divides him from the capitalist has widened. (211)

Higher wages "would therefore be nothing but *better payment for the slave*, and would not conquer either for the worker or for labor their human status and dignity" (80).

Even if many modern workers do not suffer from the poverty of *physical* deprivation, they do suffer from the poverty of *social* deprivation. Although the workers may benefit from high incomes, they still occupy an inferior position in society as long as most of the wealth is controlled by a small economic elite. Marx warned that the capitalists would be willing to bribe their workers in various ways to break their revolutionary spirit and thus protect the power of the ruling class (504–5).

Does the United States have a capitalist ruling class? Michael Parenti, a Marxist political scientist, provides evidence that this is the case:

> About one-fifth of one percent of the population, the "super rich," own almost 60 percent of the corporate wealth in this country. Approximately 1.6 percent of the population own 80 percent of all stock, 100 percent of all state and municipal bonds and 88.5 percent of corporate bonds. . . . In just about every major industry, be it steel, oil, aluminum or automotive, a few giant companies do from 60 to 98 percent of the business. Some two hundred companies account for about 80 percent of all resources used in manufacturing. . . . The wealth of America is not owned by a broadly based middle class. If anything, the trend toward ever greater concentrations of economic power is increasing.[11]

How can such inequality of power be reconciled with the human equality proclaimed by the Declaration of Independence?

One response from those who champion American capitalism would be to challenge Parenti's use of statistics and to deny that the inequality is as great as he indicates.[12] At a deeper level, however, the issue concerns not just the *quantitative* measurement of inequality of wealth but the *qualitative* evaluation of work in a capitalist society. The Marxist would criticize capitalism for degrading workers by forcing them into jobs that require only the "most easily acquired knack." But are those perhaps exactly the sort of jobs that many workers prefer? Some workers seem to want a job that doesn't demand much from them, because this leaves them free to devote their time and attention to things other than work. Those who want to commit themselves fully to their work are free to look for jobs that satisfy them. Many people prefer low-paying jobs that are personally satisfying to high-paying jobs that are monotonous. Thus it might seem that capitalism leaves the worker free to choose his work.

Marx would dismiss this as nonsense. Within the capitalist system, the freedom of the worker must always be illusory, because the workers' choices are always constrained by the capitalist's need to exploit labor for profit. True freedom for the worker—and for all human beings—can be achieved only through a socialist revolution.

4. Would socialism emancipate human beings?

In the *Communist Manifesto*, Marx presents socialist society as the first truly free society:

> In place of the old bourgeois society, with its classes and class antagonisms, we shall have an association, in which the free development of each is the condition for the free development of all. (491)

A society without class conflict will permit all people to freely develop their human powers. They will do so in such a way that the freedom of each secures the freedom of all. In expressing their individuality, human beings will also express their sociality.

But this gives us only a vague idea of what socialist freedom would be like. As a general formulation, we could say that for Marx, human freedom is the self-actualization or self-determination of humans as conscious, rational beings. (This corresponds closely to Hegel's idea of freedom.) Complete emancipation requires that human beings consciously develop their human powers by exercising rational control over both the natural and the social conditions of life. When we look, however, for a more concrete account of freedom under socialism, Marx suggests the possibility of two different kinds of freedom: the social freedom of self-expressive social labor and the political freedom of self-governing democratic citizenship.

The prerequisite for both forms of freedom is the abolition of private property. Socialism would not abolish the right to maintain personally acquired property used for individual consumption. Even in a socialist society, workers would have personal property (484–85, 490–91). But land and the means of production would be owned in common and used for the benefit of all (326–27, 438). Factory workers, for example, would not have to sell their labor to the factory owner. Instead, they would manage the factory themselves as a cooperative enterprise. Rather than working for an employer, the workers would work for themselves, which would transform their labor into self-expressive activity. "Hired labor is but a transitory and inferior form, destined to disappear before associated labor plying its toil with a willing hand, a ready mind, and a joyous heart" (518).

Marx paints an even more romantic picture of socialist freedom in *The German Ideology*:

> As soon as the distribution of labor comes into being, each man has a particular, exclusive sphere of activity, which is forced upon him and from which he cannot escape. He is a hunter, a fisherman, a shepherd, or a critical critic, and must remain so if he does not want to lose his means of livelihood; while in communist society, where nobody has one exclusive sphere of activity but each can become accomplished in any branch he wishes, society regulates the general production and thus makes it possible for me to do one thing today and another tomorrow, to hunt in the morning, fish in the afternoon, rear cattle in the evening, criticize after dinner, just as I have a mind, without ever becoming hunter, fisherman, shepherd or critic. (160)

Thoreau lived like this at Walden Pond, so did Robinson Crusoe, and — except for the literary criticism — so did Rousseau's savage.[13] But is this a realistic vision for a socialist society?

Marx says, "each can become accomplished in any branch he wishes." How can a person become accomplished in some activity without complete devotion to it to the exclusion of other activities? We might also wonder how this could be done in a modern industrialized, technological society that requires a specialized division of labor. The activities of hunting, fishing, and rearing cattle suggest a simple, pastoral existence, but Marx often implies that socialism would build upon the technological advances of capitalism (476–78).

If all the people of a socialist society are free to do as they please, will every person creatively develop all innate talents? Won't many people prefer idleness and self-indulgence?

And what is meant by the remark that "society regulates the general production" for the freedom of all? Who are the regulators? Must all the people participate in the regulatory decisions? If so, won't this interfere with their freedom to do what they please when they please?

Finally, we should note that three of the four activities of Marx's ideal socialists are directed to procuring food. The socialist waits until after dinner to study literary criticism. How can hunting, fishing, and rearing cattle be fully expressive of freedom if they are imposed by the bodily necessities of life? Marx indicates in *Capital* that even in socialist society, labor is not liberating as long as it is imposed on the laborer to satisfy physical needs.

> The realm of freedom actually begins only where labor which is determined by necessity and mundane considerations ceases; thus in the very nature of things it lies beyond the sphere of actual material production. . . . Freedom in this field can only consist in socialized man, the associated producers, rationally regulating their interchange with Nature, bringing it under their common control, instead of being ruled by it as by the blind forces of Nature; and achieving this with the least expenditure of energy and under conditions most favorable to, and worthy of, their human nature. But it nonetheless still remains a realm of necessity. Beyond it begins that development of human energy which is an end in itself, the true realm of freedom, which, however, can blossom forth only with the realm of necessity as its basis. The shortening of the working day is its basic prerequisite. (441)

This passage lends itself to various interpretations. One would be that Marx relies on the continuing expansion of labor-saving technology in socialist society to give everyone free time for "that development of human energy which is an end in itself" (406). But the realm of physically necessary labor can never be abolished completely. At the very least, people will have to produce, operate, and repair the machines.

Marx is ambivalent about whether labor can become a humanizing activity in a socialist society. At times, he argues that under socialism the productive process would be organized in such a way that labor would become a humanly self-expressive activity. At other times, he agrees with Adam Smith that the division of labor demanded by technical efficiency must be morally degrading because of the monotony of narrowly specialized tasks, and therefore moral freedom is found not in labor but in leisure. Insofar as he agrees with Smith, Marx assumes that the *technical* division of labor dictates the *social* division of labor. But such technological determinism is dubious. The technical division of labor into separate tasks does not necessarily require a social division of labor in which each worker performs only one task. Through batch production, one worker might perform different tasks at different times; and this may be more efficient than restricting a worker to one task. Neither Smith nor Marx recognizes that the monotony of narrowly specialized labor may lower the morale of workers in ways that lower their productivity.[14]

Marx's assumption that technically efficient labor must be degrading leads him to hope that automation will allow workers to escape from labor and thus fulfill their humanity in leisurely activities. This confidence in the liberating effects of technology as a tool for conquering nature should remind us of Descartes's recommendations at the end of the *Discourse on Method*. Some of the objections to Descartes's project might apply also to Marx's. It is unclear, for instance, how Marx would protect socialist society against the establishment of a technically trained elite as the new ruling class.

Marx, of course, would argue that there will be no ruling class in a socialist society because there will be no political rule at all. The revolutionary proletarians must abolish the state (200, 490–91). Who, then, should rule? This has been one of the central questions throughout the history of political philosophy. But Marx answers, *no one* should rule over anyone else. Once socialism creates a classless society — or perhaps we should say a society with only one class to which all human beings belong simply by virtue of their humanity — politics as such, which means the rule of some over others, will disappear.

Isn't it implausible, however, that any society — even a socialist one — could escape fundamental conflicts of interest among various groups? Wouldn't a government be necessary to settle such conflicts?

Another difficulty is that this idea of abolishing the state contradicts Marx's suggestions that a socialist society would promote freedom through democratic citizenship. Marx rejects the modern assumption that human beings are by nature asocial individuals, and he reaffirms the Aristotelian view that human beings are naturally *political*—or at least *social*—animals.[15] The "human essence" emerges not as an isolated individual but as "the ensemble of the social relations" (145).

> The human being is in the most literal sense a *zoon politikon* [political animal], not merely a gregarious animal, but an animal which can individuate itself only in the midst of society. Production by an isolated individual outside society—a rare exception which may well occur when a civilized person in whom the social forces are already dynamically present is cast by accident into the wilderness—is as much of an absurdity as is the development of language without individuals living *together* and talking to each other. (223)

Therefore, true freedom demands that all *individuals* become *citizens*. "Human emancipation will only be complete when the real, individual man has absorbed into himself the abstract citizen" (46).

In much of his writing, however, Marx implies that socialist citizens will fulfill their social essence in social labor rather than political participation. "Man first sees and recognizes himself in other men," Marx believes. "Peter only establishes his own identity as a man by first comparing himself with Paul as being of like kind" (317). Marx indicates that under socialism, economic production would be organized to satisfy this need for mutual recognition.

> Let us suppose that we had produced as human beings. In that event each of us would have *doubly affirmed* himself and his neighbor in his production. . . . In the individual expression of my own life I would have brought about the immediate expression of your life, and so in my individual activity I would have directly *confirmed* and *realized* my authentic nature, my *human, communal* nature.
>
> Our productions would be as many mirrors from which our natures would shine forth.[16]

If socialist individuals recognize one another as fellow workers, is it unnecessary then to seek recognition as fellow citizens? Although political power as "the organized power of one class for oppressing another" must disappear in socialist society, would a classless society create a truly democratic form of political power in which the state would not be distinguished from the people? Marx suggests this when he explains that "in true democracy the *political state is annihilated*" because "the political state *qua* political state, as constitution, no longer passes for the whole." "In democracy the constitution, the law, the state itself, insofar as it is a political constitution, is only the self-determination of the people, and a particular content of the people" (21).

Although such comments give us only a vague picture of socialist society, what we see entices us. Nevertheless, we must wonder whether such a society is practicable. In particular, we must ask about the problems in organizing a socialist economy.

5. Would a socialist economy work?

This question presses upon us as soon as we notice in the *Communist Manifesto* that Marx wants to abolish buying and selling (486). Capitalism deprives human beings of their dignity by grounding all human relationships on money (101–5). A socialist society, therefore, would have to abolish money. Economic life would be organized without a system of market prices. Although Marx is not completely clear on this point, presumably the production and distribution of goods in a socialist economy would be determined by a central plan (529–32).

Capitalist economists—like Ludwig von Mises—have argued that if socialism requires the abolition of money, then a socialist economy is impossible.[17] When Lenin attempted to establish pure socialism by abolishing money in the Soviet Union from 1918 to 1921, the disastrous consequences forced him to restore limited markets under the "New Economic Policy" in 1921.[18] Without the pricing mechanism of the marketplace, socialist planners cannot allocate resources rationally because they have no basis for economic calculation.

As a simple illustration of the problem, imagine having to choose between two ways of manufacturing the same product. One way requires ten tons of wool and fifteen tons of cotton, the other fifteen tons of wool and ten tons of cotton. Deciding which is more efficient demands a common unit of measurement between wool and cotton. In a capitalist economy, prices provide such measurement. If wool is twice as expensive as cotton, then the more efficient process of production would be the one that uses less wool and more cotton. The prices tell us that wool is valued more highly than cotton. In this way, market prices help us to make rational economic decisions.

A pricing system is superior to socialist planning, Mises maintains, because prices are spontaneous signals, because they simplify the pertinent information, and because they measure subjective needs. Prices arise from unplanned patterns of interaction, and they change quickly as the patterns change. A socialist planner, however, would have to work everything out through conscious design. Therefore, the planner would have to have absolute knowledge of all the relevant information. Instead of simply watching the fluctuating prices of wool and cotton, the planner would have to know—hour by hour, day by day—everything that might affect the relative values of cotton and wool. But how would anyone know the value of anything insofar as "value" reflects subjective human preferences? Prices register those preferences automatically.

Aside from Mises's logic, the persuasiveness of his argument has been enhanced by the failure of socialist governments to organize their economies without market prices. Many socialist economists have tried to solve the problem by arguing for market socialism—that is, some combination of central planning and a pricing system.[19] It is debatable whether this answers Mises's objections.[20] Beyond the purely economic issues, some socialists fear that market socialism is only capitalism in disguise.

Another weakness in a socialist economy is the lack of material incentives to work. The motto for a Marxist economy must be: "From each according to his ability, to each according to his needs!" (531). But if people know that what they *receive* will not be proportionate to what they *contribute*, won't they be tempted to become free riders with no motivation to work? Why would people work hard if it doesn't increase their wealth? In fact, socialist governments have been forced to allow some capitalist economic incentives to avoid economic catastrophes.

There have been some intriguing socialist experiments—in Cuba and China—designed to replace *material* incentives with *moral* incentives. The idea is to devise programs of social education to teach people that they have a social duty to work hard and that they should value the social recognition they receive for performing their social duty. The experiments have not been very successful, but that may be because they have not gone far enough.[21]

If human beings are social creatures, if they desire the approval of others, and if they tend to adopt the values instilled in them by their culture, then it would seem possible to educate them—particularly during their childhood—to work for social rewards rather than material rewards.[22] Indeed, there is evidence that even the capitalist spirit of individual acquisitiveness arose as a product of social conditioning. Adam Smith suggested this when he observed that the selfish desire for accumulating wealth reflects the social desire for the recognition of others. "The rich man glories in his riches, because he feels that they naturally draw upon him the attention of the world."[23] This man was probably taught from birth that great wealth confers high social status. Would he have turned out differently if he had been educated to believe that only those who fulfill their duties as socialist citizens win "the attention of the world"?

But if socialist citizens must be socially conditioned to think more about their social duties than their individual interests, a socialist society begins to look like a totalitarian regime that uses indoctrination and terror to stifle individual liberty. This certainly was the case under the rule of Josef Stalin.

6. Can we have Marx without Stalin?

To reject Marx because Stalin was a Marxist would be as unjustified as rejecting Christianity because the Spanish Inquisition was led by Christians. On the other hand, it would also be unreasonable to maintain that there was no connection at all between Marx and Stalin. Irving Howe, a prominent socialist writer, confesses that Stalinism "forced thoughtful socialists to reconsider the terms of their conviction."[24]

Both Lenin and Stalin justified their despotic rule as an exercise in what Marx called the dictatorship of the proletariat, which was supposed to be the transitional period between capitalism and communism (220, 538). Howe speaks of the dictatorship of the proletariat as an "uncomfortable legacy from Marx," and he notes that Marx never used that phrase in any of his major writings.[25] But even when he does not use those exact words, Marx does not hesitate to stress—in the *Manifesto*—the need for "despotic inroads on the rights of property, and on the conditions of bourgeois production" (490). Marx also insisted that the *idea* of socialism cannot be separated from its *history*, and so it would seem odd to free Marx from any responsibility for the history of Marxist regimes.

Is there a flaw in Marx's teaching that could account for the horrors of Stalinism? Some commentators have pointed to Marx's millenarianism as the crux of the problem. Marx speaks easily of communist society as the final redemption of humankind from the conflicts that have plagued all previous history: "Communism is the riddle of history solved" (84). Thus, Marx secularizes the Christian vision of salvational history (refer also to chapter 3, section 3; chapter 10, section 1). Despite its atheism, Marxism can stir in its followers all the fervor of religious zealotry. And this fanatical devotion to the redemptive transformation of human nature can easily create a messianic Machiavellianism. If the inevitable end of the Communist Revolution is the earthly salvation of the human race, then *any means is justified to that end*.

The redemptive expectations of Marxism are well illustrated by

Leon Trotsky's description of what man will look like in communist society:

> Man will become immeasurably stronger, wiser and subtler; his body will become more harmonized, his movements more rhythmic, his voice more musical. The forms of life will become dynamically dramatic. The average human type will rise to the heights of an Aristotle, a Goethe, or a Marx. And above this ridge new peaks will rise.[26]

Revolutionary leaders who take this as their goal find it hard to compromise with anyone or anything that stands in their way. If this is the inevitable outcome of the Communist Revolution, then for the sake of the Revolution *everything* is permitted.

Unfortunately, Stalin is only one of many revolutionaries who have applied this sort of logic. In the early 1970s, the communist rulers in Cambodia caused the deaths of millions of their people. One observer explained:

> Their inflexible ideology has led them to invent a radically new kind of man in a radically new society. A fascinating revolution for all who aspire to a new social order. A terrifying one for all who have any respect for human beings.[27]

Albert Camus suggested that to escape this revolutionary nihilism, we must restore a spirit of moderation founded on the recognition that human nature imposes limits on political action. When human beings strive to become gods, they become monsters. There is only one way to avoid this: "Each tells the other that he is not God."[28]

Many socialists, shocked by the brutal tyranny of Stalinist regimes, maintain that this is not the inevitable consequence of Marxism, that Marxist socialism can be, and should be, democratic.

7. Can socialism be democratic?

If not, Marx would suggest, then democracy itself is doomed, because only through socialism can we achieve a true democracy (20–21, 46, 326–27, 518, 623–29, 631–43, 647–52). Only in a classless society, where all people become workers and where the means of production are socially owned, can all participate equally in making the decisions that shape their lives. Only socialism allows us to have "an association, in which the free development of each is the condition for the free development of all" (491).

To defend this position, however, a socialist must answer the argument—perhaps best stated by Friedrich von Hayek in *The*

Road to Serfdom[29] — that a centrally planned economy must necessarily suppress individual freedom. Through the free market, the preferences of millions of individuals can be coordinated in a rational manner without authoritarian coercion. Employers and employees are free to negotiate mutually acceptable arrangements. Buyers and sellers are free to bargain with one another over prices. In this manner, the impersonal mechanism of the market organizes economic life without the coercive domination of some by others. Although the rich start out with more advantages than the poor, at least the poor have more freedom to advance in a market society than in a society where a ruling elite controls the economy.

Even some socialists — such as Robert Heilbroner — have acknowledged the force of this argument that socialism cannot be democratic.[30] The capitalist market mechanism relies on individuals pursuing their personal gain in competition with one another. But a socialist economy must force individuals to obey a central plan. Capitalism stresses individual freedom, while socialism stresses collective solidarity. It is hard to see how bourgeois individualism could be combined with socialist collectivism. Consequently, socialists like Heilbroner must admit with regret that they cannot have "a socialist cake with bourgeois icing," and therefore "socialism cannot be the best of all worlds."[31]

The example of Yugoslavia in the 1950s and 1960s was often cited by some socialists as evidence for the possibility of a democratic form of socialism.[32] Rejecting the authoritarian socialism of the Soviet Union, Yugoslavian socialists tried to create a truly democratic regime based on economic self-management and political self-government. In the Soviet Union, management of the means of production was transferred from private owners to the centralized bureaucracy of the state. But in Yugoslavia, the means of production were treated as social property managed by the workers themselves. Although there was some central planning by the state, Yugoslavia seemed to have a system of market socialism in which self-managed enterprises competed within the framework of a market economy.

In Yugoslavia, most firms were required by law to be managed by a workers' council. The members of the workers' council were elected every two years by their fellow workers. The number of members varied from fifteen to 120, depending on the size of the firm. Restrictions on the number of times a member could be reelected were designed to encourage wide participation. The workers' council met once a month to make the basic decisions for the firm — hiring and firing, production, distribution of wages and profits, and prices. Also, the council elected a management board with five to eleven members serving one-year terms. The management board met weekly to execute the decisions of the workers' council. None of these representatives were paid, and they continued as workers during their periods of service on the council or the board. Finally, the management board hired a full-time, paid director to handle the daily management of the firm in conformity with the policies set by the workers' representatives.

During the first ten years of this system (1953–1963), Yugoslavia had annual growth rates of over 9 percent, making it one of the fastest growing economies in the world. But subsequently there were high levels of unemployment and inflation. The defenders of the system argued such problems could have been avoided by making some minor changes.

Some critics, however, doubted that Yugoslavian socialism was truly democratic. Yugoslavia was a one-party state that engaged in authoritarian repression. Even within the self-managed enterprises, there was some evidence of a subtle form of authoritarianism. Upper-class men tended to be the most active participants in the workers' councils. Women and men from lower-class backgrounds were less inclined to participate. Ordinary workers were sometimes reluctant to assume the burdens of managerial responsibility; they sometimes preferred to be led by the well-educated, skilled workers or even the professional director and the director's staff. And yet, it seemed that Yugoslavia had been more successful than the capitalist countries in allowing workers to participate in management.

Another objection to the Yugoslavian experiment in socialism is that it was not really socialism at all. For insofar as they relied on a market economy, the Yugoslavian socialists seemed to concede Hayek's argument that socialist planning without free markets cannot be democratic. Some socialists thought that Yugoslavia betrayed the socialist cause.

But Yugoslavia provided inspiration for those democratic socialists who wished to combine a market economy with a socialist culture. Some American socialists have argued for simply extending the welfare-state measures initiated by Franklin Roosevelt, the aim being to moderate the excessive individualism of bourgeois society with an increasing sense of communal unity. Irving Howe, for example, speaks of "the lasting contribution of the Roosevelt era — *the socialization of concern*, the vision of society as a community, not based as yet on truly egalitarian principles but at least modulating the heartlessness of 'rugged individualism'."[33] Socialists like Michael Walzer emphasize the need to draw people into public life by giving them more opportunities for democratic participation.[34] Would this fulfill Marx's vision of human emancipation? Or would it simply continue our quest for a community in which all human beings are equally entitled to "Life, Liberty, and the pursuit of Happiness"?

Many of the critics of Marxism have become smug in asserting that the collapse of the Soviet Union and other socialist regimes proved that Marxism must fail. Mises would argue, however, that this kind of reasoning from "the lessons of history" is fallacious. "Historical facts and historical experience can never prove or disprove a statement in the way in which an experiment proves or disproves."[35] History is not a laboratory in which we can control all the relevant variables to determine causal relations. For that reason, the socialist can always argue that the Soviet experience was not a good test of socialism because the historical circumstances were not right or because the Soviet system was not truly socialist. Under different conditions, socialism rightly understood might still be possible.

If we cannot resolve the debate between socialism and liberalism by appealing to historical experience, we have no choice but to appeal to philosophical argument. Which position is the more persuasive? We have considered Marx's arguments for socialism, and we have considered some of the early arguments for liberalism by those such as Locke. But for a contemporary statement of liberal reasoning, we will turn to John Rawls.

Notes

1. Ludwig von Mises, *Socialism*, trans. J. Kahane (Indianapolis: Liberty Classics, 1981).
2. See, for example, the articles on "The Road Back from Serfdom: A Tribute to Friedrich A. Hayek" published in *The American Economic Review* 82 (May 1992): 1–36. See also János Kornai, *The Socialist System: The Political Economy of Communism* (Princeton: Princeton University Press, 1992), especially chaps. 1–4, 15, 24.
3. Kornai argues that any attempt to do this creates self-destructive contradictions in which neither markets nor planning can work well. For the opposing point of view, see Michael Harrington, "Markets and Plans: Is the Market Necessarily Capitalist?" *Dissent* 36 (Winter 1989): 56–70.
4. All of these texts can be found in Robert C. Tucker, ed., *The Marx-Engels Reader*, 2nd ed. (New York: Norton, 1978). All page references in the text are to *The Marx-Engels Reader*. For a comprehensive history of Marxist theory, see Leszek Kolakowski, *Main Currents of Marxism*, 3 vols. (Oxford: Oxford University Press, 1978). For a history of the

Russian Revolution, see Bertram D. Wolfe, *Three Who Made a Revolution* (New York: Stein & Day, 1984). See also, as a useful reference work, Tom Bottomore, ed., *A Dictionary of Marxist Thought* (Cambridge: Harvard University Press, 1983).

5. See Karl Mannheim, *Ideology and Utopia* (New York: Harcourt, Brace & World, Harvest Books, n.d.), 1–13, 124–64; Clifford Geertz, *The Interpretation of Cultures* (New York: Basic Books, 1973), 193–233; and Paul Ricoeur, *Hermeneutics and the Human Sciences* (Cambridge: Cambridge University Press, 1981). Marx often seems to assume that all moral and political arguments are merely rationalizations of economic interests. But do his own arguments condemning capitalism appeal implicitly to some standard of justice? On Marx as a moral relativist, see Allen W. Wood, "The Marxian Critique of Justice," *Philosophy & Public Affairs* 1 (Spring 1972): 244–82. On Marx as affirming the moral value of freedom, see George G. Brenkert, "Freedom and Private Property in Marx," *Philosophy & Public Affairs* 8 (Winter 1979): 122–47. For the argument that Marx and Aristotle share a common moral framework in their adherence to moral realism, see Alan Gilbert, "Marx's Moral Realism: Eudaimonism and Moral Progress," in Terence Ball and James Farr, eds., *After Marx* (Cambridge: Cambridge University Press, 1984), 154–83; and Gilbert, *Democratic Individuality* (Cambridge: Cambridge University Press, 1990). Compare Harvey C. Mansfield, Jr., "Marx on Aristotle: Freedom, Politics and Money," *Review of Metaphysics* 34 (December 1980): 351–67. For the debate over whether Marx was a technological determinist, see G. A. Cohen, *Karl Marx's Theory of History: A Defence* (Princeton: Princeton University Press, 1978); and Richard W. Miller, "Producing Change: Work, Technology, and Power in Marx's Theory of History," in Ball and Farr, *After Marx*, 59–87.

6. See Kornai, *The Socialist System*, chaps. 4, 15.

7. On the debate among historians as to whether early capitalism exploited or benefited the working class, see E. P. Thompson, *The Making of the English Working Class* (New York: Random House, Vintage, 1966), 189–212.

8. See Eugene von Böhm-Bawerk, *Capital and Interest*, trans. George D. Huncke and Hans F. Sennholz (South Holland, IL: Libertarian Press, 1959), 290–307. Compare Joan Robinson, *An Essay on Marxian Economics* (New York: St. Martin's Press, 1942); and Ronald Meek, *Studies in the Labour Theory of Value* (London: Lawrence and Wishart, 1973). For a sympathetic interpretation of Marx as a theoretical economist, see Robert Paul Wolff, *Understanding Marx: A Reconstruction and Critique of "Capital"* (Princeton: Princeton University Press, 1984).

9. In distinguishing human work as guided by conceptual thought from the work of other animals, Marx shows the influence of Aristotle's biology. Modern evolutionary biology confirms this distinction. See Harry Braverman, *Labor and Monopoly Capital: The Degradation of*

Work in the Twentieth Century (New York: Monthly Review Press, 1974), chap. 1.

10. See Studs Terkel, *Working* (New York: Pantheon, 1974); and Paul L. Wachtel, *The Poverty of Affluence: A Psychological Portrait of the American Way of Life* (New York: Free Press, 1983).

11. Michael Parenti, *Democracy for the Few*, 3rd ed. (New York: St. Martin's Press, 1980), 8–9.

12. See Irving Kristol, *Two Cheers for Capitalism* (New York: Basic Books, 1978), 194–225.

13. See Staughton Lynd, *Intellectual Origins of American Radicalism* (Cambridge: Harvard University Press, 1982), 92–96; and Jean-Jacques Rousseau, *The First and Second Discourses*, ed. Roger D. Masters, trans. Roger D. Masters and Judith R. Masters (New York: St. Martin's Press, 1964), 223–24.

14. See Adam Smith, *The Wealth of Nations* (New York: The Modern Library, 1937), bk. 1, chaps. 1–2; bk. 5, chap. 1, art. 2. See also Harry Braverman, *Labor and Monopoly Capital*; and James Bernard Murphy, *The Moral Economy of Labor: Aristotelian Themes in Economic Theory* (New Haven: Yale University Press, 1993). Braverman and Murphy develop the Aristotelian idea that work as a humanizing activity is the unity of conception and execution: "a worker first constructs in thought what he then embodies in matter." They argue that the modern assumption that there must generally be a separation of conception and execution in the division of labor, so that what is conceived by one person is executed by another, rests on a theoretically mistaken and morally impoverished understanding of productive labor.

15. Karl Marx, *Capital*, 3 vols. (New York: International Publishers, 1967), 1: 326.

16. Karl Marx, *Early Writings*, trans. Rodney Livingstone and Gregor Benton (New York: Random House, Vintage, 1975), 277–78.

17. Mises, *Socialism*, chaps. 5–6; and Mises, *Bureaucracy* (New Haven: Yale University Press, 1944), 20–56.

18. See Peter J. Boettke, *The Political Economy of Soviet Socialism: The Formative Years, 1918–1928* (Boston: Kluwer Academic Publishers, 1990).

19. See Oskar Lange and Fred M. Taylor, *On the Economic Theory of Socialism* (New York: McGraw-Hill, 1964); David Miller, *Market, State and Community: Theoretical Foundations of Market Socialism* (Oxford: Clarendon Press, 1990); and Alec Nove, *The Economics of Feasible Socialism* (Winchester, MA: Allen & Unwin, 1983).

20. See Don Lavoie, *Rivalry and Central Planning: The Socialist Calculation Debate Reconsidered* (New York: Cambridge University Press, 1985); Lavoie, *National Economic Planning: What Is Left?* (Cambridge, MA: Ballinger, 1985); and Kornai, *The Socialist System*, chap. 21.

21. See Charles E. Lindblom, *Politics and Markets* (New York: Basic Books, 1977), 276–90. Since the death of Mao Zedong in 1976, Chinese leaders

have reversed his policies by providing material incentives to stir economic productivity. Does this illustrate the failure of socialism to secure economic prosperity? Or does it rather show the need to define socialism broadly enough so that it can include some reliance on market incentives? See, on the new materialism in China, Brantly Womack, "Modernization and Democratic Reform in China," *Journal of Asian Studies* 44 (May 1984): 417–39. In *A Pattern for Failure: Socialist Economies in Crisis* (New York: Harcourt Brace Jovanovich, 1984), Sven Rydenfelt, a Swedish economist, surveys fifteen socialist countries and argues that they all fail to provide people the incentives necessary for productivity. See also P. T. Bauer, *Equality, the Third World, and Economic Delusion* (Cambridge: Harvard University Press, 1981).

22. See Joseph H. Carens, *Equality, Moral Incentives, and the Market* (Chicago: University of Chicago Press, 1981), 96–138, 164–77. Socialists draw attention to the many manifestations of human altruism. In Great Britain, for example, the sale of blood for transfusion is illegal; all blood comes from voluntary donations. Does this manifest a potentially strong and pervasive human desire to serve the needs of others, a desire that socialism would nurture? Or does it rather show the inclination of a *few* people (about 6 percent of the eligible population in Britain) to make *small* sacrifices for the good of others? See Richard Titmuss, *The Gift Relationship* (New York: Pantheon, 1971); and Kenneth J. Arrow, "Gifts and Exchanges," *Philosophy & Public Affairs* 1 (Summer 1972): 343–62.

23. Adam Smith, *The Theory of Moral Sentiments* (New Rochelle: Arlington House, 1969), 71. See also Karl Polanyi, "Our Obsolete Market Mentality," *Commentary* 3 (February 1947): 109–17; Polanyi, *The Great Transformation* (Boston: Beacon Press, 1957); and Albert O. Hirschman, *The Passions and the Interests* (Princeton: Princeton University Press, 1977).

Is the acquisitive spirit of capitalism a universal feature of human nature that appears in some form in every culture? Or is it an invention of bourgeois culture? See Max Weber, *The Protestant Ethic and the Spirit of Capitalism*, trans. Talcott Parsons (New York: Scribners, 1958); Edward E. LeClair, Jr., and Harold K. Schneider, eds., *Economic Anthropology* (New York: Holt, Rinehart & Winston, 1968); Marshall Sahlins, *Stone Age Economics* (Chicago: Aldine, 1972); and Richard A. Posner, *The Economics of Justice* (Cambridge: Harvard University Press, 1981), 146–206. Refer back to chap. 4, sec. 6.

24. Irving Howe, Introduction to *The Essential Works of Socialism*, ed. Irving Howe (New Haven: Yale University Press, 1976), 15.

25. Ibid., 7–8, 11. For the argument that Engels rather than Marx is responsible for Soviet totalitarianism, see Terence Ball, "Marxian Science and Positivist Politics," in Ball and Farr, *After Marx*, 235–60.

26. Leon Trotsky, *Literature and Revolution* (New York: Russell & Russell, 1957), 256.

27. François Ponchaud, *Cambodia: Year Zero*, trans. Nancy Amphoux (New York: Holt, Rinehart & Winston, 1977), xvi.

28. Albert Camus, *The Rebel* (New York: Random House, Vintage, 1956), 306. See J. L. Talmon, *Political Messianism: The Romantic Phase* (New York: Praeger, 1960).

29. Friedrich von Hayek, *The Road to Serfdom* (Chicago: University of Chicago Press, 1944).

30. See Robert Heilbroner, "What Is Socialism?" *Dissent* (Summer 1978): 341–48; and Heilbroner, *Marxism: For and Against* (New York: Norton, 1980), 150–72.

31. Heilbroner, "What Is Socialism?" 348.

32. For differing assessments of socialist self-management in Yugoslavia and elsewhere, see Lindblom, *Politics and Markets*, 330–43; Mark A. Lutz and Kenneth Lux, *The Challenge of Humanistic Economics* (Menlo Park, CA: Benjamin/Cummings, 1979), 255–61; Branko Horvat, *The Political Economy of Socialism* (Armonk, NY: M. E. Sharpe, 1982); Mihailo Markovic, *Democratic Socialism* (New York: St. Martin's Press, 1982); Kornai, *The Socialist System*, chap. 20; and Rydenfelt, *Pattern for Failure*, 70–74.

For an anthropological study of worker management as "utopian anarchy," see Charles J. Erasmus, *In Search of the Common Good: Utopian Experiments Past and Future* (New York: Free Press, 1985), 282–327. For a defense of "workplace democracy" as combining liberty, equality, and efficiency, see Robert A. Dahl, *A Preface to Economic Democracy* (Berkeley: University of California Press, 1985). See also John Stuart Mill, *Principles of Political Economy*, ed. W. J. Ashley (London: Longmans, 1923), bk. 4, chaps. 6, 7.

33. Irving Howe, "From Roosevelt to Reagan," *Dissent* (Winter 1983): 46. Compare Morton J. Frisch, "Franklin Delano Roosevelt," in Morton J. Frisch and Richard G. Stevens, eds., *American Political Thought: The Philosophic Dimension of American Statesmanship* (Dubuque: Kendall/Hunt, 1976), 219–35; and Theda Skocpol, "The Legacies of New Deal Liberalism," in Douglas MacLean and Claudia Mills, eds., *Liberalism Reconsidered* (Totowa, NJ: Rowman & Allanheld, 1983), 87–104.

Does the expansion of social welfare programs eventually deprive the poor of the incentives to productive work, thus worsening their condition? Did this happen in the United States in the 1960s and 1970s? Or should we rather say that the suffering of the poor in the United States is a consequence of inequitable economic conditions and inadequate welfare policies? See Benjamin Page, *Who Gets What from Government* (Berkeley: University of California Press, 1983); Charles Murray, *Losing Ground: American Social Policy, 1950–1980* (New York: Basic Books, 1984); and Jacqueline Jones, *The Dispossessed: America's Underclass from the Civil War to the Present* (New York: Basic Books, 1992).

34. Michael Walzer, *Radical Principles* (New York: Basic Books, 1980), 23–53, 128–38. For examples of democratic socialism in utopian communities, see John Humphrey Noyes, *History of American Socialisms* (Philadelphia: Lippincott, 1870); and Melford E. Spiro, *Kibbutz: Venture in Utopia* (New York: Schocken Books, 1970).
35. Mises, *Socialism*, 533.

Chapter

12

Equality and Liberty
Rawls's *Theory of Justice*

Key Readings

A Theory of Justice, sections 1–4, 11–17, 20–30, 36–37, 39–40, 43, 46, 48, 65, 67, 75, 77–82, 85–87.

In some periods of American history, socialism has had some popular appeal. In the presidential election of 1912, for example, Eugene V. Debs of the Socialist Party received 6 percent of the vote.[1] Nevertheless, American political debate has been dominated largely by the principles of liberalism broadly conceived—the Lockean liberalism of the Declaration of Independence. But despite the general agreement on the idea that government should secure equal liberty for all individuals, Americans disagree about the best way to pursue that goal.

Thomas Jefferson hoped that although previous regimes had promoted "an artificial aristocracy, founded on wealth and birth," American democracy would be ruled by "a natural aristocracy" grounded on "virtue and talents."[2] Democratic equality, therefore, would be an equality of opportunity that would allow all people to develop their talents, so that the naturally best could rise to the top. Abraham Lincoln conveyed this thought in his image of life as a race. The primary aim of popular government, he believed, was "to elevate the condition of men — to lift artificial weights from all shoulders — to clear the paths of laudable pursuit for all — to afford all, an unfettered start, and a fair chance, in the race of life."[3] This is the noble vision that elevates American political rhetoric. It's the American Dream — a fair chance for all to get ahead in life.

But doesn't Lincoln's image of the race of life suggest a possible conflict between equality and liberty? The fairness of the race demands absolute *equality* at the starting line but absolute *liberty* in the running of the race. The faster runners must be free to take the lead and leave the slower runners behind. But how can we be sure that the slower runners are not hindered by "artificial weights"? How many of the slower runners were raised in families that didn't train them to run fast? Were they perhaps born to parents who had already fallen behind in the race? Is it unfair for the fast runners to be free to give their children a head start? Does fairness require that we occasionally stop the race, bring everyone back to the starting line, and then start again? What should we do for those who from birth suffer physical or mental disabilities that prevent them from running well? And what should we do for those who accidentally injure themselves during the race? Should the faster runners be forced to help those people who are unfairly disadvantaged? Those of us who stress the fairness of *equality* would want to protect the unfortunate from unfair competition. On the other hand, those of us who stress the fairness of *liberty* would want to protect the freedom of the fastest runners to win all the trophies.

In a footrace, the competitors are rewarded according to their ability to run fast. But in the race of life, don't we want to recognize many different kinds of talent? Aren't there many human attributes — strength, beauty, courage, imagination, compassion, intelligence, and so on — that we want to reward? And don't we want to preserve the boundaries between different fields of competition? We might allow someone with a talent for making money to accumulate great wealth, but we would not want that person to run for public office with the expectation that the office could be bought.

To depict life as a race suggests that we must always compete with one another. Competition may stir us to develop some talents more fully than we would otherwise, but don't we also want to develop our capacities for cooperating with one another? Don't we want to affirm not only the natural differences that divide us, but also the natural similarities that unite us as human beings? Many of us will not excel in the various spheres of human competition. Yet insofar as we all share in the dignity of being human, we deserve equal respect.

How is it possible to secure both the liberty of each person to get ahead in life and the equality of respect owed to each person as a human being? And how is it possible to insure that the inevitable inequalities in a free society do not deprive disadvantaged people of an equal opportunity to succeed? These are the critical questions of American political debate, and they are the questions that John Rawls tried to answer in *A Theory of Justice*.[4]

Rawls (b. 1921) is a professor of philosophy at Harvard University. When his book first appeared in 1971, it created a public controversy that went beyond the normal borders of academic philosophy. Some commentators praised the book as a brilliant defense of liberal democracy that secured both liberty and equality. But critics on the political Right denounced the book for promoting a radical standard of equality that would suppress individual freedom. Critics on the political Left scorned the book as a defense of bourgeois liberty against the just claims of genuine equality.

In examining Rawls's book and the disputes provoked by it, we shall have to consider whether there is a conception of justice that respects both human liberty and human equality. To formulate such a conception, Rawls argued, we must think about how justice would appear to us if we were guided only by considerations of fairness. And we must see how justice as fairness would dictate two principles that would allow "a reconciliation of liberty and equality" (204).

1. Are the principles of justice those we would choose under certain conditions of fairness?

This is surely so, Rawls insists, because we could, presumably, rely on whatever standards of justice we would choose as free, equal, and rational persons acting under circumstances that were fair. In such a hypothetical situation, Rawls believes, we would adopt a general conception of justice as fairness requiring "that all primary social goods be distributed equally unless an unequal distribution would be to everyone's advantage" (150). We must begin by surveying the circumstances of that hypothetical choice and the principles that would be chosen. Without trying to explore all the intricate details of Rawls's book, we can still examine the general patterns of his reasoning.[5]

Rawls begins with the idea of a social contract, which he borrows from Hobbes, Locke, Rousseau, and Kant. But what he calls the "original position" is a more general and abstract idea than that of the traditional social contract (11). To construct the original position, we must imagine people restricted in both their knowledge and their motivations. Under a "veil of ignorance," no one knows anyone's particular abilities, desires, moral preferences, or social position. This insures that no one can design principles that unfairly favor anyone, and thus impartiality is secured. And yet, each person must know certain general facts about human psychology and social life. Each must know, for example, that people often need economic incentives to be productive. Each person must also understand that there are certain "primary goods"—rights and liberties, powers and opportunities, income and wealth, self-respect—that all rational people would want as the necessary means to any ends they might choose to pursue.

Concerning their motivations, people in the original position must be "rational and mutually disinterested" (13). By "mutual disinterest" Rawls does not mean egoism. Rather, he wants only to assume that people "take no interest in one another's interests" (127). In thinking about justice, we must assume conflicting interests because where there is no such conflict, there is no need for justice (129–30, 281). Moreover, in the original position, people are rational in judging how best to advance their interests. They are rational "in the narrow sense, standard in economic theory, of taking the most effective means to given ends" (14).

If we make all of these assumptions about the parties in the original position, we should be able to infer, Rawls contends, that they would choose the following two principles of justice:

> First: each person is to have an equal right to the most extensive basic liberty compatible with a similar liberty for others.
>
> Second: social and economic inequalities are to be arranged so that they are both (a) reasonably expected to be to everyone's advantage, and (b) attached to positions and offices open to all. (60)

Later in the book, "to everyone's advantage" is interpreted to mean "to the greatest benefit of the least advantaged"; and "open to all" is said to mean "open to all under conditions of fair equality of opportunity" (302).

Why would people in the original position select these principles? Fundamental to their reasoning, Rawls believes, is their desire to express their respect for one another. They do not want to force anyone to sacrifice his or her interests to advance the interests of someone else. Adopting the categorical imperative of Immanuel Kant, these people "desire to treat one another not as means only but as ends in themselves" (179). Because they do not regard persons as means, they will not "impose upon them lower prospects of life, for the sake of the higher expectations of others" (180).

Human beings are to be treated as ends in themselves because of their capacity for moral choice, which gives them a dignity that nonhuman things do not have. Not being determined simply by the physical laws of nature, human beings are separated from the physical world by their ability to choose the ends of their lives (251–57). "Thus a moral person is a subject with ends he has chosen, and his fundamental preference is for conditions that enable him to frame a mode of life that expresses his nature as a free and equal rational being as fully as circumstances permit" (561).

To secure this human capacity for free choice, Rawls argues, we must accept the first principle of justice, which protects the equal liberties of citizenship. This includes all the basic liberties of citizens:

> political liberty (the right to vote and to be eligible for public office) together with freedom of speech and assembly; liberty of conscience and freedom of thought; freedom of the person along with the right to hold (personal) property; and freedom from arbitrary arrest and seizure as defined by the concept of the rule of law. (61)

This equality of citizenship provides an equality of respect for all. Despite social and economic inequalities, each person derives self-esteem from equal dignity as a citizen (544).

Additional support for the equal moral worth of all citizens comes from the second part of the second principle of justice—fair equality of opportunity. This requires that all should have a fair chance to succeed in life through their own talents and efforts irrespective of their social class (73). The educational system, for example, should be designed so that even the poorest people have an equal chance to acquire technical training and cultural knowledge. Consequently, even those in the lowest classes of society need not feel degraded. For not only are they equal as citizens, they also have an equal chance to rise in society through work and effort.

But if the equal dignity of human beings as moral persons dictates equal liberty and equal opportunity, why does it not also dictate equality in income and wealth? Rawls answers that as long as economic inequalities make everyone better off, it would be rational for us to permit them. If unequal economic rewards provide incentives that increase economic productivity, then such inequalities are morally just as long as they improve the expectations of the least advantaged members of society (75, 151). Inequality is unjust only when it is not to the benefit of all (62).

Therefore, one of the standards of justice, which Rawls calls "the difference principle," is that social and economic inequalities must be "to the greatest benefit of the least advantaged" (302).

We can now summarize the two principles of justice as they apply to the primary social goods that are the means to any good human life — liberties, opportunities, economic resources, and self-respect. All citizens must be equal in their basic liberties. All must have equal opportunities to develop their talents and abilities. And these two kinds of equality — in liberties and opportunities — should secure equality of respect for all. Inequality in economic resources is permitted, but only as long as it benefits the least advantaged.

The critics of Rawls object that these principles do not, in fact, reconcile liberty and equality. Don't the social and economic inequalities permitted by the second principle of justice subvert the political equality of the first principle? Even if all people are formally equal in their political rights — voting, political participation, freedom of speech, property rights, equality under the law, and so on — won't the poorest citizens lack the economic means to exercise these rights fully? (We have seen that Locke is open to the same criticism.) Rawls can reply to this criticism by stressing the importance of equality of opportunity in allowing the poor to improve their conditions. But he admits that absolute equality of opportunity is impossible under his principles. For example, a child's success in life depends largely on the character of his or her family. If the family does not properly nurture the child's capacities, that child may never have an equal chance in life. Yet Rawls does not want to interfere with the institution of the family (74, 301, 511). Would equal opportunity require abolition of the family? Is this the same problem we saw in Plato's *Republic*?

Even if Rawls could guarantee equal liberty and equal opportunity, would this insure equal dignity for all? As long as there are distinctions between the rich and the poor, won't the poor feel degraded by their low economic status? Rawls insists that the poor should not envy the rich, but he admits that when economic inequality is great, the poor tend to suffer a loss of self-respect (534). In allowing some people the freedom to acquire great wealth, Rawls permits economic inequality that may violate the moral dignity of the poor.

From another point of view, however, some critics have charged that Rawls sacrifices individual liberty in his pursuit of social equality. Although Lincoln argued that we should remove the "artificial weights" that prevent people from running as fast as they can in the race of life, Rawls seems to argue for hindering the faster runners so that the slower runners can keep up with them.

According to Rawls, those whose natural talents permit them to succeed in life must not be free to enjoy all the rewards of their success. The benefits of their work must be shared with those less fortunate. Through taxation or other means, the government must transfer some of the wealth of the rich to the poor (277–80). Moreover, to overcome the natural inequalities among people, society must devote more attention to those who are naturally inferior. "In pursuit of this principle greater resources might be spent on the education of the less rather than the more intelligent, at least over a certain time of life, say the earlier years of school" (101). In his insistence on equality, Rawls seems to restrict the freedom of Jefferson's "natural aristocracy" to develop their "virtues and talents."

We shall have to reflect on how Rawls might answer these criticisms. We begin with the difference principle since it seems to be the most controversial part of his teaching.

2. Should we force the more fortunate people of our society to help those less fortunate?

Most of us would agree that we should help those less fortunate. But how far should we go in compelling those who are well-off to sacrifice some of their resources and opportunities to help those less well-off? Consider, for example, the policy of affirmative action. This policy was first proposed in the United States in the 1960s. The objective of affirmative action is that minority-group members or otherwise disadvantaged people who have suffered from discrimination or other disabilities should receive preferential treatment. President Lyndon Johnson made this a national policy in September 1965 when he signed Executive Order 11246. It stated that on all projects supported by federal money, employers had to prove that they had sought out job applicants from minority groups and that they had given special treatment to such applicants. Later, this was extended to universities and professional schools. In its most extreme form, this could establish a quota system in which a certain proportion of positions would be set aside for women, blacks, and other disadvantaged groups. To justify this policy President Johnson used his own version of Lincoln's image of life as a race:

> Imagine a hundred yard dash in which one of the two runners
> has his legs shackled together. He has progressed 10 yards,
> while the unshackled runner has gone 50 yards. At that point

the judges decide that the race is unfair. How do they rectify the situation? Do they merely remove the shackles and allow the race to proceed? Then they could say that "equal opportunity" now prevailed. But one of the runners would still be forty yards ahead of the other. Would it not be the better part of justice to allow the previously shackled runner to make up the forty yard gap; or to start the race all over again? That would be affirmative action towards equality.[6]

There may be some justice in this. But affirmative action in its most radical form—a quota system—seems unjust to most people because it appears to be reverse discrimination. If it is unjust to discriminate *against* individuals merely because they are black, is it not also unjust to discriminate *in their favor* merely because they are black? Still, there is much to be said in favor of rectifying past injustices by helping those who have suffered unjust treatment. What would Rawls suggest?

Those critics of Rawls who also oppose affirmative action charge that his difference principle would require a quota system of reverse discrimination to favor disadvantaged groups.[7] The clearest evidence is in his comments on the principle of redress:

> The difference principle gives some weight to the considerations singled out by the principle of redress. This is the principle that undeserved inequalities call for redress; and since inequalities of birth and natural endowment are undeserved, these inequalities are to be somehow compensated for. Thus the principle holds that in order to treat all persons equally, to provide genuine equality of opportunity, society must give more attention to those with fewer native assets and to those born into the less favorable social positions. The idea is to redress the bias of contingencies in the direction of equality. (100–101)

But Rawls immediately adds that this principle is only one principle of justice that must be weighed in the balance with others such as "the principle to improve the average standard of life, or to advance the common good" (101):

> Now the difference principle . . . does not require society to try to even out handicaps as if all were expected to compete on a fair basis in the same race. But the difference principle would allocate resources in education, say, so as to improve the long-term expectations of the least favored. If this end is attained by giving more attention to the better endowed, it is permissible; otherwise not. And in making this decision, the value of education should not be assessed only in terms of economic efficiency and social welfare. Equally if not more important is the role of education in enabling a person to enjoy the culture

of his society and to take part in its affairs, and in this way to
provide for each individual a secure sense of his own worth. (101)

It would not be just "to try to even out handicaps" through preferential treatment for the disadvantaged so that everyone could
compete in the same race. But it is just, Rawls suggests, to provide
sufficient opportunities—especially education—for the disadvantaged so that each person is secure in the inherent dignity of a
human being. From this point of view, special help for the victims
of past discrimination would be one principle of justice to be
balanced against others.

We should give more attention, however, to one of Rawls's
comments quoted above: "[S]ince inequalities of birth and natural
endowment are undeserved, these inequalities are to be somehow
compensated for." We can see how this could be true. No one
deserves to be born black or white, for instance, and therefore no
one *deserves* rewards or punishments as a result of race or ethnic
affiliation. Similarly, someone born with a physical disability does
not deserve the suffering it brings. But Rawls's idea is more extreme
than this.

It is commonly assumed, Rawls observed, that in a just society,
the good things of life would be distributed according to moral desert
(310). There seems to be no more obvious principle of justice—to
each what each deserves. But Rawls dismisses the idea of rewarding
merit as "impracticable" (312). Jefferson rejected as "artificial" the
aristocracy based on wealth and birth because no one *deserves* to
be born into a noble family with inherited wealth. Yet Jefferson
assumed that an aristocracy based on talents and virtue would be
"natural" because it is reasonable to reward people for such
personal merit. Rawls, however, argues that talents and virtue are
just as arbitrary as noble birth and inherited wealth. No one
deserves natural talents or moral character because these personal
attributes arise largely from genetic endowment and social circumstances, which are accidental factors that no one deserves (101–4).

Someone who is born with a great natural capacity for intellectual
activity has not earned that capacity. It's an accident of nature.
Surely, an accidental gain does not merit any reward. But we might
argue against Rawls by saying that rewards are deserved not so
much for inherited abilities as for efforts in developing those
abilities. Rawls can answer, however, that a person's capacity for
disciplined effort has been shaped largely by fortunate family and
social circumstances that have not been earned. Each person as an
infant was absolutely dependent on other human beings for
assistance in developing into an adult. Whether physical and

cultural growth would be nurtured or stunted was largely beyond the infant's control. So, insofar as a person's achievements depend on personal attributes, which are determined by the accidents of social circumstances and genetic endowment, success in life depends on "luck in the natural lottery" (75).

Believing it is unjust to allow the happiness of human beings to depend on the arbitrary workings of the natural lottery, Rawls tries to mitigate this injustice through the difference principle.[8]

> We see then that the difference principle represents, in effect, an agreement to regard the distribution of natural talents as a common asset and to share in the benefits of this distribution whatever it turns out to be. Those who have been favored by nature, whoever they are, may gain from their good fortune only on terms that improve the situation of those who have lost out. The naturally advantaged are not to gain merely because they are more gifted, but only to cover the costs of training and education and for using their endowments in ways that help the less fortunate as well. No one deserves his greater natural capacity nor merits a more favorable starting place in society. But it does not follow that one should eliminate these distinctions. . . . [W]e wish to set up the social system so that no one gains or loses from his arbitrary place in the distribution of natural assets or his initial position in society without giving or receiving compensating advantages in return. (101–2)

But isn't it hard to accept Rawls's fundamental claim here that justice cannot be based on merit or desert? Rawls asserts that justice cannot be the rewarding of desert if desert is based on undeserved attributes. Yet isn't this wrong? Doesn't it make impossible any conception of justice at all?[9]

Whatever claim a person might make to meriting or deserving some reward must ultimately rest on an unmerited, undeserved attribute. A person might argue, for example, that he or she deserves admission to law school because of exceptional intelligence or moral character. But we could ask, is this intelligence and moral character *deserved*? Of course, we could raise this question about any claim of merit. To avoid an infinite regress, we must accept some basis of desert that itself is undeserved. Because no human being is self-created, no person is ever completely responsible for the kind of person that he or she is.

In denying that justice can be based on undeserved attributes, Rawls subverts his own account of justice. If Rawlsian justice rests on the claim that all human beings deserve equal respect because of their human dignity as moral persons, then such justice rests on an undeserved base. No one can claim to be responsible for being born a human being. That we were born human beings rather than cockroaches was just a lucky break for us! Would a consistent application of the difference principle require that we compensate cockroaches for the misfortune of their birth?[10]

If it is just to respect human beings simply because of their membership in the human species, as Rawls insists, then why is it not also just to respect them for developing whatever human capacities nature has given them? That one human being has greater natural assets than another is no more arbitrary than the fact that they are both human. Isn't it just to recognize both their *equal merit* as human beings and their *unequal merit* as human beings with different human abilities?

Another way to see the implausibility of Rawls's denial of moral desert is to consider its implications for the policy of affirmative action. A Rawlsian justification for affirmative action in law school admissions, for example, would rest on the argument that no one deserves to go to law school.[11] As a society, we can decide that to promote equality we want more black lawyers. We can then require that law schools admit a certain number of black applicants even if that means that some of the blacks admitted have lower test scores and lower average grades in college than some of the white applicants who are rejected. Some people will say this is unfair discrimination because it violates the right of the white applicants to be judged on the basis of their merit alone. But presumably Rawls would argue that those with high test scores don't deserve the intelligence and discipline that permitted them to do so well on the tests. To judge applicants based on their race is no more arbitrary than judging them based on their intellectual abilities. So, when we admit a black applicant and reject a white applicant, we are not saying that the black applicant is *better* or *more deserving* than the white applicant. They are both equally undeserving! The only just standard is the judgment of society as to what admissions criteria are most likely to promote equality.

Doesn't this kind of reasoning threaten individual freedom? Rawls insists on the Kantian principle that we should always treat human beings as ends in themselves, never as means. But when Rawls says that the natural talents and moral capacities of a person should be treated as a "common asset" to be exploited for the good of all, isn't he treating this person as a means to the advancement of others? By denying that a person has a right to certain talents and abilities, and by arguing that these personal attributes are really social resources to be used as society wishes, doesn't Rawls dehumanize that person by taking away the independent nature of that person and by treating that person as a tool for the use of others?

What, then, should we say in defense of Rawls? First, we should remember that the "principle of redress," which seems to support affirmative action, is not an absolute principle for Rawls. It should be balanced against other principles. A policy like affirmative action — or any social program to compensate the victims of unjust discrimination or of other misfortunes — becomes unjust when it is pushed to unreasonable extremes. Surely most of us would agree with this principle in some form. Social programs for the poor, the sick, the handicapped, the elderly, and the unemployed or the civil rights laws prohibiting racial, ethnic, and sexual discrimination illustrate how we allocate social resources to protect people against arbitrary disadvantages.[12]

Shouldn't we admit that there is some truth in Rawls's claim that the causes of success or failure in our society arise largely from undeserved circumstances? Some empirical studies of the American economy suggest that economic success depends less on intelligence, schooling, or other factors than on sheer luck.[13] Even Friedrich A. Hayek and Milton Friedman — Nobel Prize economists who defend capitalism — have conceded that the free market distributes goods without reference to moral merit.[14]

But how should Rawls answer the charge that the difference principle would exploit the naturally talented people to benefit the disadvantaged, thus depriving the talented few of their liberty for the sake of promoting a tyrannical equality? We should remember that liberty and equality traditionally have been part of a liberal trinity — liberty, equality, and fraternity. Although supporting political liberty and equality of opportunity, Rawls also wants to use the difference principle to secure fraternity (106). A person's identity is shaped largely by the community — by the person's family, education, culture, and so on — and therefore, that person is indebted to that community for its influence. When some citizens are asked to work to improve the lives of fellow citizens who are less well off than themselves, they need not feel that they are being used as means to advance the ends of other people, because they should recognize the ends of their community as their own.

But to speak of society as a fraternal union bound together by a spirit of sharing evokes suggestions of socialism. We can therefore understand the warning of Daniel Bell, one of Rawls's most fervent critics: "With Rawls, we have the most comprehensive effort in modern philosophy to justify a socialist ethic."[15] Many of Rawls's socialist critics, however, would disagree.

3. Does justice require socialist equality?

Much of what Rawls writes appears to deny that socialism is necessary for justice. He assumes "a democratic regime in which land and capital are widely though not presumably equally held." But he notes that at least in theory, "a liberal socialist regime can also answer to the two principles of justice" (280). By "liberal socialism," he must mean market socialism in which the means of production are publicly owned and workers manage their own firms.

Socialist commentators on Rawls's theory are usually disturbed by the great inequalities that would be permissible under the difference principle. Kai Nielsen, for example, complains that because Rawls justifies any inequality that increases the material wealth of the most disadvantaged, he would deny the right of those at the bottom of society to attain equal citizenship and equal opportunity. Like most apologists for capitalism, Rawls assumes, according to Nielsen, that as long as the material standard of living rises continually for all, then economic, social, and political inequalities do not matter.[16]

This is clearly a misinterpretation of Rawls, however. Although in theory the difference principle would sanction great inequalities in exchange for small benefits to those least well-off, Rawls does not expect inequalities of wealth to be excessive (536). Indeed, the other principles of justice would severely limit inequality. To preserve equal political liberty, Rawls proposes the use of public funds to promote free public discussion and political campaigning. Moreover, the tax system and the laws of property should "prevent concentrations of power detrimental to the fair value of political liberty and fair equality of opportunity" (277). Equality of opportunity demands that even those in the lowest classes of society should have an equal chance to advance themselves. Because such equal opportunity is jeopardized "when inequalities of wealth exceed a certain limit," government should enforce that limit (278).

And we should not forget the principle of equality of respect. Rawls hopes that in a just society there would be little envy. In the absence of envy, the equality of political liberty should provide equal dignity for all despite inequalities of income and wealth. But Rawls concedes that where economic inequality becomes excessive, it might be reasonable for those less well-off to feel envious and thus experience a loss of self-respect. "To some extent men's sense of their own worth may hinge upon their institutional position and their income share" (546). In that case, equality of self-respect would dictate at least a rough equality of wealth.

In the words of one socialist writer, Rawlsian justice would require socialism of some sort "if the self-respect of the worst off could be maintained in no other way, or if the fair value of liberty could be protected in no other way, or if fair equality of opportunity would be achieved in no other way." Even if capitalism and socialism were equally justified on these points, Rawls's teaching would still support socialism "if a socialist economy were capable of providing the worst off with a higher level of wealth and income than could be provided under any other system."[17]

There is, then, a socialist undertone in Rawlsian justice, which has provoked those who advocate capitalism as the only secure basis for freedom. They worry that Rawls endorses a socialist conception of equality that would deprive us of our individual liberty.

4. Does justice require capitalist liberty?

The case for libertarian capitalism as an alternative to Rawls's egalitarian justice was set forth in 1974 by Robert Nozick in his *Anarchy, State, and Utopia*.[18] Nozick, a colleague of Rawls in the Department of Philosophy at Harvard, advocated "the minimal night-watchman state, a state limited to protecting persons against murder, assault, theft, fraud, and so forth."[19] The only just power of government is to prevent force and fraud. Beyond that, all have the right to live as they please.

The sort of government endorsed by Rawls would therefore be unjust because it would violate individual freedom. A Rawlsian government, for example, would use taxation to redistribute income and wealth to help the poor. But taxation, Nozick argues, is clearly unjust because it is a form of slavery. If I have to work a certain number of hours to earn enough income to pay my taxes, then in effect the government is forcing me to work those hours for the benefit of others.

That taxation is slavery is only one of many shocking conclusions reached by Nozick. But his arguments supporting those conclusions are often seductive in their plausibility. A good example is his story about Wilt Chamberlain.[20]

Assume that you were able to distribute property in a society to conform to your favorite conception of justice. You might want an equal distribution. Or you might prefer a distribution according to some standard of merit. Now imagine that Wilt Chamberlain is a popular basketball player. Because he is so popular, he negotiates a contract that gives him twenty-five cents from the price of every ticket of admission. People pay this willingly because they enjoy watching him play basketball. If a million people attend the home games, Chamberlain receives $250,000 for the season. This upsets your just pattern of distribution. But what is wrong with it? If each person had a just share of the wealth under your distribution, then all are entitled to whatever they have. But if all are entitled to hold what they have, are they not also entitled to freely transfer some of their wealth to someone else in exchange for some benefit? If Chamberlain has not defrauded or coerced his fans, is he not entitled to whatever they willingly pay him for his services?

At this point, however, you might want to object. If you are a Rawlsian, you would insist that Chamberlain's accumulations of wealth must not interfere with equal political liberty or equality of opportunity. You might recommend taxing Chamberlain's income to support social welfare programs for the poor. But if he has justly acquired his property, Nozick would ask, how can you force him to give it up without violating his rights?

The Chamberlain example illustrates the three basic principles of Nozick's account of justice: just acquisition, just transfer, and rectification. A person is entitled to hold property if that property was acquired without unjust injury to anyone else. If that property is voluntarily transferred to someone else in exchange for something, then the second person has a just title to the property. But if some property was originally acquired unjustly, then we would have to rectify the injustice somehow. Thus, Nozick's entitlement theory of property conforms to the usual legal procedure for determining property rights. We do a title search to insure that the property was originally acquired justly and to insure that it has been justly transferred. Notice that we do not have to ask whether anyone deserves the property or whether having it promotes any conception of justice.

We should also notice the similarities to Locke's defense of property rights. Although he departs from Locke at critical points, Nozick agrees with Locke in stressing individual freedom in the acquisition of property. Nozick's individualism, however, is more radical than Locke's because, unlike Locke, Nozick rejects the idea of individuals consenting to the establishment of society and government for the promotion of the common good. Nozick has to struggle to distinguish his position from that of the libertarian anarchists.[21]

This extreme individualism might be the best point of attack for the Rawlsian critic. Consider what Rawls might say about the Wilt Chamberlain example.[22] Nozick assumes that as long as *individual* economic transactions are just, their *collective* effects will also be just. But this is not necessarily true. It is not unjust for people to pay to see Wilt Chamberlain play basketball. But if these and other kinds of transactions eventually create a situation of great inequality in which some people have great wealth and others have little, then we might properly act to prevent that as unjust if it would deprive the poor of equal opportunity. After all, Chamberlain's freedom to succeed in sports arose in a society that secured certain conditions of equality of opportunity.

Nozick denies that there is a social entity or a social good. "There are only individual people, different individual people with their own individual lives." He concedes, nevertheless, "that we partially are 'social products' in that we benefit from current patterns and forms created by the multitudinous actions of a long string of long-forgotten people, forms which include institutions, ways of doing things, and language." He insists that this "does not create in us a general floating debt which the current society can collect and use as it will."[23] But if we are in fact "social products," how can we deny any "floating debt" to the society that produced us?

Although at times Rawls seems to accept a radically individualistic view of human nature, he goes farther than Nozick in acknowledging the social nature of human beings. Rawls describes the formation of human character through social relationships:

> The members of a community participate in one another's nature: we appreciate what others do as things we might have done but which they do for us, and what we do is similarly done for them. Since the self is realized in the activity of many selves, relations of justice that conforms to principles which would be assented to by all are best fitted to express the nature of each. (565)

Insofar as we are social creatures, Rawls suggests, we need the help of society to develop and express our human capacities. It is not unreasonable, then, to expect more than a "minimal nightwatchman state." Yet how far is a government obligated to go in providing an equal chance for all in the race of life? Many of Rawls's critics would agree with him on the need for social welfare measures to secure equality of opportunity, but some of his critics fear that his principles would require an absolute equality of conditions that would threaten individual freedom.

5. Should we seek equality of opportunity but not equality of result?

Irving Kristol and Daniel Bell—known to many as leading neoconservatives—have criticized Rawls for demanding equality of result rather than equality of opportunity. Kristol and Bell see Rawls as subverting that reconciliation of equality and liberty achieved by welfare-state capitalism, in which people have an equal opportunity to become unequal.

Kristol accuses Rawls of failing to respect the justice of the "bourgeois notion of equality":

> The founding fathers of modern bourgeois society (John Locke, say, or Thomas Jefferson) all assumed that biological inequalities among men—inequalities in intelligence, talent, abilities of all kinds—were not extreme, and therefore did not justify a society of hereditary privilege (of "two races," as it were). This assumption we now know to be true, demonstrably true, as a matter of fact. Human talents and abilities, as measured, do tend to distribute themselves along a bell-shaped curve, with most people clustered around the middle, and with much smaller percentages at the lower and higher ends. . . . [I]t is a demonstrable fact that in all modern, bourgeois societies, the distribution of income is also roughly along a bell-shaped curve, indicating that in such an "open" society the inequalities that do emerge are not inconsistent with the bourgeois notion of equality.

Moreover, Kristol explains, once this distribution of talents and abilities along a bell-shaped curve has determined the economic structure and the social structure, it then shapes the distribution of political power as well.[24] Inequalities in economic wealth, social status, and political power are justified as long as they reflect the natural inequalities in talents and abilities.

Bell makes a similar argument in defending what Michael Young, a British sociologist, has called "meritocracy."[25] In a meritocratic society, those at the top have an "earned status" based on "individual merit" or "superior competence." They are the "best men." What kind of merit or competence do they have? By what standard are they the best? Bell is unclear about this, but he does speak of them as "technical elites" who have "technical skills and higher education." More specifically, he speaks of their high intelligence as measured by IQ tests.[26] According to Young, the formula for merit is $I + E = M$ (intelligence + effort = merit). The quantity of intelligence is measured by IQ tests, and the quantity of effort is measured by modern time-and-motion studies.

Would this conform to Plato's vision of a community ruled by philosopher-kings where all members receive what they deserve? Or is it perhaps closer to the kind of society suggested by Descartes, a society ruled by scientists and technically trained elites? In any case, it does resemble the society sought by Jefferson, which was to be ruled by the "natural aristocracy."

But Rawls rejects the idea of a meritocracy (106–8). And again we must wonder why it would be wrong to reward people according to their natural talents and abilities. Consider how Rawls might reply to Kristol and Bell.[27]

First, we should challenge the assumption that all human abilities and talents can be judged by one standard of measurement — the IQ test. Even if IQ scores distribute themselves along a bell-shaped curve — a few people with very high scores, a few with very low scores, and most in the middle — why should that justify a similar distribution of economic, social, and political rewards? Modern psychological research would confirm our common-sense impression that there are many forms of intelligence that cannot be measured by IQ tests.[28] Why should a person's performance on a single paper-and-pencil test determine his or her place in society?

We might also argue that the capitalist society defended by Kristol and Bell rewards not so much intelligence as it does the talent for making money. Where money is the universal medium of exchange, it tends to become the only standard of social worth. We should remember Rousseau's complaint about this in the *Second Discourse*. Although social inequality arises generally from four kinds of differences — "wealth, nobility or rank, power, and personal merit" — eventually they are all reduced to wealth "because being the most immediately useful to well-being and the easiest to communicate, it is easily used to buy all the rest."[29] Marx made the same criticism. In a bourgeois society, what people possess is not proportioned to what they deserve, because what they possess is determined not by what they merit but by what they can buy.[30] Would Kristol and Bell say that a rich person *merits* all the things money can buy? Does a rich person merit more legal protection, more political power, or more medical treatment than a poor person?

Even if the talent for making money is rewarded in the economic sphere, there is no good reason to reward it in all other spheres of social life. Rawls would insist that with respect to "basic liberties," all citizens as moral persons deserve equal status. The right to a fair trial or the right to vote, for example, should not be distributed according to wealth. And to insure fair equality of opportunity, a certain minimal level of education should be provided equally to all, regardless of wealth. Distributive justice requires different principles of distribution for the different spheres of society.[31]

For some purposes, it is useful to distinguish equality of opportunity and equality of result. But Bell and Kristol push this distinction too far. To some degree, genuine equality of opportunity in a democracy does dictate equality of result. Democratic citizens demand equal respect and equal protection for their interests. They demand this because as human beings they share a common moral dignity. But equal respect and equal protection of interests do not necessarily require equal power or equal property. The natural differences among human beings may dictate some inequality in power and in property. Both the unity and the diversity among human beings must be respected.[32]

Rawls believes, therefore, that we need to balance equality of opportunity against other principles of justice. He does not deny the principle of careers open to talents, but he argues for limits on meritocratic inequality to insure all citizens an equal sense of self-respect. Even Bell appears to agree with this when he says we should "insist on a basic social equality in that each person is to be given respect and not to be humiliated on the basis of color, or sexual proclivities, or other personal attributes." Bell adds, "We can assert that each person is entitled to a basic set of services and income which provides him with adequate medical care, housing, and the like." He explains that a just meritocracy would rest on the belief that although all are not entitled to equal *praise*, all are entitled to equal *respect*.[33] Consequently, Bell observes, a capitalist meritocracy creates cultural tensions between the different standards governing different realms — efficiency in the economy, equality in the polity, and self-actualization in the culture.[34] But this contradicts Bell's argument that economic, political, and social goods should all be distributed according to the bell-shaped curve of technical knowledge. The idea that we should seek a balance between efficiency, equality, and self-actualization would support Rawls's conception of justice. His first principle requires political equality. His second principle incorporates the principle of economic efficiency (66–72, 79–80). And one of the needs promoted by Rawlsian justice is self-realization (84, 107, 561–66).

If we accept Rawls's complex account of justice as dictating different distributive principles for different spheres of life, then we must wonder how to settle conflicts between these principles. For example, how do we resolve the tension between the political equality demanded by Rawls's first principle of justice and the social and economic inequalities permitted by his second principle? Don't we need some single, comprehensive standard of judgment? Rawls argues for certain rules of priority for ranking the principles. Underlying these rules, there is a conception of human nature and of what human beings need to fulfill their nature. Equal liberty, for example, takes precedence over other principles because of "the central place of the primary good of self-respect and the desire of human beings to express their nature in a free social union with others" (543). And more generally, Rawls maintains, the principles of justice allow people to "express their nature as free and equal rational beings subject to the general conditions of human life" (252–53). If the aim of justice is to secure the conditions for the fullest expression of human nature, then it would seem that to agree on the meaning of justice we must first agree on the meaning of human nature. But according to some of the powerful intellectual movements of our time—such as "deconstructionism" and "postmodernism"—human nature does not exist except as an arbitrary construction of individual wills and cultural practices.[35]

6. In asking political questions, must we ask about the meaning of life?

We commonly judge the goodness of a political community by how well it promotes the flourishing of human life. A good political regime helps people to live a good life. But such a judgment presupposes an understanding of what constitutes a good human life. Traditionally, people have appealed to "the Laws of Nature and of Nature's God"; thus they have looked for natural or divine standards of how human beings ought to live.

In recent centuries, however, many political thinkers have doubted the existence of any objective moral order that is either natural or divine. Human beings do not *discover* moral values, Friedrich Nietzsche declared, rather they *create* them.[36] Yet if all values are arbitrary creations of the human will, if there are no moral absolutes, how can we reasonably adhere to liberty and equality as absolute principles of justice? It would seem that nothing has any intrinsic value, that even human life itself is worthless. That is what Nietzsche called "nihilism." And he warned that it would devastate human life in the twentieth century.[37] The question for modern liberals like Rawls is whether they can accept moral relativism without falling into the abyss of nihilism.

Rawls defends his account of justice as morally neutral, in that it does not presuppose any conception of the moral ends of life. In his John Dewey lectures, delivered in 1980, Rawls explains that because his view of justice should "serve as a shared point of view among citizens with opposing religious, philosophical and moral convictions, as well as diverse conceptions of the good, this point of view needs to be appropriately impartial among these differences."[38] But insofar as principles of justice shape the general structure of a community, won't they necessarily favor some way of life as preferable to others? Rawls comes close to conceding this in *A Theory of Justice* when he notes that as a consequence of his principles, "certain initial bounds are placed upon what is good and what forms of character are morally worthy, and so upon what kinds of persons men should be" (32). If Rawls advocates a liberal theory of justice, we would expect his principles to form the character of citizens to conform to a liberal way of life. Instead Rawls tries to avoid this. He would like to have an open society in which every way of life can be pursued freely.

In the quest for a morally neutral conception of justice, Rawls looks for purely *formal* standards of justification that do not rest on any *substantive* moral judgments. To do this, he can appeal either to the idea of formal rationality or to the idea of the autonomous self. "The theory of justice," he says, "is a part, perhaps the most significant part, of the theory of rational choice" (16). Here, he draws on the modern economic concept of rationality (142–50, 407–39). Even without making a substantive judgment about what ends people should pursue in life, we can make a formal judgment about their rationality in calculating the best means to whatever ends they might choose. We can judge whether a person has chosen means that are appropriate to specific ends, and we can judge the internal consistency of the choices that person has made. We do this, however, without judging the reasonableness of the ends themselves. Rawls offers a bizarre example:

> Thus imagine someone whose only pleasure is to count blades of grass in various geometrically shaped areas such as park squares and well-trimmed lawns. . . . [I]f we allow that his nature is to enjoy this activity and not to enjoy any other, and that there is no feasible way to alter his condition, then surely a rational plan for him will center around this activity. (432–33)

The two principles of justice as fairness are rational, Rawls suggests, insofar as they would help anyone to pursue any rational plan of life even if the aim of that plan is only to count blades of grass!

Why should we allow every person to choose an individualized, rational plan of life no matter how absurd the ends may seem to us? We must do so, Rawls answers, because to deny people such freedom would violate their human dignity as beings capable of free choice. Human beings must be autonomous in choosing their plans of life because they will thus express their nature as "free and rational beings with a liberty to choose" (256). This suggests that we can determine the meaning of justice without determining the meaning of life because justice requires that we leave each person free to determine the meaning of life. Indeed, Rawls implies that what makes a person human is the capacity for freely creating a meaningful life out of an otherwise meaningless universe.

Despite the appearance of moral neutrality, doesn't Rawls rely on some substantive judgments of human excellence? In judging that rational life plans are better than irrational ones, he assumes that rationality is good. And in judging that we should allow people to express their human nature as free and rational beings, he assumes that human life is good and that the fulfillment of human purposes is good.[39] We can easily overlook these assumptions because we take them for granted.

As products of a liberal culture, it is also easy for us to overlook the fact that Rawls's principles promote a liberal way of life as being the best life for human beings. Brian Barry has sketched the liberal conception of life implicitly endorsed by Rawls:

> A liberal . . . must hold that a certain type of man, and a society in which that type of man flourishes are superior to others.
>
> Liberalism rests on a vision of life: a Faustian vision. It exalts self-expression, self-mastery, and control over the environment, natural and social; the active pursuit of knowledge and the clash of ideas; the acceptance of personal responsibility for the decisions that shape one's life. For those who cannot take the freedom it provides alcohol, tranquilizers, wrestling on the television, astrology, psychoanalysis, and so on, endlessly, but it cannot by its nature provide certain kinds of psychological security. Like any creed it can be neither justified nor condemned in terms of anything beyond it. It is itself an answer to the unanswerable but irrepressible question: "What is the meaning of life?"[40]

Is Barry correct in saying that this liberal vision cannot be judged good or bad "in terms of anything beyond it"? Can't we judge how well it conforms to human nature? Couldn't we argue, for example, that it is justified insofar as it allows human beings freedom to develop a wide range of their natural talents and abilities, while it also provides minimal security for all based on the equality of certain natural human needs?[41]

Rawls often appeals to conceptions of human nature rooted in evolutionary biology.[42] His theory of justice requires a notion of human flourishing as conforming to the species-specific needs and

powers of human beings as products of natural selection. The very
possibility of justice as fairness presumes a natural human capacity
for reciprocity that some evolutionary biologists regard as the
biological ground for human morality. Rawls explains:

> Reciprocity, a tendency to answer in kind, . . . is a deep
> psychological fact. Without it our nature would be very different
> and fruitful social cooperation fragile if not impossible. . . . Beings
> with a different psychology either have never existed or must
> soon have disappeared in the course of evolution. A capacity for
> a sense of justice built up by responses in kind would appear
> to be a condition of human sociability. (494–95)

Thus Darwinian biology might support a revival of Aristotelian
naturalism in moral and political philosophy.[43] While showing a
prudent respect for the diverse customs and traditions of human
experience, we might still judge political communities as better or
worse in conforming to the natural needs and capacities of human
beings as rational and political animals.

If we did so, however, we would discover that such an appeal to
human nature would be not the end but the beginning of our
inquiries, because we would discover the complexity of human
nature both in itself and in its interplay with the circumstances of
individual and social history. We would find ourselves asking the
same questions about nature and convention that were asked by
Socrates. Socrates was not the first to ponder such questions. It
began many thousands of years ago, when some human being first
looked up into the night sky, shuddered in awe, and wondered how
to make sense of it all.

Notes

1. See Michael Harrington, *Socialism* (New York: Saturday Review Press,
   1972).
2. Thomas Jefferson, Letter to John Adams, 28 October 1813, in *The Life
   and Selected Writings of Thomas Jefferson*, eds. Adrienne Koch and
   William Peden (New York: Random House, Modern Library, 1944),
   632–33.
3. Abraham Lincoln, Message to Congress, 4 July 1861, in *The Collected
   Works of Abraham Lincoln*, ed. Roy P. Basler, 9 vols. (New Brunswick,
   NJ: Rutgers University Press, 1953–1955), 4: 438. For criticisms of the
   American liberal metaphor of life as a race, see Garry Wills, *Nixon
   Agonistes: The Crisis of the Self-Made Man* (Boston: Houghton Mifflin,
   1970), 234–45, 589–602.
4. John Rawls, *A Theory of Justice* (Cambridge: Harvard University Press,
   1971). All page references in the text are to this book.

5. For useful introductions to the interpretation and evaluation of Rawls's book, see Brian Barry, *The Liberal Theory of Justice* (Oxford: Oxford University Press, 1973); Norman Daniels, ed., *Reading Rawls* (New York: Basic Books, 1973); and Michael Sandel, *Liberalism and the Limits of Justice* (Cambridge: Cambridge University Press, 1982).

6. Quoted by Daniel Bell, "On Meritocracy and Equality," *Public Interest* No. 29 (Fall 1972): 44. For the debate over affirmative action, see Nathan Glazer, *Affirmative Discrimination: Ethnic Inequality and Public Policy* (New York: Basic Books, 1975); Philip Green, *The Pursuit of Inequality* (New York: Pantheon, 1981), 165–210; William Ryan, *Equality* (New York: Random House, Vintage, 1982), 148–60; and Richard A. Epstein, *Forbidden Grounds: The Case Against Employment Discrimination Laws* (Cambridge: Harvard University Press, 1992).

7. See Bell, "Meritocracy," 56–58.

8. Should Rawls apply his difference principle to international relations? Would the richer nations be obligated to help the poorer nations? See Brian Barry, *Liberal Theory*, 128–33; and Charles R. Beitz, *Political Theory and International Relations* (Princeton: Princeton University Press, 1979), 128–53. Compare P. T. Bauer, *Equality, the Third World, and Economic Delusion* (Cambridge: Harvard University Press, 1981).

9. Here I am following closely the argument of Michael Zuckert, "Justice Deserted: A Critique of Rawls's *Theory of Justice*," *Polity* 13 (Spring 1981): 466–83.

10. See chap. 2, sec. 3; chap. 6, sec. 5; chap. 8, sec. 1. See also Rawls, *Theory of Justice*, 512.

11. Some elements of Rawlsian justice appear in Ronald Dworkin's defense of affirmative action. See Dworkin, *Taking Rights Seriously* (Cambridge: Harvard University Press, 1977), 223–39; Dworkin, *A Matter of Principle* (Cambridge: Harvard University Press, 1985), 293–303; and Sandel, *Liberalism*, 135–47.

12. For a Rawlsian defense of welfare rights, see Frank Michelman, "Constitutional Welfare Rights and *A Theory of Justice*," in Daniels, *Reading Rawls*, 319–47.

   Has Rawls designed his original position to teach the Golden Rule — do unto others as you would have them do unto you if you were in their position? See Thomas Hobbes, *Leviathan*, ed. Michael Oakeshott (Oxford: Basil Blackwell, n.d.), chap. 15, p. 103; chap. 17, p. 109; chap. 26, p. 177; and Alan Gewirth, *Human Rights* (Chicago: University of Chicago Press, 1982), 128–42.

13. Based on a survey of the evidence, Christopher Jencks, in *Inequality* (New York: Basic Books, 1972), concludes: "Economic success seems to depend on varieties of luck and on-the-job competence that are only moderately related to family background, schooling, or scores on standardized tests. The definition of competence varies greatly from one job to another, but it seems in most cases to depend more on personality than on technical skills" (8).

14. See Friedrich A. Hayek, *The Constitution of Liberty* (Chicago: University of Chicago Press, 1960), 85–102; and Milton Friedman, *Capitalism and Freedom* (Chicago: University of Chicago Press, 1962), 161–66.

15. Bell, "Meritocracy," 57.

16. See Kai Nielsen, "Capitalism, Socialism and Justice," in Tom Regan and Donald VanDeVeer, eds., *And Justice For All* (Totowa, NJ: Rowman & Littlefield, 1982), 277–85; and Nielsen, *Equality and Liberty: A Defense of Radical Egalitarianism* (Totowa, NJ: Rowman & Allanheld, 1985), 78–99. For socialist defenses of Rawls, see Robert Amdur, "Rawls and His Radical Critics: The Problem of Equality," *Dissent* (Summer 1980): 323–34; and Arthur DiQuattro, "Rawls and Left Criticism," *Political Theory* 11 (February 1983): 53–78.

17. Amdur, "Radical Critics," 333.

18. Robert Nozick, *Anarchy, State, and Utopia* (New York: Basic Books, 1974).

19. Ibid., 162.

20. Ibid., 160–64.

21. See Virginia Held, "John Locke on Robert Nozick," *Social Research* 43 (Spring 1976): 169–95. For a survey of contemporary libertarianism that traces its Lockean roots, see Stephen L. Newman, *Liberalism at Wit's End* (Ithaca, NY: Cornell University Press, 1984). For philosophic defenses of libertarianism, see Ayn Rand, *The Virtue of Selfishness* (New York: New American Library, 1964); Murray Rothbard, *The Ethics of Liberty* (Atlantic Highlands, NJ: Humanities Press, 1982); Loren E. Lomasky, *Persons, Rights, and the Moral Community* (New York: Oxford University Press, 1987); and Douglas B. Rasmussen and Douglas J. Den Uyl, *Liberty and Nature: An Aristotelian Defense of Liberal Order* (La Salle, IL: Open Court, 1991).

22. See G. A. Cohen, "Robert Nozick and Wilt Chamberlain: How Patterns Preserve Liberty," in John Arthur and William Shaw, eds., *Justice and Economic Distribution* (Englewood Cliffs, NJ: Prentice-Hall, 1978), 246–62. Perhaps the best answer to Nozick's Wilt Chamberlain parable would be another parable, such as that told by Michael Walzer in "Town Meetings and Workers' Control: A Story for Socialists," in *Radical Principles* (New York: Basic Books, 1980), 273–90. For the argument that both Rawls and Nozick adhere to an individualistic conception of society that is indefensible, see Alasdair MacIntyre, *After Virtue* (Notre Dame: University of Notre Dame Press, 1981), 227–37.

23. Nozick, *Anarchy*, 33, 95.

24. Irving Kristol, "About Equality," in *Two Cheers for Capitalism* (New York: Basic Books, 1978), 184–85.

25. Michael Young, *The Rise of Meritocracy* (Baltimore: Penguin Books, 1961).

26. Bell, "Meritocracy," 30–31, 41, 65, 67.

27. For egalitarian arguments against meritocracy, see Walzer, *Radical Principles*, 237–56; Green, *Pursuit*; Ryan, *Equality*; and Nielsen,

Equality and Liberty, 132–87. For evidence that the American welfare state promotes unfair inequality, see Benjamin I. Page, *Who Gets What from Government* (Berkeley: University of California Press, 1983).

28. On the many kinds of intelligence, see Howard Gardner, *Frames of Mind: The Theory of Multiple Intelligences* (New York: Basic Books, 1983). For the controversy surrounding IQ testing, see Arthur R. Jensen, *Bias in Mental Testing* (New York: Free Press, 1979); Stephen Jay Gould, *The Mismeasure of Man* (New York: Norton, 1981); and R. C. Lewontin, Steven Rose, and Leon J. Kamin, *Not In Our Genes* (New York: Pantheon, 1984), 83–129.

29. Jean-Jacques Rousseau, *The First and Second Discourses*, ed. Roger D. Masters, trans. Roger D. Masters and Judith R. Masters (New York: St. Martin's Press, 1964), 174.

30. See Robert C. Tucker, ed., *The Marx-Engels Reader*, 2nd ed. (New York: Norton, 1978), 101–5.

31. This pluralistic conception of justice is defended by Michael Walzer, *Spheres of Justice* (New York: Basic Books, 1983). For an Aristotelian defense of this conception, see William A. Galston, *Justice and the Human Good* (Chicago: University of Chicago Press, 1980).

32. See Jane J. Mansbridge, *Beyond Adversary Democracy* (Chicago: University of Chicago Press, 1983), 3–7. A rigorous analysis of the various conceptions of equality is set forth in Douglas Rae, *Equalities* (Cambridge: Harvard University Press, 1981). Rae criticizes Rawls, Bell, and other theorists.

33. Bell, "Meritocracy," 64–66. Can social respect be distributed equally? Or is the pursuit of respect of such a nature that one person's gain must be another's loss? See William J. Goode, *The Celebration of Heroes: Prestige as a Social Control System* (Berkeley: University of California Press, 1978); and Robert H. Frank, *Choosing the Right Pond: Human Behavior and the Quest for Status* (New York: Oxford University Press, 1985).

34. See Daniel Bell, *The Cultural Contradictions of Capitalism* (New York: Basic Books, 1978).

35. For some of the debate over deconstructionism and postmodernism, see Jonathan Culler, *On Deconstruction* (Ithaca: Cornell University Press, 1982); John M. Ellis, *Against Deconstruction* (Princeton: Princeton University Press, 1989); J. G. Merquior, *Foucault* (Berkeley: University of California Press, 1985); Richard Rorty, *Contingency, Irony, and Solidarity* (Cambridge: Cambridge University Press, 1989); Stephen K. White, *Political Theory and Postmodernism* (Cambridge: Cambridge University Press, 1991); and Martha Nussbaum, "Human Functioning and Social Justice: In Defense of Aristotelian Essentialism," *Political Theory* 20 (1992): 202–46.

For evidence that modern relativism is a Nietzschean revival of the sophistic rhetorical tradition, see Friedrich Nietzsche, *Friedrich Nietzsche on Rhetoric and Language*, eds. Sander L. Gilman et al. (New York: Oxford University Press, 1989); and Mark Backman,

Sophistication: Rhetoric and the Rise of Self-Consciousness (Woodbridge, CT: Ox Bow Press, 1991). Many readers of Allan Bloom's immensely popular book, The Closing of the American Mind (New York: Simon & Schuster, 1987), have assumed that it is a conservative attack on modern relativism. A few readers have noticed, however, that Nietzsche is one of the heroes of Bloom's book. Bloom never says Nietzsche was wrong about anything, and he identifies Socrates (the other hero of the book) as a Nietzschean philosopher ("the complementary man"). See The Closing of the American Mind, 51, 98, 200–209, 266–68, 304–10, 377; and compare Nietzsche, Beyond Good and Evil, sec. 207. See below, note 43.

36. See Friedrich Nietzsche, Beyond Good and Evil, trans. Walter Kaufmann (New York: Random House, Vintage, 1966). For evidence that even Nietzsche relied on a law of nature, see secs. 22, 188, 230, 264.

37. That Nietzsche's prediction has been proven correct is the general theme of Paul Johnson's Modern Times: The World from the Twenties to the Eighties (New York: Harper and Row, 1983). The inclination to nihilism is evident, for example, in many of the assumptions that dominate contemporary art and literary studies. In contrast to the traditional belief that art somehow imitates nature, it is commonly assumed today that art is a creative activity with no reference to nature. Moreover, it may even be claimed that what we regard as knowledge of the nature of things is, in truth, a cultural fiction of our language. In its most radical form, however, this Nietzschean skepticism becomes self-contradictory. But few of its adherents are as candid as Nelson Goodman: "My outline of the facts concerning the fabrication of facts is of course itself a fabrication" (Ways of Worldmaking [Indianapolis: Hackett, 1978], 107). See E. H. Gombrich, Art and Illusion, 2nd ed. (New York: Pantheon, 1961), 291–329, 359–96; Jonathan Culler, Structuralist Poetics (London: Routledge & Kegan Paul, 1975), 137–60, 243–54; and Jacques Derrida, Of Grammatology, trans. Gayatri Chakravorty Spivak (Baltimore: Johns Hopkins University Press, 1976), 10–26, 44–51, 157–64. For a defense of the realist view of art as a representation of reality, see A. D. Nuttall, A New Mimesis: Shakespeare and the Representation of Reality (New York: Methuen, 1983), 1–98.

38. John Rawls, "Kantian Constructivism in Moral Theory," Journal of Philosophy 77 (September 1980):542–43. Compare Ronald Dworkin's argument that liberalism requires a principle of neutrality — "that political decisions must be, so far as possible, independent of any particular conception of the good life, or of what gives value to life" (A Matter of Principle, 191). He also argues — as many liberals would — for governmental support of the arts insofar as this protects "the structure of our intellectual culture" (ibid., 232). Does this contradict his principle of liberal neutrality?

39. On these points, see William Galston, Liberal Purposes (Cambridge:

Cambridge University Press, 1991), chaps. 4, 6. For the argument that economic rationality fails as a morally neutral standard for social theory, see Barry, *Liberal Theory*, 19–33, 116–27; Brian Barry and Russell Hardin, eds., *Rational Man and Irrational Society?* (Beverly Hills: Sage Publications, 1982), 367–86; and Allen E. Buchanan, *Ethics, Efficiency and the Market* (Totowa, NJ: Rowman & Allanheld, 1985).

40. Barry, *Liberal Theory*, 126–27. Alexis de Tocqueville coined the word "individualism" to denote the American character. See his *Democracy in America*, trans. George Lawrence (Garden City: Doubleday, Anchor Books, 1969), 506. For critical explorations of American individualism, see Francis L. K. Hsu, *Americans and Chinese*, 3rd ed. (Honolulu: University Press of Hawaii, 1981); and Robert N. Bellah et al., *Habits of the Heart: Individualism and Commitment in American Life* (Berkeley: University of California Press, 1985).

41. For a substantive defense of liberalism as conforming to human nature, see Galston's *Justice and the Human Good* and his *Liberal Purposes*. Many American public policy analysts assume that liberal democracy is simply a system for aggregating individual preferences taken as given. But some argue that this ignores the influence of politics in forming preferences. See Charles E. Lindblom, "The Market as Prison," *Journal of Politics* 44 (May 1982): 324–36; David C. Paris and James F. Reynolds, *The Logic of Policy Inquiry* (New York: Longman, 1983); Frank Fischer, "Methodological Foundations for Public Policy Analysis," *Policy Studies Journal* 12 (December 1983): 399–409; Aaron Wildavsky, "Choosing Preferences by Constructing Institutions: A Cultural Theory of Preference Formation," *American Political Science Review* 81 (1987): 3–21; and James Q. Wilson, *On Character* (Washington, DC: The AEI Press, 1991).

42. See Rawls, *A Theory of Justice*, 260, 398, 414, 424–25, 431–32, 456, 485–88, 490, 494–95, 502–4, 516.

43. See C. Judson Herrick, *The Evolution of Human Nature* (Austin: University of Texas Press, 1956); and Robert J. McShea, *Morality and Human Nature: A New Route to Ethical Theory* (Philadelphia: Temple University Press, 1990). Allan Bloom intimates that the crucial question for any modern assessment of "natural right" is whether "natural teleology" is still defensible; and he suggests that the clearest manifestations of teleology are biological. He cannot develop this latter thought, however, because he agrees with Kant and other moderns that human beings transcend nature through culture. See *The Closing of the American Mind*, 51, 110–18, 125–27, 130–31, 166, 181, 203, 300–301. See above, note 35. Compare chap. 2, secs. 2–3.

Epilogue

I shall not end this book with a statement of conclusions because I believe any rigorous examination of the fundamental issues of political life will always be inconclusive. It is as true for political philosophy as it is for any serious intellectual inquiry that we can never possess the final answers. Those who think they have the final answers are those who do not understand the questions. Those questions that we can answer with certainty are usually not very interesting questions. The most important questions—such as those raised in this book—are likely to be insoluble.

This must be so for two reasons. First, we cannot discover the ultimate answers to the important questions because we do not have absolute wisdom. Like Socrates, we must confess that because we are not divine, we must search for truth without ever fully possessing it. But we find the pursuit valuable in itself. Although deprived of absolute knowledge, we can still gain some limited understanding of the questions. Through studying the greatest books of the greatest minds, we can learn how to weigh the plausibility of competing arguments.

The second reason for the deficiency of our political knowledge is that the most important object of our study—human nature—is too complex to be explained in simple formulations. By nature human beings strive for diverse and conflicting ends. As a result, we can never arrange political life to fulfill all of our natural needs and capacities. We must rank what often seem to be equally worthy ends. In understanding the necessity for such choices, we gain a tragic insight into the human condition.

We should not become discouraged, however, when we cannot answer philosophic questions with absolute certainty. For we should realize that all of our knowledge, with the possible exception of mathematical proofs and demonstrative logic, consists of plausible conjectures. Through a mathematical proof, we might draw an inference from given premises in a manner that is precise and conclusive. But such demonstrative reasoning is too limited to make sense of our world, particularly politics. Our answers to the enduring questions of political life must always be to some degree imprecise and inconclusive. And yet, we can support our answers with plausible arguments. (For that matter, even mathematical reasoning properly understood may, in its own way, be merely plausible.)

As in a Socratic dialogue, plausible argumentation requires that we move through three stages of reasoning: (1) we must clarify the question at issue; (2) we must then distinguish the major answers to the question; and (3) we must survey and weigh the pertinent evidence and reasoning for each answer. In judging a political philosopher, we must look for consistency, comprehensiveness, and brilliance. Is the reasoning free of self-contradiction? Is there a comprehensiveness of vision? Does the account of politics cover the full range of human nature as manifested in political life, or are critical features of our political experience ignored? Finally, we must ask about the brilliance of the work in illuminating our understanding. Does the philosopher's thinking throw light upon areas of politics that would otherwise be obscure? Furthermore, we must ask, at every step, about the relevant evidence of human experience as recorded by poets, historians, and scientists. By asking such questions, as we have in this book, we see that, even when we cannot attain absolute precision and certitude in our knowledge, we can still judge the plausibility of what political philosophers teach us.

By relentlessly posing questions—to ourselves and to others—and by refusing to settle for easy answers, we strive to free ourselves from illusions. We devote ourselves to Socratic questioning because we seek the dignity of living without self-deception. Only as long as we are thinking can we be fully awake and thus fully alive.

If we want more than this, if we wish to transcend doubt in the discovery of the final answers, then we must move from philosophic quest to religious belief. But doesn't even religious faith depend somehow on human reason? If we appeal to faith rather than reason in our search for truth, it is because we think we understand the limits of reason. But determining the limits of reason would itself be the highest achievement of reason.

Our inescapable dependence on reason points us to an enduring feature of our nature. Surely, Aristotle was right: as human beings, we are by nature rational animals. By nature we desire to understand. We are the animals for whom to live means to think. Consequently, even if we can never resolve the fundamental questions of life, we shall continue to think about them. We are also political animals because we cultivate our natural capacity for thought by living in civilized communities. We live together by thinking together. We can therefore judge a political community according to how well it promotes this natural human end. Of course, a political regime must first secure the material needs of life. But it must also nurture the mind and the spirit if life is to be worth living. Although a political regime can never fully satisfy our deepest yearnings for meaning and purpose in our lives, it can at least accommodate our natural need to explore with one another the mystery of what it means to be a human being. That political life should foster rather than impede that pursuit is one truth that we can hold to be self-evident.

Appendix

The Declaration of Independence
in Congress, July 4, 1776[1]
The Unanimous Declaration of the Thirteen United States of America

When in the Course of human events, it becomes necessary for one people to dissolve the political bands which have connected them with another, and to assume among the powers of the earth, the separate and equal station to which the laws of Nature and of Nature's God entitle them, a decent respect to the opinions of mankind requires that they should declare the causes which impel them to the separation. — We hold these truths to be self-evident, that all men are created equal, that they are endowed by their Creator with certain unalienable Rights, that among these are Life, Liberty, and the pursuit of Happiness. — That to secure these rights, Governments are instituted among Men, deriving their just powers from the consent of the governed, — That whenever any Form of Government becomes destructive of these ends, it is the Right of the People to alter or to abolish it, and to institute new Government, laying its foundation on such principles and organizing its powers in such form, as to them shall seem most likely to effect their Safety and Happiness. Prudence, indeed, will dictate that Governments long established should not be changed for light and transient causes; and accordingly all experience hath shown, that mankind are more disposed to suffer, while evils are sufferable, than to right themselves by abolishing the forms to which they are accustomed. But when a long train of abuses and usurpations, pursuing invariably the same Object evinces a design to reduce them under absolute Despotism, it is their right, it is their duty, to throw off such Government, and to provide new Guards for their future security. — Such has been the patient sufferance of these Colonies; and such is now the necessity which constrains them to alter their former Systems of Government. The history of the present King of Great Britain is a history of repeated injuries and usurpations, all having in direct object the establishment of an absolute Tyranny over these States. To prove this, let Facts be submitted to a candid world. — He has refused his Assent to Laws, the most wholesome and necessary for the public good. — He has forbidden his Governors to pass Laws of immediate and pressing importance, unless suspended in their operation till his Assent should be obtained; and when so suspended, he has utterly neglected to attend to them. — He has refused to pass other Laws for the accommodation of large districts of people, unless those people would relinquish the right of Representation in the Legislature, a right inestimable to them and formidable to tyrants only. — He has called together legislative bodies at places unusual, uncomfortable, and distant from the depository of their public Records, for the sole purpose of fatiguing them into compliance with his measures. — He has dissolved Representative Houses repeatedly, for opposing with manly firmness his invasions on the rights of the people. — He has refused for a long time, after such dissolutions, to cause others to be elected; whereby the Legislative powers incapable of Annihilation, have returned to the People at large for their exercise; the State remaining in the mean time exposed to all the dangers of invasion from without, and convulsions within. — He has endeavoured to prevent the population of these States; for that purpose obstructing the Laws of Naturalization of Foreigners; refusing to pass others to encourage their migration hither, and raising the conditions of new Appropriations of Lands. — He has obstructed the Administration of Justice, by refusing his Assent to Laws for establishing Judiciary powers. — He has made Judges dependent on his will alone, for the tenure of their offices, and the amount and payment of their salaries. — He has erected a multitude of New Offices, and sent hither swarms of Officers to harass our people, and eat out their substance. — He has kept among us, in times of peace, Standing Armies, without the Consent of our legislatures. — He has affected to render the Military independent of and superior to the Civil power. — He has combined with others to subject us to a jurisdiction foreign to our constitution, and unacknowledged by our laws; giving his Assent to their Acts of pretended Legislation: — For quartering large bodies of armed troops among us: — For protecting them, by a mock Trial, from punishment for any Murders which they should commit on the inhabitants of these States: — For cutting off our Trade with all parts of the world: — For imposing Taxes on us without our Consent: — For depriving us in many cases, of the benefits of Trial by Jury: — For transporting us beyond Seas to be tried for pretended offenses: — For abolishing the free System of English Laws in a neighbouring Province, establishing therein an Arbitrary government, and enlarging its Boundaries so as to render it at once an example and fit instrument for introducing the same absolute rule into these Colonies: — For taking away our Charters, abolishing our most valuable Laws, and altering fundamentally the Forms of our Governments: — For suspending our own Legislatures, and declaring themselves invested with power to legislate for us in all cases whatsoever. — He has abdicated Government here, by declaring us out of his Protection and waging War against us. — He has plundered our seas, ravaged our Coasts, burnt our towns, and destroyed the lives of our people. — He is at this time transporting large armies of foreign mercenaries to compleat the works of death, desolation and tyranny, already begun with circumstances of Cruelty and perfidy scarcely paralleled in the most barbarous ages, and totally unworthy the Head of a civilized nation. — He has constrained our fellow Citizens taken Captive on the high Seas to bear Arms against their Country, to become the executioners of their friends and Brethren, or to fall themselves by their Hands. — He has excited domestic insurrections amongst us, and has endeavoured to bring on the inhabitants of our frontiers, the merciless Indian Savages, whose known rule of warfare, is an undistinguished destruction of all ages, sexes and conditions. In every stage of these Oppressions We have Petitioned for Redress in the most humble terms: Our repeated Petitions have been answered only by repeated injury. A Prince, whose character is thus marked by every act which may define a Tyrant, is unfit to be the ruler of a free people. Nor have We been wanting in attentions to our British brethren. We have warned them from time to time of attempts by their legislature to extend an unwarrantable jurisdiction over us. We have reminded them of the circumstances of our emigration and settlement here. We have appealed to their native justice and magnanimity, and we have conjured them by the ties of our common kindred to disavow these usurpations, which, would inevitably interrupt our connections and correspondence. They too have been deaf to the voice of justice and of consanguinity. We must, therefore, acquiesce in the necessity, which denounces our Separation, and hold them, as we hold the rest of mankind, Enemies in War, in Peace Friends. —

We, Therefore, the Representatives of the United States of America, in General Congress, Assembled, appealing to the Supreme Judge of the world for the rectitude of our intentions, do, in the Name, and by Authority of the good People of these Colonies, solemnly publish and declare, That these United Colonies are, and of Right ought to be Free and Independent States; that they are Absolved from all Allegiance to the British Crown, and that all political connection between them and the State of Great Britain, is and ought to be totally dissolved; and that as Free and Independent States, they have full Power to levy War, conclude Peace, contract Alliances, establish Commerce, and to do all other Acts and Things which independent States may of right do. — And for the support of this Declaration, with a firm reliance on the protection of Divine Providence, we mutually pledge to each other our Lives, our Fortunes, and our sacred Honor.

Notes

1. Reprinted from the facsimile of the engrossed copy of the original manuscript in the Library of Congress.

Index